A More Noble Cause

A. P. Tureaud, Jr.

Rachel L. Emanuel

A More Noble Cause

A. P. TUREAUD and the Struggle for Civil Rights in Louisiana

A PERSONAL BIOGRAPHY

Rachel L. Emanuel and Alexander P. Tureaud, Jr.

Louisiana State University Press

Baton Rouge

Publication of this book is supported by DeeDee and Kevin P. Reilly, Sr.

Published by Louisiana State University Press
Copyright © 2011 by Louisiana State University Press
All rights reserved
Manufactured in the United States of America
First printing

Designer: Laura Roubique Gleason
Typeface: Minion Pro
Printer: McNaughton & Gunn, Inc.
Binder: Dekker Bookbinding

Frontispiece: A. P. Tureaud, Sr., in the late 1950s.
Unless otherwise stated, all photographs are from the collection of Alexander P. Tureaud, Jr.

Library of Congress Cataloging-in-Publication Data

Emanuel, Rachel Lorraine, 1955–
  A more noble cause : A. P. Tureaud and the struggle for civil rights in Louisiana : a personal
biography / Rachel L. Emanuel and Alexander P. Tureaud, Jr.
     p. cm.
  Includes bibliographical references and index.
  ISBN 978-0-8071-3793-2 (cloth : alk. paper) — ISBN 978-0-8071-3794-9 (pdf) —
ISBN 978-0-8071-3942-4 (epub) — ISBN 978-0-8071-3943-1 (mobi)
  1. Tureaud, Alexander Pierre, 1899–1972. 2. African American civil rights workers—Louisiana—Biography. 3. Civil rights workers—Louisiana—Biography. 4. African Americans—Civil
rights—Louisiana—History—20th century. 5. Civil rights movements—Louisiana—History—
20th century. 6. Segregation—Louisiana—History—20th century. 7. Segregation in education—
Louisiana—History—20th century. 8. School integration—Louisiana—History—20th century.
9. Louisiana—Race relations. I. Tureaud, Alexander P., 1936– II. Title. III. Title: A. P. Tureaud
and the struggle for civil rights in Louisiana.
  E185.93.L6E63 2011
  323.092—dc22
  [B]

                              2011004188

The paper in this book meets the guidelines for permanence and durability of the Committee on
Production Guidelines for Book Longevity of the Council on Library Resources. ∞

To my parents, Otis W. Emanuel and the late Leon L. Emanuel, and siblings, Regina E. Martin, Judge Leon L. Emanuel III, and Judge Ramona L. Emanuel Williams, who provided guidance that has forever sustained me, and to my daughter, Lawryn Emmanuelle Owens, whom I love with all my heart.

—Rachel L. Emanuel

To Lucille Dejoie, wife, mother, and grandmother, who was the anchor and equal of her husband, A. P. Tureaud. In her own right she was a trailblazer, strong and forthright, and she taught me and many others the value of integrity and love of family and friends.

—A. P. Tureaud, Jr.

Contents

Preface   ix

Acknowledgments   xv

1. Underestimated and Misperceived   1
2. Of Creole Heritage   4
3. Educating Alex   17
4. Southern Exodus   24
5. Preparing for a Legal Career   34
6. Return to New Orleans   54
7. Meeting Lucille   66
8. Growing Community Involvement   80
9. The War Years   92
10. NAACP Lawyer   101
11. Law and Fatherhood   117
12. "Separate but Equal" Strengthened in the Face of Desegregation   127
13. Desegregation of Primary and Secondary Schools   150
14. The Politician   161
15. Desegregation Battles after *Brown*   182
16. Enforcing *Brown*'s Mandate in New Orleans Grade Schools   195
17. Catholics and Desegregation   212
18. More to the Desegregation Mandate   218
19. Reconstructing Public Education   229
20. More Direct Action   238
21. Courts Are the Way   249
22. Race against Time   257

Notes   265
Index   285

Illustrations follow page 116.

Preface

Local historians have called him one of the most important figures in twentieth-century Louisiana. The late New Orleans civil rights attorney Alexander Pierre Tureaud Sr. used his legal skills, community organizing, and sheer gumption to set the stage for civil rights gains for African Americans in the Deep Southern state of Louisiana. Long a stronghold of racial segregation, Louisiana was the very state where "separate but equal" originated, in the U.S. Supreme Court's 1896 decision in *Plessy v. Ferguson*. Tureaud's work assisted in overturning *Plessy* and eliminating the egregious acts being perpetuated against African Americans with its sanction.

This book is about a man whose life exemplified perseverance. In a series of strategic moves, Tureaud worked for civil rights throughout his legal career, which spanned more than four decades. In an address to the Ninety-second Annual NAACP Convention held in New Orleans in 2001, Dr. Julian Bond stated, "The history of the New Orleans NAACP Branch, and indeed the history of the Association statewide, is personified in the life and career of attorney A. P. Tureaud, for a time the only black lawyer in the state. His name was on virtually every NAACP lawsuit filed during those five decades of lawsuits which won voting rights; integrated schools, universities, buses, parks, and public buildings; and equalized the salaries of black teachers."

Shedding light on Tureaud's life story for a national and international audience is a meaningful endeavor. This book will supplement what we know about the civil rights struggle played out in Louisiana.

Rachel Emanuel was introduced to A. P. Tureaud Sr. through the news release archives in the LSU Office of Public Relations, where she was employed as an editor. Emanuel, a 1977 graduate of LSU, was gathering information on pioneering black students who attended LSU in order to plan a reunion with other black alumni in 1988. A. P. Tureaud represented these students in lawsuits that desegregated Louisiana's flagship institution.

Following their 1988 reunion, African American graduates of LSU honored Tureaud by naming an alumni chapter after him. Members of the A. P. Tureaud Sr. Chapter of the LSU Alumni Association joined with black students who initiated a campaign resulting in the naming of a university classroom building for him. The Alexander Pierre Tureaud Hall was dedicated on March 23, 1990, in recognition of the civil rights efforts of the late civil rights attorney. It is the first and currently the only building on the LSU campus named for an African American.

The Tureaud Chapter was the sponsoring organization for a grant proposal written by Emanuel to produce a documentary on Tureaud's life. *Journey for Justice: The A. P. Tureaud Story* was produced and co-written by Emanuel with major funding from the Louisiana Endowment for the Humanities and the Louisiana Bar Foundation IOLTA fund. The fifty-minute video documentary, which had its public and broadcast premiere in 1996, highlights Tureaud's life and career.

Interviewing civil rights leaders such as Judge Constance Baker Motley, Judge Robert Carter, attorney Jack Greenberg, and numerous others for the documentary was facilitated because of their respect and admiration for Tureaud. Lawyers, religious leaders, politicians, educators, journalists, businesspeople, and students—both black and white—speak with admiration for the man and pride in his achievements. There are those among this group who were not impressed that he was Creole and looked like a white man and that he was educated at the elitist black Howard Law School. Even those who considered him to be a conservative who looked down on the activism of black radicals admit that he was the right man to deal with the complexities of the times. They respected his integrity and compassion and lauded him for his willingness to stay the course.

Emanuel's 1996 dissertation was an ethnographic account of the making of the documentary. The author was encouraged to submit her work to LSU Press for publication. A number of fortuitous events carried the project from an initially proposed specialty textbook on how to create black documentary to a scholarly biography on Tureaud. Noting that Emanuel's study contained a wealth of information about a central figure in Louisiana's civil rights story, the staff of the LSU Press suggested a collaboration between Emanuel and Tu-

reaud's only son and LSU's first black undergraduate, A. P. Tureaud Jr., to produce a scholarly biography.

As a lawyer and historian, Tureaud realized the value of documenting his
legal efforts, as well as those of his colleagues, in their struggle to secure constitutional guarantees for black Americans in Louisiana. For more than fifty
years, he assiduously preserved his letters, speeches, and important documents.
He also collected, with an unrelenting passion, historical information regarding civil rights initiatives and significant contributions made by people of color
in Louisiana. On May 17, 1975, the A. P. Tureaud Papers were officially accepted
into the archives of the Amistad Research Center in New Orleans, at a formal
and festive ceremony attended by Tureaud's widow Lucille, children, and other
family members; friends; city officials; and members of the press. The Tureaud
Papers were an invaluable resource for this project.

The family of the late professor Joseph Logsdon offered the use of his audiotaped interviews with Tureaud, which were to be published as his memoirs, left
unfinished at his death. LSU Press suggested incorporating information from
these interviews into this book. The tapes, which provide reflections from Tureaud's own perspective, along with the recollections of his son, have added to
the biography by exploring the attorney's distinctive views of how to achieve social change.

A prominent theme throughout this book is Tureaud's motivation to work
for African American civil rights, a motivation enhanced by his family, legal
education, and community involvement. Community for him was a vast network of neighborhoods, churches, educational institutions, voting leagues,
businesses, political organizations, and his wholehearted participation in the
NAACP. The community, which initially included his Seventh Ward Creole
neighborhood and other wards within his hometown of New Orleans, later included the entire state of Louisiana, other parts of the South, and national affili-
ations.

This account encompasses not only Tureaud's legal career and service to the
bar but also his community work as an organizer of civic and voting leagues;
his leadership in race relations committees; his role as national advocate for the
Knights of Peter Claver, a fraternal order of black Catholics; and his family and
social life. It also provides information about Tureaud's role in politics through
work within the Republican and Democratic parties, as well as his foray into
national politics as a candidate for the U.S. Congress. His stance on community
activism is summed up in a statement he made during an interview with Robert

Wright: "Negroes had nothing to fight with. They didn't have any of the materials of war. They only had themselves and whatever persuasion they could bring to bear by group activity or something like that. We in Louisiana had to depend upon our own resources for whatever gains we could make."

Other individuals have contributed to cementing Tureaud's legacy in the annals of history. In 1981, New Orleans mayor Ernest "Dutch" Morial dedicated the Central Office Building of the Housing Authority of New Orleans as the A. P. Tureaud Building. Morial also spearheaded the renaming of London Avenue after his mentor. In 1994, at the request of parents of children attending the Marie Couvent School, the Orleans Parish School Board renamed the school after A. P. Tureaud.

On January 20, 1997, the A. P. Tureaud Civil Rights Memorial Park in Tureaud's Seventh Ward was dedicated. In the middle of this minuscule park stands an impressive, larger-than-life bronze statue of Tureaud. The statue was created by Sheleen Jones, a young black sculptor and a 1991 graduate of Xavier University of New Orleans. The statue stands impressively on a large cement base covered with polished rose-colored marble. The artistic configuration represents Tureaud opening the gates of prejudice, leading the way to justice and freedom. The wrought-iron gates, replicas of ironwork made by African slaves that adorn many buildings in the Vieux Carré, are a celebrated trademark of New Orleans architecture. In addition to Tureaud, the names of nine civil rights crusaders, black and white, including Dutch Morial and Judge J. Skelly Wright, are etched into the marble facing that covers the base of the monument.

Other posthumous honors include recognition by the National Bar Association, the Louis Martinet Legal Society, and NAACP branches; and the naming of legal fraternities (such as the American Inn of Court in New Orleans), law school student organizations, and scholarships after him. On February 26, 1999, on the cusp of the new millennium, the Tureaud family and the city of New Orleans celebrated the one hundredth birthday of A. P. Tureaud Sr. at the Civil Rights Memorial Park. In 2008, the U.S. Department of the Interior designated the Tureaud home on Pauger Street as a historic landmark. An A. P. Tureaud Legacy Committee was established in February 2010 to honor the legacy of the preeminent Louisiana civil rights attorney, to educate the public about his remarkable contributions to social justice, and to inspire future lawyers to use the law as a tool to further social equality.

Tureaud's personality, talent, and legal accomplishments motivate Emanuel and A. P. Tureaud Jr. continually to share his story. Those who presently work for civil rights and justice are encouraged to remember that Louisiana achieved civil rights goals through the work of individuals like Tureaud. Emanuel and coauthor A. P. Tureaud Jr. sincerely hope that they have done his story justice.

Note on Sources

The authors have relied heavily on family reminiscences and the taped interviews of A. P. Tureaud Sr. conducted by the late University of New Orleans professor Joseph Logsdon. Beginning with Tureaud's childhood in the Faubourg Marigny and continuing through his incredible forty-six years as a civil rights lawyer in Louisiana, Logsdon captured, in amazing and colorful detail, the salient events in Tureaud's life. If not otherwise cited, information in this book comes primarily from these two sources.

Acknowledgments

Our sincere thanks to all who have taken this extended and exciting journey with us. At every crossroad, as the book developed, it was our good fortune to improve our writing and research, which confirmed our belief that we were destined to create the biography of this unique man. Although it is not possible to mention everyone who helped, we would like to salute and thank the following individuals.

To those who provided superb professional guidance and resources: our editors Ayan Rubin and Grace Carino; Gilbert King; Dr. Huel Perkins; Jackie Bartkiewicz; Dr. Jewel Prestage; Dr. John Butler; Dr. Max McComb; Dr. America Rodriguez; Dr. John S. Butler; Dr. Denise Barkis-Richter; Maureen Hewitt; Sheila Cooper; Dr. Gaines Foster; the Dr. Joseph Logsdon family; Harold Isadore and Ruth Hill, SULC Law Library; the Amistad Research Center staff, especially Brenda B. Square and Christopher Harter; the New Orleans Public Library, especially archivist Irene Wainwright; the Moorland-Spingarn Research Center at Howard University; the *Shreveport Sun;* the Harry Ransom Center at the University of Texas at Austin; Xavier University (La.) Archives and Special Collections; the Louisiana Endowment for the Humanities staff; the Louisiana State Bar Association staff; the Louisiana Bar Foundation; Chase Bank, especially Mary Durusau; the LSU Special Collections staff, especially Faye Phillips; Anne M. Saba, Historic Preservation Officer of the Office of Public Affairs, U.S. Customs and Border Protection; Dr. I. Bruce Turner, head of Special Collections, Edith Garland Dupré Library at the University of Louisiana at Lafayette; and the LSU Press, especially MaryKatherine Callaway and Rand Dotson.

To those who provided valuable insights: Dr. Barbara Worthy, the late Dr. Joseph Logsdon, the late judge Constance Baker Motley, Judge Robert Carter, attorney Jack Greenberg, Prof. Raphael Cassimere, Dr. Roger West, Sherman Copelin, Prof. Charles Vincent, Prof. Vanue B. Lacour, attorney Lolis Elie, Prof. Donald DeVore, the late Ernest "Dutch" Morial, Sybil Morial, Judge D'Army Bailey, Judge Carl E. Stewart, the late dean Louis Berry, the late Dr. Jesse N. Stone, the late attorney Norman Amaker, Dr. Leonard Burns, attorney Leo C. Hamilton, Prof. Maurice Franks, Prof. Evelyn Wilson, Prof. Stanley Halpin, Vice Chancellor John Pierre, the late C. C. and Julia Dejoie, Emily Leumas, Philip "Duke" Rivet, Jari Honora, Dr. and Mrs. Trent James, Greg Osborne, Anna Dejoie Daniels, the late Stafford and Evelyn Tureaud, Susie Brown Waxwood, and Dr. Maurice Martinez.

All of the Tureaud daughters, Sylvia, Carole, Elise, Jane, and Janet, contributed important information, serious and often humorous, which helped to expand and enrich accounts of the day-to-day activities and adventures of this social, political, and gregarious family. Numerous relatives, including a cadre of grandchildren, neighbors, friends, colleagues, and clients, also shared their personal experiences with Tureaud, allowing greater insight into his personality and aspirations.

To those who gave encouragement and moral support: Otis W. Emanuel, Ken and Regina E. Martin, Judge Leon and Frenchie Emanuel, Judge Ramona Emanuel and Ken Williams, Lawryn E. Owens, Mary K. Scott, Allison Young, Darrell Patterson, Chancellor Freddie Pitcher Jr., Carla Ball, members of the Kueleza Literary Book Club, Jonn Hankins, Victor Labat, Caryn Cossé Bell, Castro Spears, Ronda Tureaud Raymond, Alexander Tureaud III, Michelle and Andrew Tureaud, Dr. Connie Atkinson, and Nancy Oschenschlager.

A special acknowledgment to Fay Tureaud, a librarian and lover of books, for her knowledge and patience in proofreading and providing constructive criticism over the long haul.

Special thanks for financial support from attorneys Walter C. Dumas and Ike Spears.

A More Noble Cause

1
Underestimated and Misperceived

He sat in that chair day after day, reflecting on his life as he spoke haltingly into the tape recorder. He was a man whose erect bearing had once projected calm assurance and deep human insight and whose physique had once reflected his lifetime enjoyment of the rich Creole cuisine of New Orleans.

He looked much older than his seventy-three years, and a casual visitor might have thought that his lack of movement and energy reflected a mental exhaustion as well. Despite the fact that he was now gaunt and barely had enough strength to rise from a chair without assistance, he refused to give in to the constant pain that increasing doses of medication could not relieve. As he ruminated over his life, he recalled names, dates, places, and events with unerring accuracy.

The depth of knowledge and perseverance the old man exhibited seemed implausible for one in his condition. But then his entire life had been one impossible challenge after another. Through sheer will, he had changed the face of Louisiana forever. He had helped to stifle rampant segregation through a series of historic lawsuits. He had altered attitudes and conquered adversity with a disarming but unyielding demeanor. The wizened old man in the chair did not look as if he had done any of those things. But then Alexander Pierre Tureaud had been consistently underestimated and was often misperceived by others.

Knocking on the doors of houses in the Faubourg Marigny of New Orleans, whose owners awaited their early morning deliveries of French bread and other baked goods, Alexander Pierre ("Alex") Tureaud, nine years old, cheerfully greeted the customers as he delivered purchases to their doorstep. The white woman who managed the neighborhood store where he worked assumed, when hiring the curly-haired boy, that he was white.

When the owner of the store later discovered that Alex was a Negro, he instructed the manager to fire him. It did not matter that Alex did a good job, was conscientious, punctual, polite, and liked by the customers. In fact, the store manager paid him a little extra each week, called "lagniappe" by Creoles, because she was more than satisfied with his performance. Following the directive of the owner, the manager fired Alex, and the boy's initial opportunity to earn his own money was taken away because of racial discrimination.

A wide-eyed, hopeful young Creole experienced his first painful rejection as a colored person during the early 1900s in the segregated South.[1] The wages from the part-time job, though only $1 a week, enabled him to contribute to his family's meager household income and allowed him to have his own spending money.

Years later, Alexander P. Tureaud greeted two white men with a collegial tip of his hat as he walked by them and entered the courthouse. "Seen that nigger lawyer, yet?" one of the men asked. Realizing that the man was addressing him, Tureaud shook his head, chuckled to himself, and proceeded up the steps without a second glance in their direction. As he entered the building, he overheard the man's next remark: "We're gonna have some fun with that nigger today." It was then that Tureaud realized that these men were his opposing counsel.

Instead of being angered by their racist comments, Tureaud was amused. Their off-the-cuff statements would create a psychological advantage when he confronted them later in court. Their remarks served to fuel his enthusiasm for the legal battle ahead.

Once inside the courtroom, the two white lawyers could not conceal their surprise when Tureaud introduced himself as the attorney for the plaintiffs and smiled respectfully at the opposing counsel. Tureaud had been mistaken as white many times before, and he knew he could use it to advance his objectives.

Ironically, many of Tureaud's potential black clients expressed the opinion that a Negro lawyer in the South could not handle their cases. Tureaud was confident that he could and worked diligently to prove them wrong. Facing the opposing white counsel as he represented his trusting black clients strengthened Tureaud's resolve and provided opportunities for him to hone his courtroom skills.

With each courtroom appearance, Tureaud became more secure in his role as an attorney and as a civil rights advocate. With each victory he increased his caseload. In the long and arduous pursuit of equality and justice, Tureaud was armed with the law and trained to fight in the legal battle for justice. He would never consider being removed from a case because he was a Negro and convinced clients, judges, and his opposition that he was a capable and skilled lawyer.

Born three years after the U.S. Supreme Court's decision in *Plessy v. Ferguson,* which declared racial segregation the law of the land, Tureaud, in addition to his legal career, became a student of history. He was particularly inquisitive about his lineage as a New Orleans Creole of color.

The desire to fight racial injustice had been set long ago in the Creole culture of Louisiana. Tureaud found within his culture role models of activism and aligned himself with men and women determined to achieve equality. Pride in his heritage taught him that it is more noble to fight injustice, no matter what, than to resign oneself to it.

2
Of Creole Heritage

The Creole community of New Orleans, into which Alex Tureaud was born, began as a distinct ethnological culture as early as 1724, during the French colonial period.[1] Alex's maternal ancestors, free people of color, or *gens de couleur libres,* were individuals of French, Spanish, and African heritage. They spoke French, Creole (a dialect of French with Afro-Caribbean words and phrases), and English and were members of the Catholic Church. His paternal ancestors were French and African, and most were slaves until freed by the Emancipation Proclamation of 1863.

The Afro-Creole culture evolved in Louisiana as the French and Spanish settlers cohabitated with African slave women, producing mulatto children.[2] Native Americans, indigenous to the region, were also active participants in this process of multiracial blending, as runaway slaves frequently found refuge among local tribes.

The Code Noir (the Black Code) of 1724, promulgated by Jean-Baptiste de Bienville, the appointed governor of the province of Louisiana, prescribed the rights and restrictions of slaves and free people of color.[3] According to the Code Noir, free people of color had the same rights as any citizen of French Louisiana, except the right to marry and receive legacies from white citizens.[4] Thus, preceding the Civil War, free persons of color enjoyed the privileges of voting, owning property, attending school with white residents, and owning slaves. The code also required baptism for all slaves, allowed slaves to sue masters for mistreatment, recognized slave marriages by the church, and protected slave families from separation by sale.

The Louisiana Black Code of 1724 also allowed slaves and free people of color to get a religious education. Religious study or catechism, often referred to as "religion with letters," included basic instruction in reading, writing, and arithmetic. Catechism classes prepared children for first communion and confirmation. Thus, in the eighteenth century, a sizable number of black residents in southern Louisiana were literate.

By 1830, after the state had been under American control for some time, Louisiana law prohibited the secular education of slaves and imposed prison sentences for violators. It was not until after the Emancipation Proclamation, during the Reconstruction period of the South, that education for black residents was again legalized.[5] In 1864, a year after the Emancipation Proclamation, New Orleans organized the first free public school for Negro students.

After the Civil War, particularly during the Reconstruction period, with the protection of the Thirteenth, Fourteenth, and Fifteenth Amendments to the Constitution and the Civil Rights Act of 1866, all people of color, including freed slaves, were allowed to vote, actively participate in the political process, acquire land, seek their own employment, and use public accommodations. Following the era of Reconstruction, people of color living in the South experienced an increasing erosion of these privileges. The lines became blurred between the status of free people of color and that of freed slaves. Their rights were significantly diminished after the infamous 1896 U.S. Supreme Court decision in *Plessy v. Ferguson,* which established the "separate but equal" doctrine. This decision legalized segregation of the races, relegating Negroes (the term for people of color used at the time) to second-class citizenship.

The tradition of privilege for people of color began in the parishes of Louisiana, where black and brown slaves toiled to make white men prosperous. It played out in the same parishes where free men of color, intent upon protecting their ambiguous status in a segregated society, continued the struggle for racial and economic equality.

Tureaud, pronounced "Too Row" with a silent "d," was an uncommon name in New Orleans but not in St. James Parish. There were white Tureauds who owned sugar plantations in that parish, and many were influential in the government of Louisiana as far back as 1803. Some were judges, notaries, and pharmacists. Several were involved in the political life of the community. Young Alex's relatives often spoke of a Tureaud in the Reconstruction legislature, the legislative body that served during the twelve-year period 1865–77, immediately following the Civil War. Reconstruction was a time for defining the means by which white and black Americans could live together in a nonslave society.

Augustin Dominique Tureaud was the first Tureaud to set foot on the shores of North America.[6] The son of a courtier from La Rochelle, France, Augustin was sent to Santo Domingo to manage his father's sugar plantation. Not long after his arrival on the Caribbean island, the slave uprising led by a free black man, Toussaint L'Ouverture, began. Augustin, his mulatto housekeeper, and her two children fled the island in a rowboat. After the first night adrift, the youngest child died from exposure and was buried at sea. The three survivors were rescued by the U.S. Coast Guard and taken to Baltimore, Maryland.

With financial support from his father, Augustin, called "A.D.," purchased several ships and began a new career as a sea captain. While in New Orleans, he met Emanuel Marius Pons Bringier, called Marius, a wealthy planter of White Hall Plantation in St. James Parish. During an extended visit at the plantation, Bringier offered A.D. a business partnership and asked if he would marry his youngest daughter, fourteen-year-old Elizabeth ("Betsy"). A.D. accepted both offers.

The thirty-eight-year-old A.D., finding that his bride-to-be needed time to adjust to the unexpected proposal of marriage, left St. James Parish. In 1803, twelve months after their betrothal and the year that France sold Louisiana to the United States, Betsy wed A. D. Tureaud at White Hall Plantation. Marius Bringier and his wife, Aglae, gave the newlyweds Union Plantation in honor of the joining of the two families.

A.D., who was later elected as a judge in St. James Parish, and Betsy had seven sons and one daughter. Their oldest child and firstborn son, Augustin Marius Tureaud, called "A.M.," married Aurora Mather, of Belle Alliance Plantation. Together they had eight children; however, A.M. fathered several slave children. In 1843, A.M., age thirty-three, executed a contract of sale to purchase a young mulatto slave woman, Josephine Mather, and her three-year-old son, Adolphe Tureaud, from his mother-in-law.[7] Josephine was manumitted by A.M. shortly after he purchased her.

Genealogical information and family documents strongly support that Adolphe Tureaud was one of A.M.'s mulatto offspring. According to the 1870 Louisiana census, Adolphe was born in 1840 in St. James Parish; he was identified as a mulatto who lived on Bagatelle Plantation with his mother, Josephine Mather; his brothers, Henry and Edward; and his sister, Marie. All of Josephine's children were baptized and given the surname Tureaud. Edward and Marie were probably also the progeny of A.M.; however, Henry was the son of A.M.'s younger brother, Benjamin Tureaud. Parish records, specifically Henry's death certificate, documented Benjamin Tureaud's paternity of Henry. No records were found to determine that any of Josephine's children were manumitted.[8]

Ancestry of Alexander Pierre Tureaud

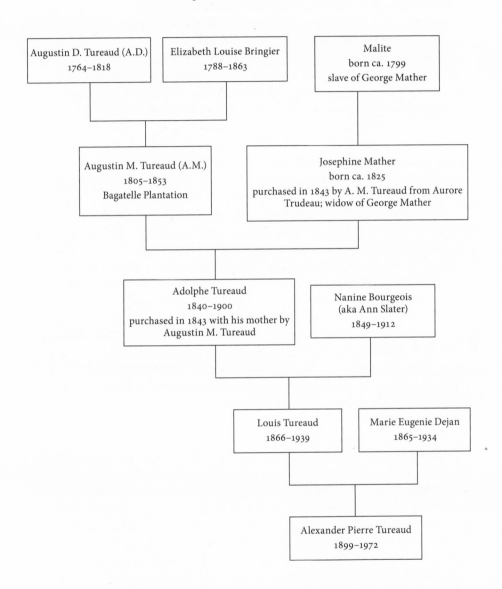

Augustin D. Tureaud (A.D.)
1764–1818

Elizabeth Louise Bringier
1788–1863

Malite
born ca. 1799
slave of George Mather

Augustin M. Tureaud (A.M.)
1805–1853
Bagatelle Plantation

Josephine Mather
born ca. 1825
purchased in 1843 by A. M. Tureaud from Aurore
Trudeau; widow of George Mather

Adolphe Tureaud
1840–1900
purchased in 1843 with his mother by
Augustin M. Tureaud

Nanine Bourgeois
(aka Ann Slater)
1849–1912

Louis Tureaud
1866–1939

Marie Eugenie Dejan
1865–1934

Alexander Pierre Tureaud
1899–1972

During the Civil War, Adolphe Tureaud left Bagatelle Plantation and joined the Corps d'Afrique. Consisting of twenty-six regiments of black men, slave and free, approximately 10,000, the corps fought courageously for the Union in decisive battles of the Civil War.[9]

After serving in the war, Adolphe returned to St. James Parish and began to reconstruct his life as a freedman. He was trained in farming and the building trades, which would afford him opportunities to make a living. He had a relationship with Nanine Bourgeois, a former slave from a nearby plantation. At the age of seventeen, Nanine gave birth to their son, Louis, born in 1866 in St. James Parish, one year after the Civil War ended. Adolphe acknowledged paternity but never married Nanine, who remained with her son in the rural sugar plantation region for a number of years.

In 1868, two years after the Civil War ended, Adolphe and his uncle, Noel Mather, purchased a tract of land in St. James Parish, on the left bank of the Mississippi River in Convent, Louisiana. Also in 1868, at the age of twenty-eight, Adolphe was elected to a two-year term as a representative from St. James Parish in the Louisiana Reconstruction legislature. After completing his first term, he was reelected and served his second and last term, from 1870 to 1872.

In a civil ceremony on May 13, 1869, and several years later in a religious ceremony at St. Michael's Catholic Church on April 8, 1872, Adolphe was married to Celestine Mather. Celestine was a former slave on the Mather plantation, Belle Alliance, where Adolphe and his mother, Josephine, had lived before they were sold to Augustin Tureaud. Although Josephine and Celestine have the same surname, a review of the limited parish documents does not support their kinship. While serving in the legislature with distinction, Adolphe farmed the land in the rural sugar plantation region for ten years and then leased it to his brother Henry for ten years.[10]

Eventually, Nanine left the plantation with her son, Louis, to make a better life in New Orleans, where she met Alexander Slater, a native of Baltimore living in the Creole community there. The couple married and had two sons, Robert Manuel and James Alexander. In 1885, when Louis was nineteen years old, his stepfather died.

Literate in French and English, Louis received his religious training and grammar school education in New Orleans. He attended racially mixed schools established by the Reconstruction legislature. Following in the footsteps of his father, he also had an apprenticeship in carpentry, and he joined the New Orleans Creole tradition of working in the building trades. In addition to hiring himself out for general carpentry work, he worked on the river as a screwman, the forerunners of longshoremen, tightening and packing bales of cotton in the holds of ships so that they would not list. He also made cisterns and installed spiral staircases in homes in the Vieux Carré, New Orleans's French Quarter. As his skills increased, he began seeking work as a subcontractor.

Louis, a handsome mulatto, married a beautiful Creole woman, Marie Eugenie Dejan, on June 1, 1886, in St. Augustine Church in the Faubourg Tremé of New Orleans. His bride had thick black hair and dark eyes. Eugenie, as she was called, was often considered to be a white person when she ventured outside her Creole neighborhood. Like her husband, she was fluent in English and French, but she also spoke Creole. As a child of the Reconstruction era, Eugenie attended a private, racially mixed grammar school; however, it is not known how many grades she completed. Upon leaving grade school, she, like many Creole girls, continued training at home, preparing for marriage and motherhood. A devout Catholic, Eugenie was a regular communicant at St. Augustine Church, where she was baptized in 1865.

The marriage was rocky. During Louis's frequent separations from his wife, he would return to his mother's home, staying for months at a time, which created problems between Nanine and her daughter-in-law. Nonetheless, in fewer than twenty years of marriage, Eugenie and Louis Tureaud had twelve children. All but two survived childhood.

Their surviving sons were Adolph; Louis, who was called "Willie" to distinguish him from his father; Edward; Alexander; and Emile. One son, whose name is not known, was the victim of an unfortunate accident as a toddler.[11] He was severely burned when his nightshirt caught fire while he warmed himself too near an unprotected fireplace. He died of pneumonia a few days later. The daughters were Carmen Louise, Marie Louise, Blanche, Corinne, Victoria, and Virginia. Blanche died when she was in her teens.

Alexander Pierre Tureaud, the fifth son, born on February 26, 1899, enjoyed the special attention afforded the "baby" of the family by his mother, older siblings, two grandmothers, and numerous relatives for two years until his sister Virginia was born on March 26, 1901.[12] A few years later, Emile, the sixth son, twelfth and last child of Eugenie and Louis, was born. Emile would always be the baby of the family, but as an adult he would grow to be the largest in stature.

By the time Alex was born, Louis was a self-employed contractor who specialized in building homes. He hired other carpenters and skilled craftsmen, such as bricklayers, cement finishers, and plasterers, as the individual jobs required. He was respected for his skills and his devotion to work. Theirs was a working-class household, struggling as Louis's income fluctuated and as escalating racism in New Orleans challenged the economic well-being of many Negro families. Eugenie became a very frugal housewife. Fortunately, all of her working children were resourceful and shared a portion of their earnings with her.

Building houses, in rows or as single dwellings, was what Louis did best. However, he often made mistakes in estimating materials and the amount of time needed to complete a job, which prevented him from securing many contracts or earning a profit. Alex and his three older brothers were often recruited to complete jobs when their father ran out of money to pay his workers. Top salaries at that time were $3 a day for skilled laborers. His brothers, hired as carpenters, were fortunate to get $3 a week when working for their father. Once Louis paid his son Willie with a quart of milk for a week's work. Often when their father's cash flow was low or work was slow, the sons received no pay at all for their labor.

As one of the younger children in a large family, Alex was rarely without the company of one or more of his siblings. Their home, small and compact, provided limited space and privacy. At an early age Alex learned the art of compromise and accommodation. Consideration of others was necessary to maintain family harmony. Although the Tureauds' household was full of activity common in large families, their home environment was seldom chaotic or unsettling. Loud and rowdy behavior, even in pure enjoyment, was not tolerated.

Soft spoken and respectful of others, Eugenie became a role model for her children. Alex developed a strong bond with his mother, which continued throughout their lives. His accommodating and compassionate nature matched hers. Alex almost never lost his temper or shouted in anger at others, as a youth and as an adult. These personality traits developed in his formative years had a significant impact on his personal and professional life. His calm demeanor helped to keep him focused on his goals, his schoolwork, his family, his career, and his decades-long pursuit of equal rights.

Alex's relatives in the Seventh Ward, the Faubourg Marigny, and the Faubourg Tremé provided support and protection from the harsh racial prejudice prevalent in the segregated South. The Faubourg Marigny, a suburb of the Vieux Carré, which hugs the bank of the Mississippi River in an area barely above sea level, is bounded by Esplanade Avenue, St. Claude Avenue, Press Street, and the river. One of the original extensions of the city of New Orleans, historically Marigny was home to many free men and women of color who owned homes and businesses there.

Marigny was developed in the early nineteenth century, about 1810, by Bernard Xavier Philippe de Marigny de Mandeville, an eccentric white Creole millionaire. Just downriver from the old city limits of New Orleans, the triangular piece of land was a plantation owned by the Marigny family. Prior to being laid out and developed as the first suburb of the city, its irregular shape allowed it to claim three wards, the Seventh, Eighth, and Ninth. A significant number of Creoles of color inhabited Marigny, particularly in the Seventh Ward, and lived harmoniously with immigrants from Europe, the Caribbean, and Central and South America. With their close proximity to the river, many residents of Marigny were employed in the shipping industry as seamen, skilled laborers, longshoremen, screwmen, haulers, and mechanics.

Another significant resource for the inhabitants of Marigny, especially those living near Alex, was the French Market, with its myriad of businesses and employment opportunities. Several of Alex's Italian playmates boasted that their families owned shops and stalls selling fruits, vegetables, fish, exotic foods, and household goods in the bustling market.

Louis and Eugenie rented half of a two-family Creole cottage at 907 Kelerec Street, which came to an abrupt end at Dauphine Street. Their home was in the Faubourg Marigny, one block below Esplanade Avenue, within the same block of the father of Marie Laveau, who was later to be known as a voodoo priestess. The Tureaud side of the cottage strained to accommodate the family of twelve. Squat and square, with high-pitched roofs and thick walls of brick covered with cement, Creole cottages were popular in the Vieux Carré and the older suburbs of Marigny and Tremé. These houses were built in working-class neighborhoods in the early 1800s.

Built flush to the banquette, or sidewalk, many of these houses featured gas lanterns at the front doors and had four rooms downstairs and two upstairs. The flickering golden glow of the lanterns lit the streets of the neighborhood with mini orbs like dancing sunsets. As evening approached, the glow from the lighted lanterns was a signal for Alex and his siblings to come inside. The Creole cottages had no hallways, and their high ceilings helped reduce the discomfort from the heat and humidity of New Orleans's subtropical climate. The kitchen and a small bathroom were usually located at the rear of the building. Sometimes these rooms were detached from the main house. The backyard patios, often luxuriant with tropical foliage, provided space for play, drying laundry, and evening socials. Many residents grew edible plants, like plantains, a fruit that resembles a large banana, in their patio gardens.

Creoles of color who were residents of the Seventh Ward were often referred to as "downtown Creoles." As with other downtown Creoles, the Tureauds' family life frequently revolved around their church activities. Christenings, first communions, confirmations, and weddings were occasions for celebrating with family and friends. The imposing white stucco Catholic church that the Tureauds attended, St. Augustine, was around the corner from Alex's maternal grandmother, Louisa Dejan, called "Mamere," who lived on Barracks Street. Its first mass was celebrated in 1842, fifty-seven years before Alex was baptized there in 1899. The church was built at the request of free black residents, who wanted a place where they could sit and worship. At the time, black parishioners were relegated to standing or kneeling in the rear of St. Louis Cathedral and were prohibited from purchasing pews. The black residents of Faubourg Tremé collectively contributed $25,000 to build St. Augustine as their house of worship.

Before construction was completed, however, white residents in the area began purchasing pews in an attempt to gain control of the church. Black parishioners joined in the "War of the Pews," purchasing half of the pews in the center aisles and all of the pews on the two side aisles. St. Augustine Church became the first mixed Catholic parish in New Orleans and the first Catholic church where slaves could sit and worship. Free black parishioners purchased the side aisles for their black brethren who were not yet emancipated. Here slaves participated in religious rituals on an equal footing with free men and women, black or white, for the first time in the United States.

The glorious beginning of St. Augustine Church was tarnished a half century later by the lack of courage shown by the leaders of the Archdiocese of New Orleans, who allowed racial segregation to prevail in its parishes. Many Creoles changed their religion and withdrew from the Catholic Church. However, the majority practiced their beliefs devoutly and attended segregated churches with regularity.

Except for the baptism of his children, Louis Tureaud rarely attended church services. He refused to endure the humiliation that accompanied sanctioned segregation. He was critical of the pastoral leadership of the bishop, who allowed these racist practices.

When attending church or social events as a family, with or without Louis, the Tureauds commanded attention, not just for the size of their family but also because of their impeccable attire. The boys wore standup collars and ties, and the dresses worn by the girls were complemented with matching gloves and hats. Alex's sisters had gently rounded figures and attractive faces, offset by dark eyes and thick, silky hair. Two of the girls had freckles. The boys of the family, including Alex, were all of average height, solidly built, and considered very handsome. Keeping well groomed in the heat and unrelenting humidity of New Orleans in the early 1900s was a major challenge. Most people changed clothes twice each day during the hot months, which were practically three-fourths of the year. Eugenie taught her daughters to sew, and as a result of their handiwork, they dressed stylishly on a limited household budget. Managing laundry for such a large family was a monumental task, and washed clothes were perpetually hung on the outdoor lines that crisscrossed the Tureauds' small backyard garden. Sheets, shirts, and other articles flapped in the wind, providing shade from the sun as children darted in and out at play.

As the parish church of his family—where he and his mother were baptized, his parents and grandparents were married, and where he attended Sunday mass—St. Augustine Church embodied Catholicism for Alex. Yet, like his father, he felt strongly that the archbishop's policy of racial segregation was not serving him well. Young Alex satisfied his mother's admonition to practice his religion throughout his childhood, but upon reaching adolescence, he withdrew from the church. By this time, a majority of St. Augustine's parishioners were Italian. Several decades later the parish experienced significant change again as white residents moved out of the area and black residents, who were not Catholic, moved in.

St. Augustine Church remains an important Tremé institution. Near the massive wooden doors at the main entrance of the church, a bronze plaque placed by the pastor, Father Jerome Ledoux, summarizes its illustrious past and includes the following: "Alexander P. Tureaud, Attorney and Noted Louisiana Civil Rights Leader, was baptized here April 2, 1899."

Private clubs and benevolent societies, which organized for social, economic, and later political purposes, sponsored dances, picnics, hayrides, Mardi Gras balls, and special events for their members and invited guests. These social activities were another important aspect of the Tureauds' family life. Alex's father did not belong to any private clubs or societies. Nonetheless, the Tureauds and their children were often invited to the dances and social events sponsored by these groups. Exchanging invitations with members of other clubs provided opportunities for parents to have their daughters and sons included in Creole society. "In the Creole community, we were more or less given to social activities that were privately hosted, privately operated. You had to subscribe to a list that was made for a dance," Tureaud later recalled. "This list helped to keep out the undesirables."[13]

It was rumored that some clubs refused to admit guests whose skin was darker than a brown paper bag. Whether fact or fiction, the brown paper bag test emphasizes the fixation with color that was prevalent within the Creole community. Alex knew that color was not the only determinant of Creole privilege. Straight, wavy, or curly hair was also a valued asset in many Creole social circles.

While playing in the streets in his neighborhood that were shaped by the crescent bend of the Mississippi River, Alex was surrounded by houses and shops built in the Caribbean-colonial architectural style. These structures displayed ornamental works of wood, iron, and brick, created by skilled craftsmen and artisans like his father. Louis Tureaud and his three older sons worked on many construction jobs in the French Quarter and nearby neighborhoods. Many of Alex's Creole uncles and cousins built homes and stores in the historic sections of the city. As he grew and became familiar with other areas of the city, Alex observed the impressive ironwork that graced many of the stately houses in the French Quarter. He later learned that African slaves were responsible for much of this exquisite work. The initial pride that he felt upon learning about the hallmarks of his Creole heritage soon expanded to include an appreciation for the accomplishments of all people of color.

New Orleans has celebrated a love affair with food since its beginning during the French colonial period. The herbs, spices, and traditional foods utilized by French, African, and Caribbean cooks produced unique recipes, which have been prized and protected for generations. Alex's mother and sisters, all outstanding cooks, prepared this spicy, richly flavored Creole cuisine of gumbo, jambalaya, okra, and étouffée. Alex had a healthy appetite and, as a growing boy, never seemed to get quite enough to eat.

As a teen, Alex and his friends danced to the music of King Oliver and Eric Petite at the Jeunes Amis Hall, a popular Creole dance club in the Seventh Ward. Emerging jazz musicians and local bands were also regulars in the clubs on the shores of Lake Pontchartrain. The south shore of Lake Pontchartrain, which forms the northern boundary of New Orleans, was popular for picnics and hayrides. Providing an escape from the city's heat and humidity, clubhouses were built by some Creoles on pilings over the oval-shaped lake. These clubhouses offered opportunities for Alex and his friends to socialize safely outside the boundaries of the Seventh Ward. Alex, a good swimmer, loved the relaxed atmosphere and cool breezes of the lake. Although it was not an ideal place to swim, Lake Pontchartrain, which was wide but not particularly deep near the shoreline, was safer than the muddy water and swift currents of the Mississippi River, where Alex sometimes swam without his parents' knowledge.

The lakeshore environment was more than just an enjoyable recreation spot. It also provided a means of income for builders, musicians, and waiters. Alex and his older brothers, Adolph, Willie, and Eddie, helped their father build a house for a family friend on the shores of the lake.

Louis instilled in his children an interest in the activities of the world about them, as they read newspapers and kept abreast of the events of the day. Eugenie, a meticulous housekeeper, was resourceful in providing basic necessities for her family, even during lean times. She orchestrated a multitude of daily chores in ways that gave each child an opportunity to contribute to the well-being of the family. Working as domestics was sometimes necessary for the girls in order to supplement the household income, as the boys secured regular employment in the building trades.

The Faubourg Marigny was an ideal neighborhood for a curious and inquisitive boy like Alex. He romped with his playmates in and around the Vieux Carré, climbed the levee banks of the Mississippi River, and enjoyed the bright colors and pungent aromas of the French Market. Playing outside in bare feet until dusk, Alex and his friends would have preferred the nearby parks to the banquettes or the streets, but the public parks were clearly marked with "White Only" signs.

The Tureauds lived in a racially mixed neighborhood. A white bachelor fireman, who was known to them only by his last name, Clark, lived in the rear of Alex's home, in separate quarters. Alex played with neighborhood boys and girls whose parents were immigrants from Europe and the Americas. Many of the European immigrant families, primarily Italians, spoke little English. As a child, Alex got along well with his neighbors; they all went in and out of each other's homes and sometimes shared meals together. As he moved about the neighborhood playing with his friends, racial issues were often overlooked because he looked like he was white. As he grew older, Alex noticed that girls no longer played freely with boys outside their racial groups when they reached puberty. He also heard white residents use harsh words and racial epithets when speaking of their Negro neighbors.

Alex, like other people of color, learned early the rules of legalized racial segregation that required Negroes to play in parks, drink from water fountains, ride on streetcars, use public restrooms, and even enter their physicians' and dentists' offices through doors specifically designated for "Colored Only." Those who violated the Jim Crow laws could be fined, jailed, victimized by the police, and sometimes even lynched by a mob of angry white vigilantes.

The childhood activities of give and take, winning and losing, with peers who were Creole, Italian, Latino, and Filipino helped Alex develop a broader understanding of people. He was also a keen observer who kept an open mind and formulated his own opinions about others, regardless of their racial or ethnic affiliation.

Eugenie assumed primary responsibility for monitoring family activities. Louis, though eager for his children to achieve, distanced himself from the daily requirements of parenting and directed his energy toward earning a living. Alex's parents valued success in school, attendance at catechism classes, and active participation in family gatherings. Since the State Constitution of 1898 outlawed racially mixed public schools, services, and accommodations in Louisiana, Eugenie and Louis agonized over the increasing restrictions and discrimination that confronted their children as they attended school, sought employment, and socialized with their friends.

3
Educating Alex

When Alex began his public school education in 1906, there were two primary schools for black students in his neighborhood, the Marigny and the Bayou Road schools. The administrators, clerical staff, and teachers in both schools were white. The Bayou Road School was closer to his home, so his mother enrolled him there. At seven years of age, Alex entered the first grade already familiar with the routines of classroom instruction as a result of his regular attendance in catechism classes.

Miss Bridgette Hines, the principal, often accompanied Alex on his short walk to school. If she didn't see him on the banquette in front of his home, she would knock at his door to inquire if he was ready for school, a friendly gesture that demonstrated her interest in his education. Alex enjoyed school, finding the white teachers very pleasant and patient as they helped students through the learning process. Alex excelled in every class.

About a year after his enrollment, the entire faculty and staff, including the principal, were replaced with black women. Alex was aware of the change in the leadership and faculty of the school, but he was too young to recognize its significance. The new Negro principal was Miss Dora Coghill, a graduate of Straight College in New Orleans, an institution of higher education founded in 1869 as a place for freedmen and women to receive an education. Agnes Leonie Bauduit, Priscilla Waterhouse, and Fannie C. Williams were among Alex's teachers. Proud, emerging feminists, a few generations ahead of their time, Coghill, Bauduit, Waterhouse, and Williams exemplified a new breed of educated women of color, whose numbers would increase dramatically as professional training and jobs became more accessible to them.

Miss Waterhouse was tall and heavyset. Her masculine-sounding voice commanded discipline, even though Alex and his classmates giggled behind her back because she had a mustache. Alex was an active and leading participant in Miss Waterhouse's weekly spelling bees. He became excited and challenged by the spelling contests and emerged as one of the best spellers in the school.

He was recognized as a student with great potential, and many teachers extended themselves to help him expand his horizons, increase his knowledge, and sharpen his skills. The teachers at the Bayou Road School exposed their students to the accomplishments and contributions of Creoles and African American men and women. This awareness allowed Alex to broaden his perspective on history and to view the fight for racial equality less parochially. The seeds of his cultural consciousness were sown during his years at the Bayou Road School.

Often sent on errands for Principal Coghill, Alex delivered messages to other schools in the area. One school to which he walked frequently was called the Bucket of Blood School. Located on Galvez Street near Annette Street, a considerable distance from his school, it was a substandard tenement house converted into a school that was painted blood red. Several years later, Fannie C. Williams, one of his favorite Bayou Road School teachers, was appointed principal of that school.

Like the Bucket of Blood School, academic facilities set aside for Negro residents of New Orleans were shabby, dilapidated, and in need of major improvements. There were deficiencies not only in the number and condition of schools in the city but also in the availability of equipment, books, and supplies. Despite the deplorable conditions in the black public schools in the Crescent City, Alex benefited from the instructional program at his school because of the skill and dedication of his teachers.

Other aspects of Alex's life were broadened in his walks to and from school. Taking an alternate route home, he would occasionally stroll past a public park designated for whites only. The park, formerly Congo Square, was once known as Place du Cirque and Place des Negres. His father explained to young Alex that as early as 1805, in this open, grassy plain on the northern edge of the French Quarter, African slaves were permitted to sell produce from their gardens or other staples, such as fish or meat, on Sunday, which was their day off. Singing, dancing, and tribal traditions prevailed, allowing Africans the unique opportunity to share and preserve their cultures and languages, as well as earn money.[1] Knowing the historical significance of this now segregated park, Alex was critical of the leadership in his city that sanctioned such restrictions. Today this property is named Louis Armstrong Park in honor of the legendary black New Orleans jazz musician.

Occasionally after school, Alex would visit his maternal grandmother, Mamere Dejan, on Barracks Street. Her house was a family gathering place where aunts, uncles, cousins, and close friends, viewed as "almost family," would socialize regularly. Here, Alex was exposed to family traditions, loving relatives, tasty Creole meals, and the lively discussions of current events and political issues. He learned about the impact of the "separate but equal" Jim Crow laws that angered and frustrated the Creole community. Included in these conversations were references to historic acts of courage by Creole men and women who challenged segregation. Alex remembered the names of those he would later come to revere as early civil rights activists: Louis A. Martinet, a politician, lawyer, educator, journalist, and medical doctor; Rodolphe Desdunes, a lawyer, educator, journalist, and historian; Marie Couvent, a businesswoman who helped build St. Augustine Church and established the first free school for indigent black students; and Homer Plessy, the lead plaintiff in the legal case *Plessy v. Ferguson.* When he grew up, Alex recognized the breadth of their contributions and developed an abiding respect for their courageous persistence and sacrifice.

When Alex was nine years old, his oldest brother, Adolph, was hired as a merchant seaman for the Morgan Line. His ship made regular runs up the Atlantic coastline to New York City. Because he was the oldest child in the family, Adolph's time away on his new job was a significant family experience. Weary from the uncertainties of sporadic employment with his father and eager to earn a decent and regular wage, Adolph was ready to set out on his own. Articulate and loquacious like his father, with a passion for current events and politics, the twenty-year-old was extremely excited about the adventures that awaited him as he left the Port of New Orleans bound for Manhattan.

For Eugenie, Adolph's new job provided a dependable financial contribution, which helped to keep the family afloat. Initially, Adolph continued to live at home in New Orleans. As he matured and as the South became more segregated, he settled in Harlem, in 1913. His departure signaled the beginning of the gradual dissolution of the family unit. For Louis, Adolph's departure represented the loss of a reliable and skilled employee and the comradeship of his firstborn. For the younger children in the family, it stimulated their imagination to dream of life in places beyond New Orleans. Eventually, Adolph resumed his career in the building trade, working as a cabinetmaker, and purchased a home in Brooklyn. He remained in touch with his family and would invite his siblings to visit him in New York.

Before completing the seventh grade, Alex and his cousin Jules Haywood developed an interest in the performing arts and created a vaudeville escape act, patterned after that of the renowned Harry Houdini. They were intrigued by men in blackface, stand-up comedians, singers, dancers, and magicians. Once again, Tureaud's interests and talents paralleled those of his Creole heritage. New Orleans's first theater had mulatto stars.[2] Alex and Jules were booked into several Negro vaudeville houses in and around New Orleans for one-night stands. As they made the local circuit, they dreamed of hitting the "big time" in cities in the North. In an attempt to secure engagements, they contacted a relative in the business, who informed them it would be difficult for them to find work because they were minors. Disillusioned, they ultimately abandoned their act. Some time later, Alex would have the opportunity to pursue his interest in the entertainment industry with his brother Adolph in New York.

As Alex progressed through each grade, his academic achievements boosted his self-esteem and confidence. It was obvious to his parents that, unlike his older brothers, Alex was an intellectual and had neither an interest in nor the stamina for a life in the building trades. Enjoying the challenges of the classroom, he wanted to continue his education and graduate from high school. Upon completion of the seventh grade at the Bayou Road School, Alex enrolled in the Thomy Lafon School for the eighth grade.

Thomy Lafon, who was born in New Orleans in 1810 and died in 1893, was a well-known and widely esteemed Creole philanthropist. He had contributed sizable sums to political movements, including the American Anti-Slavery Society and the Underground Railroad.[3] Lafon is thought to be one of the greatest Negro benefactors of education and charity in the United States.[4]

The Thomy Lafon School, located at Seventh Street and Magnolia Avenue, was in a densely populated Negro neighborhood in uptown New Orleans. At the time, downtown Creoles and uptown black residents disliked, but tolerated, each other. The animosities between the two groups were long standing and focused on gradations of skin color and perceptions that Creoles considered themselves a privileged group. Altercations over territorial disputes occurred frequently. These fights were serious and occasionally deadly. Alex was not keen on the idea of attending a school uptown. However, there was no public school downtown that offered an eighth grade program.

Traveling on the segregated streetcar each day to school was distasteful to

Alex. A wooden sign reading "For Colored Patrons Only" was routinely moved up and down the row of seats, and the Negro passengers were required to sit behind this partition—a demoralizing daily reminder of white supremacy. For Alex, paying the full fare to ride a segregated streetcar in order to attend an inferior black school was disheartening. He would often stand, rather than sit, behind the screen as an act of defiance.

Alex became the target of an uptown gang and had to leave the Thomy Lafon School near the end of his first academic year there. At a picnic sponsored by the Bulls Aid and Social Club, a distant relative, a downtown Creole with the same last name, was involved in an altercation with students who lived uptown. Remembering the name Tureaud, the uptown students swore vengeance and threatened to attack Alex after school. The principal, Miss Sylvanie Williams, intervened before the confrontation could take place and personally escorted Alex to the streetcar before school dismissal. After that incident, Alex did not return to the Lafon School.

Determined to continue his education, he appealed to his father to pay his tuition at a private school in their neighborhood. Louis refused, not wanting to spend his money on tuition. Alex had already completed more schooling than any of his brothers and sisters. Louis suggested that his son work for him during the day and attend school at night, paying his tuition out of his wages. Alex learned of the Medard Nelson School from his Italian neighbors who were students there. Disappointed by his father's suggestion, he enrolled in the Medard Nelson School as an evening student.

Medard Nelson, owner and instructor, was a Creole of French and Indian ancestry. Professor Nelson, as his students respectfully called him, was admired for his intellect and his successful teaching strategies. His students, who were mostly Creole and white, worked in family businesses during the day and attended school at night. Professor Nelson operated an integrated school, despite laws prohibiting them.

Exhausted at the end of each day by his long hours as a carpenter's apprentice, Alex dropped out of the Nelson School after only one week. Even at fifteen, he knew that his current plan was not viable. Although it seemed as if Alex was stuck in a "no win" situation, he never abandoned his desire to obtain a high school education. With his hopes of becoming a high school graduate temporarily sidetracked, he focused his energy on his carpentry training.

During slow periods of employment, his father apprenticed Alex to a bricklayer or a cement finisher. Although he was young and strong, the work was demanding, and his obvious lack of interest in the trades made each task seem more tedious. He disliked physical labor and realized that he lacked the motivation of his brothers, who enjoyed their work. He was willing to learn the trade as a steppingstone to securing a high school diploma. His father had suggested for him a career in medicine. Alex knew that if he wanted to go to college, having a skill could help pay the bills.

Louis and Eugenie Tureaud separated several times during Alex's school years. He and his siblings watched their parents reconcile their differences and resume their relationship, only to separate again. Eventually his parents' marriage failed, and his father became estranged from the family. Some time later, Louis left the Crescent City and settled in New York City with his mother, who had joined his brothers, Robert and James. His departure initiated a series of dramatic changes for the family.

Eugenie and her children were forced to vacate their rented house on Kelerec Street and move into a small building on Eugenie's mother's property. It was a distressing experience, especially for the older girls. There was no privacy and no place to entertain their friends. Willie (Louis Jr.) and Eddie were struggling to find steady carpentry work. In addition to helping their mother and younger siblings, the two had wives and their own growing families to support. Fortunately, the older girls in the family were able to make their own clothing and earned money as accomplished dressmakers.

All of Alex's older sisters and brothers did the best they could to support their mother and younger siblings. Young Alex, too, felt a personal responsibility to see that his mother would always have money for food, clothing, and rent.

A neighbor and friend, Francisco Richard, whose father was an officer of the Grand Army of the Republic, a social and political organization of Civil War veterans, encouraged Alex to take a civil service exam to gain employment with the federal government. Francisco had passed the exam and was appointed to a job in Washington, D.C. Alex sat for the exam, but before the results were posted, he decided to leave New Orleans to seek work elsewhere.

Eric Bigard, a brother of Barney Bigard, the well-known jazz musician who played in Louis "Satchmo" Armstrong's band, informed Alex that a labor recruiter was seeking men, age twenty-one and older, to work in Chicago and would provide free transportation to get there. Alex knew that labor recruiters frequented the uptown neighborhoods, around South Rampart and Gravier streets, soliciting black workers for factories and mills in the North. In 1916, as World War I raged in Europe, the untapped southern black labor force was an attractive resource for these industries. Many southern states, including Louisiana, prohibited this type of recruitment, although that did not keep the recruiters from luring workers north.[5]

Alex's decision to leave home was made in haste. He felt that this move was the opportunity of his dreams. The uncertainty of the unknown excited him. Attuned to the risks and potential dangers ahead, the seventeen-year-old knew he had to keep his wits about him. To qualify for a job he told the recruiter that he was twenty-one. Perhaps the recruiter knew that he was being less than truthful because Alex, though mature for his years, had a youthful appearance. Nonetheless, a deal was struck and a dishonest contract, serving the needs of both parties, was mutually agreed upon.

Eugenie did not approve of her son's plan to join the Great Migration, the long-term exodus of southern African Americans to the North, Midwest, and West; however, she did not try to persuade him to remain in New Orleans. It was obvious that Alex was bent on seeking a future apart from that of his brothers and other male relatives in the building trades. In addition to creating a better life for himself, Alex was also deeply committed to helping his mother and younger siblings. He knew he could earn higher wages up north.

Totally dependent on the largess of her children and the generosity of her family, Eugenie persevered with dignity. She found comfort in the myriad of activities and adventures of her maturing children and relied upon her religious faith to ease her heartache and fears. For Alex and his siblings, the lessons of his childhood, as taught by his mother, were invaluable. As they experienced life, the Tureauds were able to confront their problems in a calm, rational manner, without malice or self-loathing.

Once his decision was made and his mother consoled, Alex and his friend Eric Bigard boarded the Illinois Central for Chicago. When he put his foot on the cast-iron steps of the train's boarding platform, Alex knew his life would change forever.

4
Southern Exodus

"Riding the blinds" to Chicago, as the trip was called by the hordes of Negro, Mexican, and Polish men who were Alex's counterparts, was a uniquely disturbing experience for a sheltered seventeen-year-old. Having ventured no farther than a few miles from New Orleans, Alex now traveled through the backwaters of Mississippi, the hills and valleys of Tennessee, the tobacco fields of Kentucky, and the farmlands of Illinois.

The year was 1916. He witnessed desperate men who ran to board the moving train, often risking life and limb in an attempt to exchange the peonage of the South for the promise of freedom and opportunity in the North. This experience was Alex's first exposure to the harrowing events occurring in the rural sections of the country as a result of the Great Migration. This exodus of people of color fleeing poverty, unemployment, and increasing racial restrictions would significantly increase the minority populations in urban centers above the Mason-Dixon line.

When the train reached Kankakee, a river city not far from Chicago, many of the men in the group were ushered off the train. A determined Alex did not budge until he reached his preferred destination, Chicago. Once there, he was assigned to a work crew and housed in a hut on railroad property a few miles from the Loop, the center of downtown. Laying tracks, driving spikes, and securing cinder beds, the men worked as a team, crawling out of the hut at different hours of the day and night. For their labor, the men were paid $1 an hour. Alex was thrilled with his rate of pay and proudly shared his weekly earnings with his mother.

Alex's fellow workers affectionately called him "Yellow Kid" because of his complexion. Although "Yellow Kid" was one of the youngest in the group, his peers respected him. He could read and write, and he was willing to keep the others, many of whom were illiterate, informed about work requirements and other job-related information outlined in written communications that were circulated in the rail yard.

One evening while he was reading the local newspaper, a headline about the Illinois Central Railroad labor strike currently taking place in the very yard where the men worked caught Alex's attention. Reading further, he realized that the Illinois Central Railroad had hired him and the other workers as strike-breakers. He knew that strikes were lightning rods for violence. His home on Kelerec Street in New Orleans was a few blocks from the docks along the Mississippi River, where disputes between labor and management were frequent. In 1913, three longshoremen in New Orleans picketing the docks of the United Fruit Company were shot by policemen; one died. Civil unrest followed, and the aftermath of broken bones, bloody heads, and destruction of property was widely reported in the local newspapers and gossiped about in his home and neighborhood.

There had been no demonstrations or violence in the Chicago rail yards. With time, tensions mounted between the strikebreakers, called "scabs," and the striking union workers. The federal government eventually took over the operation of the railroads. Yet Alex knew that he and fellow "scabs" were vulnerable and the potential for violence was ever present. They felt trapped, enticed by the dollar-an-hour wage, which was considered very good pay in 1917. With housing provided by the railroad, only food and clothing were their major expenses.

Three dollars a week was the highest wage Alex had ever earned while working for his father in New Orleans. Yet Alex knew that his father and brothers were skilled craftsmen who supported the labor movement. That knowledge made him more perplexed, feeling that he should walk off the job. When sending money home, he shared information about the situation with his mother. Concerned about his welfare, she contacted Alex's uncle and godfather, James Slater, and her older son, Adolph, residents of New York City. Slater contacted his friend Oscar Delarosa, a New Orleans Creole who lived with his family in Chicago. Delarosa, a cigar maker, had abandoned New Orleans for Chicago to seek a career and a life free of racial segregation. He visited Alex in the rail yard and quickly recognized that this was not a suitable place for the young man to work. He encouraged Alex to quit and invited him to live in his home on East Forty-second Street. Delighted, Alex accepted the invitation, never wanting to be on the wrong side of a picket line again.

Oscar Delarosa and his family socialized with other Creoles from New Orleans who had established a social and economic network in the northern cities where they now lived. Some could pass for white and did so, living in better neighborhoods and securing jobs unavailable to people of color. Alex knew that some of these people were too dark skinned to pass for white in Louisiana, but in places like Chicago, which had little exposure to Creoles, the difference between light-skinned Negroes and European immigrants often went undetected. If hair texture provided a clue to their racial background, Negroes would cut their hair short. Some even spoke with a foreign accent to disguise their black identity.

Alex discovered that many relocated Creoles were clannish, as they were known to be in New Orleans, and kept to themselves even in their new surroundings. However, they were industrious and supportive of each other and willing to help those who moved into their community. Delarosa continually encouraged Negro youths to go to school. Through his connections, he helped Alex get a job in a steel foundry.

The Western Steel Foundry was a huge workplace. Alex was awestruck at the process used to make steel. Ore was mixed with other materials at extremely high temperatures to produce molten steel, which was then poured into small forms in a large work space, sometimes called the pit. It was extremely dangerous work. Alex witnessed several accidents in which workers suffered severe burns on their arms and feet. Clocking out at five in the afternoon, exhausted, he would stop on his way home to get a meal. Afterward, he would go straight to bed. Up at five the next morning, he would return to the foundry for another grueling day's work.

Few restaurants or bars near the foundry served Negro patrons. It was well known that local bartenders would discard a glass used by a Negro. A bar located in the western section of Chicago, near the stockyards, was the one eatery where many ethnic groups were served without incident. For the price of a beer, the bar offered all-you-could-eat sausages, sardines, crackers, and cheese. Alex would buy a big stein of beer and devour all the free food he could. He also enjoyed the soup that was occasionally served. Thick with vegetables, it reminded him of the gumbos of New Orleans.

In the foundry, Negro men worked side by side with white workers, many of whom were recent European immigrants who did not speak English well. In Alex's opinion, these immigrants seemed to be more socially and economically deprived than Negroes when it came to securing employment and better housing. Many female immigrants were typically hired as maids in public buildings, scrubbing floors by hand. Alex discovered that a co-worker was making more money and had better working conditions because he was a union member. A policy against Negro membership in the union prohibited Alex from representation and these benefits.

One day after suffering a pulled muscle on the job, Alex missed work to seek medical treatment. When he returned to the foundry the next day, his foreman was angry that he had missed a day's work and reassigned him to the pit. Alex felt that his pay was not enough to undertake such a dangerous and demanding job. Realizing that he was shut out of union membership and the protections it provided, he quit his job at the foundry a few days later.

European immigrants and Negroes from the South were attracted to Chicago by the vast number of jobs for unskilled laborers. Expecting better housing, increased employment opportunities, and decent schools for their children, many became disillusioned when their expectations were not realized without discrimination.

On his first outing to enjoy his favorite pastime, swimming, Alex found that Negroes were allowed on the public beaches only in the section around Thirty-fifth Street. In his pursuit of other leisure-time entertainment, he discovered that segregation was also practiced in the theaters in downtown Chicago. Public transportation, however, did not require separate compartments on the trains and seats on streetcars for white and Negro riders. So as he explored the city, Alex could sit where he wanted, which was not the case in New Orleans. Additionally, social functions brought him into contact with young people from a variety of backgrounds.

Alex enjoyed theatrical productions and attended theaters and vaudeville houses, where he often encountered Negro men accompanying white women. Local policemen, repulsed by interracial dating, harassed these couples, although they rarely stopped them from socializing in public venues throughout the city. Believing that white women were interested in Negro men primarily for their money, many Negroes looked down upon these women, considering them to be no better than prostitutes.

The Catholic churches in Chicago were predominantly white until Negro Catholics from Gulf Coast communities moved to the city in large numbers. Negro children attended Chicago's Catholic schools in and near Hyde Park and around Nineteenth Street near Dalton Station. Alex did not go to church much during his stay in Chicago because he didn't want to pay for public transportation to the neighborhoods where the churches were located.

Negro-owned businesses were clustered in a section along State Street and monopolized vaudeville, the theater, and the nightclubs. Other common sights on State Street were the black peddlers who had a variety of merchandise to sell and the numerous public speakers on their soapboxes. The office of the *Chicago Defender,* a Negro-owned daily newspaper, was located in the same section of town. From his days as a *Defender* delivery boy in New Orleans, Alex was a regular reader of the publication. Editorials published in the *Defender* informed black residents of their responsibility as newcomers to Chicago. The paper urged Negro immigrants to talk clean, act clean, and literally keep themselves clean, often pointing out specific communities where residents were not living up to the prescribed standards.[1]

While a guest at the Delarosa home, Alex was friendly with their son, Augie, a nightclub piano player. Augie enjoyed riding in "big, fine" cars, which he and many other entertainers felt elevated their social status. Alex wrote to his family back home, joking that Augie's car was so long that even when driving in the broad streets of Chicago he had to turn around a corner two times.

Alex was fascinated by the politics of the city, believing that some positive changes were taking place for Negroes. The Republicans controlled Chicago. Local politicians had Negro neighborhood ward bosses, who obtained power and patronage in these positions. One of the ward bosses who rose to prominence was Oscar DePriest, a well-known Republican committeeman who later served as a member of the Chicago Parole Board. DePriest became the first Negro to serve on the Chicago City Council, having been elected alderman of the Second Ward in 1915, and was also a Cook County commissioner and assistant Illinois commerce commissioner. In 1928, he became the first Negro since Reconstruction to win a seat in the U.S. House of Representatives. DePriest was called the grand high chief of the People's Movement in the Second Ward and represented his Negro constituents ably throughout his five years of service. Alex was privileged to hear support for the elective franchise urged by DePriest.

Becoming more politically aware as he moved about the neighborhoods where Negro residents lived, Alex regularly attended the YMCA, where civic matters were discussed. The activities of the Negro press, the number of Negro candidates seeking public office, and the increased political activity stimulated by World War I impressed him. With regularity, Negro residents appealed to local, state, and national officeholders to improve public accommodations, housing, employment opportunities, and public education.

The city's Negro leaders, who had applauded President Woodrow Wilson's election in 1912, voiced their concerns about the quality of life for Negroes directly to members of his administration, although little changed. During Wilson's first term in office, the U.S. House of Representatives passed a law making racial intermarriage a felony in the District of Columbia. The president also allowed his cabinet members to segregate government offices—his new postmaster general being the first. Photographs were required of all applicants for federal jobs. Wilson reportedly explained that segregation would eliminate friction between the colored and white clerks and that this policy was not enforced to injure or humiliate the colored clerks. If what they heard of Wilson's explanation of this policy was true, many in Alex's political and social circles expressed deep disappointment.

Despite the active political environment and the excitement generated by the countless social activities available, Alex eventually decided that Chicago was not for him. A timely invitation from his oldest brother, Adolph, to come to New York City was welcomed. Alex began to plan his trip eastward.

Leaving Chicago for New York was a far different experience than leaving New Orleans for Chicago. Because he had limited funds, Alex bought a reduced-rate ticket that took him only as far as Ohio. When he reached Ohio, he was supposed to get off the train, but the young passenger hid his face in a newspaper and remained on the train all the way to Erie, Pennsylvania, where he then paid his way to Buffalo, New York. Alex financed the remainder of his trip by working for two weeks washing dishes in a hotel. In addition to his salary, his employment at the hotel provided him with four free meals a day.

While in Buffalo, Alex went to a see a motion picture, entering the darkened theater after the movie had started. When the lights came on, he found it interesting to see that other Negroes had seated themselves in rows separate from white patrons even though they were not required by law to do so.

Frugal as ever, Alex, on the last leg of his extended odyssey from Chicago to New York City, decided to ride the Erie Line, instead of the New York Central Railroad, because it cost $1 less. The Erie Line turned out to be a train transporting milk instead of passengers, and he arrived more than twelve hours later than he expected. Delighted to be in New York City at last and thankful that his brother Adolph had the patience to wait for him, Alex was finally able to relax as they traveled uptown to Harlem. Chicago had been a big step up from New Orleans for Alex, but New York was an even greater one. En route from the train station to Adolph's apartment, the younger brother was amazed by the number of Negroes he saw on the crowded streets of the then largest black community in America.

He enjoyed learning his way around town. Excited to be in New York, he visited relatives and internalized the energy and fast-paced activity of the city. Grandma Slater and his uncles Robert and James were all living in Harlem. At this time, the Harlem Renaissance, a "New Negro Movement," celebrated racial pride through poetry, prose, art, and music and challenged institutionalized racism through legal action. Alex reveled in this atmosphere.

This renaissance reminded Alex of the Creole antebellum renaissance that occurred during the mid-1800s in New Orleans, often referred to as the golden age of Louisiana literature. Men and women of color, poets and writers such as Rodolphe Desdunes, penned an insightful and significant body of literary work during the era. In 1845, the first anthology of verse written by free people of color in America was published. The 215-page volume, *Les Cenelles,* represented the collaborative efforts of seventeen New Orleans poets. In the 1930s, a Creole couple in New Orleans gave Alex a handwritten copy of the *Les Cenelles* manuscript. He would later collaborate with Dr. Edward Maceo "Red" Coleman, a fraternity brother from Howard and historian at Morgan State University, to reissue the poems in the edited volume *Creole Voices,* celebrating the centennial of the original publication.

Harlem, the best-known Negro community in the United States, was originally settled by Dutch immigrants and was named for a major city in the Netherlands, Haarlem. During the first decade of the twentieth century, Harlem in New York became a black enclave. Its population exploded by more than 200,000 before and after World War I, during the Great Migration. As northern ghettos grew in size, discrimination and prejudice intensified, and more and more hotels, restaurants, and theaters refused to admit or serve Negro patrons.

Once Alex arrived in New York, his primary objectives were to secure employment and review his options for settling down and continuing his education. To satisfy his immediate need for cash, he accepted a day job washing dishes. For fun and pocket change, he and Adolph performed in a local theater at night. The young and handsome bachelors, with attractive physiques, wore their stage costumes well. They enjoyed the attention of those who liked vaudeville, including the young women who frequented the Republic Theatre, where they performed.

Around this time Alex's sister Victoria was experiencing problems with her husband, a Creole from the Daste family. When the marriage failed, she moved to New York, where she completed high school and was trained in shorthand and typing. She worked as a secretary but left that job for higher wages in a local factory. While in New York, Victoria met and married her second Creole husband, whose last name was Floyd. That marriage also ended in divorce.

In Harlem, Alex involved himself in the Negro protest movement. He attended meetings and rallies with his uncle Robert Slater, who was active in the Republican Party. He also witnessed the pandemonium created by a parade featuring Marcus Garvey, a native of Jamaica and the self-proclaimed leader of the "Back to Africa" movement of the early 1900s. Garvey sought to instill black pride in the hearts of despairing lower-class men and women of color. He believed that he was the equal of any white man and encouraged his followers to feel the same way.

Bolstered by a large black following and flush with contributions from the Ku Klux Klan and other white racist groups, Garvey envisioned himself as the champion of the downtrodden. He proposed building a great black nation in Africa. He challenged the existing civil rights organizations, including the NAACP, which Garvey felt supported integration by amalgamating the races. Although the emphasis on racial equality resonated with Tureaud, Garvey's separatist and back-to-Africa rhetoric did not impress him. The New Orleans native's desire for an inclusive society in America and his desire to join forces with others who espoused this ideal strengthened. Garvey's movement collapsed in the late 1920s after he was imprisoned for mail fraud.[2] Tureaud would eventually witness Garvey's deportation from the United States, which took place from the Port of New Orleans in 1927.

In addition to his burgeoning political interests, Alex kept abreast of current events in theater and music. In 1918, he attended a performance of Madame Florence C. McCleave of Detroit, Michigan, the first Negro to sing at the old Aeolian Hall in New York City. Upon learning that Joe "King" Oliver was in town, Alex visited him and enjoyed the music of the Creole Jazz Band, which was quickly gaining popularity in northern cities. Proud of this musical form, which originated in the city of his birth, Alex was excited by the reception New York fans gave fellow New Orleanian King Oliver and members of his band.

Growing weary of his dishwashing job, Alex sought a more suitable and lucrative position. Good news arrived from New Orleans. He learned he had passed the civil service examination that he had taken prior to departing for

Chicago. His grades on the exam qualified him for a position as a junior clerk in the library of the U.S. Department of Justice in Washington, D.C.

Giving up the dishwashing job was easy. Moving to a new city where he had no friends or family was not. Even so, Alex accepted the job. After packing his meager belongings, he boarded a train for the nation's capital. Instead of "riding the blinds" to an uncertain future, as he had done months before, Alex headed for Washington to accept a job he had earned solely on his merit.

As he rode south on the train, the rich farmlands, sprawling factories, and the populous cities in New Jersey, Pennsylvania, Delaware, and Maryland impressed Alex and confirmed for him the wealth and power of the industrialized Northeast. In addition to the grandeur that he saw from the window of the train as it barreled south toward Washington, Alex observed the squalid tenements in the overcrowded ghettos, populated by destitute immigrants and disenfranchised Negro residents, that flanked the railroad tracks.

From his first day on the job in the nation's capital, Alex could hardly believe his good fortune. As a clerk in the law library of the U.S. Department of Justice, he was immersed in the law and worked in the presence of members of the U.S. Supreme Court and their staffs. This prestigious library served the nation's highest court, where such luminaries as Oliver Wendell Holmes and Louis Brandeis sat on the bench. Alex was stimulated and challenged by the responsibilities of his job, his colleagues, and the vitality of the law library. He worked diligently to improve his research skills. Once he acclimated to his new environment, he enrolled in Dunbar High School (formerly M Street School).

With the boundless energy of an eighteen-year-old, Alex explored the historic and governmental attractions in the District of Columbia, worked full-time in the Justice Department library, and attended high school at night. He met U.S. attorney general Thomas Ralph Gregory and Chief Justice of the Supreme Court Edward Douglass White. Justice White had been his New Orleans neighbor, having once lived on Esplanade Avenue, a few blocks from the Tureauds' home on Kelerec Street.

In Washington, Tureaud found the career path that his mother envisioned for him and that his father challenged him to seek out. Reading newspaper articles in the *New Orleans Times-Picayune* or the *Chicago Defender* did not compare with his daily experiences involving federal bureaucrats, politicians, and other powerful national leaders.

In 1920, at the age of twenty-one, Alex graduated from Dunbar High, achieving his childhood dream of becoming a high school graduate. Anxious to expand his knowledge and further his skills, he enrolled in a school operated by the Knights of Columbus. He attended, but did not graduate from, St. John's College in Maryland and also studied law privately under the tutelage of William Henry Harrison Hart, a Howard Law School professor.[3] Studying law was essential to Alex's continued intellectual growth. He never forgot the Creole cigar maker Oscar Delarosa telling him how important it was to get a good education.

During his years in Washington, Alex maintained regular contact with his family in New Orleans. He honored his commitment to his mother and regularly sent her money. When he could afford it, he would travel to New York and New Orleans. Alex matured into a handsome man, with thick straight hair, dark eyes, and a trim athletic body. He was always well groomed, appropriately dressed, and enjoyed an active social life.

5
Preparing for a Legal Career

Alex lived in several places around town when he first moved to Washington, D.C. A colleague at the Department of Justice found a temporary housing arrangement for him at Parkland Place, between Fourteenth and Fifteenth streets. Within months, Alex discovered that many of Washington's middle-class Negroes took in boarders or roomers. He was grateful for this practice because Negroes encountered racial discrimination when they tried to obtain housing or hotel accommodations even in the nation's capital at that time.

Alex found new accommodations in a home in a middle-class neighborhood on Thirteenth Street at the corner of Wallach, across the street from a fellow New Orleanian, Howard University professor William Bauduit. Professor Bauduit's sister, Agnes L. Bauduit, had been one of Alex's teachers and later became principal of McDonogh School No. 6 in New Orleans. This residence was also near the home of James A. Cobb, a professor at the Howard University Law School, who subsequently became Alex's teacher and mentor. Cobb would become a role model and a lifelong friend. Alex described William Fletcher, his landlord for the Thirteenth Street residence, as a "fine gentleman." Fletcher was a letter carrier and his wife a housekeeper. The couple had a six-year-old daughter.[1]

After enrolling in night classes at Howard University Law School, Alex moved to a rooming house on U Street, which offered board, was closer to the school, and was less expensive. Unfortunately, that arrangement was "quite a disappointment." "We were working students and we would come home tired and hungry and the landlord would never have anything to eat," he said. "She lived in a fine home, but she used our [rent] money to enhance her lifestyle."[2]

He moved into another rooming house on Ninth Street near T Street, where many other Howard Law School students boarded. Meals were served twice a day, once in the morning and once in the evening, at a cost of about $5 a week. Dinner consisted of "a lot of bread and white gravy," he grumbled. "Sunday dinner was sometimes served with a piece of cake."[3] In 1921, Alex was promoted to first-grade clerk at the library of the U.S. Department of Justice and for the final time while in law school he moved, this time into the home of a fellow law classmate, Eugene "Gene" Davidson.

Howard University was founded in a former beer and dance hall in 1867 as a theological seminary. The law school opened in 1869, and soon after other departments and professional schools were established. In 1895 Congress subsidized the institution over the objections of its southern members, who seemed to prefer ignorance rather than education for black Americans.

When Alex enrolled at Howard, tuition was $100 per year, plus a matriculation fee of $5.00. A library and athletic fee of $7.50 was also collected. Tuition could be paid in two installments, even though the university was organized on the quarter system. In 1924, tuition was increased to $125.[4] Rooming with the Davidsons cost less than campus housing, as the rate for students in the professional schools was $27 per quarter, plus a linen fee of $2 and a deposit of $1. Law students taking special exams were charged $2.

The Davidsons lived in northwest Washington, a middle-class neighborhood of single-family homes. Most of the houses were brick and had front and back yards. The back yards in many of these homes also had gardens. Alex was impressed that these homes had modern conveniences, such as central heat, hot water, and indoor bathrooms. More notable, the people who lived in these homes owned them. Alex and several other law students occupied the third floor of the Davidsons' home. Here, Alex enjoyed a lifestyle that provided not only the finest material comforts he had ever experienced but also tremendous intellectual stimulation and emotional support, the latter reminiscent of the environment he left back home in New Orleans.

Soon the Davidsons were regarded as extended family, and the father, Shelby Davidson, was in many ways a surrogate father to the young law student. Alex admired Davidson's devotion to his family, as well as his success as a businessman. Davidson was a lawyer and owner of a real estate business and a weekly newspaper, the *Washington Daily American*. His path to personal and professional success as one of the D.C. Negro elite was intriguing to a young man like Alex. As he grew older and matured, Alex bore a resemblance to Davidson, as they were both 5'5" and bald.

Born in 1868 in Lexington, Kentucky, Shelby Davidson had been a federal employee, an experience he had in common with Alex. In 1896, Davidson was employed as an unclassified laborer for the Treasury Department. It was the same year that he was suspended indefinitely from enrollment at Howard University. Davidson was suspended for violation of Rule XI, accused of having a relationship with a married woman.[5] Davidson fought the university, as he was convinced that a degree from Howard University guaranteed social and financial success.[6] By June 1896, the same year he and the university came to terms and Davidson received his Howard degree, he had read the standard texts for law students. He was admitted to the Kentucky State Bar in 1899 and to the District of Columbia Bar in 1900.[7]

Government jobs were highly coveted and among the most stable and respected occupations for Negroes during the late nineteenth and early twentieth centuries. Within a few years, Davidson was transferred with a promotion from his first job with the U.S. Department of the Treasury to the Office of the Auditor's Post Office Division. He invented improvements to the adding machine and designed tables and lamps that increased efficiency in the office. As the result of the segregationist policies of the Wilson administration, Davidson experienced the segregation of white and black workers in the workplace and saw many Negroes demoted to dead-end jobs.[8] He ended his government career after nineteen years.

He and his wife, Leonora Coates Davidson, were an enterprising couple. Davidson's law practice, real estate business, and newspaper, along with his wife's career as a beauty culturist and chiropodist, allowed them to live very comfortably. Leonora also taught at the National Institute for Women and Girls. As an entrepreneur, she marketed her own liniment and owned and managed a cafeteria.[9]

Shelby Davidson was a member of Washington's most prestigious and elite Negro clubs, including the Pen and Pencil Club of Washington. Initially formed as a literary society, the club quickly transformed into a societal cloister. Davidson was also a member of the Mu-So-Lit Club, a group financially solvent enough to own and maintain a lodge, which was a retreat for upper-class Negro men.[10] He was president of the Bethel Literary and Historical Association (BLHA). This organization grew into one of the most important public forums for the discussion of race issues in Washington, D.C.[11]

Davidson also was actively involved in the NAACP. The Davidsons often hosted NAACP meetings and conducted fund-raising activities for the organization in their home. While living in the Davidsons' home, Alex encountered many NAACP activists and prominent educators, including social reformer and scholar W. E. B. Du Bois. Du Bois had cofounded the organization with a white southerner, William English Walling, in 1909.[12]

Alex was fascinated by the history of the NAACP. Early in the twentieth century, Du Bois's Niagara Movement revived the call for civil rights in America. The Niagara Movement was named for the meeting place where fifty-nine well-known Negro intellectuals and businessmen met with Du Bois to form an organization that would provide a militant approach to ameliorating America's racial problems and the escalating violence toward Negroes. The original site for the conclave was Buffalo, New York, but the group was denied accommodations by white hotel managers in that city and moved to the Canadian side of Niagara Falls.

Du Bois, then a professor at Atlanta University, was exasperated by Booker T. Washington's conciliatory policies toward whites. Washington, a former slave turned activist, leader, and college president, was a major spokesperson for the Negro in the eyes of white and Negro Americans in the early nineteenth century until his death at the age of fifty-nine. Self-reliance born of hard work was the cornerstone of Washington's conservative social philosophy.

One of the most influential black men of his time, Washington, who in 1881 founded Tuskegee Normal and Industrial Institute in Alabama, was a confidential adviser to a number of U.S. presidents. For years, presidential political appointments of African Americans were cleared through him. Alex never met Washington, as the Negro leader died in 1915 before Alex became involved in civil rights activities.

Du Bois's Niagara Movement issued a manifesto, a Declaration of Principles. After reading and discussing the manifesto, Alex agreed with its basic principles, which supported the right to vote, rejected segregation in public transportation and public accommodations, and promoted for Negroes the right to other liberties enjoyed by whites. Owing to a lack of financial growth, insufficient communication, and Booker T. Washington's denouncement of its strategies, the Niagara Movement did not sustain itself as a viable organization and disbanded in 1910. It left in its wake the building blocks that became the foundation for Du Bois to construct a stronger and more focused organization, the NAACP. Du Bois, with a nucleus of Niagara militants joined by a number of liberal white supporters of equal rights, developed the guiding principles that allowed the NAACP to become one of the most enduring social forces in America.[13]

At the Davidsons' home, Alex also met minister Robert Bagnell; educator

William Pickens; poet James Weldon Johnson and his brother, Robert Johnson; Rhodes scholar and Howard philosophy professor Alain Locke; and attorney Archibald Grimké. Grimké, a Harvard Law School graduate, was a diplomat, author, editor, publisher, and vice president of the NAACP. He also held the distinction of being one of the first recipients of the Spingarn Medal, a prestigious award given by the NAACP to an American Negro for distinguished merit and achievement. In his lifetime, Alex would come to know a number of the Spingarn medalists, including Du Bois, inventor George Washington Carver, historian Carter G. Woodson, singer Marian Anderson, Dr. Charles Drew, musician/composer Edward "Duke" Ellington, legal giant Thurgood Marshall, and fellow New Orleanian Andrew Young.

Archibald Grimké; his brother Francis, a Presbyterian minister; and Grimké's daughter Angelina were also boarders at the Davidsons' home. Although Angelina was nineteen years older than Alex, they developed a close friendship. The teacher, poet, and playwright was born on February 27, 1880. She celebrated her birthday the day after Alex's. Having the love of family history in common, Angelina and Alex shared stories about their ancestors. Alex enjoyed Angelina's interest in New Orleans culinary specialties, recalling that he discussed with her the use of filé. He explained that filé is a type of seasoning, powdered sassafras leaves, put in gumbo with other ingredients such as crab meat, shrimp, sometimes veal and pork.[14]

Alex was fascinated by Angelina's life story. Her parents, Archibald and Sarah Stanley Grimké, had been a prominent biracial couple whose family members included slave owners, slaves, free Negroes, and white abolitionists. Two of her great-aunts, Angelina and Sarah, were prominent abolitionists in the North. Angelina Weld Grimké was named for her aunt, who had died the year before she was born.

In 1883, Angelina's mother left her husband, first taking three-year-old Angelina with her, only to return the young girl to her father four years later. Sarah's parents never approved of her interracial marriage, and possibly their granddaughter was a constant reminder of that marriage. Although Angelina and her mother corresponded, they never saw each other again.

When Alex met Angelina, she was an English teacher at Dunbar High School, his alma mater, a position she held until her retirement in 1926. Angelina began writing at an early age, subsequently penning 173 poems, of which 31 were published, a good number in *The Crisis*, the magazine of the NAACP. In addition to poetry, she wrote short stories, essays, and plays.

Angelina's best-known work, *Rachel*, a three-act drama, was produced as a vehicle for the NAACP to rally allies against the effects of D. W. Griffith's motion picture *The Birth of a Nation*. The NAACP strongly denounced the Griffith film, which depicted Negro men, particularly mulattoes, as brutes and rapists determined to destroy white American civilization. *Rachel* premiered in 1916 at the Myrtilla Miner Normal School in Washington, D.C. Angelina showed Alex the production's program, which noted, "This [production] is the first attempt to use the stage for race propaganda in order to enlighten the American people relating to the lamentable condition of ten millions of Colored citizens in this free republic." After several more theater productions in 1917, the play was published in 1920.

Angelina never married, and Alex never discussed whether he heard that reportedly she was a lesbian. Such a revelation was alluded to in her work and widespread news after her death.[15] She retired from teaching and left Washington in 1930, after the death of her father. Angelina lived out her retirement in seclusion in New York and died on June 10, 1958.

Alex enjoyed the camaraderie and fellowship of the many exceptional Negro men and women who attended Howard University. The Washington, D.C., in which he lived in the early 1920s was a thriving social and educational center for the Negro elite, though it was deeply racially segregated. Recreational facilities, for instance, were limited for Negro residents. Public parks and golf courses were segregated or sometimes not open to them.

Neighborhood theaters and private clubs that sponsored dances provided social activities for Alex and his friends. On holidays, many Negro clubs, sororities, and fraternities hosted picnics in nearby Virginia, on privately owned land, because public parks were for whites only.

A significant part of Alex's social life was spent in the company of Gene Davidson and Frank W. Adams, another law school classmate who after graduation would take a position with the D.C. municipal court and later become an assistant U.S. attorney. Adams was a protégé of George W. Crawford, a Negro who was the city attorney of New Haven, Connecticut. "Social life in Washington did not permit a dull moment if you were in the swing of things—and I was," Alex recalled.[16]

While at Howard, Alex joined the Alpha Phi Alpha fraternity. He became friends with several men from Louisiana, many of whom were classmates and fraternity members. The fraternity was founded in 1906 by seven Negro students at Cornell University in Ithaca, New York. While continuing to stress academic excellence among its members, Alpha men also recognized the need to help correct the educational, economic, political, and social injustices faced by African Americans. Alex and other fraternity brothers, such as Du Bois, New York black politician Adam Clayton Powell Jr., Thurgood Marshall, and Dr. Martin Luther King Jr., would put the organization in the forefront of the fight for civil rights.

As a New Orleans Creole accustomed to an active social life, Alex fit easily into the Washington social scene. He regularly attended formal and informal social functions on and off campus. Alex and several of his law school friends established the Informal Club. The primary function of the club was to sponsor social events and not require those attending to wear the expensive formal attire traditionally required at fraternity functions. Alex often jokingly claimed that he had only one suit and "that one was rented."[17] A rare personal photograph of his college days reveals a mixed group of revelers at a picnic in front of a wooden cabin in the Virginia countryside. Alex, casually dressed in cotton slacks and a collarless shirt, smiled for the camera. Because he could organize a good party, the law student was voted president of the club and served in that capacity until he left Washington.

Alex frequented the Howard and Dunbar theaters, located in the vibrant U Street District, in the northwest section of Washington.[18] After hearing a rousing speech by James Weldon Johnson at the Howard Theatre, Alex joined the NAACP. In its early years, the NAACP leadership was predominantly white. Du Bois, as editor of the association's official publication, *The Crisis,* served the only prominent Negro role. Between 1916 and 1920, however, a concerted effort was made to recruit Negro members in every region of the country. As a result, membership rolls increased tenfold during that four-year period. The organization's efforts to promote antilynching legislation and challenge state-supported disenfranchisement and residential segregation achieved enough success to establish the NAACP as a significant civil rights organization.

The stage of the Negro-owned Howard Theatre at Seventh and T streets served another important purpose in improving race relations as it cultivated the young art form from Alex's native Louisiana known as jazz. The motion picture theaters and live shows downtown were not open to Negroes. From time to time, however, when a big production came to Washington, Negroes who wanted to see it either had to attend separate shows held for them or had to be relegated to separate seating, apart from the white patrons. When showcasing black talent, the Howard Theatre allowed white patrons to attend and provided seating without color barriers.

Gene Davidson edited his father's paper, the *Washington Daily American,* and he and Alex frequently wrote articles about racial injustices. Once, Alex infiltrated a segregationist meeting held in the basement of a Catholic church by passing for white. He reported in the newspaper the secret pledge made by members of the all-white group to block potential black buyers from purchasing homes in the neighborhood. Vivid in Alex's memory of that meeting was the American flag, prominently displayed as the white audience members expressed their grief over the Negroes' attempt to invade their neighborhoods as residents.

On another occasion, Alex attended a meeting called by the District of Columbia Advisory Council. This council was composed of representatives from different sections of the city. Alex surmised that the government of the District of Columbia was in the hands of commissioners appointed by the president of the advisory council. Many of these commissioners were not D.C. residents. They commuted to Washington and were engaged in government services but lived in the suburbs in Maryland and Virginia. In most cases, the local Negro citizens had no involvement in the policy making or the government of the District of Columbia, but whites from surrounding communities did.

Alex was secretary to one of the founders of the Thirteenth Street Boundary Association, which sought to get representation on the D.C. Advisory Council. Before the group could be admitted, a meeting was held to discuss the matter. The advisory council eventually gave favorable consideration to the membership of the Thirteenth Street Boundary Association, but not before Alex had to listen to the speeches of antagonists in the meeting. One speaker said, "Mr. Chairman, the president of the United States is a white man. The judges of the District of Columbia are all white. The commissioners of the District of Columbia are white. I don't see any reason in the world why we need to have any Negro membership on this advisory council."[19]

After the meeting, Alex was asked by a white man also in attendance what he thought of "Negroes" wanting to be allowed on the advisory council. "Well, that seemed like a logical thing to me, seeing that I'm a Negro," he replied with amusement. The gentleman seemed taken aback but offered no apology.[20]

Alex temporarily left his job at the Justice Department to join the staff of the Mutual Housing Association, organized by Arthur W. Mitchell. Mitchell had come to Washington, D.C., in 1921. Interested in this venture because housing for Negro residents was greatly needed, Alex also was attracted to the possibility of making more money. He initially felt Mitchell was a sharp businessman; however, if he had had prior knowledge of his partner's background, perhaps the law student would have declined to join the venture. Early in his career, Mitchell, a native of Alabama, was founder and administrator of several agricultural primary schools of questionable purpose, and he arrived in Washington after several ventures in real estate that left a record of lawsuits against him.[21]

The Mutual Housing Association purchased apartment buildings, selling stock to various individuals who wanted to move into them. Mitchell was impressed with Alex's ability to make excellent sales pitches. In a matter of months, the new recruit was promoted from stockholder to codirector of stock sales with Joseph F. Singleton, also from New Orleans, to secretary of the association, at which time he became dissatisfied with Mitchell's business methods. Mitchell, who also operated a poolroom from the basement of this real estate office, insisted that prospective tenants purchase stock in the apartment in order to move in. Once all the apartments in their buildings had tenants, the company would sell the building and go on to buy individual homes.

It was frustrating to have Mitchell use strong-arm tactics, and Alex felt pressured to do his bidding in managing the properties. Although he and four other men owned stock as original stockholders in the company, Mitchell was the only one making a salary and monopolized the company's stock. Alex Tureaud later stated: "Arthur Mitchell reminded me of the [1933 film] *Emperor Jones* in his first lines, in which Paul Robeson [the actor who played Jones] said to Smitty, the Englishman: 'You see, Smitty, it's like this. The little stealing that you does, it puts you in jail. But for the big stealing like I does, I winds up as Emperor.'"[22]

Disgruntled, Alex and the other original stockholders hired Charles Houston to file a suit to try to remove Mitchell from the presidency and the control of the corporation. "We filed the suit in the District of Columbia and lost it there because the court, the Supreme Court of the District of Columbia, held that the corporation was a Delaware Corporation and all matters affecting the administration and the management and control of the Corporation would have to be filed in the court of jurisdiction, which was Delaware. Nothing else was done about it," Alex explained.[23] Fortunately, Alex had taken some wise advice to take a leave of absence from his job at the Justice Department, instead of resigning, allowing him to return to the job without any difficulty.

Mitchell was admitted to the Washington, D.C., Bar in 1927 and practiced law there for almost two years; in 1928 he also accepted a position running the Chicago campaign for Republican presidential nominee Herbert Hoover. Mitchell eventually left Washington, moving in 1929 to Chicago, where he continued the practice of law but also pursued his own career in politics. He became a pioneering Negro politician as a Democrat, and his work as a leading black campaigner for Franklin D. Roosevelt helped to secure his election to the U.S. House of Representatives from the Illinois First District in 1934, in which he defeated incumbent Negro Republican Oscar DePriest. He was reelected three times and served through January 3, 1943.

During his congressional tenure, Mitchell distanced himself from the NAACP on antilynching and other issues deemed offensive to members of Congress from southern states. As the only black member of Congress, he refused to assume a role as the nation's "Negro representative." While in his fourth term in Congress, Mitchell filed a lawsuit against the Illinois Central and Rock Island railroads after he was forced from first-class accommodations into a segregated train car just before it passed into Arkansas. His suit was advanced to the U.S. Supreme Court, which ruled that the railroad violated the Interstate Commerce Act of 1887, a federal law designed to regulate the railroad industry, but its jurisdiction was limited to companies that operated across state lines. Mitchell's victory against discrimination and later his outspoken objections to discrimination by defense contractors angered the Chicago party officials, prompting the end of his political career when they would decide to back another candidate for his congressional seat in 1942.[24]

He resumed the practice of law and enjoyed farming near Petersburg, Virginia. Tureaud held ownership in Mitchell's housing company as late as 1969, noting that shortly after Mitchell's death in 1968 his widow contacted him requesting that he sell the stock to her as she was settling her husband's estate.[25]

The law professors at Howard traditionally called students by their last name, so Alex, the aspiring attorney, was known as Tureaud. From this time forward, practically all of his friends, male and female, as well as his frat brothers and associates addressed him as "Tureaud." Only his parents and siblings addressed him by his first name.

Unlike Tureaud, many of his fellow law students were second-generation college graduates. A majority of his classmates were Negro males; however, during the years Tureaud matriculated, both black and white females attended the Howard Law School. Ollie May Cooper, a 1921 graduate, worked as secretary to the dean and later was appointed to the faculty, becoming the second black woman to teach law in the nation. By the early 1920s, Howard Law School had trained more than 75 percent of the black lawyers in the United States.[26] Howard helped Negro lawyers define their role in the profession using the law to achieve equal rights for Negroes.

Tureaud was impressed with his law professors and felt he received an outstanding legal education at Howard. Louisiana native James A. Cobb was Tureaud's constitutional law professor. Cobb, a former special assistant to the attorney general of the United States (from 1907 to 1915), later sat on the Municipal Court of the District of Columbia for ten years (from 1926 to 1936). One of the first black judges in the nation, he was first appointed to the position by President Calvin Coolidge and reappointed by President Herbert Hoover. Cobb's eloquent but emotional lectures on the Thirteenth, Fourteenth, and Fifteenth Amendments motivated many aspiring black lawyers, including young Tureaud, to devote themselves to securing equality and justice for all, as promised in the U.S. Constitution.

The Thirteenth Amendment made slavery unlawful within the United States or any place subject to American jurisdiction. The Fourteenth Amendment prohibited state laws that abridged the privileges or immunities of citizens of the United States; deprived any person of life, liberty, or property without due process of law; or denied to any person within its jurisdiction the equal protection of the law. The Fifteenth Amendment granted voting rights to U.S. citizens regardless of race, color, or previous condition of servitude. On the occasion of the 1922 dedication of the Lincoln Memorial in the nation's capital honoring the memory and deeds of President Abraham Lincoln, Cobb, a member of the Republican Party, reminded his students of the importance of the sixteenth president of the United States, who made these amendments possible.

Tureaud was a frequent target of Cobb's humor. He enjoyed verbally jousting with his law professor about law students' ties to the South. During initial class meetings, Cobb would ask his students where were they from. Most were from the South, but occasionally a student would say that he or she was from a northern city. Cobb would ask again, "Where are you really from? Not where do you live," musing that everyone wanted to identify with a large city, like Tureaud, who claimed that he was from New Orleans.[27] Tureaud would acknowledge proudly that he really was from New Orleans and didn't know much about any other places in Louisiana, particularly Arcadia, Cobb's native town. "That shut him up on that," Tureaud exclaimed with satisfaction.[28]

Tureaud admired Cobb's ability to speak with power and compassion, but above all else he was fascinated with his professor's thoughts about the freedoms that were guaranteed to all people under the Constitution. Cobb, tall and handsome, wore horn-rimmed glasses even when they were no longer popular.

He stuttered a bit when he tried to make a point. "Yet, when he got to the crux of the decision that he was interested in, he could put a great deal of emphasis on it and stir up our emotions," Tureaud recalled.[29]

William Henry Richards, who taught property, pleading and practice, evidence, and equity, was another professor who impressed young Tureaud. Richards, who was black, was the mayor of a town in Tennessee during Reconstruction. Like Cobb, he was a Howard Law School graduate and taught at his alma mater for thirty-eight years.[30] Richards instructed Tureaud on evidence, an important subject for which the textbook was *Greenleaf on Evidence*. "Most of his examinations were given out of the footnotes, rather than out of the regular text, because he wanted to see how extensive your study of the law was," Tureaud remembered.[31] As a conscientious law student, Tureaud always exceeded the basic requirements for each course of study. Even as a student in grade school, he set a higher standard for himself and seemed to enjoy the challenge of mastering difficult material. Discipline and fortitude were characteristics evident throughout his professional career. He would have been unable to work methodically and diligently year after year, challenging the status quo of the segregated South, without these virtues.

Recognizing that many of the Howard Law School students came from hometowns in the South, where they received limited preparation in reading, spelling, writing, and oration, Richards focused on remedial instruction in these areas as well as on his students' legal training. "He would always make us read from the text and then recite our interpretation of the text we read," Tureaud recalled. "And he did this largely to make us conscious of the necessity for being able to read and read with understanding. It was quite an experience, and for me it was torture to hear some of my classmates try to read those provisions of the textbook, because they were not good readers. I didn't have trouble with reading. I was always proud of myself as a speller and a reader and I could read almost anything at first sight. . . . I just seemed to have a natural ability in reading," Tureaud stated with pride.[32] According to Tureaud, Richards was a very strict professor, and his examinations weren't easy.

Judge Robert Heberton Terrell, an 1889 Howard Law School graduate who earned his undergraduate degree, magna cum laude, from Harvard University in 1884 and earned a master's degree in law from Howard in 1893, taught jurisprudence, pleading and practice in inferior courts, legal ethics, and domestic relations. A law school classmate of Judge Cobb's and class valedictorian, Terrell formerly taught at the M Street High School (later renamed Dunbar High School) in Washington. He later practiced law with John R. Lynch, a former member of the U.S. House of Representatives from Mississippi. Terrell maintained his practice until he received four successive four-year presidential appointments as judge of the Municipal Court of the District of Columbia, where he remained until ill health forced him to retire.

In 1891, Terrell was married to Mary Church of Memphis, Tennessee, whom he met while both were employed at a school for colored youth in Washington. Mary Church Terrell became active in the feminist movement, founding the Colored Woman's League in Washington in 1892. This club merged with the National Federation of Afro-American Women in 1896 and adopted the name National Federation of Colored Women. Mary Church Terrell was elected this group's first president.

Judge Terrell, whose light complexion often caused others to mistake him as white, entertained his students with humorous anecdotes about the absurdity of racial prejudice reflected in his personal life, as well as his experiences on the bench. One of Tureaud's favorite stories recounts a time when Terrell was returning home from the municipal court. The judge got out of his car near his residence at Seventh and S streets and noticed a number of younger Negroes whom he did not recognize milling about on the corner. To protect himself against potential violence, he called a Negro boy to come to him. "Are you so and so?" Terrell asked. Before he could get an answer, he said, "I know your daddy," smiling widely, all the while walking along with the boy, hoping not to be suspected of being white. Judge Terrell served on the Howard Law School faculty until his death in 1925.

Tureaud felt that Judge Terrell was a very good judge, having the appropriate temperament and educational background. Tureaud respected the Terrells for the contributions they made to the social and civic life of Washington.

Another of Tureaud's law professors, William Henry Harrison Hart, an 1887 Howard Law School graduate, was recognized for his expertise in the areas of criminal law, torts, and corporations. Through his political connections, Hart secured funds from the U.S. Congress for Howard's first law building and $10,000 a year to operate it. Hart earned the admiration of his students and the entire civil rights community when he was prosecuted, convicted, and fined for refusing to move to the "colored section" on a train traveling between the District of Columbia and Maryland. Hart appealed this conviction and won.[33] He left the law school in 1922, after thirty-two years of teaching.

Tureaud described his criminal law professor as a "very interesting character," and he and other students remembered that Hart enjoyed telling his classes that he walked from Alabama to Washington to get an education. Given to casual dress, Hart didn't fit the stereotype of a professionally dressed Howard Law School professor. "He had a short, stocky, thick neck . . . too big for any [shirt] collar that he could buy," Tureaud mused.[34]

Tureaud delighted in hearing Hart's firsthand account of his attack on the Jim Crow car laws. Hart, the plaintiff, argued his own case in court, and Tureaud enjoyed retelling the story as much as he enjoyed hearing it: "He went to trial court and was given forty minutes. Being the unusual lawyer that he was, his defense took two hours. And when the case reached the court of appeals, he was given unlimited time to present his argument to the court. [Hart] started during the daylight hours and by the time he concluded they were turning on the lights in the courtroom. . . . That was how effective he was!" Tureaud laughed.[35]

A forceful orator, Hart was interested in using the law to obtain equal rights for Negroes. Tureaud felt fortunate to have Hart as a law instructor, and Hart made a lasting impression on the young student. Tureaud listened intently when Hart encouraged students to study law so that they could return to do pioneering legal work in the South, where there was a great need for lawyers. "I always had an interest in returning home, even though I had opportunities elsewhere. I felt that I might be able to make a contribution in that particular area," Tureaud stated.[36]

Being exposed to these outstanding scholars, who were also men of uncommon principles, set the bar high for Tureaud. Justice, equality, and fairness were additional ideals that became an inherent part of Tureaud's persona. Several of his professors followed his career as a young lawyer, but none of them lived to appreciate the volume and scope of his accomplishments.

Tureaud had a white law professor, Charles Birney, whose grandfather had been a Civil War army officer. The relationship between the white teachers and black law students was cordial, though there was little camaraderie, he recalled. Tureaud believed that the white professors came to Howard University to teach out of a sense of duty to help educate Negroes. They were friendly and did not seem patronizing. "Besides, they were getting paid and they didn't mind earning the extra money," he said, recalling that many were either employed by local governments or in the legal department of the federal government.[37]

During Tureaud's years at Howard, Mason N. Richardson served as the law school's dean in 1921, and Judge Fenton Whitlock Booth served from 1921 to 1930. Booth, who was white, was nominated by President Theodore Roosevelt to the U.S. Court of Claims. He served as chief justice of the court from 1928 until he retired from active duty in 1939. Judge Booth died in 1947. A 1911 graduate,

James C. Waters Jr., returned in 1921 to serve as the school's secretary, librarian, and professor of law.

In their junior year, Tureaud and his classmate Frank Adams served as monitors in moot court. In this position, the two were not only overseeing the moot court cases, which were being tried by the seniors, but were actually showing the upperclassmen how to present their cases. Tureaud boasted, "At one point, we were bold enough to challenge the seniors and to try a case in the moot court as juniors, we did pretty well. Why, I thought we won."[38]

According to Tureaud, monitoring the moot court was like being the clerk of court. "I made up a docket and assigned all the students their cases, selecting them by alphabetical order. I prepared a brief summary of what the case was about and posted it on the bulletin board. I prepared a calendar of the cases and the trial schedule, so that each student would know far enough in advance to which case he was assigned," appreciating his commitment to the task.[39] Additionally, Tureaud was prepared to argue either side of a case if a student failed to come prepared. He not only helped fellow students but also impressed many visitors to the school's moot court session at that time. His recollections of these moot court cases included the *Collector v. Day,* in which the collector of the internal revenue filed suit against Day, who objected to paying a tax to the judge. Tureaud would never forget the concept "The power to tax is the power to destroy."

Known to be frugal, Tureaud did not buy case law books, opting to complete his assignments by studying the original cases, which he researched at the library where he worked. Using the original cases required him to do more reading. Tureaud didn't mind the extra work. His case abstracts or briefs for classes not only had more substance but also included procedure of the law that was involved. "It took a much longer time. But I spent all my time studying law. I didn't waste any time doing anything else," he joked.[40]

His love of the law and his respect for the Constitution motivated Tureaud to have many extended conversations about the law outside the classroom. He became a member of the Blackstone Society, a student organization whose members advanced the interests of the legal profession in lectures and debates on the role of common law in American and English society put forth by Sir William Blackstone. Blackstone was an English jurist who in 1758 became a professor of law at Oxford University, where he inaugurated courses in English law. He published his lectures as *Commentaries on the Laws of England* (4 vols., 1765–69). Blackstone's *Commentaries,* called the "Bible of American lawyers," shaped the principles of law in both England and America when its first volume appeared in 1765.

Tureaud studied Blackstone's *Commentaries* under Professor Hart the summer before he entered Howard. He felt that the course was "very helpful in understanding common law." Because of Hart, Tureaud often repeated the seminal Blackstone quotation "Law is the embodiment of the moral sentiment of the people."

According to Blackstone, "Civil law is given, not to create rights, but to protect already pre-existing natural rights." Wherefore, says Blackstone, the "primary object of law is to maintain and regulate these absolute rights of individuals." Blackstone defined absolute rights as those "such as would belong to man in a state of nature, and which EVERY MAN is entitled to enjoy, whether in society or out of society." These natural rights include "life and *liberty,* and which *no human legislature may abridge or destroy, unless the* OWNER himself shall commit some act that amounts to a forfeiture."[41] America's founding fathers were familiar with Blackstone's work and used it as a foundation for the U.S. Constitution.

In monthly meetings held on the third floor of the Davidsons' home, which Tureaud and his roommates, Gene and Frank, called "Blackstone Hall," society members expounded on the value of constitutional law in improving Negro life in America and provided support to each other in their rigorous law studies. After his father became ill, Gene was unable to devote as much time to studying law because he was responsible for the family businesses. Tureaud quipped, "Gene prepared for his law classes by sticking around some of us who were around the house" and "by osmosis."[42] These young law students debated weighty issues within a stone's throw of the statue of Sir William Blackstone that was erected in 1920 in the Federal Triangle at the corner of Constitution Avenue and Third Street.[43] Regarding his valuable time spent in Blackstone Hall, Tureaud stated, "It seemed like the fellows from Blackstone Hall had been singled out for honors at Howard's law school, something that the school did not do gratuitously."[44]

Charles Hamilton Houston, who later became one of the school's most celebrated deans and founder of the civil rights laboratory at the law school, began teaching during Tureaud's last year. In 1924, the Harvard Law School graduate joined the Howard law faculty and began his calculated assault on Jim Crow. All of the students, including Tureaud, recognized that Houston was working to bring the Howard Law School into national civil rights prominence. Hous-

ton substituted for the regular professor in a course in which Tureaud was enrolled. Tureaud, the student, was not impressed with Houston's teaching style
and demanding research requirements. Houston began teaching agency, surety
and mortgages, jurisprudence, and administrative law to first- and second-year
law students; thus Tureaud, a graduating senior, was able to avoid his classes.

Houston demanded a lot from his students, having no tolerance for laziness
and rejecting complaints that his assignments were too long. He told first-year
students, as he had been told at Harvard, "Look to your left and look to your
right because next year one of you won't be there." When he became the school's
vice dean, Houston lengthened the school year, improved the curriculum and
standards, and eliminated the evening program. Everyone who knew Houston
conceded that he demanded even more from himself than from others. Hard
work, integrity, principled conduct, thoroughness, and intellectual rigor were
standards that he expected from others as well as from himself.

Houston became known for telling his students that "a lawyer is either a social engineer or he's a parasite on society."[45] He defined a social engineer as a
lawyer who used his knowledge of the law to better the lot of the nation's indigent citizens. Tureaud would cross paths many times with Houston in his lifetime. He would witness Houston's career shift from a full-time law professor
and dean to a strident advocate for civil rights as the legal counsel for the national office of the NAACP.

Houston evolved into the kind of social engineer that mirrored his classroom definition: he helped build the legal foundation that enabled the NAACP
to successfully attack and destroy racial segregation in the United States. Houston nurtured and trained Thurgood Marshall, who inherited the mantle of leadership after Houston's untimely death.

In June 1925, Tureaud graduated with honors from law school and was
awarded a Bachelor of Laws degree. He also received a set of law books, valued
at $500, for earning the highest grade in legal research. As a graduate of Howard
Law School, Tureaud was the first person in his family to finish college. His father, then living in New York, must have felt a tremendous sense of pride. Louis
proclaimed when his son was in elementary school that he should pursue a career in medicine. Negro doctors prospered almost everywhere, even in Louisiana. Surely he thought that his son, now the lawyer, would work and live above
the Mason-Dixon line. Negro lawyers struggled to earn a decent living in the
segregated South.

Tureaud's mother, Eugenie, free from the responsibility of caring for her
children, all adults now and on their own, celebrated her son's graduation.

Supported by her children, Eugenie lived comfortably in the Seventh Ward on Mandeville Street. Over the years, the bond between mother and son grew stronger as Tureaud kept in touch regularly, often visiting her in New Orleans. He even convinced his mother to visit him in Washington, D.C. It was her first and only trip there.

Soon after graduation, Tureaud sat for and passed the District of Columbia bar exam. He was one of only two Howard grads that year to pass the D.C. exam, believed to be one of the most difficult bar exams in the country. Tureaud became a minute clerk for Judge Cobb, his former law professor, in D.C. Municipal Court Division 5. With the prospects of two other jobs, one as assistant attorney for the U.S. Department of Justice and the other as assistant U.S. attorney in the District of Columbia, he briefly considered remaining in Washington. In 1926, Tureaud's devotion to his mother, who was ill, drew him back to New Orleans and a job at the U.S. Customs House under the patronage of Walter Cohen, comptroller of customs and a leader of the Black and Tan, a group of Creole and Negro Republicans.[46]

Before his departure, Tureaud witnessed the historic 1925 Ku Klux Klan march on Washington. He observed the parade at his usual viewing spot at Fourteenth Street and Pennsylvania Avenue, which provided him with a better vantage point because the parade route turned at the Treasury Department before moving toward Pennsylvania Avenue and the White House. He was among very few Negroes watching the parade, which he dismissed as more amusing than anything else. He laughed at the costumed group of white participants disguised in sheets and pointed hats. He listened to the jeering and cursing by Negroes and a number of white onlookers. Although many Negro and white leaders in Washington were trying to discredit the Klan, the appointment of admitted Klansman Hugo Black as a justice of the Supreme Court in 1937 would raise the issue of the group's connection to the Democratic Party. The importance of the event was not lost on the young law school graduate, who would confront many extreme racists throughout his extended legal career in the Deep South. In addition to the KKK, he would have to contend with the Knights of the White Camellia, an organization of racists who vehemently opposed equality for Negroes in Louisiana.

During his absence from New Orleans, many changes had occurred in his family. Adolph was married and had moved from Harlem to Halstead Avenue in Brooklyn, New York, where he lived with his wife and daughter, Gladys. He was a successful cabinetmaker and was saving to buy the apartment building in which he and his family lived. Willie had purchased a home at 2211 Mandeville

Street, a duplex in downtown New Orleans, where he lived with his wife, Florestine, who was called "Ket," a Creole-speaking housewife. They would eventually have four children. Mother Eugenie and younger brother Emile lived in the duplex with Willie and his family. Tureaud joined their household upon his return to New Orleans. Brother number three, Eddie, a carpenter, was married and had one daughter, named Juliette. Unfortunately, Eddie died of spinal meningitis during the Carnival season of 1928.

While Tureaud was away, his sisters Carmen, Marie, Corinne, and Virginia "crossed the color line" and were living as white women. In the Creole vernacular, they were *passé blancs,* passing for white. At their request, all photos and documents that would identify them as colored were destroyed. Tureaud's nephew Stafford Tureaud remarked, "Their decision to live as white women was more economic than social. Times were tough back then and black people did not have access to decent jobs, only menial ones."[47] All of the sisters completed primary school and were taught to cook, sew, and prepare themselves for marriage. Although his sisters frequently worked as domestics, they wanted more and left to secure the better jobs that were available to white women. Victoria, the one sister who did not join her four sisters as they crossed the color line, left New Orleans and resided in New York.

Tureaud's mother and siblings agreed not to reveal information about the new identity of the four girls to anyone. For all intents and purposes, Carmen, Marie, Corinne, and Virginia no longer existed as members of the Tureaud family. The deep sense of loss that Eugenie and her other children felt after the four girls departed was akin to experiencing a death in a family, multiplied by four.

During the years that followed, only Eugenie and her children knew details regarding the lives of the four departed sisters. Victoria, Tureaud, and Willie's wife, Ket, secretly kept in touch with them. Corinne lived in New Orleans, married, and became the matriarch of a sizable family. It is believed that two sisters married and settled in the Carolinas. One was thought to be living in Chicago. Members of the family surmised that three sisters were married to white men and one was married to a Latino man.

Victoria, the only sister who maintained her Creole identity, was two years older than Tureaud. As children they played together and developed a very close and caring relationship. As a woman in her forties, twice divorced and weary of New York, Victoria eventually returned to New Orleans and lived with Willie and his family on Mandeville Street. She worked as a secretary in Tureaud's office and devoted a large part of her life to her brother's career.

Victoria was a loyal and trustworthy employee who could be depended upon at all times. She enjoyed being with her family again and was a loving aunt to a platoon of nieces and nephews. Anatole "Nat" Moliere, a Mason and lodge brother of Willie, became her third and last husband. Nat was a highly skilled blacksmith who shoed racehorses and was paid well for his work by successful stables, often traveling the racing circuit in the United States. Fluent in French, he was also frequently hired as a toolmaker and often forged parts for antique cars.

Emile, the baby of the Tureaud family, was a plasterer. He and his wife reared six children, eventually moving them all to California in the 1980s.

Although the illness of Tureaud's mother, Eugenie, was a compelling reason for him to return to New Orleans, there were other reasons as well. While studying law at Howard, Tureaud was again exposed to discussions of the heroic efforts of the Creole lawyers Louis Martinet and Rodolphe L. Desdunes, who protested racial discrimination in the courts and in the press. Martinet and Desdunes were among the prominent New Orleans Creoles of color who in 1890 formed the Comité des Citoyens to fight against racial discrimination. As a Creole, Tureaud felt connected to both men, and they became his role models. As a lawyer, he felt compelled to follow in their footsteps and to satisfy a yearning to "right the wrongs."

6
Return to New Orleans

It is more noble and dignified to fight, no matter what, than to show a passive attitude of resignation. Absolute submission augments the oppressor's power and creates doubt about the feelings of the oppressed.

—Rodolphe L. Desdunes, *Our People and Our History*

When he returned to his hometown in 1926, attorney A. P. Tureaud encountered fertile territory for legal work in constitutional rights (later known as civil rights). Legalized racial segregation, which resulted in second-class citizenship for Negroes throughout the South, was rampant in New Orleans. Black residents were not allowed to vote, and local, state, and national politics left them with little access to the public services most white residents took for granted. Schools, parks, transportation, housing, sewers, street lights, medical services, job opportunities, and police and fire protection were woefully lacking in black neighborhoods. The Creole leaders in Tureaud's Seventh Ward organized in order to improve living conditions in their community. In the tradition of the Comité des Citoyens that raised funds to attack Jim Crow laws in *Plessy v. Ferguson,* Creoles sought to improve their community by organizing civic leagues, which actively challenged the status quo.

Eager to get involved, Tureaud met Rodolphe L. Desdunes, fifty years his senior and accidentally blinded fifteen years prior to the young lawyer's return to New Orleans. Tureaud felt an intense kinship with Desdunes because of their similar backgrounds. Desdunes's father had been forced to leave Haiti in a political struggle. Born in New Orleans, Desdunes grew up in the Creole section of the city, was an employee of the U.S. Customs Service, studied law, and was interested in preserving Creole history. Throughout his career as a lawyer, Creole historian, and newspaper owner, Desdunes, like Tureaud, dedicated himself to the pursuit of racial equality.

Desdunes was an 1882 graduate of Straight College's law school, located on the corner of Esplanade and Burgundy streets in New Orleans. In 1869, Straight University, later renamed Straight College, was established by the Congregational Church "for the education and training of young men and women, irrespective of color or race."[1] The university was named for Seymour Straight, a produce merchant in New Orleans and Ohio who donated the land for the school and was its chief benefactor. Between 1874 and 1886, Straight operated a law department. Louis A. Bell, a Howard Law School graduate admitted to the bar in New Orleans in 1871, was responsible for the development of plans for the department.[2]

Although the law department existed for only twelve years, it played a critical role in graduating the first group of Negro lawyers in Louisiana. During this time, a number of black lawyers became members of the bar of Louisiana and began to redress the injustices to which people of their race were subjected across the nation. One of Straight's faculty members also wrote a handbook on admiralty law, a textbook that Tureaud had used at Howard and treasured. "That was and still is a very important subject of the law in Louisiana, because we do have admiralty jurisdiction," he stated. "We have in New Orleans the sea, the river, and ocean going vessels."[3]

Desdunes was well known locally as founding editor of the black newspaper the *New Orleans Crusader*. He was also the author of a history of black Creoles titled *Nos hommes et notre histoire* (Montreal, 1911), translated as *Our People and Our History*. Desdunes, who died in 1928, advocated equality before the law and used the influence of the press to promote his views. He sought the power of the legal system to bring about justice. The *New Orleans Crusader,* which was first published in 1889 by another Straight Law School graduate, Louis A. Martinet, called for assertive civil rights efforts in the local, state, and federal courts from 1890 from 1896. Tureaud identified with this approach, having had firsthand experience with advocacy through his writings during his Howard Law School days. As an attorney, he would use the press to advocate for civil rights for all Americans.

Tureaud's employer at the U.S. Customs House was Walter Cohen, comptroller of customs. Cohen was appointed to the position by Republican president Warren G. Harding in 1922.[4] A successful businessman, Cohen was president of the People's Industrial Life Insurance Company in 1910. As a result of his accomplishments in the Republican Party and his insurance business, he welded a significant amount of power for a Negro in Louisiana. As comptroller of customs, his patronage extended to the ports of New Orleans, Texas, and Florida.

Walter Cohen liked Tureaud and hired him as a customs liquidator. In this position, Tureaud was responsible for the accounting of merchandise entering the New Orleans port, verifying and computing the total dutiable value, and applying the appropriate customs duty assessment rate. He had to know the provisions of the Tariff Act, regulations and rulings under the act, applicable decisions of the U.S. Treasury and the Customs Courts and provisions of the Internal Revenue Code, and pertinent regulations of other government agencies, which applied to customs work and to the varieties of merchandise typically involved. It was a full-time job, yet the young lawyer was determined to secure the necessary contacts to establish his career practicing law, even if it was only part-time at the start. Cohen encouraged his young protégé to join social clubs, as well as civic and political organizations, in order to meet the current Negro leadership in New Orleans. Eager to be included in the inner circle, Tureaud associated with Creole businessmen and civic leaders, such as the Labat brothers, Emile and George, who were undertakers. George was president of the San Jacinto Club, a Seventh Ward social club with 100 members, and the New Orleans branch of the NAACP.

James Lewis Jr., whose father was the commissioner of public works, welcomed Tureaud's community involvement. Dr. George W. Lucas of the NAACP and Antoine M. Trudeau, general manager of the Safety Industrial Life Insurance Company, also became friends of Tureaud's. Trudeau's son, A. M. "Mutt" Trudeau, later became a lawyer in Tureaud's law office. Dr. Joseph A. Hardin, a well-known practicing physician, lived one block from Tureaud. Hardin, a native of Mississippi, was also the president of a locally owned insurance company that was sold to Metropolitan Life Insurance Company.

Tureaud entered into a community of like-minded men, many who welcomed the enthusiasm of a younger generation who shared a common philosophy and approach to solving legal, social, and economic problems. These men were inspirational role models who helped direct Tureaud in his civic involvement and legal career. Yet there were some who viewed eager young professional men as a threat to their positions of leadership in the political arenas of the segregated city.

The Seventh Ward Creole community was self-sustaining in many ways, with several businesses owned by its more industrious and resourceful residents. However, no matter how much the Negro community nurtured its youth and provided for the needs of its residents, local leaders knew they depended upon resources from outside their community. White people controlled these resources, and racial discrimination resulted in the denial of many services to people of color, despite the fact that all taxpaying citizens in America were entitled to them.

Tureaud witnessed firsthand the result of the decisions that white leaders made to protect their homes and business interests in New Orleans from devastation during the flood of 1927. The white leaders of the city agreed to breach a section of the levee with dynamite to protect the central business district, the Vieux Carré, and the affluent white neighborhoods in New Orleans from being flooded by the Mississippi River. They blatantly disregarded the havoc that would be caused by intentional flooding in surrounding parishes, namely, St. Bernard and Plaquemines, where the poor and less politically active residents, white and Negro, lived. Reparations were promised, but what was eventually provided to victims was woefully lacking, even though city leaders publicly promised that citizens would receive sufficient funds to rebuild their homes and businesses.[5]

Despite many disappointments regarding racists' policies and actions, Tureaud was proud that Creole leaders organized to remedy the situation. He embraced their strategies of using the law to fight for their rights. When Tureaud returned to New Orleans, Frank B. Smith, Renee C. Metoyer, and Joseph A. Thornton were the only Negro lawyers practicing in the city. Smith practiced in the recorder's court and was an attorney for the Knights of Pythias, an international, nonsectarian fraternity founded in Washington, D.C., by lawyer Justus H. Rathbone in 1864. The primary goal of the Knights of Pythias, which was the first fraternal order chartered by an act of Congress, was to rekindle brotherhood throughout the country following the Civil War years. All of the lodges that were established throughout the country were for white men only. However, a group of Negro men in New Orleans petitioned the organization for membership and became the only lodge for people of color. The segregated local unit of this fraternity was founded in 1881.

Metoyer, a graduate of Straight Law School, was one of Louisiana's first black notary publics. Nearing retirement, he relied on notary public work as his major source of income. Thornton, a 1914 graduate of Howard Law School and a World War I veteran, offered Tureaud space in the law office he shared with Metoyer. The law office Tureaud occupied with the two elder Creole lawyers was located at 612 Iberville Street. The advantages of this French Quarter office were its close proximity to the Customs House and to the courthouse. His nephew and later his driver, Stafford Tureaud, remarked, "At that time the civil district court was just down the block from his office. It was easy for him to walk in either direction if he had a problem."[6]

Thornton was admitted to the Louisiana Bar after passing an oral examination. He would consult with and refer cases to the young lawyer. However, the deaf and aging Thornton spent most of his time in the veterans' hospital. Tureaud felt that Metoyer, who died in 1937, and Thornton had not handled the type of legal work that the majority of Negro residents needed. He felt that cases needed to be litigated to establish a body of jurisprudence that would put an end to segregation and legalized racial discrimination. Tureaud would have the opportunity to involve his senior partner, Thornton, in initial civil rights cases he pursued for the NAACP, including a significant voting rights case. The case would be decided in their favor in 1946, the same year that Thornton died.

Tureaud was hired as legal counsel for the Safety Industrial Life Insurance Company, which was founded by Robert Brokerson, A. M. Trudeau, and Sydney Brandon. Through this association, Tureaud became a member of the Autocrat Social and Pleasure Club, was appointed to its board of directors, and in the 1930s served as club president. Founded in 1915, the Autocrat Club was located in the heart of the Creole neighborhood on St. Bernard Avenue. The club was a place where Creole men socialized, played cards, and shot pool. The club also sponsored dances, social events, and carnival balls, which Tureaud remembered attending as a young man with his siblings. The Autocrat Club was also a rallying place for legal and social activism.

The young attorney joined the club hoping to increase his visibility in the community and to expose its members to his ability to provide legal services. He studied the needs and desires of his people, finding them interested in the right to vote and in improving their community. Additionally, members of the Autocrat Club helped organize the New Orleans chapter of the Urban League.

Tureaud admired and respected the leadership skills of S. W. Green, a local and national officer in the Colored Knights of Pythias, who organized Negro residents to rally for a new hospital for veterans in New Orleans in 1932. Green, like many other Negro leaders with whom Tureaud worked, was active in civic organizations and the NAACP. Many other civic activists were married, and their wives were an integral part of the community as well, organizing and leading women's auxiliaries of their husbands' civic groups, holding membership in the NAACP, and working in the family business or in their own professions.

Green made his fortune as a grocer in New Orleans and later became president of the Liberty Independent Life Insurance Company. He organized and built the Pythian Temple in New Orleans, located in the heart of the central business district with a roof garden that was used for social events. The impressive twenty-story building on Common Street, near Gravier and Simon Bolivar streets, was built at a cost of $225,000. Louisiana boasted 9,000 Pythians and 81 lodges. Green's service to the New Orleans NAACP branch included assistant secretary in 1920 and member of the executive committee, as well as chairman of other committees throughout the 1920s and 1930s. Mrs. S. W. Green, born in Alexandria, Louisiana, was general manager of her husband's office at the Pythian Temple. She was also the bookkeeper, cashier, and purchasing agent for her husband's businesses. Mrs. Green organized the women's auxiliary of the Knights of Pythias, the Star of Calanthe, No. 27, and was the first Worthy Counsellor of the Court. She was also a member of the New Orleans NAACP branch.

In addition to his job at the Customs House and part-time legal practice, Tureaud focused his efforts on the activities of the civic leagues, which evolved from neighborhood social clubs. The Seventh Ward Civic League was one of the first to be organized, by Dr. Joseph Hardin and retired postal worker Alexander Mollay in 1927. Hardin and Mollay met with interested persons at the Autocrat Club to form the league. Taking their lead, Tureaud, A. M. Trudeau, and Arthur J. Chapital Sr., who would serve as president of the New Orleans branch of the NAACP from the mid-1950s to 1962, addressed gatherings in other neighborhoods and ultimately encouraged the founding of leagues in eleven of the city's seventeen wards. Tureaud also collaborated with activists in the neighborhoods below the Industrial Canal in the Ninth Ward. Johnson Lockett, treasurer of the local NAACP branch, who later had a school named for him in the Ninth Ward, was an outspoken leader active in league work.

The civic leagues called on the young lawyer to draw up their constitutions and bylaws. The leagues were active in stimulating community pride and fostering a desire for community improvement. Tureaud devoted part of each day to league involvement, once he completed his work at the Customs House. Not yet married and unencumbered by the demands of family life, Tureaud spent his evenings going to the various areas of the city, talking with residents and pointing out to them the benefits of civic improvement. This bachelor was able to get good meals at these meetings. Tureaud would note years later that the civic leagues were the nearest things the black community had to participating in the political process at the time because these groups elected officers.

Tureaud was involved in the formation of the Federation of Civic Leagues, which was composed of the eleven individual leagues. The federation, whose charter Tureaud assisted in writing, brought together representatives of each of the wards to serve as a clearinghouse for all of the needs in the city. An initial project of the federation was to clean up neighborhoods, which had been neglected by the city. Ditches needed to be dug so that water could properly drain off the sidewalks. The streets required grading, and sidewalks had to be built. At the same time, a numbering system for houses in certain sections was needed to facilitate mail delivery and response by firefighters and police. A significant achievement of the leagues was obtaining streetlights. League leaders also emphasized the need for playgrounds and schools in their neighborhoods.

Tureaud's lifelong journey to improve educational conditions for Negro children began with his work establishing the civic leagues. At the beginning of the 1920s, there were eighty-six public schools in New Orleans; of that number fewer than twenty were designated for Negro students; only two were recently built. There was only one four-year public high school, McDonogh No. 35, which opened in 1917.[7] Tureaud and other civic league leaders appealed to the New Orleans school board for new schools, improvements for the existing schools, and the hiring of an attendance officer. White schools got the lion's share of the money appropriated, and the Negro schools received what was left over. Few, if any, new school buildings were constructed for Negroes after *Plessy v. Ferguson*. When Tureaud and other civic leaders began to point out that fact, many white politicians claimed that the separate schools were equal. Tureaud agreed that they were separate but they were in no way equal. The civic league leaders were initially unsuccessful in trying to improve public schools. School board officials even maintained that not enough classrooms existed to accommodate all the children who would be forced to attend school by truant officers if they were hired.

The new Joseph Craig School, built on the site of the Bayou Road School, which Tureaud attended as an elementary student in the racially mixed Sixth Ward, was completed in 1927. White residents had opposed plans for this new construction because the site was not in a Negro section of town. To address the opposition, the school board decided that Negro students who would have transferred to the Craig School would be assigned temporarily to Bienville and Valena C. Jones schools until the new building for the Joseph Craig School would be built on Phillips Street.

Tureaud was supportive of Seventh Ward Civic League president Dr. Joseph Hardin's 1928 appeal to school officials to build a replacement for Valena C. Jones School. The school was named for one of the most celebrated Negro female educators in the South. Its principal, Fannie C. Williams, a leading black educator in her own right, worked with the leadership of the Seventh Ward Civic League, including Tureaud and Hardin, to sponsor fund-raising events for the school. Eventually, Principal Williams, with the backing of the Seventh Ward Civic League, was successful in petitioning the Orleans Parish School

Board for a three-story brick building and a playground. In 1928, the school board voted a quarter of a million dollars for the project. The school was rebuilt on the site of the Bucket of Blood School, which had been opened when Tureaud was in grade school but closed in 1915 when its building was destroyed by wind and flooding.

In October 1929, more than 2,000 people attended the dedication ceremonies of the new school, located at Annette and Miro streets. In attendance were school board member Isaac Heller, who gave the keynote address, and Principal Williams.[8]

The league officers were viewed as determined men and were highly respected by residents in their communities. However, these men received no salaries for their league work. In fact, residents had to pay to belong to the leagues, and many were willing to join because they appreciated the efforts being made. "These groups enabled Negroes to acquire skills in running organizations— writing constitutions, keeping minutes, and learning bookkeeping . . . and were vehicles for an ideology aimed at strengthening and unifying the Negro population."[9]

From 1928, when the civic leagues were started, Negro residents experienced harassment, public embarrassment, and intimidation when trying to register to vote. Becoming registered voters, paying poll taxes, and participating in the elective process were the focus of civil leagues for black residents, and progress was made on these fronts.

The league members began to combine their resources and volunteers with those of the New Orleans branch of the NAACP in order to raise money to attack the unconstitutional voter registration requirements. Each ward organization paid a $10 fee for NAACP membership. Financial resources were strained. At the same time the New Orleans NAACP leaders were preoccupied with trying to raise money to pay lawyers to assist Negroes who were falsely accused of crimes. The reports of police brutality were so numerous and the number of Negroes falsely accused of crimes was so high that Tureaud knew the local NAACP leaders could not possibly raise all the money that was needed. The NAACP had to be selective in the cases it agreed to represent. Generally, the branch took on cases only if its members felt that there was sufficient shock and outrage in the community. The civil rights issues stirred up the community's interest.

Tureaud felt his return to New Orleans was an opportune time for getting the local NAACP branch involved in legal action for civil rights. In 1927, he became a board member of the New Orleans branch of the NAACP. As chairman of its Committee on Publicity, he promoted the civil rights activities of the local branch, which was founded in 1915. Tureaud had developed a deep appreciation for the organization while a student at Howard Law School.

In courts throughout the country, the NAACP was the only national legal advocacy organization representing Negroes against the injustices of racial prejudice. The national office identified a group of Negro attorneys as legal representatives in several states during the 1920s and 1930s to prosecute lynchings, police brutality, and other criminal offenses against Negroes. A. P. Tureaud's name appeared in the NAACP national office's legal directory in 1928 as a representative in Louisiana.

The eager young attorney was a likely choice for several reasons. Tureaud was one of only four Negro lawyers in New Orleans and one of five in the state of Louisiana. While at Howard Law School, he had been a member of the Washington, D.C., branch of the NAACP and often was included in meetings with the group's founders and branch officials, such as W. E. B. Du Bois and James Weldon Johnson. As a Howard Law School graduate, Tureaud was a member of the network of alumni that Charles Hamilton Houston, special counsel to the NAACP, and later Thurgood Marshall often tapped. Most of all, Tureaud was a willing local representative for the organization. "I started out with NAACP work from the very first day I was admitted to practice law. The other lawyers [in Louisiana] were not active in NAACP work," Tureaud stated.[10]

A number of black lawyers throughout the South who worked with the NAACP Legal Defense and Educational Fund (LDF) acknowledged Tureaud's courage in associating with the NAACP early in the movement. One such individual was black attorney Lolis Elie of New Orleans, a graduate of Loyola University School of Law, who became a civil rights lawyer in his own right. "For Tureaud to become a lawyer was a major step. And to become a civil rights lawyer and identify with the NAACP and the NAACP Legal Defense and Education[al] Fund with Thurgood Marshall took a great deal of guts and a great deal of courage," Elie noted.[11]

Former NAACP Legal Defense Fund counsel Constance Baker Motley remarked that the NAACP staff respected Tureaud because "it took a lot of courage in those days to identify publicly with the NAACP. As Thurgood used to say, 'You know, he's putting his life on the line. We're getting the next plane out of here. But he has to stay here and face whatever reprisals there might be for our activity.'"[12] The young lawyer would be tested many times in his philosophical views and political strategies, but he would persevere.

Tureaud initially worked with James Weldon Johnson, the NAACP's first black executive secretary. His work continued with former Howard Law School dean Charles Hamilton Houston, who directed the NAACP's legal campaign as special counsel in 1930. Houston introduced Tureaud to Thurgood Marshall when they were visiting the South to experience firsthand the blighted conditions caused by rampant racial segregation.

The New Orleans native was enthusiastic about using his legal skills to help the local branch fight racial discrimination and assert the equal rights of colored people. The types of civil rights issues that brought Negro lawyers to the forefront were beginning to be addressed in New Orleans. When Tureaud joined the New Orleans branch, the local leadership, headed by president George W. Lucas, had won a victory against a city ordinance that mandated residential segregation. In 1927, the U.S. Supreme Court declared unconstitutional Louisiana legislation that granted cities with a population of 14,000 or more the power to mandate segregation in residential housing.

The 1930 murder of a fourteen-year-old black female by a white man, despite its horror, hardly surprised many in the Negro community. When an all-white jury convicted Charles Guerand for shooting and killing Hattie McCray, who had resisted his sexual advances, the Negro community was shocked and hopeful that justice would eventually prevail in the South. The New Orleans NAACP branch conducted a fund drive to support the litigation on behalf of McCray. Guerand was sentenced to death.

Within a short time, Tureaud became frustrated with the local leadership of the NAACP that had initially inspired him to get involved. The leaders of the local branch refused him the opportunity he most wanted, that of using his legal training to fight for equal rights. Twice the local branch sought the services of white lawyers instead of calling upon Tureaud. His boss, Walter L. Cohen, also was a member of the NAACP's executive committee. The executive committee members hired a white attorney to handle one of the branch's first voter registration suits. Expressing his dismay to the local branch leaders, Tureaud wrote, "I find it quite embarrassing to be taking one stand publicly that we privately do not subscribe to. It is difficult for me to subscribe to the action taken by our executive committee with reference to our test case of the registration laws."[13]

The test case to which Tureaud was referring, *Trudeau v. Barnes,* was one of the first court cases challenging Louisiana's discriminatory voter registration procedures. Writing to NAACP executive director Walter W. White, Tureaud reported that the first attorney retained by the branch was white and resigned before seeing the case through. "He submitted a $105 bill for services rendered and entered the Louisiana gubernatorial race." Tureaud wrote.[14]

The second white lawyer selected by the local branch was Henry Warmouth Robinson, a prominent member of the New Orleans Bar. This selection angered Tureaud and other local branch members. Robinson was unsuccessful in winning the case. In *Trudeau v. Barnes,* the federal courts stated they had no jurisdiction over registration complaints when the plaintiff failed to use all remedies available in the state courts, clearly pointing out Robinson's lack of legal knowledge.

Although the same Creole leaders at this time thought of Tureaud as quite capable in many respects, it was a challenge convincing them that a Negro lawyer could command the same respect from the courts as a white member of the bar. "Colored attorneys are sought only on occasions when free services are required," he complained, "or to make speeches for the cause."[15]

Branch president George Labat had berated colored lawyers for banality during a Republican Party meeting. Tureaud, five years out of Howard Law School, was incensed and angrily quit the NAACP executive committee in disgust. Tureaud called the existing branch a "self-perpetuating body" that never seemed to hold any elections for officers. In 1931, disillusioned, he appealed to the national NAACP office to either invalidate George Labat's recent move as local branch president or approve the creation of a second New Orleans branch. "We believe the NAACP to be a creative as well as a protest organization. Personal ambition is not a part of our makeup. Our desire is not for self, but for the cause. Unfortunately, the older men about these parts seek honor and glory for themselves first, and the organization's progress afterwards."[16]

His request to the national office did not receive the response against the Old Guard that Tureaud and the other Young Turks had hoped for. The national office stated that it was against policy to have two branches in the same city. Despite the national office's response, Tureaud maintained his association with the national NAACP and waited for the opportune time to effect change. He found himself squarely in a struggle between the conservative and conciliatory actions of the Old Guard members, who were not willing to allow him to use his legal training for the cause of civil rights, and the enthusiastic demand for more radical actions by the Young Turks, who were.

Historians Arnold Hirsch and Joseph Logsdon wrote that by 1931, following the deaths of Old Guard NAACP leaders Walter Cohen and George Lucas, the fragmentation of the black leadership, the defeat in the *Trudeau* case, and the onset of the Great Depression, local clamor for civil rights in New Orleans waned.[17] The economic catastrophe of the 1930s precipitated an ideological struggle within the national NAACP. Du Bois resigned from the editorship of *The Crisis* magazine in 1934, charging that the organization was dedicated to the interests of the black bourgeoisie and ignored the problems of the masses.

During this transitional time, Tureaud continued his association with the NAACP, but to a lesser degree. His work at the Customs House, a marriage and family life, and his leadership activities in social, civic, and religious organizations became his primary focus. These obligations certainly were enough to challenge any young man. However, Tureaud remained dedicated to a more noble cause and never lost faith in the belief that his legal education should and would be used to fight the injustices of racial prejudice and discrimination.

7
Meeting Lucille

At a dance held at the roof garden of the Pythian Temple, Tureaud was introduced to New Orleans debutante and Howard University graduate Lucille Dejoie in 1928. The roof garden was a place where men and women like Tureaud and Lucille could enjoy dancing to live music and was similar to the entertainment spots of their college days at Howard. Unlike the dance halls and clubs in Washington, D.C., that were privately owned and catered to the general public, the Pythian Temple's roof garden, owned by the Colored Knights of Pythias, was rented out for dances sponsored by individuals and organizations. Most of the white-owned clubs in the city were off limits to Negroes. Those that allowed Negro patrons did so with restrictions on seating and had separate entrances.

Young, attractive, and energetic, Lucille was working in her chosen profession, pharmacy, and was involved in the business affairs of her family. The two began dating and discovered many common interests, including their experiences at Howard University. Because he was seven years her senior, Lucille's girlfriends referred to Tureaud as the "Old Man."

Lucille Albertine Dejoie, born on September 26, 1906, in New Orleans, was the oldest daughter and second child of Louise Burel and Joseph Jules Dejoie. Her parents were descendants of *gens de couleur libres* and lived uptown at 3313 Danneel Street, one block from Louisiana Avenue. Lucille had three sisters, Marie, Myrtle, and Anna, and six brothers, Joseph Jr., Leonidas, Alvin, Byron, Burel, and Wellington. With ten children all born in rapid succession, Lucille's mother joked that she was embarrassed to be seen in public because she was often pregnant before her last child was walking.

Lucille's mother, Louise, was the only child of Lucille Boutee and Joseph

66

Burel, both of whom were born in New Orleans in 1851. According to the census of 1890, they were married in 1882. Joseph Jules Dejoie, Lucille's father, was the son of Octavie Segue, born in 1845, and Jules Dejoie, born in 1840. They were married in New Orleans in December 1870, and Jules worked as a pastry chef. The ancestors of the Dejoie family immigrated to New Orleans from Haiti.[1]

In 1904, Lucille's parents were married in a Catholic mass. They lived near their relatives, the Boutees, Segues, and Burels. Joseph was educated in the Crescent City and attended New Orleans University (opened by Protestants during Reconstruction), where he received his pharmaceutical training. Joseph and Louise, considered modern Creoles, lived a more Americanized lifestyle compared with many downtown Creoles. In fact, Lucille referred to herself as an American Negro, not as a Creole. Lucille, named for her maternal grandmother, inherited many of her mother's features. Both could have passed for white.

Lucille's family lived in a predominantly Negro neighborhood, where her father owned a drugstore and rental property. Her father and several of her male cousins were successful businessmen. In collaboration with his Dejoie cousins, the Louisiana Life Insurance Company was launched, with Joseph as a founding stockholder. A cousin, C. C. Dejoie, started the *Louisiana Weekly,* a black newspaper, in 1925. Dejoie's Pharmacy, located on the corner of Danneel and Third streets, served the Negro community living uptown. Initially, Joseph and Louise lived above the store. Within a decade, Joseph borrowed money from his mother-in-law and built a large, comfortable two-story house on Danneel Street a few blocks upriver from the drugstore. Joseph invited his widowed mother-in-law to live with them, which she did until her death.

Smart and enterprising, Joseph was a good businessman. After completing his new house, he converted their previous living quarters on the second floor of the store into offices, which he rented to doctors. He also owned an apartment building with four units and a grocery store on the ground floor.

Joseph's customers respected him as a caring professional. Everyone called him "Mr. Joe," and many of his customers regularly sought his advice, particularly regarding financial matters. With Mr. Joe's help, several longshoremen, who were hard workers but were not very well educated, opened bank accounts and eventually purchased homes.

Joseph provided a comfortable middle-class lifestyle for his wife and children, including live-in domestic help. Louise, his wife, could not drive and disliked using public transportation. Too frequently the streetcar driver would inform her that she was sitting in the section reserved for Negro passengers and would usher her to a seat above the screen, which separated white and black passengers. Even when Louise protested, the conductor would insist that she move, assuming that she was one of those liberal white women out to cause trouble. She refused to be humiliated in public, so Joseph hired a driver for her.

Louise had exquisite taste, and her home was adorned with porcelain vases and figurines, which she loved. An ebony grand piano and an oversized dining room table reflected her penchant for entertaining her large family and many friends. She enjoyed family gatherings, especially when her children and, later, her grandchildren converged at her home on Sunday afternoons to eat, socialize, and enjoy the camaraderie of kinship.

Lucille attended Thomy Lafon Elementary School. She then attended Xavier Preparatory High School for one year before enrolling in Talladega High School, a boarding school in Talladega, Alabama. Her older brother Joseph was also enrolled at the school. Lucille attended the School of Pharmacy at Howard University, in Washington, D.C., earning a Bachelor of Science degree in pharmacology in 1927. Joseph preceded her at Howard and returned to New Orleans, where he helped his father run the drugstore. He, too, was a pharmacist.

Also returning to New Orleans after graduation, Lucille worked in the family drugstore. With three pharmacists in the family, Joseph Sr. opened a second store on South Rampart Street in the heart of a thriving black business district. Leonidas, a younger son, was enrolled in the School of Pharmacy at Xavier University of New Orleans, a private Catholic institution of higher learning for Negroes established in 1915. After graduation, Leonidas also joined the family business.

While preparing an elixir for a patient one day, "Mr. Joe" collapsed. The victim of a massive stroke, he never regained consciousness and died within a few days. He was only forty-four years old. Joseph Jr. and Lucille took over during this time of extreme family crisis. Their mother, a consummate homemaker, knew little of the day-to-day operation of the drugstores or of the other family businesses. Her eldest son and daughter worked together to secure the family's welfare, keeping both stores and the rental property in the black. Louise was not coping well at home without her husband's support and guidance, so Joseph Jr. arranged for several of the younger children to attend boarding school in Virginia. Lucille helped her mother organize the household, and slowly the family regained its equilibrium until a second tragedy occurred. Joseph Jr., not yet thirty years old, was diagnosed with tuberculosis and eventually moved, with his wife and son, Patrick, to Arizona. Unfortunately, his illness did not respond to the climate, and within months he was dead. After the funeral, Joseph's wife and son moved to her hometown of St. Louis, Missouri.

Lucille was left to manage the family businesses alone. She also provided needed support to her mother. When it seemed that the family was near the breaking point, Lucille prevailed. She closed their second store and awaited the graduation of her younger brother Leonidas from the School of Pharmacy at Xavier University. Lucille's younger sisters and brothers had jobs either in the store or at home, which she arranged and supervised.

Regrettably, Lucille's sister Marie did not believe that her brother's tuberculosis was contagious. Against medical advice, she drank from cups and glasses that Joseph had used and contracted the disease. She lingered for several years before dying. Again, ever dependable Lucille was there to help her mother and siblings weather another family crisis.

Tureaud, no doubt, saw in Lucille a very attractive partner, referring to more than just her good looks. Not only did the two have similar family, religious, and educational backgrounds; Lucille, like Tureaud, also had a no-nonsense, practical side that displayed itself when handling the demands of life's challenges with her emotions in check. Lucille was a smart, strong, opinionated woman with a vibrant personality, who readily expressed her ideas.

Like many professional black men of the time, Tureaud used his initials, A.P., to keep white people, especially his adversaries in court, from knowing and calling him by his first name. Lucille called him by his last name, which sometimes gave the impression that they were business partners; however, they shared a deep love for each other, and their relationship was truly a partnership of equals.

Tureaud and Lucille enjoyed socializing with friends and family. Their popularity in social circles resulted in their names showing up on the guest lists for dances, balls, picnics, and other social gatherings. If it was true that color-conscious Creole residents often administered the "brown paper bag test" for admittance to the dances they sponsored, Tureaud and Lucille would not have been denied entrance to these affairs. Lucille was a member of Alpha Kappa Alpha sorority, the sister Greek organization to Tureaud's fraternity, Alpha Phi Alpha. Lucille, like Tureaud, pledged the Greek organizations while enrolled at Howard.

When Lucille joined the AKA sorority, she embraced a sisterhood of college-trained women that began in 1908 at Howard University. This sorority sought to improve the socioeconomic conditions in the community, at home, and abroad. The members of America's first Greek-letter organization established by black college women believed that it was critical to have an association that cut across racial, international, physical, and social barriers to help individuals and communities develop and maintain constructive relationships with others. The sorority organized the first civil rights lobby to ensure decent living conditions, to help secure permanent jobs, and to improve the conditions under which Negroes lived and worked. Lucille organized the New Orleans chapter of Alpha Kappa Alpha when she returned to the city from Howard. Throughout her life, she was a loyal *soror* who supported the traditions and practices of her beloved sorority.

Lucille's mother approved of her daughter's relationship with Tureaud because he was a Creole, reared a Catholic, and a professional who had a secure federal job. During their courtship, the country was on the brink of the Great Depression. Although many people felt that being a Negro civil rights attorney in the Jim Crow South was risky, Tureaud's income from the Customs House was sufficient to support a wife.

Their three-year courtship called for proper decorum and propriety. The popular couple was always accompanied by friends and relatives on their outings together. Lucille's mother frowned on her daughter being picked up by Tureaud in his old, unkempt Ford. She once volunteered a bedspread to cover the car seats in order to protect the beautiful dresses her daughter and Lucille's best friend, Suzie Brown, were wearing to a dance. Louise had to make this gesture only once. Tureaud got the message.

It might have been said that when Lucille accepted his proposal, Tureaud would be "marrying up," a term used for those who married into a higher socio-economic status than their own. Lucille's relatives were professionals, including pharmacists and businessmen. Tureaud's career path was unique among his immediate family; only he and his sister Victoria were formally educated beyond the eighth grade. His father, brothers, and other male relatives were all tradesmen and skilled laborers. He didn't pursue a career in law to become rich, as Tureaud was not interested in or impressed by the accumulation of material possessions.

Perhaps Lucille saw that Tureaud was rich in pride and ambition. He was a hard worker and willing to fight for a noble cause. Between 1928 and 1931, Lucille witnessed Tureaud's significant interest in and growing involvement with the community and civil rights activities, particularly his work with civic leagues and the NAACP. She realized that her husband-to-be would devote a great deal of his time to community service and that this work would keep him busy and often away from home. She also saw in Tureaud a person who enjoyed and was truly concerned about his family. She hoped that his commitment, like hers, would allow them to build a life together that would accommodate both family and career.

Their courtship ended on December 21, 1931, at Corpus Christi Church. "Teel," Lucille's nickname from childhood, at twenty-five, and Tureaud, now thirty-two years old, were married in a simple ceremony attended by immediate family and a few close friends. Because of the Great Depression, the Tureauds and Dejoies, like other families celebrating marriages at this time, decided that a small wedding would be more appropriate. Immediately after the ceremony the newlyweds boarded a ship bound for Cuba, where they enjoyed a weeklong honeymoon.

During their absence, the bride's mother sent engraved wedding announcements to family and friends. Upon their return to New Orleans, the couple moved into a newly renovated home at 1973–75 Rocheblave Street. The two-story double was located in the heart of the Seventh Ward, where Creoles lived in substantial numbers. The house was also convenient to shopping areas and near a local bus line. It was a short distance from the Valena C. Jones Elementary School and six blocks from Corpus Christi Church, often called the soul of the downtown Creole community. Lucille had formerly attended Holy Ghost Church on the corner of Louisiana Avenue and Danneel Street, in the uptown New Orleans neighborhood where she grew up. Now Corpus Christi Church became an important institution in her life.

Founded in 1916, by the 1950s the church was the largest black parish in the United States, serving approximately 12,000 Catholics.[2] For Lucille and A.P., not only was it the church where they were married, but it would also be where their children were baptized and confirmed. Catechism classes, Saturday afternoon confessions, Sunday mass, and the feast day celebrations were regularly observed by the Tureaud family at Corpus Christi Church. Eventually, it was also the church where several of their daughters would be married and funeral masses for family members, including Tureaud and Lucille, would be celebrated.

The two sides of their Rocheblave Street house were identical; each unit contained a living room, two bedrooms, and one bath on the top floor, and a kitchen, dining room, sitting room, laundry room, and garage on the ground floor. Accessible from each kitchen was a large yard, where the fragrance of honeysuckle and sweet olive filled the air in springtime. The Tureauds' move to the semi-rural Seventh Ward in the early 1930s proved to be a difficult adjustment for Lucille. The house was on a dirt street that was resurfaced once a year with clamshells covered with hot black tar. With a dairy farm one block away, a neighbor who had a dancing bear, and the unique lifestyle of the downtown Creoles, Lucille realized that living in this milieu would be a challenging experience.

Not surprisingly, Tureaud was proud to bring his young bride to the Seventh Ward. In comparison with other downtown neighborhoods, the Seventh Ward was viewed as politically and socially progressive. The list of residents from the Seventh Ward was impressive, including not only the leaders of the Seventh Ward Civic League, members of Corpus Christi Church, and schoolteachers and administrators, with whom Tureaud associated, but also such famous musicians as Jelly Roll Morton, Lizzie Miles, Manuel Perez, and Buddy Petit. Tureaud admired many of these individuals for their community pride and willingness to work for the betterment of all Negroes.

The Tureauds were a professional black couple, which was rare in those days. NAACP colleague Constance Baker Motley later acknowledged this. "Talk about a two-family income, they had it."[3]

Tureaud's mother, Eugenie, occupied half of the house on Rocheblave Street, and a door in an upstairs bedroom permitted easy access between the two units. Within months of his marriage Tureaud grew concerned about Eugenie's deteriorating health and invited his older brother Willie, Willie's wife Ket, and their three sons, Louis, Stafford, and Leonard, to live with their mother. Since Tureaud and Lucille both worked, Eugenie would be in good hands with Ket, a devoted daughter-in-law. Tureaud and Lucille often relieved Willie, Ket, and the boys on weekends by assuming responsibility for Eugenie's care.

At the time of the move to Rocheblave Street, Willie and Ket were grieving the sudden death of their teenage daughter, Marguerite, who died of tuberculosis. Coming to live with Eugenie, who was ill with cancer, was a painful reminder of their tragedy. However, their support was needed, and the move allowed them to rent their house on Mandeville Street, which provided additional income for Willie and his family during the height of the Great Depression.

Lucille continued to work as the primary pharmacist in the family drugstore, sharing that responsibility with her younger brother Leonidas. She alternated between day and night shifts, often working until 9 p.m. With the assistance of her brothers and sisters, the store was able to remain open from 9 a.m. to 9 p.m., six days a week. On Sunday the store closed at 3 p.m.

At least one Sunday a month, after closing the drugstore, Lucille and Tureaud joined the Dejoie family for dinner. "Mother" Dejoie would put both extensions in the dining room table to accommodate her dinner guests. She cooked and served large quantities of well-seasoned food to a lively and sizable gathering of her children, in-laws, and friends.

While working full-time at the Customs House, Tureaud continued to devote time to community and political activities and often spent evenings in his law office. He converted the downstairs sitting room in their home on Rocheblave Street into a home office with a separate entrance, so he could confer with clients without disturbing the family. Lined with an impressive collection of law books, Tureaud's home office was furnished sparingly with a large desk, an upright Underwood typewriter, a convertible sofa, and a few chairs. A large steel safe sat in one corner of the room. During the years when he was establishing his reputation, Tureaud often placed clients' legal papers in the safe before they left. This act was designed to impress upon them the importance of their legal problems and his commitment to confidentiality.

The home office provided easy access to locals who needed legal assistance. A Creole lawyer in the Seventh Ward, with an office in his home, was an anomaly. Tureaud needed work and was eager to establish a positive reputation as a competent lawyer. He valued opportunities that allowed him to expand his practice and enhance his reputation. Being available in the evening, at home, allowed clients who had jobs to meet with him after work.

Tureaud's private law practice was restricted during his more than fifteen years at the Customs House. In 1936 the Bureau of Customs inquired whether he was representing clients in matters that involved the U.S. government.[4] Careful not to jeopardize his federal job, the young lawyer wrote to the comptroller of Customs, stating, "I have an extremely limited practice carried on mostly for the purpose of keeping up with current problems in the law in which I am interested from the student's view point."[5]

For more than a decade after returning to New Orleans, Tureaud eked out a meager living as a lawyer. Initially, his practice involved civil, criminal, and civil rights work. Criminal cases usually dominated the dockets of Negro lawyers, especially in the South, because of the high rate of arrests of Negro men. He also handled wills for both Negro and white clients, and it was widely believed that white men who wanted to provide for their illegitimate children by Negro women chose Tureaud to prepare the appropriate paperwork. Trying to establish himself as a practicing Negro lawyer in the segregated South during the Depression was not easy. Despite many disappointments, Tureaud persevered because he was convinced that the law was the best means of fighting injustices and providing opportunities for a better life.

The Tureauds' home was a busy place. Relatives and friends dropped by to visit, often unannounced. Lucille and Tureaud, both from large families, were accustomed to a household full of people. They enjoyed being in the company of friends and relatives. Visitors were often invited to sit around the kitchen table and share a meal or a drink with the family. Many times social visits provided opportunities for relatives and friends to confer with Tureaud about personal issues that need legal remedies. Generous and discreet, he often provided his services pro bono.

As Eugenie's health worsened in the early 1930s, Tureaud and his brothers Willie and Emile were the only children in New Orleans available to assist her. Adolph and Victoria were living in New York. Eddie was dead. In their first and only visit since they had left the family to live as white women more than twenty years earlier, Carmen, Marie, Corinne, and Virginia came to their mother's bedside. They came together in one car, which they parked in Eugenie's indoor ground-floor garage. Once the car was inside, the garage doors were closed from within. The four women remained inside the house for the duration of their visit, spending time with only their mother and members of the immediate family. During this all-too-brief visit, the four women learned all they could about the events in the lives of their brothers, sister, nieces, nephews, and other relatives that had transpired since their departure. In the quiet moments between conversations, the Tureauds probably agonized over the fact that this unique family gathering would be the last for Eugenie and her errant daughters. After a few days the four visitors departed, as they had arrived, in secret.

Victoria kept her promise to her sisters. She destroyed photographs of them and other personal items of identification. Many years later, after she died, the birth certificates of the four sisters were found in Victoria's house by relatives. All four certificates were originals and were laminated.

Despite the anxiety and sadness that weighed heavily on Tureaud during the final stages of his mother's illness, he was ecstatic when Lucille informed him that she was pregnant with their first child. Sylvia Louise Tureaud was born on January 18, 1934, at Flint-Goodridge Hospital. The hospital, located on Louisiana Avenue in the uptown section of the city, was owned by Dillard University, a private school created in 1930 for Negro students by merging Straight University and Union Normal School. Union, founded in 1869 by the Freedman's Aid Society of the Methodist Episcopal Church, was renamed New Orleans University. A medical department, including a school of pharmacy and a school of nursing, was established in 1889. The medical department was discontinued in 1911, but the nursing school was allowed to continue. Flint-Goodridge Hospital was operated by Dillard until 1983. It was the only hospital in the city that allowed black doctors to attend and operate.

Sylvia's middle name, Louise, was chosen in honor of her maternal grandmother. From the moment of her birth, she was believed to be Louise Dejoie's favorite. Several months after Sylvia's birth, Tureaud's mother, Eugenie, died at the age of sixty-nine. Her passing was quiet and peaceful, following months of agonizing pain. She had been the significant adult in Tureaud's life. She taught him perseverance and the meaning of commitment. He deeply grieved the loss of his mother, whom he described as his most perfect jewel.

Letters and calls poured in from friends and colleagues of the NAACP and Alpha Phi Alpha fraternity from throughout the country expressing their condolences to Tureaud and his family. Their kind gestures, and those of Tureaud's friends, church members, and family in the Seventh Ward, helped sustain him and reflected Tureaud's widening scope of close and meaningful relationships and his ever extending community of professional, civic, and personal supporters. Following a morning funeral mass celebrated at Corpus Christi Church, Eugenie was buried in an aboveground family crypt at St. Roch Cemetery.

In 1936, two years after Eugenie's death, Lucille gave birth to a son, who was named for his father and would be called "A.P." He would be the couple's only son and would become more intimately involved with his father's civil rights work than any of the other Tureaud children.

In the spring of 1939, Tureaud received word from his brother Adolph that their father had died in New York. Prior to his death, Louis worked as a carpenter at an upscale Westchester County country club in White Plains, New York, located thirty miles north of Manhattan. At the time of his death at seventy-three years of age, Louis lived on the grounds of the club. Willie was able to join his sister Victoria and his older brother Adolph for their father's funeral. Louis was buried in Yonkers, New York.

During the summer of 1939, Tureaud and Lucille, expecting their third child, traveled to New York with their firstborn daughter and their son, Sylvia and A.P. Jr., to visit Adolph and Victoria and to see the World's Fair. While in New York, they also visited Nanine Slater, Tureaud's grandmother, and her sons, Robert and James.

Tureaud's mother had died the year his first child was born. The same year his father died, Tureaud's third child was born. Carole Lucille, whose middle name was given in honor of her mother and her great-grandmother, Lucille Boutee, was born on September 8, 1939.

Two years later, on July 7, 1941, Lucille gave birth to her third daughter, Elise

Eugenie. Selecting her middle name was easy. Upon seeing his new daughter for the first time, Tureaud remarked that Elise looked like his mother because of her light complexion, fine black hair, and freckles. Elise's skin was particularly sensitive to the sun and heat, which was quite uncomfortable during New Orleans's summers. Prickly heat caused a rash that covered her body. Sylvia and A.P. Jr. applied powdered starch to Elise's face and body in an attempt to ease her discomfort. Laughter followed because they thought it made Elise look like a ghost! Now that their household included four children, Lucille reduced her hours at the pharmacy and encouraged Tureaud to look for a larger house.

Tureaud's mother was the consistent role model for the development of his spirituality. His father, on the other hand, was a constant and well-informed critic of the political and social injustices that were legal in the segregated South and exposed his children to the issues controlling their lives. Always a Catholic, even though he chose not to go to church, Louis advocated commonsense leadership that was honest and moral. His children respected and benefited from his social and political activism.

When he returned to New Orleans after law school, Tureaud joined a Roman Catholic fraternal organization for black laymen, the Knights of Peter Claver. The organization was founded in 1909 in Mobile, Alabama. Its headquarters was in New Orleans. Just like the civic leagues and NAACP, the order brought together men, women, and children to promote community improvement. The Ladies' Auxiliary of the Knights of Peter Claver was founded in 1922, the Junior Daughters in 1930, and the Junior Knights of Peter Claver in 1971.[6]

Tureaud was a member of the Corpus Christi Council No. 60 of the Knights. In the early 1930s, he was elected the first national advocate to the Knights of Peter Claver from Louisiana. It is not surprising that Tureaud would be a committed member of the order. The organization espoused religious, civic, and social goals that the young attorney felt were worthwhile, and early in its existence, it went on record as supporting human rights and condemning governmental and religious laws and policies that limited those rights.

The national officers of the order include a supreme knight, a secretary, a treasurer, and an advocate. The national board of directors comprised appointees from the order's districts. New Orleans, Chicago, New York, and Los Angeles all had significant numbers of Negro Catholics. Each district had a local council, which was headed by a grand knight; each council sent delegates to the national convention. At the time Tureaud became a national officer, the group boasted more than 15,000 members, representing 22 states.[7] The order today is international, having councils in a majority of the states in this country and in other countries, comprising more than 18,000 Catholic family members.[8]

Tureaud was readily tapped for a leadership role as national advocate in the organization, which provided a number of social services to its members, including life insurance, loans, scholarships, and limited medical assistance. In addition to religious and social services, the organization informed its members of activities and policies that threatened the advancement of colored Americans and kept them apprised of the work of the NAACP and other groups that they could support in efforts to combat racism. The organization provided moral and financial support to the NAACP and other human rights groups.[9]

As national advocate, Tureaud represented the order in legal matters, including the settlement of insurance claims. He also helped to secure certification in several states so that insurance policies could be issued. Tureaud helped to publish the order's official organ, *The Claverite*. It reported the membership news, and through its editorial pages members of the order expressed their concerns about political, business, and religious leaders throughout the country whose actions they believed did not foster goodwill and progress for all.

In addition to receiving a salary for his position as national advocate, Tureaud's association with the Knights of Peter Claver enabled him to network on a national scale and gave him an opportunity to shape and influence the group's activities. On November 3, 1936, *The Claverite* reported that a fund, established by the Knights of Peter Claver, awarded scholarships to Archibald T. LeCesne, who later served as national advocate, and Vincent Malveaux to attend Howard Law School. Tureaud was instrumental in securing scholarships for these men, who were graduates of Xavier University in New Orleans and desired a career in law. Impressed by their ability and diligence, Tureaud became their mentor, later celebrating their graduation from his alma mater and keeping abreast of their successful legal careers. Tureaud became a role model and adviser to many aspiring young men and women who were interested in the law. Many of his protégés became trailblazers, the first Negro lawyers to achieve important political, judicial, and corporate positions in Louisiana and in several other states.

During his tenure as national advocate, Tureaud served with Louisiana's first elected supreme knight, Dr. Beverly V. Baranco of Baton Rouge, Louisiana. Tureaud's friend and fellow New Orleanian Dr. C. C. Haydel was national physician for the order in 1936 and served in that capacity for two years.

During 1939, the same year that Tureaud would litigate his first cases as local counsel for the NAACP, he investigated a charge of embezzlement of more than

$8,000 in funds from the order. It was one of the most difficult tasks he had to perform up to this time. Revelations in the yearlong investigation weighed heavily on the attorney and exposed him and other national leaders to a great deal of criticism. In August 1940, Tureaud provided a Special Report on Transactions in the "Glapion Affair" and recommendations to safeguard against such a situation occurring again. Tureaud's investigation of the matter was thorough; he meticulously laid out the facts in the case and made every effort to clear up misunderstandings and dispel rumors. Periodic reports during the investigation were published in *The Claverite* and were discussed at meetings of the board of directors throughout 1939 and 1940. A weary Tureaud noted that by October 12, 1939, the investigation represented fifty-two days and nights of work by him and fellow knights.

The final report issued by Tureaud in August 1940 had a conciliatory tone. He thanked the order's members who offered their assistance in checking the records and stated that without their help it would have been impossible for him to complete the investigation. Clearly, Tureaud sought to promote healing throughout the order and knew that it was necessary to foster continued support for the organization and its programs. In time, with the widespread circulation of the August 1940 report, the healing occurred. Tureaud's recommendations provided a more efficient and accountable method of running the order's business.

His work in the leadership of the order continued for nineteen years during the period between 1934 and 1963. In 1950, Tureaud was elevated to the position of national secretary and served in that position until 1954. As national secretary he was responsible for the organization's records and the handling of its funds.

During this time, the order continued to support community improvement efforts and was aligned with the activities of the NAACP. At the Thirty-seventh Annual Convention of the Knights of Peter Claver held in Baton Rouge, on August 5, 1952, Louisiana Education Association president J. K. Haynes addressed the convention. Haynes praised the legal work of Tureaud and other NAACP attorneys and leaders for the cause of civil rights. A number of these noted attorneys and leaders were in attendance, including Thurgood Marshall, Archibald Carey, John G. Lewis, James M. Nabrit Jr., Daniel Byrd, Professor I. B. Augustine, and Arthur Chapital.

The order's members formally expressed their dissatisfaction with the continued racial segregation in Catholic schools and churches. Their 1956 resolution presented to Archbishop Joseph Francis Rummel of New Orleans reminded him of "the ageless principles of the Catholic Church on the matters of brotherhood and the unity of men."

Tureaud sought the position of supreme knight in several elections, from 1956 through 1964. Dr. E. B. Perry proved to be stiff competition. In each election, Tureaud carried out an extensive campaign, at least as extensive as he deemed appropriate for the order. He discouraged New Orleans supporters who wanted to produce campaign buttons, believing that such an expense would set an undesirable precedent. Typically, Tureaud garnered support in the New Orleans area. Despite the attorney's efforts and the support of Supreme Knight Baranco from Louisiana in an extensive letter-writing campaign in 1958 and again in 1960, Tureaud was never elected to the order's top position.

He received the St. Peter Claver award of merit at the Golden Anniversary Convention, August 3, 1959. Tureaud confessed that his not being elected to supreme knight was one of the great disappointments in his life.[10] Throughout his adult life in New Orleans, he practiced his religion in his unassuming manner and was respected for his devotion to his faith. Tureaud believed that those who revered God, upheld the sanctity of the family, were faithful to both their friends and their commitments, were sensitive to the needs of others, and willing to come to the aid of those less fortunate would be both successful and happy in life. He sought to instill these ideals in his children. He was willing to obey the laws of this country until they could be changed. He advocated this idea to the Negro lawyers that he would mentor.

"Success requires temperance in all things, being thorough, and in having courage and determination to see things through to their happy conclusions," he said.[11] These are the ideals he would recommend to all who would listen and by which he chose to live his life.

8
Growing Community Involvement

Tureaud became involved with other Negro leaders who shared his goal of racial equality, which was pursued through the concerted efforts of the local black schools, their PTAs and scouting groups, the civic leagues, the YWCA, fraternities and sororities, the church, professional organizations, and the NAACP. Civil rights campaigns seeking better schools, community playgrounds, swimming pools, community centers, hospitals, health clinics, and municipal facilities, such as paved streets and refuse collection, encouraged Negroes to unite and work together irrespective of religion, class, or skin color.

When parish and city resources were woefully insufficient and even denied to Negro residents, the religious, civic, professional, social, and civil rights groups in the black community conducted fund-raising campaigns, and their collective resources benefited schools for their children. Typically, these benefits varied with individual schools based on the size of the neighborhood organizations and leadership strengths therein.

The Valena C. Jones School earned the respect of parents and students alike and became an outstanding educational resource in the downtown Creole community of the Seventh Ward. All the Tureaud children benefited from attending the Jones School, which was established in 1923 and also housed the first black normal school in New Orleans.[1] Principal Fannie C. Williams supplemented the enriched curriculum of her school with organized festivals, concerts, and dance recitals celebrating the traditions and language of the Creole community. Jones was the first public school for black students in New Orleans to provide free dental services to its pupils.

Many of the teachers from Jones School eventually assumed positions of leadership as principals, supervisors, and administrators throughout the New Orleans public school system. Dr. Mack Spears, for example, became the first Negro superintendent of schools and later president of the school board. Former U.S. congressman and longtime civil rights activist and aide to Dr. Martin Luther King Jr., Andrew J. Young, who served as mayor of Atlanta, Georgia, and U.S. ambassador to the United Nations, attended the Jones School.

Self-help campaigns were conducted by the school and included community-wide seminars and communication for maintaining clean and attractive homes and neighborhoods; for promoting better child rearing and character building; and for improved personal health and hygiene. Furthermore, they sought to eradicate adult illiteracy in the belief that enhanced education would lead to proper "citizenship." Pride in black history developed in tandem with the self-help focus.

Negro teachers taught black history as part of their professional commitment to instilling racial pride and nurturing positive self-images for their students. By the late 1930s New Orleans had a branch of the Association for the Study of Negro Life and History. Gertrude Green, a teacher at J. W. Hoffman High School, was its president. Tureaud and Dr. C. C. Haydel coauthored a book, *The History of Negro Physicians in New Orleans,* for this association.

There was still much more work to be done. Specialist Alonzo G. Grace of Connecticut, hired by New Orleans educators, produced a 1939 report for the New Orleans Citizen Planning Committee for Public Education titled "Tomorrow's Citizens: A Study and Program for the Improvement of the New Orleans Public Schools, General Program for Colored Children." The report confirmed what Tureaud and others already knew: that there was a "wide gulf in educational opportunity" between Negro and white students in New Orleans going far back into the history of the state and region.[2] Tureaud had personally experienced the limited educational opportunities available for Negro students. He knew firsthand that schools for Negro children were dilapidated and overcrowded. Secondhand books, furniture, and equipment discarded from classrooms serving white students were sent to schools for Negro students.

Lucille was active in the Valena C. Jones School Parent Teacher Association and served as its president for two terms. The Jones School PTA was affiliated with the national PTA, which provided support focused on the health and education of children through the relationship of parents and teachers in the school.[3]

While Tureaud devoted much time to fighting racial injustices, Lucille fulfilled her own commitment to community service and improvement. Many of her interests revolved around her children's educational and religious activities, such as the Girl Scouts and the Ladies' Auxiliary of the Knights of Peter Claver. She maintained an active interest in her sorority, Alpha Kappa Alpha. Her involvement with the sorority included scholarship support and later participation in the Ebony Fashion Fair fund-raiser. She belonged to several garden clubs and bridge groups and socialized with the wives of other Negro leaders.

Lucille was a participant in the YWCA during its initial attempts to tear down the barriers between black and white women in New Orleans. Julia Dejoie, wife of Lucille's cousin C. C. Dejoie, recalled that when the two groups of women first began to meet together in 1945, it was hard to resolve the habitual segregation even when seated in the same room. Dejoie mentioned that one way in which she and other Negro members were able to break the ice was to read the society pages of the local dailies. At subsequent gatherings, inhibitions could be laid aside and an easy conversation could be started by congratulating the white women on a recent engagement or other social accomplishments of their children.

Tureaud believed that segregation, like slavery, required Negroes to be dependent on white patronage because both systems denied power to Negro people. Segregation perpetuated a paternalistic relationship between Negro and white persons. The attorney detested paternalism in race relations. He saw it as demoralizing, a direct threat to one's self-esteem, and the cause of the poor public perception of Negroes. Tureaud also believed that segregation was evil, "separate but equal" policies and practices were ineffective, and the denial of any citizen's rights in a democracy was indefensible. With these views on segregation and his legal training at Howard Law School that prepared him to be a social engineer, Tureaud was highly motivated to fight segregation and its legal barriers to opportunity and choice.

Other circumstances and influences earlier in his background also motivated Tureaud to fight segregation and its perpetuating paternalism. Fiercely proud of his heritage, Tureaud discriminately identified with the best parts of it. The Creole history that the Tureaud family shared was rich with examples of Negroes who had job opportunities for which they were paid for their labor, had access to education, and other freedoms denied to most slaves. When stripped of many of the freedoms that they had enjoyed following Reconstruction, they did not acquiesce but instead used their job skills, education, and financial resources to fight for change. Tureaud's parents and grandparents shared these stories with him and his siblings, heightening their pride.

Tureaud's exposure to civil rights activists from an early age validated his

philosophy on equal rights in adulthood and taught him civic and legal strategies that would serve him well. His immediate family supported the young attorney's civil rights activities. They admired and looked to him for support not
only for themselves personally, but also for all people of color.

During Tureaud's quest for civil rights, he would not show reckless disre-
gard in his activities, maintaining respect for the legal system and all parties,
including his opposition. He was cautious in his actions for the benefit of himself and others. For example, a pragmatic Tureaud recognized the need for a
good working relationship with those in authority when he returned to New
Orleans to practice law.

Poring through the accounts of current events in the daily newspapers and
attending meetings and participating in discussions with civic, political, and
legal leaders in a variety of venues, Tureaud satisfied his thirst for knowledge.
He recognized then, and would experience personally later, that many Negro
leaders with longevity were only as aggressive as the times permitted. According to Tureaud, there were those who "appealed personally to the white power
structure in individual cases. . . . In these cases someone on the board of the
NAACP knew someone who was an authority or had influence, sometimes it
was the editor of *The Times-Picayune*. Through these personal interventions
our grievances would be made known."[4]

He saw what happened when having respect on a superficial level was not
enough. Tureaud knew that Negroes, as a whole, were poor, with little access
to the country's riches. Negroes had businesses that provided essential services
in their segregated communities; they also provided black people with pride in
ownership and a degree of self-reliance. But segregation and discrimination isolated Negroes from equal opportunities in the corporate world. And in this respect, Tureaud felt that Negroes didn't have businesses that "amounted to anything."[5] He was, therefore, opposed to voluntary separatism.

Experiencing a time in the segregated South when Negroes owned insurance companies, funeral homes, drugstores, and professional offices for dentists, medical doctors, and attorneys, Tureaud lamented, "Negroes didn't own
banks and expansive homesteads." He believed that another telling aspect of
their disenfranchisement was the fact that Negroes were not heads of any industries that received government subsidies: "The only subsidies we get from
the government are through the poverty programs and that's only for subsis-
tence, maintenance, and shelter."[6]

During his time as a federal employee in Washington, Tureaud observed
that the federal government provided white businessmen with subsidies such

as tax exemptions and procurement services. He realized that local, state, and federal governments contracted with white-owned businesses, helping them to profit from government investments. Tureaud felt that the services of big business provided for the operation of government. The building of a post office, or the construction of a ship or an airplane, for example, he saw as great undertakings with millions of dollars involved. When these ships and airplanes are built with government money and private funds, they are placed under contract for governmental services. Tureaud explained, "Big business in America, owned by white men, reinvests in small white-owned businesses, helping these businesses maintain a level of capital far above the small businesses owned by Negroes."[7] He knew that Negroes could not petition to the government for redress of grievances, for the Negro race had no representation in government.

"Being new in the community and not having anyone I could turn to who was an authority," Tureaud felt that his handling of police brutality cases would inevitably make him or his prospective clients the target of police abuse.[8] When he went into court to represent a Negro victimized by police officers or arrested for no readily apparent cause, Tureaud asked that his client be set free. Some judges admitted that there was nothing they could do for a black client. "They were quick to tell you that 'I couldn't afford to do that. These white people who are sitting in this courtroom are the people who put me in office. You don't vote. I couldn't do that.'" Tureaud heard these excuses repeatedly.[9]

Without quoting specific cases, Tureaud stated that on some occasions judges who had compassion for his clients would publicly announce a conviction of the accused but would officially record a dismissal of the case. It was customary that when a white person helped a Negro, the black community members publicly recognized that person and often presented a gift. Small tokens of favor were appreciated because they were so few and far between. These are the kinds of things that the young attorney witnessed on far too many occasions.[10]

Negro residents experienced significant restriction when using public accommodations. There were "White Only" signs on water fountains and restrooms. Public transportation was also segregated. Negroes spending their hard-earned money to buy food at a restaurant were not allowed to sit and eat; in many instances they had to use take-out service through a back window. The courts were not the initial avenues for addressing these problems. Tureaud and other Negro civic leaders sought solutions first by appealing to business owners and managers. They asked that the "White Only" signs be taken down only to be told that it was against state law.

With much frustration, those seeking jobs in record shops, five-and-dime stores, grocery stores, and furniture stores that were thriving on Negro patronage found that they could not be employed. The Negro civic leaders campaigned for jobs with little success. During the Depression, Negro leaders asked owners of large chain stores, such as the five-and-dimes, to employ them. Again, the storeowners would say they couldn't do it because it was against the law. Tureaud knew that the next steps would be to change the laws.

Many of the cases were initiated when local residents came to Tureaud or to the local branches of the NAACP with their complaints. "When we found that they were something of a serious nature, which probably needed the services of the NAACP, we would communicate it to the National office," Tureaud said.[11] He remembered numerous cases early in his career involving beatings, lynchings, and other kinds of criminal behavior, most often in the rural areas of the state.

In 1938, the U.S. Supreme Court's decision in *Pierre v. Louisiana* addressed the exclusion of Negroes from Louisiana juries. Hugh Pierre, a crippled black farmer living in St. John the Baptist Parish, was sentenced to death for shooting Constable Ignace Rousell, who attempted to arrest him for the theft of a plow. On an appeal to the Louisiana Supreme Court, the lower court's conviction was upheld. The state justices concluded that since only about 100 Negro men who lived in St. John the Baptist Parish could read and write, having 4 potential Negro residents considered for grand jury and the trial jury, out of a total of 300 residents, seemed reasonable. None of the four Negroes in the jury pools was actually selected.

The NAACP appealed the case to the U.S. Supreme Court, where the conviction was reversed and a new trial was ultimately ordered. Justice Hugo L. Black delivered the Court's opinion, stating that the Louisiana court's estimate of black literacy was unworthy of belief. Applying the precedent in *Norris v. Alabama* (1935), one of the cases in which nine Negro males, age thirteen to twenty-one, were tried for the rape of two white women in Scottsboro, Alabama, the Court decided that Pierre had been deprived of a fair trial because "Negroes had been systematically excluded--because of race--from the Grand Jury."[12] However, Pierre was convicted in a retrial and subsequently executed.

Despite setbacks like these, Tureaud was encouraged by each case in which the NAACP attacked racial discrimination and pursued civil rights for Negroes in Louisiana. In association with the NAACP lawyers across the country, Tureaud felt strongly that his involvement in Louisiana could have a significant impact on the matter of requiring fair trials for Negro citizens.

His disaffection for the Old Guard of the local branch of the NAACP continued. He felt that the leadership throughout the late 1930s under James Gayle, a publisher of church music, and his successor, Dr. Aaron W. Brazier, a physician, was ineffective and showed "little or no aggressiveness at all."[13] Tureaud felt that the two were barely keeping the organization alive. Criticism of the branch leadership reached a high point following the loss of a lawsuit the NAACP brought against the City of New Orleans for denying Rev. R. W. Coleman of the First African Baptist Church in New Orleans permission to rent the Municipal Auditorium for a concert.[14]

To Tureaud's great dismay, Brazier retained a white lawyer, Watson Meritt, to handle the suit. When the younger members of the NAACP branch, who were known to the older members as the "Young Turks" but who called themselves "the Group," heard of this arrangement, they went to Dr. Brazier and requested that the NAACP branch consider using Tureaud as their lawyer. Brazier and the members of the Old Guard maintained that Meritt would probably have a better chance of success with the case than Tureaud because the Negro lawyer had not been in town very long. Dr. Brazier suggested that he work with Meritt.

Tureaud refused to let the NAACP branch officers place him in a subservient position vis-à-vis a local white attorney and said that Meritt probably wasn't any better qualified than he was to handle the case. The Negro attorney unwaveringly rejected the idea of associating himself with a white attorney in this circumstance. He vehemently objected to doing the work and having the white lawyer as a front man. "I wouldn't have a white lawyer hanging around for anything," he asserted. "I wouldn't want that image to get out."[15]

Meritt was not successful in trying the case, which became "the laughing stock in the civil court" because the white attorney had excluded the issue of race in the discrimination case and the federal court dismissed it.[16] "You know, he only had to say that he [the plaintiff] was a nigger," the judge told A. P. Tureaud, "then we would have had to hear the case."[17] Tureaud stated, "It was quite disheartening to me because I had left so many opportunities behind (in Washington, D.C.) to return to my native state, only to find the going very hard."[18] As the result of the failed court case, Tureaud, along with a group of some twenty young members of the New Orleans NAACP branch, joined together to recruit new members to vote the branch officers out of office. This group, led by postal clerk Donald Jones, included truck drivers, insurance agents, and letter carriers. The only professionals involved were Tureaud and a few schoolteachers.

Tureaud's association with working- and middle-class Negro residents was atypical for a Creole professional. Historically, the downtown Creoles of the

Seventh Ward socialized almost exclusively with each other. They found comfort with their neighbors, who were predominantly people of mixed-race backgrounds and shared similar values, religious practices, and social life in closed circles or organizations. However, Tureaud knew that in order to achieve his goals, all Negroes had to be included in the struggle. He proved to be a consensus builder, reaching out to all segments of the black community, seeing the fight for civil rights as something in which all Negroes needed to participate. Although he was a professional man, Tureaud was not a member of the Creole upper class. He was the only member of his immediate family to earn a professional degree, but he readily identified with the financial struggles of his working-class family of skilled laborers. His status would change as he established himself as a competent lawyer and committed civil rights leader, but he would continue to fight for all Negroes, regardless of class.

In the garage of Donald Jones's home, sitting on chairs borrowed from neighbors, members of the executive committee would meet on Sundays to develop strategies for improving the local branch. Tureaud realized that the executive committee was divided into three distinct groups, the Old Guard, the Progressive Ticket, and the Group. James Edward Stewart, a supervisor for the Louisiana Insurance Company, was suggested as president; however, there were members of the executive committee who wanted a professional at the helm. J. Edwin Wilkins, a pharmacist at Flint-Goodridge Hospital and president of the Autocrat Club, was the choice of those opposing Stewart. The Progressive Ticket, supporting Wilkins, was favored by prominent Creoles, including Dr. Rivers Fredericks, chief surgeon at Flint-Goodridge Hospital and president of the Louisiana Industrial Life Insurance Company.

Thurgood Marshall and NAACP national president Walter White, aware of the Group's planned coup, warned Donald Jones and his associates to play by the rules. Marshall, comfortable with the loyalty toward him and the NAACP that Tureaud and the others displayed, believed new leadership in the New Orleans branch would rejuvenate the organization. By 1939, 318 new members had joined, and the branch developed a slate of new officers that included Creoles and non-Creoles, from downtown and uptown areas of the city. A jubilant Tureaud participated in the pre-election parade through the Seventh Ward. The excitement and fanfare, which culminated in a rally at Jeunes Amis Hall, were contagious, increased interest in the election, and added visibility for the NAACP and the young lawyer.

Tureaud received permission from the national NAACP office to continue admitting members into the organization until the day of the election. The Masonic Hall on South Rampart Street was rented as a voting site because a large number of voters was anticipated. The 618 voters and almost as many onlookers attracted the attention of the local police chief, who sent out a special squad to monitor the situation.

Wilkins won by a narrow margin of thirty votes, as did most of the businessmen and professionals on the Progressive Ticket. It was rumored that the victory was supported by a bloc vote from members of the International Longshoremen's Association (ILA). It was also rumored that the ILA had purchased NAACP memberships for all its men. The seventeen-member executive committee now consisted of thirteen from the Progressive Ticket, three members of the Old Guard, and one member of the Group. The Group, with only one member on the executive committee, was still able to wield influence through the large number of members it had recruited into the local branch. Clarence Laws was the Group's elected representative on the board. Laws was the executive secretary of the New Orleans Urban League. In a departure from the Old Guard's opposition to using Negro lawyers, Wilkins invited Tureaud to be the branch's legal adviser. This overture also served to bridge the division between the Old Guard and the younger members of the Group.

Membership in the Group remained at ten following the election. Insurance agent Daniel Byrd; letter carrier Arthur Chapital; postal clerks Donald and Victor Jones; executive secretary of the New Orleans Urban League Clarence Laws; writer and insurance agent Octave Lilly Jr.; schoolteacher Winston Moore; postal clerk and journalist John E. Rousseau; labor organizer Raymond Tillman; and attorney A. P. Tureaud became a force to be reckoned with as they helped the NAACP in New Orleans evolve into a unified Negro organization that crossed class and cultural lines. Tureaud's active involvement with the NAACP was a natural outgrowth of his desire to continue the fight for equality that his Creole ancestors and heroes had begun.

In 1940, a controversy arose involving the local branch of the NAACP when Marian Anderson, acclaimed contralto vocalist, was scheduled to sing at the New Orleans Municipal Auditorium to a "white only" audience. A year earlier on the national scene, the Daughters of the American Revolution (DAR) refused to allow Anderson to sing in Constitution Hall, which the DAR owned. First Lady Eleanor Roosevelt and Secretary of the Interior Harold Ickes made it possible for Anderson to sing on the steps of the Lincoln Memorial. The event drew an audience of 75,000.

Anderson's scheduled performance in New Orleans was met with protest when the organizers conceded only to allowing Negroes to sit in the balcony, a form of "horizontal" segregation. The NAACP, led by executive director Roy Wilkins and supported by the Group, voted to boycott the concert; however, members of the local Negro fraternities and sororities wanted the concert to go on. The controversy was played out in an editorial in the *Louisiana Weekly*, which accused Wilkins of "fighting to keep Negroes from hearing a great Negro artist."[19]

The NAACP lost the fight, and Anderson's concert was held as scheduled, with designated seats in the balcony for Negroes. Anderson accepted the invitation to sing in New Orleans despite the organizers' treatment of Negro patrons. Tureaud felt that, although Anderson was aware of the controversy, art and career for her came before racial crusades and political activism. By taking the position it did, the NAACP garnered increased support from other sectors of the Negro community, including the Interdenominational Ministerial Alliance, later to be led by Rev. A. L. Davis, and the Southern Negro Youth Congress.

The Group's dissatisfaction with the editorial direction of the existing Negro-owned newspapers in New Orleans led it to publish its own newspaper. The *Louisiana Weekly*, founded in 1925 by the Dejoie family, was sold to white owners during the Great Depression but was reacquired by a family member in the late 1930s. It and the *Sepia Socialite*, another weekly, were a disappointment for the more progressive members of the Group. The Group was interested in providing a more challenging perspective regarding news, events, and information for people of color in New Orleans.

The first issue of the *New Orleans Sentinel* hit the streets of the city in June 1940 and was financed by $100 from each of the Group's ten members. Tureaud's nephew Stafford operated the printing press for the publishing enterprise and recalled that the Group bore the hardship of not only financing the paper, but writing articles, selling advertising, printing, and delivering it. Stafford, a recent high school graduate seeking a career path, was very excited about working with his uncle's newspaper. John E. Rousseau, its editor, would later be nominated for a Pulitzer Prize for his series of articles he wrote as a reporter for the *Louisiana Weekly* on the desegregation of schools in New Orleans in the 1960s.

One of the first big stories reported in the *Sentinel*, penned by labor organizer Ernest J. Wright, prompted the circulation of a petition to potential residents of the Magnolia Housing Project. This new project was to serve Negro tenants exclusively, and the newspaper reported no plans for hiring Negro workers to manage the property or work there. When these facts were published, several thousand residents signed a petition indicating that they would not move into the housing project unless a Negro office staff was hired. As a result of news reports and the petition, the Housing Authority of New Orleans (HANO) agreed to hire Negro personnel. Many years later Tureaud would serve on the board of the HANO, and after his death its office building was named the A. P. Tureaud Housing Authority Building.

As he did in his law school days, Tureaud used his skills as a reporter to uncover injustices. He wrote many *Sentinel* articles and columns. The newspapermen relied upon Tureaud for information in legal cases and the activities of the NAACP. Rousseau noted, "We were careful not to identify him as the author of these articles because he wanted to make a living as an attorney."[20]

"Tureaud did not want people to think he was forsaking that profession to take up journalism. Back then it was hard enough getting work as a black attorney," Rousseau recalled. Tureaud realized the value of Negro newspapers and was skillful in using them throughout his career. The Negro newspapers gave him eight column headlines on civil rights cases. "A lot of the times I had to write some of the damn news stories because they didn't have anyone there who could write the stories or would write them if they could," he said.[21] "I naturally tried to build up two things, the NAACP and myself as a lawyer, and that was part of the secret of my success as a lawyer with Negroes," Tureaud exaggerated with a laugh.[22]

The members of the Old Guard of the NAACP were not the only ones reluctant to use Negro lawyers. "Negroes didn't believe a Negro lawyer could practice in court when I came here, in spite of the fact that they had had Negro lawyers in New Orleans since the 1860s," Tureaud explained. "It was kind of agonizing to see a Negro come to you with a little $5 claim and in half an hour come back and get his claim," he said, laughing the laughter of disappointment.[23] The potential client would have subsequently talked to someone who had convinced him that a Negro couldn't handle his case.

Tureaud understood the apprehension of potential black clients. He knew that they saw a legal system that was white—white judges, white juries, and white court administrators—and they wanted a white lawyer. Tureaud knew that he had to prove his legal competency. He sought more business for himself as a Negro lawyer and campaigned to recruit more Negro people into the legal profession by inviting them to watch him whenever he appeared in court. Sometimes Tureaud extended his interrogation of witnesses just to demonstrate that a Negro could, indeed, practice law successfully in New Orleans.

Those who had a chance to watch him in action acknowledged the tremendous pressure on the young Negro lawyer. The white lawyers knew the white judges in ways, professionally and personally, that a Negro lawyer like Tureaud could not have in a segregated society. His professional manner in the courtroom was serious yet extremely cordial. "He didn't demean himself when he called the judges 'Sir.'"[24] He showed respect and eventually won the admiration of many in the legal profession, including his opponents. Collegiality was not difficult for someone with Tureaud's deportment.

As his experience and reputation as a master litigator grew with the success of each civil rights case he handled during his lengthy career, Tureaud's confidence increased as well. New Orleanian Raphael Cassimere, a founding member of the NAACP's Youth Council, imagined that Tureaud would be a Perry Mason type, but he was not. Recalled Cassimere, "He was very calm and quiet; in fact, sometimes you could barely hear what he was saying, but there was a method to the madness."[25] Tureaud never incited the white judges and lawyers who were in a position to determine the fate of civil rights for Negroes. He was unapologetically respectful.

9
The War Years

When the United States declared war on Germany and Italy in December 1941, black Americans found themselves in a serious dilemma. Could they fight with their country for freedom in Europe while their civil rights were denied them at home?

Tureaud chose to support the war effort. Such a decision was in line with his philosophy that one must work within the system while using the legal avenues it offers to correct injustices. Many Negroes were willing to go to war to gain respect as Americans. Tureaud expressed that "we must love our country and respect the U.S. Constitution and the laws that were created through adherence to the Constitution."[1]

Tureaud served as a volunteer ward leader in the civil defense effort. He and Lucille were also active in the war bond drives and activities that supported the U.S. troops. Three of Lucille's brothers, Alvin, Burel, and Wellington De-joie, were in the armed services in segregated units, stationed in Europe and the South Pacific.

Segregation, even in a patriotic celebration, was ingrained in the culture of America in 1942, and Negroes realized the hypocrisy of the slogans regarding freedom during the war. In the same year, black residents across the country resisted exclusion from patriotic activities held in their communities, and New Orleans residents were no exception. Andrew I. Smith, president of the $10,000 War Bond Drive Dinner, announced that the goal had been doubled thanks to the purchases of patriotic citizens of New Orleans. Smith said that Negroes who purchased bonds during the campaign were invited to attend a dinner, which was scheduled for November 19, 1942, at the Booker T. Washington High School.[2]

Plans for white residents called for an "I am an American Day" rally at the New Orleans Municipal Auditorium. A parallel ceremony for the Negroes was planned at Xavier University. Black residents boycotted the event, protesting racial segregation. Insulted by a white-only meeting of war bond personnel, editorial writers of the *Louisiana Weekly* urged black residents to fight for a victory over Nazism abroad and "white supremacy" at home. Black newspapers all over the country pitched the "Double V" campaign of World War II. Double V stood for victories over white supremacy overseas and in America.

In his keynote address to the fourth annual NAACP youth conference, Buell G. Gallagher, president of Talladega College, a private college for Negroes in Alabama, suggested that an additional "V" be added to the Double V campaign title to signify that democracy is needed within the colored race as much as it is needed abroad and at home. "If we really want democracy, we must ourselves be democratic," said Gallagher, calling for fighting on a third front for democracy within the Negro race. "The decisive sword of color prejudice, which the white man has forged, thrusts itself through the Negro group, separating the light-skinned from the dark, the straight-haired from the kinky. With notable exceptions, the social circles of every city and hamlet from Beale Street to Lenox Avenue are organized along the lines of color," President Gallagher went on with obvious concern.[3]

The college president was speaking of the conflict between Negroes with light and dark complexions that had its roots in slavery, when slave owners favored the mixed-race children they fathered with their slave women over the other slave children. These slaves were believed to have been given preferential treatment in work assignments in the masters' homes rather than in the fields. Many were educated and sometimes given an inheritance or manumission before or after the death of their masters. After slavery, the conflict manifested itself in the perception that Negroes preferred having a lighter skin tone and European features because these attributes eased acceptance by whites. Tureaud was familiar with the slang phrase that mockingly depicted this preference: "If you are black, step back: if you are brown, stick around."[4]

Subsequently, during and after slavery, lighter skin tones and European features determined the model of beauty, with its preferred and more desirable characteristics. This esoteric preference had further consequences beyond mere physical appearance. This prejudice came to the forefront for the damage it caused when those who looked more like white people were viewed as the more educated, accomplished, cultured, and privileged among the Negro race.

The color issue within the Negro race would play out in a number of scenarios throughout Tureaud's lifetime. As with many Creoles, Tureaud's insistence on identifying with his European ancestry, such as the French Tureauds of St. James Parish who were judges, legislators, and successful entrepreneurs, became increasing problematic for him, particularly with the young black lawyers during the 1960s.

The militant years of the civil rights movement would prompt the change in terminology for identifying people of color from "colored" to "Negro" to "black." Tureaud had his own ideas about how he wanted to be identified. As a person who looked like a white man, he never considered himself to be anything but a Negro. His objection to the term "black" as a cultural designation for all Negroes stemmed from his view that the term did not accurately represent the range of racial mixture and diverse cultures that he thought were important for people of color in America. As a Creole, he was proud of the racial and cultural heritage that made New Orleans a unique and special city. He acknowledged the African, European, and Native American blending that created this culture and throughout his life celebrated his ancestry as a Creole and as an American Negro.

Tureaud also disagreed with his colleagues who demanded that Negro organizations exclude white people from becoming members. According to Tureaud, this model of voluntary segregation is as bad as "the very thing that white people did—putting themselves apart (from other races)—in order to create superiority."[5] The call for ending the long-standing conflicts in the Negro community during wartime may not have fallen on deaf ears, though it hardly received more than a confirming "Amen" from many Negroes leaders and their followers. Considering the magnitude of the race problem in America, color prejudice among Negroes was a minor concern at the time.

During the war, newspapers reported a growing number of conflicts between white policemen and black servicemen throughout the South. One such case was handled by the NAACP, which ultimately had a happy ending, unlike many others. In 1942, Privates Lawrence Mitchell, eighteen, and Richard P. Adams, twenty-five, and Sergeant John Bordenave, twenty-eight, were sentenced to death for allegedly raping a white waitress, Anna Mae Mason, in Camp Claiborne, located in Rapides Parish in central Louisiana.

The original three attorneys on the case were white and had been reported as not being strong advocates for their clients. The soldiers were found guilty and sentenced to be executed. Tureaud assisted the LDF when Thurgood Marshall decided to take over the case. The U.S. Court of Appeals granted a stay of the scheduled execution of the three men pending further orders. Marshall and his team asked for ninety days to write and file an appeal. They contended that the verdict was contrary to the law, stating that the court erred in overruling a motion to quash the indictments when testimony about guard duty at Camp Claiborne was permitted but such regarding the victim of the attack was not. The attorneys also charged that the district court erred in overruling a motion for severance of trial.[6]

Medical evidence showed that the alleged victim, Anna Mae Mason, was so severely infected with gonorrhea that it was impossible for three men to have intercourse with her without at least one becoming infected. None of the defendants had gonorrhea.

The case was argued before the U.S. Supreme Court on May 10, 1943, and decided on May 24, 1943. Marshall was the counsel for the defendants, and Robert L. Stern, of Washington, D.C., was the counsel for the United States. Marshall convinced the U.S. Supreme Court to set aside the verdict of the U.S. District Court on a technicality.[7]

Justice Hugo Black delivered the opinion of the Court. It was determined that the federal court had no jurisdiction over the proceeding because the government had not accepted jurisdiction over the area at Camp Claiborne where the crime of rape had allegedly committed, as required in the Act of October 9, 1940. The Court viewed it to be immaterial that Louisiana statutes authorized the government to take jurisdiction, since at the critical time the jurisdiction had not been taken. The defendants were retried before a military tribunal in Texas and again found guilty. President Roosevelt commuted their sentences to life imprisonment; they were paroled in 1947.

This well-publicized NAACP case and its subsequent ending five years later were overshadowed by growing publicity of conflicts between Negro soldiers and local white authorities throughout the South, including two Louisiana incidents in 1942 that did not end well. In what became to be known as the Lee Street Riots, on January 10, 1942, Negro soldiers were subjected to brutality in the name of white supremacy; a suspected military cover-up ensued.

The arrest of a drunken Negro soldier in Alexandria, Louisiana, caused a rush of white military policemen, the local police, and a contingency of state troopers to the Lee Street bars, called "Little Harlem," resulting in more than two hours of explosive mayhem. Thousands of civilians were herded off the streets, and more than 3,000 Negro GIs were escorted at gunpoint back to Camp Claiborne. According to the local newspapers, thirteen black residents were shot. The military authorities denied reports of any fatalities. The War Department stated that civil policeman and one military policeman indulged in indiscriminate and unnecessary shooting.

The debate continues about how many people were killed in the incident. Whatever happened created a reign of terror for several months by white mobs over Alexandria's Negro residents. NAACP branch president Georgia Johnson's determination to investigate the causes attracted the hostility of white authorities and the city's white residents alike. Johnson was editor and manager of a local black newspaper, the *Alexandria Observer*. She also wrote articles for Negro-owned newspapers throughout the state. Because of these roles, Johnson said she was called to the Alexandria police station once and the city courts twice to give an account of what she was reporting and to explain her defense of the NAACP's position regarding the incident. She also received threatening telephone calls and was stopped on the streets and questioned by angry white residents.[8]

In this atmosphere of fear and heightened racial tensions, eyewitnesses to the event refused to publicly share information; however, there were rumors that Negro-owned funeral homes in the area received payoffs for handling the bodies of those massacred. A newspaper boy reported that customers he had served on Saturday morning were customers no longer on Monday.[9]

Later in the same year, an article titled "150 Soldiers Jailed in Rampart Street Riot" made the front-page headlines in the *New Orleans Sepia Socialite*'s November 7, 1942, edition. The incident occurred when city policemen entered a Rampart Street saloon and tried to arrest a soldier for disorderly conduct. Tureaud, writing to the NAACP national office, attributed disorder at New Orleans's Jackson Barracks to "cracker over-lords who are . . . resentful of 'northern' Negroes who were stationed there while serving their country in the armed forces."[10]

Despite these and numerous other racial incidents throughout the country, the NAACP publicly supported the war effort. Nonetheless, the FBI monitored members of the NAACP, including A. P. Tureaud, and other civil rights groups for signs of "foreign-inspired agitation." FBI records on Tureaud from 1944 until his death included reports regarding his activities in the war bond drive, as well as later references to potential Communist involvement.[11]

It is doubtful that Tureaud would have been surprised that the FBI maintained a file on him. He had the occasion to discuss the activities of suspects and defendants with FBI agents and felt that local agents held racist views. FBI director J. Edgar Hoover and the national FBI office were monitoring civil rights groups for un-American activities. Tureaud was aware that the New Orleans office monitored the black population associated with the NAACP and compiled reports on alleged "Communists."

Hoover had become the federal intelligence organization's director in 1924 while Tureaud was attending Howard Law School. Both men were employed with the U.S. Department of Justice at the same time. In fact, Tureaud recalled meeting Hoover when he came into the Justice Department's law library. He told Tureaud that he was studying Russian. While serving as special assistant to the attorney general, A. Mitchell Palmer, from 1919 to 1921, Hoover directed the so-called Palmer Raids against suspected radical Communist aliens.

Hoover was a lawyer and, like Tureaud, would doggedly devote the rest of his life to one vocation. Both illustrated by example that one person can make a difference. The two men would die the same year, Hoover six months after Tureaud.

As FBI director, Hoover instituted a number of changes to correct criticisms of his predecessor's administration. He ordered background checks, interviews, and physical tests for new agent recruits, and he reinstated previous FBI policies requiring agents to have legal or accounting training. Beginning in the 1930s, Hoover investigated alleged Communists and leftists whether for national security or his own interests. The FBI garnered headlines for its staunch efforts against Nazi and Communist espionage. During World War II, the FBI took the lead in domestic counterintelligence, counterespionage, and countersabotage investigations.

Like other members of the NAACP, Tureaud organized and headed the war loans drives. In part, this show of patriotism was done in the hope that overt identification with the war effort would lead to easier passage of civil rights legislation, less difficult social integration into mainstream American society, and access to defense industry jobs for black workers.[12]

Tureaud was vice chair to Chairman George Longe of the Fourth War Loan Orleans Parish Drive (Negro Division) of 1944. The secretary was Naomi Borikins, who was a public relations representative for the Jackson Brewery Company. The assistant secretary was Myra U. Hayward, a McDonogh No. 37 schoolteacher. The effort's office manager was Julia B. Dejoie. The New Orleans black community raised $585,000 buying war bonds in 1944.

"What Can *You* Spare That They Can Wear?" was the slogan for the United National Clothing Collection for War Relief of 1945. The New Orleans NAACP established a committee that supported the clothing drive with George Longe as chairman and Tureaud as vice chairman.

In 1946, Tureaud led the Negro Division of the Second War Loan Drive. This organization again saw leading Negro business and professional men in New Orleans supporting the sale of war bonds. Despite the widespread public awareness of Tureaud's work on behalf of war bonds, FBI informants accused him of discouraging Negroes from purchasing the bonds.[13]

Tureaud did not have a secretary for the bond drive effort and relied on the clerical support given by Julia Dejoie, who worked for him in his Iberville Street law office. Dejoie was a volunteer who assisted several chairmen of the war bond drive throughout the war years. Campaign events staged by the war bond drive included dances and balls in facilities owned by local black businessmen. Dejoie recalled a parade down Canal Street featuring such prominent national black celebrities as world-famous singer Billie Holiday.[14]

The FBI's entries following the war years reflected its interest in expanding the monitoring of black leaders throughout the country. It was reported that a former member of the Communist Party in Louisiana and the newly formed Louisiana Progressive Educational Association (LPEA) had been introduced to leading Negroes in New Orleans. As a result of these introductions, a civic association was being formed by the LPEA to serve as a front until sufficient strength had been obtained for the new organization to come out in the open. A. P. Tureaud was a member of this civic group. The LPEA was considered radical at the time for having unorthodox views on the education of children.[15] Individuals who joined or showed interest in this group opened themselves up to accusations of being suspected subversives and were placed under FBI surveillance.

During World War II and the New Deal era, several other events focused FBI attention on the NAACP, including its association with trade unions and an attempt by the Louisiana branches of the NAACP to organize a state conference to coordinate their civil rights efforts. The NAACP was often placed under FBI surveillance. In the following testimony before the House Un-American Activities Committee on March 26, 1947, Hoover explained the destructive nature and intent of Communists in the United States:

> I would have no fears if more Americans possessed the zeal, the fervor, the persistence and the industry to learn about this menace of Red fascism. I do fear for the liberal and progressive who has been hoodwinked and duped into joining hands with the communists. I confess to a real apprehension so long as communists are able to secure ministers of the gospel to promote their evil work and espouse a cause that is alien to the religion of Christ and

Judaism. I do fear so long as school boards and parents tolerate conditions whereby communists and fellow travelers, under the guise of academic freedom, can teach our youth a way of life that eventually will destroy the sanctity of the home, that undermines faith in God, that causes them to scorn respect for constituted authority and sabotages our revered Constitution.

. . . I do fear the palliation and weasel-worded gestures against communism indulged in by some of our labor leaders who should know better, but who have become pawns in the hands of sinister but astute manipulations for the communist cause.

The NAACP's affiliation with trade unions was linked to the branches' interest in securing better jobs for Negroes. The benefits of union membership carried weight with Tureaud because of his family history and his work in the Chicago foundry. He subscribed to union literature and was featured in a trade publication, *The Worker*. In 1944, when the New Orleans branch membership rolls exceeded 7,000 members, more than 2,000 members were reported to be from the General Longshoremen Workers (Local 1419) and 700 from the International Longshoremen's Association (Local 854).

A confidential informant, who was acquainted with Communist-front activities in the New Orleans area and who had furnished reliable information in the past, advised on April 10, 1951, that he never knew A. P. Tureaud to be connected with the Communist Party and stated that, in fact, Tureaud had been distrusted by the Communist Party as being too conservative.[16]

Likewise, an FBI informant advised in August 1951 that "A. P. Tureaud, who was then president of the New Orleans chapter [branch], National Association for the Advancement of Colored People, was not known to him to be a member of or active in the Communist Party."[17] Tureaud was aware that some people sought to link the NAACP with the Communists in order to discredit the organization and defeat its civil rights agenda. He was cautious in his activities and did not associate with known Communists. Marshall appreciated his effort to keep suspected Communists from infiltrating the NAACP in Louisiana.

On the national scene, NAACP founder W. E. B. Du Bois had returned to a research position at the national NAACP office in New York in 1948, which raised eyebrows because he had moved steadily left politically since his departure from the organization in the early 1940s. Du Bois identified with pro-Russian causes and was indicted in 1951 as an unregistered agent for a foreign power. Although a federal judge directed his acquittal, Du Bois had become completely disillusioned with the political leadership of the United States. In

1961, he joined the Communist Party, moved to Ghana, and renounced his American citizenship.

As World War II was coming to an end, Thurgood Marshall held NAACP legal conferences across the country to look for new approaches to thwart discrimination and reactivate legal action. He found a new breed of civil rights lawyers, many of whom had served in the war and were more aggressive in their legal approach. Tureaud attended these conferences often and shared insights about his work in Louisiana. Letters to staff members in New York showed that he actively referred specific cases, conducted research, wrote briefs, implemented and suggested changes in strategy, and generally kept the lines of communication open between him and the national office. Tureaud's role as premier NAACP local counsel in Louisiana was cemented during this time, and the types of cases in which he provided assistance would vary widely and often be conducted simultaneously throughout his work for more than four decades.

10
NAACP Lawyer

I t was a warm spring afternoon in 1942, and the Tureauds were hosting a party at their residence on Rocheblave Street. According to Lucille, her husband's decision to practice law full-time was cause for a spur-of-the-moment celebration. Amidst the joking, laughter, eating, and drinking, Lucille caught Tureaud's eye and gave him a nod of approval. They shared anxious moments as they anticipated the exciting and bumpy road that lay ahead. Surrounded by relatives and close friends, Tureaud felt that he made the right decision.

A close family friend and a respected colleague, Daniel Ellis "Dan" Byrd, acknowledged that he and Thurgood Marshall had persuaded Tureaud to resign from his job at the Customs House to practice law full-time and to allocate more time to civil rights work. In 1936, at the age of twenty-eight, Marshall had given up his struggling practice in Baltimore to work full-time for the national legal office of the NAACP under the tutelage of his forty-one-year-old mentor, Charles Hamilton Houston. From the early 1940s on, Tureaud's legal work followed precisely the NAACP strategic road map for equal rights. He so firmly endorsed Marshall's ideological goals that he placed his professional life at his colleague's service repeatedly and selflessly.

Marshall was named the first director-counsel of the NAACP Legal Defense and Educational Fund (LDF) in October 1938. Marshall and Tureaud initiated the teacher salary equalization cases in Louisiana on behalf of the New Orleans Citizens' Committee in the 1940s. The committee, made up of teachers and civic leaders, was led by four black school principals: George Longe, Israel Augustine, E. W. Sorrell, and Veronica Brown "Connie" Hill. The cases were not directly associated with the local chapter of the NAACP at this time because Tureaud feared that he would again be overlooked as legal counsel for the services of a white lawyer. Marshall agreed to take the cases only with the understanding that Tureaud would serve as local counsel.

Teachers were a natural constituency of the NAACP. In 1940, there were more than 4,000 Negro teachers in Louisiana. As historian Adam Fairclough has explained, "Well educated and upwardly mobile, they responded positively to the NAACP's call for educational improvement and greater social militancy."[1] The idea of getting equal facilities was an incentive for teachers to join the NAACP education campaign. Negro teachers lacked many of the essentials for instruction, such as blackboards, tables, and schoolbooks. School districts in cities and rural parishes had their own unique problems, but everywhere there were major inadequacies. Most school buildings were old wooden structures in poor condition.

In St. Charles Parish, one two-room structure sufficed for Negro students. In East Carroll Parish, there were no libraries in the Negro schools and no buses for the students to get to classes from remote rural areas. In Caddo Parish, there were Negro schools that had no electricity and could not accommodate all the students, so church buildings were used.

High schools were often available only in the cities and the larger towns of Louisiana. Twelve parishes had no high schools for Negro students at all. School terms in rural areas were shortened by the cotton harvest. The curriculum taught in those abbreviated semesters prepared students for menial jobs and lacked academic courses for college entrance.

On May 9, 1941, Tureaud filed a petition with the Orleans Parish School Board on behalf of Joseph P. McKelpin and other Negro teachers requesting equalization of salaries for the school term beginning that fall. Henry C. Schaumburg was school board president. The petition stated that salary discrimination based solely on race and color had been declared unconstitutional and that unless salaries were equalized the matter would be litigated. McKelpin was an untenured teacher for four years at the F. P. Ricard School. A graduate of the Valena C. Jones Normal School, a teacher training institution in New Orleans, he was scheduled to receive a bachelor's degree from Southern University in June 1942.[2]

Tureaud was informed that the school board would consider the petition at its June 10, 1941, meeting. When no substantive action was taken by the board at that meeting, Tureaud filed a lawsuit, on June 14, 1941. The school board's lawyers immediately filed a motion to dismiss the suit on the grounds that the federal court lacked jurisdiction. The motion was argued before Judge Wayne G. Borah on November 19, 1941. Assuring Tureaud that the motion was only a delaying tactic, Marshall fumed that other school boards had raised the same point in similar cases and had been dismissed. Tureaud was instructed to prepare a brief in case one was needed. Aware that the suit would set a precedent for other parishes in Louisiana, Marshall wrote to Tureaud, "I stand ready to come down at a moment's notice."[3]

It was not until February 1942 that Tureaud reported to Marshall that, as he had predicted, Judge Borah had denied the motion to dismiss and granted the board additional time to prepare its defense. The school board filed its brief asking for dismissal "for lack of evidence, stating it was not sure that McKelpin was an American citizen!"[4] Tureaud realized that the board's strategy was a delaying tactic because it expected the state legislature, which would convene in May, to pass legislation to circumvent the teachers' lawsuit. Included in the legislative action was the Rainold bill to increase pay for nondegree teachers. Tureaud filed a motion to speed up prosecution of the case. He wanted the school board to include the salary adjustments in its budget for the 1942–43 school term.[5]

Finally, in the June 1942 trial, Judge Borah ruled in favor of the plaintiffs and all other black teachers in Orleans Parish and asked the plaintiffs and defense counsel to submit briefs suggesting remedies. The NAACP requested equalization immediately, but the school board wanted gradual equalization over a five-year period. The teachers rejected this proposal and the board's counter of a three-year plan, effective September 1941.

Tureaud wrote to Marshall that the school board's position was that there was not enough money to handle an across-the-board equalization in one year. He explained,

> Your letter states that you are opposed to three years, and that you advise taking the matter up with the teachers for a plan as of September 1941. If we are disposed to granting the school board any time in which to equalize, it is my opinion that we should be governed by a study of their ability to meet the requirements, rather than to arbitrarily say we will not accept three years.
>
> I do not favor a cut. . . . I favor working the thing out to the best interest of all concerned. This can only be done by a complete knowledge of what faces us under any terms submitted.
>
> If you have a notion that this school board will not cut white teachers, let me say that it has been done to all teachers before and it can be done again.[6]

Marshall immediately expressed his concern to Tureaud in a pointedly terse manner, which became well known to NAACP attorneys whenever they compromised more than Marshall felt was necessary. Negro lawyers in the South viewed Marshall "affectionately" as a troublemaker.[7] In the NAACP attorney conferences, southern lawyers felt that they knew their legal and political environments better than outsiders. They often questioned whether they should follow the dictates of the NAACP on how to litigate cases in their hometowns or whether they should they try to work things out as southerners sometimes did.

Tureaud knew the local turf, and Marshall viewed the civil rights cases from a national perspective. Herein lay the differences in the approach to remedies sought by the two men. Tureaud's approach was conciliatory while Marshall's was much more provocative in nature. Marshall wrote to Tureaud,

> Your letter of July 29 [1942] . . . is alarming, to say the least. Maybe I do not know the New Orleans School Board, but I do know about 50 other school boards throughout the country, and they all pull the same stuff. As to the Rainold bill, this bill will raise salaries for white non-degree teachers the same as it will raise Negro non-degree teachers; and I, for one, am not willing to hold back the equalization of the salary of Negro non-degree teachers in order that white non-degree teachers may receive a raise. It looks to me like the school board is taking the Rainold bill, which they thoroughly dislike, and using it as a weapon against the Negro teachers, whom they dislike even more.
>
> As to my unwillingness to accept either a five- or a three-year plan starting this September, it is not for any arbitrary reasons. I know that many of the teachers now in the system will not be in the system five years from now.
>
> I know school boards well enough to know that they always have loose money lying around which you can not put your hands on, but which they can use for whatever purpose they see fit.
>
> Please bear in mind that the ultimate decision on this point is not left with you or me, but with the teachers who have financed the fight, and who will either lose or benefit by it.[8]

The new school year was near, and the school board had adopted its budget for 1942–43 without providing for salary equalization. To avoid possible pay cuts to teachers, Tureaud proposed a two-step compromise plan that would equalize salaries over a two-year period, beginning in September 1942. The board initially rejected Tureaud's compromise plan but then accepted it at Judge Borah's urging. The compromise was signed by all parties on September 1, 1942. The school board was ordered to increase the salaries of all black teachers by 50 percent of the difference between the present salary of Negro teachers and their white counterparts effective fall 1942. Additionally, Judge Borah ordered that all teachers, Negro and white, with the same credentials receive the same salary beginning in the 1943 school year.

Considering the time limitations, Tureaud made the best decision possible. Not only would all Negro teachers receive immediate increases averaging between 26 percent and 32 percent, but the school board decided not to appeal, which could have delayed implementation of the increases for several years.[9] A jubilant Tureaud wrote Marshall, stating, "No appeal of the judgment is contemplated by school officials."[10]

Tureaud submitted a bill for $3,500 for his legal services to Donald Jones, chairman of the Citizens' Committee. Some committee members maintained that they had no financial obligation to the local attorney because the committee had retained Marshall, not Tureaud. Others felt that his services had not really been crucial because Marshall had done the bulk of the work. Tureaud's bill covered services such as research and preparation of the initial petition, filing the brief, court appeal, and so on.

When the matter was reviewed with Marshall, he declined to intervene and advised the committee to work it out directly with Tureaud. The NAACP special counsel explained variations in attorneys' fees for similar cases but made it clear that the decision on whether to pay Tureaud's fees rested with the local committee.[11] Marshall's annual salary was raised to $2,600 in 1938, when he took over as counsel-director of the NAACP legal office from his mentor, Charles Hamilton Houston, who made only $4,000 a year. In the 1940s, following the incorporation of the NAACP Legal Defense Fund, Marshall's annual salary was only about $10,000, and he practically lived on his expense account.[12]

The committee decided to officially thank Tureaud for his help and to give him a $200 gift. Tureaud, upset and deeply offended, wrote to Jones, "It is surprising to learn that those for whom I worked would now consider me an object of charity."[13] The editor of the *Sepia Socialite* alleged that "a deal" had been made in reaching a settlement in the teachers' case and that Tureaud received several hundred dollars for the compromise, which he used to finance some investments in real estate.[14] The *Socialite* editorial claimed that Tureaud had acted unilaterally without consulting the teachers.[15]

Tureaud was furious. Considering the charges false, defamatory, and malicious, he feared that they could injure him professionally. He sent copies of the editorials to the city's district attorney for possible litigation. A complaint was drawn up against the paper's owners, but the suit was never filed.[16] In a subsequent editorial, the *Sepia Socialite* made a concession to him. In "An Open Letter to the Public School Teachers of New Orleans," the November 7, 1942, editorial stated:

> Teachers, you won a great victory only because you had competent race lawyers handling your case. Now that it is all over, there seems to be some disagreement as to payment of the attorneys' fee. Certain leaders and certain teachers (Not many, I understand) are so selfish and small that they would spoil this great victory of ours by quibbling over the bill presented by our local attorney, the only Negro lawyer in the whole State of Louisiana.
>
> This man has helped you to be justly paid "worthy of your hire," and now you would permit a committee to deny him the worth of his hire.
>
> . . . Pay this lawyer.

The editorial continued:

> It seems an earlier attempt was made once to fight a teachers' salary case, and I recall that another lawyer was paid the highest fee on record for writing one letter to the school board. I also recall the *Trudeau* case and the fee there—$5,000. I remember the segregation case, too, and another big fee and the Hugh Pierre case and another big fee. All were paid with no questions asked—and to white lawyers.
>
> . . . Teachers, maybe you don't know it, but the NAACP lawyer could never have taken your case without first associating himself with some local counsel. Did it ever occur to you that except for our lone local lawyer your case may have never come to trial?
>
> If it had been necessary to associate with a local white lawyer for want of a colored one, I wonder what the fee would have been and I wonder if the committee would be squabbling about his fee.

The Citizens' Committee subsequently paid Tureaud $2,000 for his services.

Disappointed but not discouraged, Tureaud remained hopeful that the legal system would provide the necessary ammunition against injustices. After taking the advice of Marshall and Byrd to work as a civil rights lawyer full-time, Tureaud began to realize the challenge of making a living during these initial years of working on behalf of Negro teachers. His commitment to the fight for equal rights and loyalty to organized efforts directed by the NAACP never wavered. Invoices and receipts for his NAACP legal work confirmed that he did not make much money considering the long hours of dedicated work he did for the teachers' union. During his early years, his hopeful outlook and steadfast labor were spurred on in small but steady legal victories. Tureaud's determination was fueled by these victories and his personal philosophy that success requires temperance in all things.[17]

Tureaud filed sixteen suits to equalize teachers' salaries over a period of about seven years during the 1940s.[18] Another highly publicized case involved Eula Mae Lee, a teacher at Kenner Colored School in Jefferson Parish. Tureaud challenged school board members who maintained that they were not against higher salaries for Negro teachers but that the budget for the academic year 1942–43 did not allow for such an expenditure.

A Citizens' Committee for Improving Educational Opportunities in Jefferson Parish was organized and attempted to garner greater teacher support and financial backing for Eula Mae Lee's case. However, Lee was dismissed from her teaching post in August 1944 for "wilful neglect of duty." She was charged with excessive tardiness. Her dismissal stifled the activism of many teachers in other parishes who could not afford to lose their jobs to further the cause of equal rights.

Although the action against Lee sent a clear message to potential Negro plaintiffs, Tureaud saw Lee's case through the court process, with other cases such as *Wiley Butler McMillan v. Iberville Parish School Board* in 1942 and *Malcolm S. LaGarde v. East Baton Rouge Parish School Board* in 1943. In the *McMillan* case, eleven probationary teachers were discharged because of their involvement in the salary equalization case in Iberville Parish; however, all were rehired in other parishes.[19]

After four years of legal sparring between Tureaud and the parish school board, Judge Borah ruled for the plaintiffs in the *McMillan* case. The existing salary schedule, he decided, clearly discriminated against black teachers, notwithstanding the "merit system" devised by Superintendent Linus P. Terrebonne.[20] In 1948, Judge Herbert W. Christenberry signed a consent decree in the *Lee* case in Jefferson Parish. The plaintiff, Eula Mae Lee, had married and moved to Washington, D.C., after her dismissal. Although she obtained a job in D.C., she kept in touch with Tureaud about her case in Louisiana. Christenberry's agreement represented a complete victory for the Negro teachers. The board agreed to full equalization and offered Lee her job back. Furthermore, she was awarded back pay from the 1947–48 academic year equaling $1,791.[21]

As a result of Tureaud's litigation on the teachers' behalf, in 1948 the Louisiana State Legislature adopted a minimum salary schedule for all public school teachers, whether Negro or white. Tureaud also handled a successful salary equalization case in Mississippi, *Gladys Noel Bates v. John C. Batte,* in 1948. Batte was president of the Jackson Separate School District. For the most part, plaintiffs in the teacher salary equalization cases described Tureaud as capable, caring, relentless, and undaunted by the obstacles put forth by parish officials in the opposition to equal salaries. Tureaud admitted that he was not asking for very much in the way of rights for Negro teachers. He asked for only what they were entitled to under the "separate but equal" ruling.

J. K. Haynes, president of the Louisiana Education Association (formerly the Louisiana Colored Teachers Association), hired Tureaud to serve as LEA legal counsel from 1942 to 1971. Haynes and Tureaud collaborated on civil rights issues and became supportive colleagues. They were also good friends who were cut from the same cloth. Their demeanor remained gentlemanly and even-tempered as they dealt with the most racist opponents. Haynes, an educator and articulate community leader, was a loyal friend to Tureaud throughout their lives. Lucille would tell A.P. Jr. years later that Haynes continued to send a check to Tureaud even when her husband could no longer work because of illness.

While working on teacher salary equalization and jury exclusion cases in Louisiana, Tureaud and Marshall had cultivated a very close relationship. LDF staffer Constance Baker Motley said the two were "buddies," not just business partners. "There were certain people that Thurgood truly liked and Tureaud was one of them."[22]

Marshall was more than a foot and a half taller than Tureaud. Both men wore hats. Tureaud, a stylish dresser in his youth, gained more than a few pounds around the middle as he grew older and was not as clothes conscious as he had been. A.P. Jr. often had to remind his dad to straighten his tie and tuck in his shirttail. Tureaud and Marshall made an attention-grabbing pair as they strolled down the long corridors of the courthouses throughout the state of Louisiana. Swinging their overstuffed briefcases in one hand and holding their hats in the other, they carried on a constant verbal exchange about their current legal affairs.

Although the courtroom techniques of the two men differed, each was equally impressive in court. Marshall was challenging and direct. Colleagues often described him as fiery. Tureaud, on the other hand, was soft spoken and calm. LDF attorney Jack Greenberg once said, "Gentle is what comes to mind. . . . He was the kind of person that could talk to his opponents within the limits that they would accept." Greenberg noted that Tureaud "could get agreements from them about things like times in which to file briefs, or dates that hearings would be held or accommodations for witnesses, and things of that sort."[23]

Like many of his fellow New Orleanians, Tureaud had an affinity for good food and drink. Marshall's appetite for the same put him in good company with his associates in New Orleans. The hospitable Tureaud would think his job incomplete if he did not take Marshall and other visiting NAACP lawyers to Negro-owned restaurants or to his own kitchen during their frequent trips to the Crescent City. Tureaud reveled in the intense strategy sessions with Marshall and others, which lasted well into the night, and savored the camaraderie of those whose goals and ambitions matched his.

Tureaud's French Quarter law office, while not in the most fashionable section of the Vieux Carré, was in a location that provided discreet access for Negroes, Creoles passing for white, and white clients seeking his assistance. One block from Canal Street, the office was located several blocks from the more respectable businesses in the French Quarter. Near the river and located in the western edge of the Quarter, it shared the block with a bar and restaurant; a single-room-occupancy hotel, which served as a seedy flophouse for seamen; and several small businesses. Policemen did not harass Negroes as they walked along the narrow banquettes or sidewalks of Iberville Street, which was not the case when Negroes walked on Bourbon Street or in areas with clubs and restaurants that attracted white tourists.

The office, housed in an old building constantly in need of repair, was upstairs above a white barroom. On Saturday mornings, half-naked men and women, still in bed, could be seen through the open windows of the hotel across the street from Tureaud's office. The smell of fried seafood, liquor, and cigarette smoke wafted up to the law office from the barroom below.

It was to this bar that Thurgood Marshall decided to go one day to take a break from his work with Tureaud and have a drink. Despite being told that the barroom was for whites only, Marshall went downstairs and stayed much longer than his colleague expected. Upon his return, Thurgood informed Tureaud that he had been joking and laughing with the patrons. The white owner, oblivious to Marshall's identity, later asked Tureaud when his friend was coming back.

Marshall attracted attention everywhere he went. A born raconteur, Marshall had an infectious and boisterous laugh. He was a social drinker and he smoked cigarettes. In the company of men, he would spin a yarn, remember a saucy joke, and swear like a sailor. In mixed company, he was a charmer, describing the tales of his escapades less graphically but always with much humor. He was genuinely liked by both men and women.

Tureaud was a practical joker with a dry wit. He played the straight man to the comedic Marshall. Friends and relatives never ceased to be surprised when it was revealed that Marshall was not the lone prankster. He was delighted when those who accused him of being the sole perpetrator of a practical joke found out that Tureaud was the true initiator, egging Marshall on.

Dan Byrd, a native of Marshall, Arkansas, athletic and handsome, became a close family friend and gained Tureaud's respect as an NAACP associate. A born rebel, Byrd challenged the injustices of racial segregation while attending high school in Gary, Indiana, and college at Northwestern University. He came to New Orleans to live after playing professional basketball with the Harlem Globetrotters. Byrd was the perfect complement to the more conservative but equally determined Tureaud. Together with a small but committed group of men and women, which included Byrd's energetic and outspoken wife, Mildred, they spearheaded the civil rights movement in Louisiana in the 1940s. Dan Byrd relentlessly traveled the state organizing community groups into NAACP chapters, investigating problems, and reporting his findings to Tureaud and the NAACP national office.

Access to the ballot was at the center of most NAACP battles in Louisiana during the first three decades of the twentieth century. The teacher salary equalization lawsuits were the NAACP's first step toward desegregation. However, the right to vote was viewed as critical to realizing all other NAACP goals. Civil rights leaders in Louisiana learned all too well the grueling demands of taking cases parish by parish throughout the state as they were required to do in the teacher salary equalization litigation. Voting rights efforts needed to be addressed in the sixty-four parishes of Louisiana, and Tureaud felt it would be best if the litigation was consolidated.

As early as 1928, Tureaud heard persistent complaints from black residents who were trying to register as Republicans. White registrars used a variety of dishonest methods designed to keep Negroes off the voting rolls. They were asked to fill out extremely complicated application forms, to calculate their ages to the year, date, and time of birth, or to interpret a provision of the U.S. Constitution as conditions to register to vote. They were asked ridiculous questions, such as how many bubbles could be made from a box of washing powder. In Bossier Parish, registrar Mary K. Brice required Negro applicants to give the names of two white voters to verify their identity. Many registrars closed their offices for the day whenever Negroes showed up to register. Tureaud noted, "A lot of Negroes were frustrated because of these simple-minded modes of discrimination."[24]

On rare occasions Negroes were allowed to register to vote in Orleans Parish, but only if they presented notes to the registrar from Black and Tan Republican leader and comptroller of customs Walter Cohen or other intermediaries on their behalf. The term "Black and Tan" has been used by historians to describe a coalition of the southern Republican Party composed of Negroes and Creole Republicans who, at one time, played an influential role in the party's decision-making process, particularly during the Reconstruction Period.

On one occasion, Tureaud went to the voter registration office to renew his registration. Registrar Samuel Bonds and his deputy manned the registration desk, and when Tureaud handed in his completed application, the deputy registrar told him, "You can come back some other time, your application is not correct."[25] Asking what part of the application he did not correctly answer, Tureaud received no response. In a rare public display of anger, Tureaud snatched the card from the deputy's hand. He informed the deputy that he was going to keep the card as evidence when he took the matter to court. The deputy called over a policeman stationed in the office, attempting to intimidate Tureaud. He calmed down but vowed that he would make a case of it. He successfully registered when he returned to the registrar's office the next day.

Voter registration was not only an important civil right but also often a requirement to qualify for employment or important civic activities, such as jury duty. It was increasingly difficult to persuade Negroes to face humiliation in order to register to vote and even more difficult to ask them to subject themselves to threats of physical harm every time they tried to cast their vote.

Tureaud won a significant victory in the lawsuit *Edward Hall v. T. J. Nagel* in 1946, which challenged restrictions on voter registration for Negroes. A delegation led by Edward T. Hall, president of the NAACP branch in St. John the Baptist Parish, came to Tureaud's office on Iberville Street in 1944. The members of the delegation informed him of their inability to register in that parish. They complained that the registrar, T. J. Nagel, at first refused to give them applications and then refused to meet with them in his office.

On another occasion, the registrar rejected Hall and the others before they could fill out the appropriate application forms. Negro applicants were asked to read a provision of the Louisiana Constitution, which stated that the "Louisiana Supreme Court shall by writ of certiorari have authority to certify certain cases . . ." When the readers got to the word "certiorari," the registrar would ask them what the term meant. The purpose of the interrogation was to have a reason to deny registration.

Tureaud and senior law partner Joseph A. Thornton took Hall's complaint. They sent the complaint to Thurgood Marshall, and a lawsuit was filed in the U.S. District Court. Judge Adrian Caillouet dismissed the case for lack of jurisdiction. The federal courts were "very conservative" in assuming jurisdiction in voter registration matters. In *Trudeau v. Barnes* (1933), the federal courts had decided that they had no jurisdiction over registration complaints when the plaintiff had failed to use all the remedies theoretically available in the state courts.

Marshall was eager to test the Supreme Court's ruling in the 1939 case *Lane v. Wilson*. The ruling stated that a plaintiff alleging deprivation of voting rights on the grounds of race had standing in the federal courts "without first exhausting the judicial remedies of state courts." Tureaud, Marshall, and Thornton appealed *Hall v. Nagel*, along with an Alabama case, *Mitchell v. Wright*, to the U.S. Fifth Circuit Court of Appeals. At Marshall's request, Howard Law School graduate Louis Berry also participated in the case. Like Tureaud, Berry, a native of Alexandria, Louisiana, had to attend law school outside the state because there were no schools in Louisiana that would accept Negroes. After earning his degree, Berry worked in private practice in St. Louis, Missouri, and then returned to Louisiana and sought to associate with Tureaud. At that time, Tureaud was not able to accept him into his meager practice. However, the fellow Howard graduate joined Tureaud on cases he handled in cooperation with the Legal Defense Fund, like the *Hall* case.

In April 1946, Marshall argued the cases before a standing-room-only audience of practically all Negroes in the courtroom. The *Louisiana Weekly*'s correspondent wrote a flattering portrayal of Marshall. He wore a "dark suit and polka dot tie, his unusual height towering above others and his . . . speeches touched off with a sparkling bit of dry, sarcastic humor." The correspondent reported that one of the white defense attorneys, with his southern drawl, mangled the word "Negroes" into "Nig-gras."[26]

The Alabama registrars were represented by attorney Richard Rives from the law firm headed by Joseph Lister Hill of Montgomery County, Alabama. Hill was a longtime liberal politician, serving as U.S. representative from 1923 to 1938 and as U.S. senator from 1938 to 1969. He was among a relatively small group of white Alabamians who, before the civil rights era, supported racial equality in government programs promoting civil rights. Sometime later, Rives would become one of the staunchest advocates of civil rights on the federal bench.

Both the *Hall* and *Mitchell* cases were decided on the same day. Judge Edwin Holmes of Mississippi wrote the unanimous opinion for the court that reversed Judge Caillouet's decision and affirmed the plaintiffs' right to sue in federal court without first going through the state courts. Tureaud admitted, "It was not until 1947 that we actually knocked out the requirements of Louisiana law with respect to the treatment of Negroes differently from whites in registering. We had many battles over that thing before the voting rights act came about."[27]

Only four hundred black New Orleanians were registered voters in 1940; by 1952 registered black voters numbered in the thousands. Throughout this time, black residents' indifference about registering was heightened by the fact that even when they were successfully registered, the likelihood of getting their vote to count was slim. There were numerous substantiated reports that black votes were often thrown out by white poll workers.

The same year the *Hall* case was decided, Tureaud was a member of a three-man team investigating the lynching of a black army veteran in Minden, Louisiana. This incident resulted in the first federal involvement in a Louisiana lynching. In February 1939, southern senators had filibustered an antilynching proposal in Congress. Louisiana congressman Allen J. Ellender contributed to a twenty-six-hour speech, holding the floor for a record six days. During the course of his "speech," Ellender openly disparaged black Americans, advocated repeal of the Fifteenth Amendment, and urged federal legislation to ban interracial marriages.

Daniel Byrd, John Rousseau, and Tureaud drove through the unfamiliar back roads of north Louisiana to gather information on the Minden lynching. This investigation proved to what lengths the men were willing to go for their work, despite the physical danger they faced. Only ten years old at the time, A.P. Jr. recalled that his mother was visibly upset and concerned about her husband's absence. In a telegram sent from Shreveport to his wife, Tureaud wrote, "No matter what, you and the children are my only consideration."[28]

The three men found local residents who did not want their names published in a newspaper account but who were willing to take them to the scene of the lynching, a place called Dorcheat Bayou. Details of the horrific activity differ from one person's account to the next, just like the testimonies that were eventually brought to the courtroom before an all-white jury in Shreveport.

From the viewpoint of the NAACP's three-man team, Rousseau recalled, "We found out that John Jones and his cousin . . . 'Sonny Man' [Harris] . . . were picked up . . . accused of being peeping toms."[29] Jones, earning the rank of U.S. Army corporal, had survived the "unfriendly" soil of the war overseas fighting for his country only to be lynched on the unfriendly soil of his native America. "The men were in jail for several days when a mob car[ried] them out and brought them out to Dorcheat Bayou and . . . lynched him [Jones]. They beat

'Sonny Man' and he pretended to be dead. . . . They used a blow torch on Corporal John Jones . . . on all of his genitals and everything and they killed him and they left."[30] Albert "Sonny Man" Harris Jr., Jones's seventeen-year-old cousin, later escaped to another state with his father.

Byrd, Rousseau, and Tureaud returned to New Orleans before their investigation was completed, taking a less direct route through Shreveport, believing that a number of would-be lynchers were in hot pursuit. However, they had uncovered enough information to report the names of thirteen suspects to Thurgood Marshall and obtain the LDF's support in securing an FBI investigation.

Following the Webster Parish grand jury's refusal to bring an indictment, the Department of Justice instructed Malcolm Lafargue, the U.S. attorney for the Western District of Louisiana, to institute federal proceedings. A subsequent grand jury in Monroe, Louisiana, a city in neighboring Ouachita Parish, indicted six men after the Harrises appeared to testify. Thanks to the Legal Defense Fund's involvement, the two black men's travel to and from the courthouse was conducted under tight security. Minden chief of police Benjamin Geary Gantt was one of the six originally indicted, but the charges against him were later dropped because of his cooperation with the federal authorities.[31]

The trial took place in Shreveport in the courtroom of Judge Gaston Porterie and lasted approximately five days, February 25 through March 2, 1946. Lafargue was the prosecutor. The four-man defense team, including the well-known, charismatic attorney Harry V. Booth, used the right of peremptory challenge to eliminate the only Negro on the jury.

As Tureaud and the other NAACP representatives looked on, they were not surprised by the defensive strategies typically used by white lawyers against Negroes in the South. The defense sought to discredit "Sonny Man" Harris's testimony by accusing him of having killed Jones himself and by linking him with the NAACP to provoke the ire of the jury. The defense attorneys dismissed the prosecution's accusations—that the rule of law had been violated when Jones and Harris were jailed without charges and convicted without a fair trial—by pointing out that such was "the custom throughout Louisiana for generation upon generation."[32]

Lafargue fired back that custom could not override the provisions of the state or federal constitutions and that the court would uphold the right of civil liberties. Judge Porterie agreed with Lafargue and warned that neither a private citizen nor a law enforcement officer may take the law into his or her own hands.

In its summation, the defense counsel professed to the jury his resentment
of the federal government's intrusion in local affairs, particularly in the matter
of racial segregation, and implied that the overzealous FBI investigators had in-
timidated the witnesses. Also representing the defense, attorney Allyn Sidney
(called "A.S.") Drew characterized the prosecution as a case of politically motivated federal meddling designed to undermine white supremacy:

> This is the most important case you jurors ever sat on. It will decide
> whether we people in the South can run our own business . . . whether we are
> to set up a federal police court over here in Shreveport; whether we will be
> over here day after day to satisfy the whim of some organization up North.
> . . . There will be no co-mingling of white and black. They will always be
> treated well. No force in the world can bring us to co-mingling. I say that is
> [what is] being tried [here].

A little more than three months later and 227 miles away in southern Louisiana, Tureaud would encountered a similar argument against "outside inter-
ference," this time from a white attorney, who was representing a black youth
on death row for a second time after surviving a botched electrocution. St. Martinville attorney Bertrand DeBlanc, in a show of white supremacy at its worst,
would order the black attorney off the case and demand that he "stay out of St.
Martinville and leave the matter for local handling."[33] DeBlanc did not save the
black youth from being executed.

Despite the eyewitness account by the Negro residents in the Minden lynching trial, Rousseau regretfully announced: "They found the defendants not
guilty."[34] On August 15, 1947, Jones's widow, Carrie Lee Jones, filed a $50,000
lawsuit against Sheriff Oscar Haynes for failure to protect Jones while he was in
custody. The suit was dismissed.

The harsh environment that Tureaud and other Negro attorneys had to work
in would be illustrated many times. According to John P. "Jack" Nelson, a white
civil rights attorney who was acquainted with Tureaud, segregation created significant logistical problems. "Lodging, dining facilities, restrooms, and opportunities to discuss strategies with fellow white attorneys were limited at best,"
Nelson explained.[35]

Nelson served with Tureaud on a biracial Catholic laymen's organization
that sought to prepare parishioners for desegregation. The white civil rights attorney was later involved with the New Orleans school desegregation issue as
a pro-integration candidate for the school board. He subsequently represented

plaintiffs in a desegregation suit against Tulane University, a private school in
New Orleans, and would serve as director of clinical education at Loyola University School of Law.

Tureaud wanted to remove the logistical problems caused by Jim Crow, but
what motivated him most was the desire to eliminate the imprimatur of white
supremacy evident in trials like the one held in Shreveport. If life for Negroes
in a racially segregated environment was hard, white supremacy made their existence unbearable. Tureaud was necessarily consumed—weekdays and weekends—with his growing law practice.

As his civil rights activities received increasing media coverage, Tureaud
began getting negative attention from segregationists. In the face of harassing
early morning phone calls and bomb threats to his house and office, the attorney's sense of humor helped ease the tension felt by his family. His son recalled
that the bedroom of his two older sisters was situated at the front of the house
and that he and his father would joke, although the girls didn't think it was very
funny, that "if a bomb was thrown on the front porch, they would be the first to
go."[36] Tureaud's and A.P. Jr.'s bedrooms were in the rear of the house.

Tureaud's sense of humor was also helpful while he was traveling throughout the racist South, as was his Caucasian appearance. He and his friend Dr.
Robert Adams, a New Orleans physician, often traveled outside the city in the
doctor's Lincoln Continental. Whenever they stopped at a gas station, they tried
to select one with a diner. On one occasion, the white gas station attendant assumed that Dr. Adams, because of his dark complexion and Negroid features,
was Tureaud's chauffeur. He said, "Ordinarily, we would not serve your driver,"
but since it was just the two of them, "y'all can eat over there and nobody will
ask any questions." Adams handed $20 in payment for the gas to the attendant,
who refused it, saying, "I will get it from your boss." Tureaud, who admittedly
didn't even have $20, told the attendant that he had given Adams the money to
pay for the gas.[37]

Tureaud's Caucasian appearance wasn't always helpful, however: it sometimes put him in more serious situations. In one instance, while he was a passenger on a train to Lake Charles, Louisiana, he was removed from the train because somebody told the conductor that there was "a white man in the colored
section bothering the Negroes."

Tureaud joked often about being mistaken for a white man. Yet he found it
ironic that those who were convinced that Negroes were unfit to associate with
whites couldn't tell the difference.

Bagatelle Plantation, ancestral home of A. P. Tureaud, built by A. M. Tureaud. The house was moved from its original location in St. James Parish to its present location in Baton Rouge.

Tureaud's paternal grandmother, Nanine Bourgeois Slater, in 1901, with (*from left*) her grandson Willie (Alex's older brother); Alex, age ten; his uncle James Alexander Slater; and Alex's younger brother Emile. Photo was taken in the courtyard of the Tureauds' home on Kelerec Street in New Orleans.

A. P. Tureaud's father, Louis Tureaud, ca. 1900.

Victoria, one of A.P.'s older sisters, ca. 1920. After two unsuccessful marriages in New York, "Vict," as she was called, returned to New Orleans and was a secretary in Tureaud's law
office until his death.

Actor A. P. Tureaud solicits the assistance of his sister Vict as they ham it up before he goes to the theater in New York City, 1919.

Tureaud enjoys the company of friends at a picnic in Virginia celebrating the Fourth of July in 1921.

A. P. Tureaud as (*left*) a law school student
at Howard University, 1924, and (*right*) a
teenager.

A. P. Tureaud, recent Howard Law School graduate, in downtown Washington, D.C., 1925.

Portrait of the young lawyer taken in New Orleans, ca. 1930.

Tureaud as guest speaker for the Senior Day program at Joseph S. Clark High School in New Orleans, 1953. In attendance were the graduating seniors, including his son A. P. Jr.; their parents; and faculty members. Tureaud's elementary school, the Bayou Road School, was demolished in the 1920s, and the building that became Clark High School was constructed on this site.

LSU Athletic Association student ticket (1953–54) of A. P. Tureaud Jr., LSU's first black undergraduate.

A. P. Tureaud, Class of 1925; Edwin B. Henderson, Class of 1930; and Julius A. Thomas Jr., Class of 1918, were honored at the eighty-seventh anniversary of the founding of Howard University, March 2, 1954.

Celebrating Mardi Gras in the typical New Orleans style, Tureaud and Lucille attend a gala ball in 1960.

A. P. Tureaud walks with Thurgood Marshall, New Orleans, August 31, 1960. Photo © 2010 The Times-Picayune Publishing Co., all rights reserved. Used with permission of The Times-Picayune.

From left: Unknown, Ernest Morial, A. P. Tureaud, Walter Morial, Dr. Leonard Burns, and Marcus Newstadter at a meeting of Alpha Phi Alpha Fraternity, ca. 1960.

A. P. Tureaud placing robe on Ernest "Dutch" Morial during his swearing in as first African American to serve as judge in the Louisiana Juvenile Court, 1970. Photo courtesy Sybil Morial.

A. P. Tureaud and Lucille at an audience with Pope Paul VI at Castel Gandolfo, the papal summer residence, in 1964. An interpreter introduced Tureaud and his wife to the pope, highlighting Tureaud's civil rights career, including his service as a Catholic layman.

A. P. Tureaud (*center*) is pictured with several generations of his family at the Split Rock Lodge in the Pocono Mountains of Lake Harmony, Pennsylvania, for Thanksgiving 1969, one of the last family gatherings of his life. In attendance were all of his children, their spouses, and seven grandchildren. *First row, from left:* Vanessa Nicholls, Lucille Tureaud holding Ronda Tureaud, Tina Patterson, Sylvia Patterson with Chavis Patterson, Fay Tureaud with Alex Tureaud III, Louie Patterson, and Carole Tureaud. *Second row, from left:* Jane Tureaud, Doward Patterson, Janet Tureaud, A. P. Tureaud Sr., A. P. Tureaud Jr., Elise Nicholls holding Lisa Nicholls, Theodore Patterson, and Gina Patterson.

Mrs. Lucille Dejoie Tureaud, seated in wheelchair, holds the cord that will unveil the name of her late husband, A. P. Tureaud Sr., at the dedication of the LSU classroom building named after him, March 23, 1990. Her daughters Elise Tureaud Nicholls, Jane Tureaud, and Sylvia Tureaud Patterson and a granddaughter, Monique Davis, are among those observing the ceremony. Photo from LSU University Relations.

A. P. Tureaud Jr., Nicole Moliere, and Kirt Bennett, LSU Student Government Association officers, at the dedication of A. P. Tureaud Sr. Hall. It remains the only building on the LSU campus named for an African American. Photo from LSU University Relations.

Statue unveiled at the dedication of A. P. Tureaud Civil Rights Memorial Park on January 20, 1997, honoring Tureaud and nine other civil rights leaders who fought for equal justice: Louis Martinet, Homer Plessy, Alvin Jones, Arthur Chapital, Oretha Castle Haley, J. Skelly Wright, Ernest Morial, Earl Amedee, and Isreal Augustine.

11
Law and Fatherhood

During the morning of August 20, 1944, Lucille was again admitted to Flint-Goodridge Hospital and this time gave birth to identical twin girls. She and A.P. had given their respective families their first set of twins. Burel, one of Lucille's younger brothers, jokingly commented, "If anyone in our family could produce twins, it would be Teel [Lucille's nickname]."[1]

Sylvia and A.P. Jr., upon hearing the news of the birth of their siblings, sat together in the living room and cried. When asked why they were upset, both feared there wasn't room at home for two more children. "Where would the twins sleep?" they wanted to know.[2]

The twins, healthy and adorable, were named Jane Victoria and Janet Katherine. When Tureaud saw his twin daughters for the first time, he thought to himself that they looked like his sisters who had left the family to live as white women. His daughter Carole noted years later that "he [her father] never elaborated and these phantom sisters were never discussed, so I thought that only two sisters were involved in the crossover. I was amazed and disappointed to discover that I had four aunts that I did not have the privilege of knowing. What a waste, what a loss."[3]

With the arrival of the new babies, Lucille ended her career as a pharmacist and became a full-time housewife. The Tureauds, now a family of eight, moved from Rocheblave Street to a larger two-story, single-family house on Pauger Street in the mid-forties. The house was located three blocks from their former home, making the move an easier transition for the family. There was no need to change their parish church and the children's schools.

A. P. Tureaud was a bundle of energy, arising early and going to bed late. Up at the crack of dawn, he would read both morning newspapers, drive to Dixiana Bakery for sweet cinnamon rolls and crusty French bread, and then return home to prepare eggs, grits, bacon, and ham. Milk, coffee with chicory, fresh fruit, and orange juice were always on his breakfast table.

After breakfast, Lucille combed and braided her daughters' hair. In the bathroom, using the toilet as a chair, Tureaud would polish six pairs of Buster Brown shoes before sending his children off to school. Formal education was important to the attorney. He had decided early in his own life that he would pursue the best education possible. But unlike his father, Louis, Tureaud was able to provide an academic foundation for all his children that would prepare them for college. He boasted when his children did something special in school and earned good marks.

Tureaud drove his daughters to high school most mornings. Until his car could hold no more, he also picked up many of the neighborhood children he saw walking along the way. "Mr. Tureaud is coming through," the teenage boys shouted when they spotted his car barreling through the streets and roaring around the corner.[4] He was a fast driver, making sudden starts and stops like a driver not entirely focused on the road. He seemed more intent on getting to his destination than on providing a smooth ride for his passengers. His car radio was always tuned to a news station, never music. Turning the dial constantly from one station to another, he sought the latest local, state, or national news. He often reported the news to his children, encouraging their discussion of the day's events. Sometimes Tureaud used their time in the car to quiz the children on their plans for the school day. He encouraged them to be attentive to their teachers, to study hard, and to visit the library.

Helping his children work through their problems and supporting them in their decisions was Tureaud's style. As involved as he was with his children, Tureaud reprimanded his children rarely, preferring to let Lucille discipline them. He was generous with his time, money, and affection. He was a "soft touch," and his children felt they had a better chance of getting their way with him than with their mother. When they needed extra money to buy things, they asked their father first, knowing that their mother would question their intentions. In these instances, Lucille became the lawyer and the children had to prove their case to her.[5]

On one rare occasion, Tureaud was extremely upset with A.P. Jr. when his son narrowly escaped being struck by a car as he ran across a busy street while playing, despite repeated warnings of the dangers and constant admonitions not to do so. Tureaud and Lucille were not overprotective parents, as they allowed their children the independence to make mistakes, but they always emphasized the harsh realities and dangers of thoughtless behavior.

With six children, there were always incidents that Tureaud and Lucille realized needed a calm and reassuring response. Upon moving into the house on Pauger Street, Tureaud cautioned his children against touching the coal-burning furnace in the basement. Undoubtedly, he wanted to prevent a childhood mishap with fire similar to that which had caused the death of one of his brothers. One evening, his daughter Carole was injured while attempting to shovel more coals into the furnace. An uncontrollable puff of smoke from the furnace covered her with soot and badly singed her eyebrows, eyelashes, and hair. Tureaud convinced Lucille that Carole had learned her lesson, but he realized the inherent dangers and replaced the coal furnace with a gas heater.

Tureaud gladly did the grocery shopping for his family. He also took his son shopping on Canal Street, near his office. Accompanying his son to department stores to buy new clothes gave the father and son personal time alone together. A.P. Jr. wasn't required to wear school uniforms like his sisters who attended the Catholic school. "I usually got the clothing that I wanted," A.P. Jr. recalled years later. "We were taught to buy quality items . . . a rule learned from my mother, who was more involved with the girls' shopping and encouraged them to buy the more classic styles," he said.[6] For very special events, A.P. Jr. recalled, his sisters would have dresses or gowns made by a family friend who was a modiste.

Tureaud teased his daughters and enjoyed seeing them react to his practical jokes. He once accompanied one of his twin daughters, Jane, to court for a speeding ticket. After pleading her case, she was fined several dollars. Happy with being handed such a small fine, Jane was alarmed when her father asked if she had the money to pay it. Pouting, she answered, "No," thinking he was going to pay her fine. Tureaud asked, "Well, why'd you come to court without any money? You have to pay my fees and the courts fees, plus your ticket, you know." Jane handed over the money but woke up the next morning to find $1 bills thrown on the floor around her bed. She knew that it was her father who put them there.[7]

In the 1930s, Lucille and Tureaud, with eleven other married couples, had organized a bridge club, which they named the Eatmores. Members of the Eatmores included many of the most promising young Negro couples in the city of New Orleans. Bonna and Archie Arnaud, Daisy and Osceola Blanchet, Anna and Ernest Cherrie, Evelyn and Haydel Christophe, Pearl and Prudhome Dejoie, Dora and C. C. Haydel, Helen and Walter King, Jeanne and Victor Labat,

Mildred and Ferdinand Montegut, Louise and Henry Sindos, Anna Mae and Edward Spriggins, and Daisy and Andrew Young joined Lucille and Tureaud as members of this group.

All of the husbands and many of the wives were working professionals. They were teachers and administrators in public schools and universities, medical doctors, a dentist, insurance executives, a contractor, a lawyer, and a pharmacist. Most of the women in the group were college graduates, and several worked with their husbands, helping them establish and maintain successful businesses. All of the women were involved with charitable activities in the community and were deeply committed to providing enriched social and educational opportunities for their children—in, they hoped, a nonsegregated environment.

The Eatmores rotated the responsibility of hosting their bimonthly Saturday night meetings in their homes. They played contract bridge, and the competition was fierce but friendly. Host couples sought to impress their fellow club members, crafting unique menus and hours of enjoyable camaraderie and unabashed fun. At meetings held during holidays, the hosts would decorate around appropriate themes and sometimes require guests to wear costumes, which made these occasions even more amusing.

These gatherings also provided the group with opportunities to get away from the pressures of their careers and the constant responsibility of child rearing. They were successful businesspeople and community leaders who, when in the company of their friends, let their guard down and, in the spirit of good fellowship, teased and joked with one another.

Two rubbers of bridge were played, and substantial prizes were awarded to the lucky winners. Mounds of gourmet delights were served, usually in several courses, washed down by a variety of liquid refreshments. Good jokes, often at the expense of another member, and humorous stories, often at the expense of the teller, filled the room. Throughout the evening, there was constant laughter and serious merrymaking.

After dessert and coffee, the husbands removed their coats, donned aprons, loosened their ties, and claimed absolute control of the kitchen. Until their work was done, the kitchen was off limits to their wives. The men were responsible for cleaning up, regardless of how long it took. They would wash, dry, and put away all of the kitchenware and in the process had a grand time, sharing stories, political gossip, and bawdy jokes. Cigars, cigarettes, drinks, and male bonding accompanied the task of cleanup, while the wives enjoyed their time together in the living or dining room. The wives confessed that despite the chances of getting caught they couldn't resist placing an ear to the kitchen door to listen in on what the men were saying.

Occasionally Osceola Blanchet, a professional vocalist and musician, would organize and lead a quartet, which sang a few songs before everyone else joined in the singing. The Tureaud children knew there was something special about the Eatmores' gatherings. They often heard their father whistle while typing or doing office work, but he almost never sang. As the adults adjourned their meetings, well after midnight, club members agreed that the musical interlude was the perfect way to end such very special evenings.

Over the years the Eatmores became more than bridge enthusiasts. In many ways, they became a large extended family. Family picnics emerged as an extension of the club's activities. Birthday parties, sleepovers, vacation trips, and assorted social activities provided opportunities for the club members' children to interact with each other. Many of the children became best friends and would maintain their relationships over the years.

The Eatmores collectively produced thirty children, who refer to themselves today as the Junior Eatmores. The Junior Eatmores residing in New Orleans meet occasionally; however, they are not as cohesive a group as their parents. The racial, cultural, and economic revolutions that transpired after the civil rights movement of the 1960s created unlimited social and professional opportunities for black Americans like the Junior Eatmores. Many left New Orleans, living and prospering in communities throughout the world. Although the Junior Eatmores have not maintained the club traditions of their parents, their allegiances to each other are still strong. The legacy of the Eatmores is a tribute to these Negro men and women who created an enriched social and family milieu in spite of the significant racial restrictions in place at the time.

In 1952 the Knights of Peter Claver purchased the French Hospital, a large, white three-story stucco building at 1821 Orleans Avenue. The hospital had provided medical services to white patients and closed its doors when the racially mixed neighborhood in which it was located became predominantly black. The construction of an expansive public housing project for Negroes, the Magnolia Housing Project, across the street from the hospital hastened the decision of the hospital board to close the facility and sell the building.

The renovated and painted hospital became the Knights of Peter Claver Building. Former patient rooms and doctors' offices were converted into usable office space for the society and Tureaud's legal practice. A few years after the purchase, the second and third floors were transformed into offices for rent. Tureaud represented the order at the closing. The following day, his wife and children, armed with buckets, brooms, and dust cloths, went with Tureaud to the hospital. More than one hundred years old, the Greek Revival–style building was a fortresslike structure, with thick walls and oversized front doors, and was a community landmark. The "White Elephant," as the neighbors called the hospital, had been vacant for several years and was sorely in need of repairs and a fresh coat of paint. Covered by several years of dust, everything on the inside had been left in place as if staff and patients would be returning at any moment. The Tureauds were overwhelmed by what they saw. Jane remarked, "It looked like we had entered the set of a horror film."[8]

Desks in the nurse's stations were stacked with patient records and notepads with messages. A pair of worn slippers was neatly placed under a chair. When Tureaud turned on the floodlights in the operating room, the family discovered surgical instruments displayed on trays and operating gowns and masks folded on tables. Private rooms and wards contained personal items left by patients. Hundreds of towels, sheets, and blankets, all stamped FRENCH HOSPITAL in prominent black letters, were stacked in closets or folded on carts in the hallways.

The most interesting discovery occurred in the pathology department, a suite of three small rooms that opened into a large conference area, located near the main entrance to the hospital. As Tureaud opened the door to his future office, the odor of formaldehyde and decay overwhelmed everyone. Shelves lining the rear of the rooms were stacked with a collection of jars and bottles containing human organs and bearing the names of patients. Alarmed but fascinated by the discovery, A.P. Jr. said, "It was a gruesome and provocative experience. Reading the names of the patients on the specimen jars seemed like an invasion of their privacy."[9] A human brain discovered inside one container provoked nightmares for several of the Tureaud youngsters. Tureaud and Lucille were sorry that their children saw it.

Within a few weeks after the closing, the contents of the hospital were discarded or liquidated. The Tureaud house received a large quantity of towels, sheets, operating room suits, and hospital gowns, which were used for years. Guests at the Tureaud home often asked why the towels and linens bore the name French Hospital.

Located one block west of Claiborne Avenue, a wide boulevard lined with hundred-year-old dueling oaks, the Knights of Peter Claver Building became a social and business center in the bustling downtown Creole community of the Seventh Ward. The area surrounding Claiborne and Orleans avenues was a major business district for the black residents of the downtown community. Insurance companies, doctors' and dentists' offices, private businesses, restaurants, and bars, all black owned and operated, thrived along both avenues.

The Grand Hall of the Claver Building, an ideal setting for social events, was frequently rented. Wedding receptions for three of the Tureaud daughters, Sylvia, Elise, and Jane, were celebrated there. For many years, Lucille and Tureaud hosted an open house for relatives and friends on Mardi Gras Day at the building. The grassy allée—called neutral ground in New Orleans—of Claiborne Avenue, shaded by the old oak trees, became a festive picnic site for families and groups of revelers. Food stalls and makeshift bars lined the avenue. The Zulu Social Aid and Pleasure Club and many of the black Indian tribes paraded along Claiborne Avenue. From sunrise to sunset, this magnificent boulevard was densely populated with thousands of costumed fun seekers, enjoying the hedonistic rituals of Mardi Gras. The Claver Building was also within walking distance of the Vieux Carré, Canal Street, and the Municipal Auditorium, all major venues for watching parades and gawking at revelers in unusual costumes.

As Tureaud's civil rights activities increased and his legal victories received media coverage, he felt more secure celebrating Mardi Gras in the company of family and friends at the Claver Building. Mardi Gras reveling did not attract the same disapproval it once did for the black upper class. Historian Adam Fairclough would write years later that "the arguments that swirled around the annual Mardi Gras parade of the Zulu Social Aid and Pleasure Club typified this conflict between lower-class hedonism and middle-class respectability. As the Zulus and their 'second-liners' reveled in a display of drunken buffoonery, the people whom they regarded as 'stuck-up Negroes' condemned the spectacle as grotesque and distasteful."[10]

Tureaud recalled from the perspective of old age, "Once we climbed the so-called ladder of middle-class America, we . . . felt that that was not a good image of middle-class life—to be parading and having men and women in the streets carrying on these body gyrations: 'shaking' as they'd say on the street." The persistence of "h[v]oodoo" evoked similar disdain, especially among the physicians and pharmacists who felt they had to contend with the "credulity and faith of the ignorant."[11]

The masking, drinking, and general mayhem of the day provided the perfect cover for planned acts of violence, often reported as random occurrences.

Although not widely publicized, stabbings, shootings, and frequently murders were an unfortunate by-product of Fat Tuesday in a city gone mad for the day. Mardi Gras Day was the only occasion when members of Tureaud's family heard him express feelings of vulnerability, and they were pleased that he wisely did something about it and remained off the streets.

Tureaud occupied three small offices in the Claver Building, formerly the pathology department. Years later, black attorneys would reminisce about the early morning gatherings with Tureaud, who would share with them the legal news of the day. The spartan waiting room, with its large conference table, wooden chairs, and walls of law books, became the workspace for many of the local, regional, and national civil rights crusaders who came to New Orleans. Thurgood Marshall, Constance Baker Motley, Jack Greenberg, and Robert Carter, during their days working for the NAACP Legal Defense Fund, accompanied by Tureaud, A. M. Trudeau Jr., Ernest Morial, and others, would write briefs, discuss strategies, share jokes, and toil many long hours in this room. A favorite restaurant they frequented was Dooky Chase, a few blocks from Tureaud's office. Just as he opened his law office to the NAACP national staff, the generous Tureaud later opened it to younger, struggling black lawyers who sought his advice and the use of his law library. However, Tureaud faced several years of challenging work with the local NAACP branch before such landmark civil rights efforts began in earnest.

Tureaud was dedicated to these legal pursuits and often acted alone until he was able to get assistance from younger lawyers, like Morial and Trudeau, who joined his law practice in the mid-1950s. They were eager for the experience and did not get paid initially for the assistance they gave. In fact, the senior attorney imagined that Trudeau and Morial "wondered what the devil I had them in the case for because I saw to it that in every situation I was present."[12]

Tureaud loved to travel, and fortunately, Lucille did too. A lack of public accommodations for Negro travelers did not deter the couple from taking their six children on trips throughout the country. When traveling to business conferences and conventions, Tureaud encouraged his wife and children to accompany him and to enjoy the resources of the places visited.

Negro motorists were allowed to purchase gas but could not use the restrooms in gas stations. Motels and hotels refused to accommodate Negroes. Occasionally a restaurant had a separate room with its own entrance, usually at the rear of the building, for black patrons. Many restaurants provided a window for take-out service and often charged black customers higher prices than they charged white customers.

Because of the lack of accommodations in the southern states, the Tureauds frequently arranged overnight stays with friends. These reciprocal arrangements, jokingly referred to as "the underground railroad" by the Tureaud children, eased the humiliation and anxiety of traveling in the segregated South.

A trip to Mexico City by train, a long car ride to New York City, and a plane flight to London all provided opportunities for the Tureaud children to broaden their life experiences. Summer trips were the most enjoyable time that the family spent together. Each day was a new adventure as they drove along the highway, planning their strategy for securing meals and places to sleep. With impressive skill, Tureaud bargained with the local vendors when traveling in foreign countries. These family trips provided this father with the opportunity to watch his children learn about the customs and cultures of people different from themselves and to celebrate those differences.

On a trip to the Northeast, Tureaud decided to stop for the night as dusk approached while driving through Tennessee. Finding a place to sleep for a family of eight was the biggest challenge of the day. A motel was selected, and Tureaud parked a comfortable distance from its office. Jane, Janet, and Elise, the three youngest, who also had the lightest skin tone, accompanied their father to the lobby to register. Because the family had stopped at a restaurant with take-out service, once inside their motel room they would not be seen until checkout time the next morning. As the family departed, a desk clerk remarked she would not have let any of them check in if she had seen Sylvia, Carole, and A.P. Jr., the three oldest and darkest-skinned children.

Yearly trips to Knights of Peter Claver conventions included the entire family. Depending on the location of the convention, Tureaud would rent an apartment or a house for the week. A 1955 photo taken in front of a yacht, the *Fla-Joe*—owned by Dr. Joseph Thomas, a well-known, successful black general practitioner from Dundalk, Maryland—showed the family enjoying an outing. It was taken while the Tureauds were returning from a Claver convention in Rochester, New York, after which they had also taken a detour to enjoy the theater in New York City.

A.P.'s oldest daughter, Sylvia, was dating Theodore Patterson, a resident of Maryland, and the relationship was getting serious. So a visit with the Patterson family was planned in a stopover in Maryland. Sylvia met "Pat" when he accompanied Dr. Thomas's wife, Flavia, on a trip to visit a friend in New Orleans.

Joseph, Flavia, and their son, Joseph Jr., lived on the Chesapeake Bay on an estate that had originally been a country club. The main house was a large Georgian, with a guesthouse, surrounded by extensive grounds and two deepwater piers. The Tureauds and Pattersons were among those invited to go boating on Dr. Thomas's yacht, a converted LST from World War II.

It would not be the family's last visit to the eastern shore of Maryland. A year later, Sylvia and Pat were married. The grand wedding was emotionally charged for Tureaud, who felt he was "losing" his first daughter. The newly-weds spent their honeymoon in Nassau, the trip being Tureaud's gift to the couple. His colleague Judge Frederick Thompson, who was from the Bahamas and whose son, Fred, was also Sylvia's classmate at Xavier, made good on his promise to Tureaud that he and his family would show the couple around the island.

Upon their return, Sylvia and Pat, who was in medical school, moved into Dr. Thomas's guesthouse. The two resided there until their first child, Gina, was born. After they moved out, Tureaud's protégé Ernest "Dutch" Morial and his wife, Sybil, moved into the guesthouse. Morial was in the army, stationed at Fort Holabird, an army intelligence base, in Dundalk. Pat graduated from medical school and took over the successful practice when Dr. Thomas retired.

Tureaud's lifestyle provided a variety of experiences for his children that would broaden their perspectives on life outside the New Orleans Seventh Ward. His dream for his children was that they not be limited in what they could accomplish in life because of racial discrimination.

12

"Separate but Equal" Strengthened in the Face of Desegregation

When Thurgood Marshall called an April 1946 meeting in Atlanta, Georgia, with lawyers from the South who had worked on local NAACP cases, A. P. Tureaud was there. Marshall and the lawyers agreed to bombard eleven southern states and the District of Columbia with simultaneous lawsuits demanding equal educational facilities for existing Jim Crow schools, a strategy proposed by the former NAACP legal counsel Charles Hamilton Houston.[1] Despite doubts that a significant number of cases could be generated because of the lack of willing plaintiffs, Marshall adjourned the conference with an agreement to file "as soon as possible" university cases in Louisiana, Oklahoma, Texas, Tennessee, and South Carolina and cases dealing with high schools in Louisiana, Arkansas, Florida, Maryland, and Virginia.[2]

Tureaud and Louis Berry initiated the first university desegregation case, against Louisiana State University's School of Law. "It was one of the greatest thrills of my life at that time, to know that I had a chance to argue a case in a state where I had been barred from studying law. . . . And it's a thrill that I never forgot," Berry stated years later with great enthusiasm.[3]

Tureaud filed the 1946 lawsuit on behalf of postman Charles Hatfield of New Orleans, a Negro veteran and soon-to-be graduate of Xavier University who wanted to enter LSU Law School. At that time the NAACP targeted the desegregation of public higher educational institutions based on the "separate but equal" doctrine. If there were no separate facilities for Negro students, the states' existing institutions needed to be opened to them. Tureaud, Marshall, and Berry were already working on a suit filed on behalf of New Iberia, Louisiana, native Viola M. Johnson, who wanted to attend LSU's Medical School.[4] Johnson, who had completed one year at Meharry College of Medicine, a Negro school in Nashville, Tennessee, sought to complete her last two years of medical school closer to home. She was denied admission to the LSU Medical School in New Orleans.[5]

According to NAACP attorney Robert Carter, the strategy was such that it would prove too costly for southern states to set up "these separate schools and would on their own open the doors to the existing schools."[6] Houston's rationale for targeting segregated law schools first included an additional premise that white judges who had matriculated in the nation's finest law schools could not in good conscience suggest that black lawyers in segregated schools received "equal" legal training.

State-supported, historically black law schools were set up in Pennsylvania (Lincoln University School of Law, 1854) and North Carolina (North Carolina Central School of Law, 1940). They were woefully underfunded, understaffed, and established only to deter black students from seeking admission to white institutions.

Tureaud believed that Houston may have had a point; however, litigation in the former states of the Confederacy—Alabama, Arkansas, Florida, Georgia, Mississippi, North Carolina, South Carolina, Tennessee, Texas, and Virginia, as well as Louisiana—did not initially achieve the victory that the Legal Defense Fund had attained in *Pearson v. Murray* (1936) and *Gaines v. Canada* (1938). In *Pearson*, the Maryland Supreme Court ruled that the University of Maryland had to admit Negro students to its law school if no other law school was available to them. In the *Gaines* case, which involved the University of Missouri School of Law, the U.S. Supreme Court ruled that Missouri had to educate Negro law students within its state borders. The state of Missouri, like other southern states, had instituted a program of out-of-state tuition for Negroes to attend colleges and professional schools in states that would admit them. The Supreme Court ruled in the *Gaines* case that the out-of-state tuition program did not constitute equal education.

Tureaud carefully monitored the cases of other southern attorneys working in association with the Legal Defense Fund. Ten years passed before additional lawsuits targeting higher education desegregation in other southern states achieved success in defeating Jim Crow laws in state supreme courts and in the U.S. Supreme Court. Lois Ada Sipuel was admitted to the University of Oklahoma School of Law with success in *Sipuel v. Board of Regents of Oklahoma* in 1948.

With the lawsuits against LSU, Tureaud knew he was taking on the premier public institution of higher learning in the state of Louisiana. Founded as the Louisiana State Seminary of Learning and Military Academy on January 2, 1860, in Pineville, Louisiana, the institution provided educational training to a student body that joined the Confederate forces during the Civil War in 1861. Ironically, the students were fighting against the command of their academy president, William T. Sherman, who resigned the post to lead the Union army. The state seminary was closed during the war and reopened in 1865 under the leadership of David French Boyd. In 1870, the seminary was designated as Louisiana State University. Seven years later it merged with the Agricultural and Mechanical College, which was previously located in New Orleans. Louisiana State University and Agricultural and Mechanical College moved to its present campus in Baton Rouge in 1925.

Boyd, who fought for the Confederacy in the Civil War, met with Louisiana's newly elected governor, Henry Clay Warmoth, who took office shortly after the state was readmitted into the Union in 1868. Warmoth assured Boyd that as governor he "would do nothing toward forcing the admission of Negroes" to the seminary.[7]

In 1872, William Pitt Kellogg was elected governor of Louisiana, replacing Warmoth. Kellogg, who supported efforts to integrate the state's public schools, led the state legislature's withdrawal of all support to LSU in 1872 because Boyd refused to admit Negro students. Article 135 of Louisiana's 1868 constitution, which prohibited racial segregation in Louisiana's public schools, provided Kellogg and the supporters of public school integration with the authority to eliminate state funding to LSU.

In the 1876 gubernatorial election in Louisiana, both candidates, Democrat Francis Nicholls and Republican Stephen B. Packard, claimed victory. Each convened his own legislature. At the national level, the Democratic candidate for president won the popular vote but was short one electoral vote. The Compromise of 1877 gave the U.S. presidency to Rutherford B. Hayes and gave the state of Louisiana to the Democrats. The remaining Federal troops were removed from the state, and Reconstruction ended in Louisiana in April 1877. With the Democrats in control, funding to LSU was restored and the threat to desegregate LSU brought on by Reconstruction was over.

The Louisiana Constitution of 1898 specifically provided for separate public schools for "the white and colored races" for children aged six to eighteen and stated that higher education for colored students was provided by the public institution Southern University. Southern University and Agricultural and Mechanical College began in New Orleans in 1880 when a group of black politicians petitioned the Louisiana State Constitutional Convention to establish a school of higher learning for "colored" people. Southern University was opened on March 7, 1881, and the Agricultural and Mechanical Department was established in 1890. With the continuing growth of the institution and lack of land for expansion, the university relocated to the Scotlandville area, north of Baton Rouge, along Scott's Bluff facing the Mississippi River, on March 9, 1914.

For the 1946 *Hatfield* case against LSU's law school, LDF staff attorney Robert Carter and Louisiana attorney Berry prepared the substantive argument on the constitutional violation. Tureaud presented information on the number of professional schools organized and operated by the state that prohibited the enrollment of Negro students. Southern had no law program, and Straight College, which did, had closed. Seeking to open the doors of the all-white Louisiana State University School of Law caused more strident opposition than Tureaud had anticipated. Hatfield received threats by telephone day and night. He was even threatened on his job as a postal clerk and advised to quit, which he did.

Motivated by anger rather than common sense, Hatfield on one occasion refused to heed repeated warnings to act cautiously to stay out of harm's way. He agreed to meet with an anonymous person who had written an unsigned letter asking him to come to the thirteenth floor of the Pythian Temple to discuss his lawsuit. Hatfield met the caller at the appointed place and time. In 1946, the Pythian Temple was practically abandoned, and such a meeting could be held undetected. A man whom he could not identify approached and held out money, promising more if Hatfield would drop the lawsuit and attend school out of state. When Hatfield refused the offer, the man quickly left.[8]

Hatfield headed for the elevator and realized at the last minute that, although the doors were open, the elevator was not there. He paused just in time to keep from falling into an empty shaft.[9] Fearing for his client's life, Tureaud suggested that Hatfield accept an offer made to him to attend graduate school at Atlanta University in Georgia.

In a summary judgment motion, Hatfield's lawyers believed the judge would rule in their favor. Judge G. Caldwell Herget continued the case to allow the state to open a law school for Negro students at Southern University in Baton Rouge. B. B. Taylor, representing LSU, told the court that "the mingling of the two races in the past has always resulted in friction and trouble."[10]

Judge Herget dismissed the *Hatfield* case on April 9, 1947. In his opinion, Herget stated that, just as in the *Johnson* case against the medical school, the complaint should have been directed at Southern University for not offering a law school and medical school.[11] The judge noted that the legislative act creating Southern University permitted the university to create both law and medical departments.[12] Southern University had not been made a party to the litigation, so no mandamus was issued.

This lawsuit was the impetus to the opening of a law school at Southern University in 1947. Tureaud felt that his efforts helped increase the number of Negro lawyers in Louisiana. "They didn't have any Negro lawyers until I opened up a law school at Southern University," he said years later.[13] Despite Tureaud's initial efforts, the appeals in the *Hatfield* and *Johnson* cases were considered abandoned and dismissed by the Louisiana State Supreme Court on June 11, 1953.

Louisiana became another exception to the rule that LDF attorneys had not expected. The exception did nothing to change the strategy of the LDF staff, which turned its focus to parallel litigation in Texas and Oklahoma. In 1950 the U.S. Supreme Court went steps further in the higher education desegregation effort by ruling in *McLaurin v. Oklahoma State Regents for Higher Education, et al.* that students in graduate schools of education had to be treated equally. Separate seating could not be assigned in classrooms, libraries, or other facilities. That same year in *Sweatt v. Painter, et al.* the U.S. Supreme Court ruled that a legal education had to be "substantially equal." Because such equity did not exist in the separate law school set up in 1947 at Texas Southern University as a consequence of the 1946 lawsuit brought by Sweatt, black students had to be admitted to the white law school at the University of Texas.

The first four years of the 1950s were professionally charged for A. P. Tureaud. In January 1950, the newly elected officers of the New Orleans branch of the NAACP were sworn in. Tureaud, who was elected president, along with the other officers and board members, pledged, "after careful consideration and by divine help," to accept the sacred challenge before them. They also promised: "With purity of motive, we will endeavor to the best of our individual ability, to prove ourselves worthy of the sacred honor which has been placed upon us."[14]

Opting to quickly get down to the matters at hand, Tureaud acknowledged, "One of the biggest tasks facing the NAACP is the need of workers to solicit funds to carry on the work of the organization."[15] Widespread admiration and support for Tureaud as NAACP president were reflected in an editorial appearing in the *Louisiana Weekly*. "His keen legal mind plus his genuine interest in the welfare of underprivileged people makes him especially well-suited to the many-sided and perplexing aspects of his new responsibility [as NAACP branch president]."[16]

Charles Hamilton Houston, the former Howard Law School dean with whom Tureaud had initially worked at the NAACP Legal Defense Fund and who had introduced Tureaud to Thurgood Marshall, died on April 22, 1950, from a heart attack. The previous year, at Christmas, Tureaud had first received distressing news regarding Houston's health. Houston, diagnosed with acute myocardial infraction (a heart attack), had been released from Washington's Freedmen's Hospital in time for the holidays.

The loss of a brilliant strategist and civil rights warrior gave Tureaud the renewed determination to continue his efforts to fight injustice and to broaden opportunities for Negroes in the fight for civil rights. Tureaud served three consecutive terms as president of the New Orleans branch of the NAACP, from 1950 to 1953. During these same years, he successfully challenged desegregation in Louisiana's higher education system. In four lawsuits he methodically and persistently used the courts to open the doors of Louisiana State University's law, medical, graduate, and undergraduate schools to Negro students. All of the LSU schools are located in the state's capital, Baton Rouge, except the medical school, which has its campus in New Orleans. The lawsuits involved Roy Wilson (law school), Lutrill A. Payne (graduate school), Daryle Foister (medical school), and Alexander Pierre Tureaud Jr. (undergraduate school). The *Louisiana Weekly* reported these cases in much detail and compared them to the NAACP efforts in cases setting legal precedence across the nation.

The LSU Board of Supervisors was poised to handle the desegregation issue in its August 1950 meeting. LSU president Harold Stokes announced that "the question of the rights of Negro students to be admitted to LSU under recent Supreme Court decisions will be presented to the Board of Supervisors at its next meeting." Tureaud commented, "These applications are in line with cases now in process all over the South and which will be pressed in the courts by the NAACP unless these students are admitted."[17]

The U.S. Supreme Court decisions in three important cases—*Sweatt, Gaines,* and *McLaurin*—were used to support Tureaud's lawsuits against LSU. The *Gaines* decision relied on the "equal protection" constitutional doctrine and said that a state had to furnish, within its borders, educational facilities for Negro students substantially equal to those offered to white students. It further maintained that in the absence of such facilities the Negro petitioner was entitled to take advantage of those offered to white students.

Sweatt was argued on April 4, 1950, and decided on June 5 of that year. It defined "substantially equal" in terms of the education and reputation of the faculty, variety of courses offered, physical plant, library facilities, position and influence of alumni, standing of the institution in the community, tradition, and prestige. The decision resulted from a case in which Heman Marion Sweatt filed suit to gain admission to the University of Texas School of Law.

The *McLaurin* case was argued on April 3 and 4, 1950, and also decided on June 5, 1950. That decision stated that not only were Negroes entitled to equal facilities but they also had to receive equal treatment. It ruled out segregation within an institution, banning such common practices as special seats for Negro students and special tables in the library and dining halls.

According to *Louisiana Weekly* reporter Clarence A. Laws, "Not since the Supreme Court upheld the 'separate but equal' doctrine 54 years ago has its decisions provoked as much comment and as much hope as the three decisions made on June 5 on the question of racial segregation."[18] Tureaud's comments were cited in that front-page article: "I am disappointed with the decision of the Supreme Court. I had hoped that it would strike down the 'separate but equal' doctrine, which it had established in the case of *Plessy v. Ferguson*. As it now stands we will have to attack each case of racial segregation on its own merit, insofar as school and public facilities are concerned." Tureaud was more optimistic about the Court's decision in the *Henderson* case,[19] regarding the matter of transportation, stating that the decision "practically wipes out segregation of passengers in interstate commerce."[20] Tureaud saw this Supreme Court decision as an opportunity to redeem itself from *Plessy*.

Tureaud continued his appeal for NAACP support and hope for the struggle: "I am not unmindful, however, that in these cases our cause had been strengthened, but we will still need financial support for cases through the NAACP which has for more than 40 years been chiseling away these inequities based on race, creed, color, and national origin." He concluded, "In our own state we have much to do to remove these badges of slavery and second-class citizenship."[21] His statement rang true just a month later when, "by unanimous vote on July 27, the Board of Supervisors of LSU denied the admission of 12 Negro applicants.[22] The board's action followed a daylong session. The vote was open to the press and the public; however, all discussions were held behind closed doors. LSU president Stokes made the board's task less difficult by presenting a resolution requesting that Negro applicants be denied admission. Tureaud was quoted in the *Louisiana Weekly* as saying that such action was "expected."[23]

A front-page "News Flash" in the *Weekly* on September 16, 1950, announced: "Tureaud Filed Suit against LSU." The previous day, a three-judge panel heard arguments in the suit filed against Louisiana State University. The suit asserted that there was no institution where Wilson and the eleven other plaintiffs were able to obtain legal education equal to that available at LSU, and it requested a permanent injunction restraining the state from barring these students. The suit also maintained that equal justice was being denied under the Fourteenth

Amendment of the U.S. Constitution. The trial was reset for September 30, 1950, because the defense needed more time to prepare for the case.

Unlike in the state courts, Negro and white spectators occupied desegregated seats in the federal court during the trial. On September 30, educators, business leaders, and representatives of various religious groups, as well as lawyers, crowded the court. During the trial, circuit judge Wayne Borah called more technicalities on Marshall than on LSU's chief counsel, Lawrence W. Brooks. District judge Herbert W. Christenberry called into question Brooks's objectivity when the attorney referred repeatedly to the "excellent facilities" at Southern.[24]

Tureaud and Marshall did not have many complaints with either Borah or Christenberry. Ultimately, they and other civil rights attorneys viewed the two as conscientious jurists with a sense of fair play and respect for the U.S. Supreme Court.[25]

Borah, a native of Baldwin, Louisiana, served as a U.S. District Court judge before his appointment to the Fifth Circuit Court by President Calvin Coolidge in 1928. The two civil rights attorneys had come before Borah's court in the Eastern District of Louisiana and received an unfavorable ruling in a case challenging the unconstitutionality of a Louisiana voter registration case. His rulings proved more favorable to civil rights in the teacher salary equalization cases of the 1940s.

A 1915 LSU Law School graduate, Borah practiced privately in New Orleans from 1915 to 1923, with a two-year interruption in his practice when he served in the U.S. Army (1917–19). He served as an assistant U.S. attorney for the Eastern District of Louisiana from 1923 to 1925 and as the U.S. attorney for the Eastern District from 1925 to 1928.

Judge Herbert W. Christenberry was a New Orleans native born two years before Tureaud. Christenberry was nominated to the U.S. District Court by Earl Long and appointed by President Harry S. Truman in 1947 and would serve as chief judge of the court from 1949 until 1967. The U.S. Navy veteran and 1924 Loyola University School of Law graduate practiced privately in New Orleans from 1924 to 1933, before being named assistant attorney for the Board of Commissioners for the Port of New Orleans. He formerly served as deputy commissioner of the Louisiana Debt Moratorium Commission and assistant district attorney of Orleans Parish, as well as assistant U.S. attorney and U.S. attorney for the Eastern District of Louisiana. His mother served as secretary for Huey Long, and he was a loyal Long supporter. Early in his career while handling police brutality cases, Tureaud became acquainted with Christenberry, who was assistant district attorney and later U.S. attorney. He was impressed with Christenberry's knowledge of and his concern in these matters.

Negro spectators were in awe of Marshall's performance in the courtroom. "It was very exciting to see Marshall and the other black lawyers, including Tureaud, argue their cases in court. We were proud to see Marshall looking strong and tall and handling himself so effectively against the white lawyers and judges," recalled Dr. Raymond Floyd, a professor from Southern University in Baton Rouge.[26]

Tureaud's courtroom style—though vastly different from Marshall's—boosted the pride of Negro onlookers, who knew him as a local lawyer. LDF counsel Jack Greenberg said that Tureaud was generally very good in most areas of the legal practice, including negotiating, conducting trials, and making appeals; he was quiet, composed, and not very demonstrative in court, but he was effective. Greenberg also noted that "Tureaud seemed to be more amused than angered by his opponents and their views about black people and the need for Jim Crow laws."[27]

LDF attorney Constance Baker Motley observed during her first courtroom appearance with Tureaud that "he was very highly respected by the judges and the other lawyers." She felt that he was so well respected because the judges realized that he was being "quite courageous in taking these cases." Motley recalled, "The lawyers involved in civil rights cases were experts in the field and there were so few."[28]

In a pretrial meeting, Tureaud confirmed that Wilson's petition was not a class action and that the ruling on the case would apply only to the law school. However, the attorney reminded the court that the outcome of the case would immeasurably affect the general principle of "race disqualifications" in Louisiana.[29] Concluding the plaintiff's argument, Tureaud presented comparative information about the LSU and Southern law schools. He explained that the value of the physical plant of the LSU Law School was more than $34 million, while that of the SU Law School was merely $3.5 million. There were 12,300 volumes in SU's Law Library, compared with LSU's more than 70,000 volumes. Moreover, unlike at LSU, the SU law faculty had no advanced degrees and no previous teaching experience.

The plaintiff's lawyers won. Roy Wilson, the sixteenth child of a northern Louisiana farmer, enrolled at LSU in the 1950 fall semester on a Tuesday afternoon. Wilson was expected to arrive in the LSU registrar's office at 2 p.m. but was delayed two hours because of car trouble. Tureaud flew into Baton Rouge about 1:30 p.m. the same day. When Wilson arrived, a number of photographers and newspapermen from the daily press and wire services were already present.

Tureaud was the first to enter the office of law dean Henry G. McMahon. Dean McMahon gave a cordial smile when he was presented with the court decree. He explained the registration and class attendance procedures to Tureaud and Wilson. Reporters interviewed the two men as they left the dean's office. In a prepared statement, Wilson said, "I can sincerely say that I have been treated wonderfully and I expect it to continue for the most part. And I am happy not only for what it [enrollment in LSU's Law School] means to me but what it means for democracy from the standpoint of our form of government."[30]

Tureaud's first triumph in the court against LSU was confirmed. The lower court's decision ordering LSU to admit Wilson to the law school was upheld. However, the excitement of the victory was short lived. The *Weekly*'s January 20, 1951, issue carried the headline "R. Wilson Quits LSU, Lack of Funds Reason." The article stated that Wilson did not have the money to continue his education at LSU. It did not report the more negative details being carried by other news media. The *Daily Reveille,* LSU's student newspaper, reported that lawyers representing the LSU Board of Supervisors discovered that Wilson had been released from the army with a Section 8, or "blue discharge." Blue discharges are issued for either ineptitude or insubordination. Therefore, the board ruled that Wilson was "not morally qualified" to enter the LSU Law School. The *New Orleans Times-Picayune* reported that on January 4, 1951, LSU documented eight charges against Wilson that he did not deny, including the Section 8 discharge.

The *Weekly* reported Tureaud's dismay with those who criticized Wilson for not telling the NAACP attorneys about his past. Tureaud fired back:

> It is easy to stand on the sidelines and criticize players in a game. It is my opinion that the public should not be so critical of Wilson without first knowing the true facts in the case as they really are.
>
> We should not be ready to censure or condemn Wilson. He made it possible for others of his race who have all the necessary qualifications to be admitted to any department of the school; if they are eligible, the same as he did to the school of law. Wilson left LSU with no bitterness and with no regrets.
>
> It is now left to his critics to take up where he left off.[31]

Marshall, however, expressed his disappointment with Tureaud's selection of Wilson as a plaintiff, stating in a letter to his friend and colleague, "You sure did pick one this time."[32]

Lesson learned, Tureaud was more careful in his choice of plaintiffs for future cases. Employing a more thorough process of investigation, he interviewed potential plaintiffs for social, emotional, and academic strengths and began to identify support systems for those who would become plaintiffs. Marshall became more involved in the plaintiff selection process. He urged professional training for those making selections and discussed these matters in conference with the NAACP lawyers, explaining how important it was that plaintiffs have appropriate academic standing, no criminal record, and the ability to perform under pressure.

In 1951, LSU rejected Natchitoches, Louisiana, schoolteacher Lutrill A. Payne's application for admission to its graduate school. Tureaud, again the local counsel on the case, petitioned for an interlocutory injunction on Payne's behalf. Judge Christenberry granted the injunction and ruled that Payne was to be admitted without delay. Payne attended summer classes, living in an off-campus apartment. He later wrote to Tureaud that he took two courses and received two Bs. He also reported that he was treated cordially during his stay at the university and looked forward to returning the next summer. The trail blazed by Roy Wilson and Lutrill A. Payne was beginning to attract more and more travelers. Two Seventh Ward residents, Robert Collins and Ernest Morial, who had both grown up not far from Tureaud's home, entered the LSU Law School in 1952.

Tureaud worked out an agreement with LSU Medical School officials to admit Daryle Foister, head of nursing at Flint-Goodridge Hospital in New Orleans, pending official approval by the LSU Board of Supervisors. Documents were filed before Judge Christenberry, who on March 26, 1952, signed a judgment making permanent the injunction restraining LSU from refusing to admit qualified Negro applicants to its School of Medicine. With this ruling in Foister's favor, Tureaud had his third win against LSU.

The LSU Board of Supervisors was accused of "violating the law and indirectly showing disrespect for it by forcing legal action (which costs the taxpayers heavily) each time a qualified Negro wants to enter a different school at LSU." The board members were described as "those who are still fumbling around in the dark as to what democratic ideals really mean."[33]

The *Louisiana Weekly* reported continuing progress of Negro students attending LSU. In "Collins, Morial Win Moot Court Trials at LSU," it was reported that for the first time in the ninety-two-year history of LSU, two Negro freshman law students won the first round of the Robert Lee Tullis Moot Court Competition. Collins and Morial defeated their opponents in the hearing of an appeal concerning the decision in a murder case.[34] Although the *Louisiana Weekly*'s articles described hard-fought struggles against racial discrimination in the courts, once Negro students were enrolled and attending classes at LSU, the paper reported that they were treated respectfully and cordially. These accounts were the strategies used to continue support for desegregation and not alarm potential civil rights litigants. Major abusive and unfair treatment of black students in formerly all-white schools would be widely reported after that time. Even the psychological toll on these first Negro students would later become well documented.

The year 1953 marked Tureaud's court fight against the undergraduate division at LSU. NAACP attorney Constance Baker Motley remembered being in Louisiana during the undergraduate school desegregation case. "[Tureaud's] son, A. P. Tureaud Jr., was a plaintiff," she recalled. "Guess he couldn't get anybody else to be the plaintiff, so he made his son the plaintiff."[35]

Opinions vary as to whether Tureaud ever planned for his own son to take this role in the desegregation case against the LSU undergraduate school. From experience, Tureaud knew the potential danger in which he was placing his son in defiance of the Jim Crow laws. Repeated threats to Negro plaintiffs in the previous desegregation cases included ugly exchanges of words and cruel gestures. Some plaintiffs had been spit upon, beaten by fists and clubs, and even threatened with murder after their physical likenesses hung in effigy as a warning. Yet Tureaud felt strongly about the right to equal justice and was willing to allow his son to be placed in harm's way to achieve it.

History would only repeat itself with A.P. Jr. being forced out of a public educational institution where the traditional social structure of the Jim Crow South was in place, just as his father was forced out of a public institution where the issue of class was in play. This time, a predominantly white public college and an entire group of people, rather than young boys in revelry, rejected young A.P. Jr.. The sting of personal prejudice was just as emotionally painful. Such rejection caused limitation of one's choices and a hindrance of one's rights.

Tureaud whispered to Lucille about his concerns as they lay in bed one night, knowing that she would express her feelings and then listen carefully as he worked out what he should do about the situation. No doubt, Tureaud remembered a letter A.P. Jr. had written to both his parents while away at summer camp in Pennsylvania. Unlike other letters in which their son had described the wonderful time that he was having, the other campers he had met, and the contests he had won, in this letter A.P. Jr. wrote that he felt bad that his parents did not tell him that they loved him. Noticing no change in his parents' behavior toward him on his return home, A.P. Jr. asked if they had read what he had expressed in his letter from camp. He recalled that his father and mother confirmed that they had but that they simply went about parenting as usual. It was not long before A.P. Jr. would understand just how much his parents loved him.

During his junior year of high school, A.P. Jr. discussed with his father his need to prepare for the guidance counselor a list of potential colleges he would like to attend. At the top of his list was Howard University. Fearing that his first choice was out of reach because of cost, A.P. Jr. listed Xavier University and Tulane University in New Orleans and Southern University and LSU in Baton Rouge. Agreeing that these were all good schools, his father assured him, "You got the grades; you should get in."[36]

Together, the father and son decided LSU was the best school for the money. Although A.P. Jr. did not want to study law and told his father so, the senior Tureaud advised his son to select the combined English and pre-law curriculum, unique to LSU, so that the admission could be reinforced under the "separate but equal" law. He told his son, "You can always change your major later after you are enrolled."[37]

A.P. Jr. attended the 1953 hearing of the LSU undergraduate school desegregation case, sitting with his mother and father. "There sits the most ungrateful niggra in the State of Louisiana," LSU attorney Leander Perez of New Orleans snarled, pointing an accusing finger at A. P. Tureaud Jr.[38]

Perez proclaimed that the state provided several colleges for its "niggras" and that this plaintiff should enroll in one of them. He also claimed, "LSU's refusal to admit young Tureaud does not constitute an irreparable injury to the youth . . . the harm is done to LSU by having the institution hauled before the court."[39]

Perez was lead counsel for the defense, in concert with seventeen attorneys, all graduates of LSU. Fred LeBlanc, the state's attorney general, and two of his assistants added to this number. A large number of lawyers didn't necessarily make for a better defense, however. "They're all in there for some political, personal reason, just to sort of show the flag I guess, and they're not contributing to the outcome of the case at all," LDF attorney Jack Greenberg stated. He explained further, "It's not like you're outnumbered because of their 20. In fact you're probably better off not to have 20. They just get in each other's way, that's all."[40]

Federal judge James Skelly Wright, a New Orleans native, presided over the proceedings in New Orleans in the fall of 1953. Tureaud met Wright in the mid

1940s while working on a case in St. Martinville, Louisiana, and another time when Wright was an assistant U.S. attorney. Following a brief stint in Washington with the Department of Justice, Wright was made U.S. attorney, and it was not long before he was considered as a possible appointee for a judgeship in the U.S. District Court.

Wright had visited Tureaud to inform him that segregationists were opposing his nomination. In addition, several other individuals were interested in the position. Wright's more liberal stance on civil rights was the primary area of criticism from the conservative white southern politicians. Seeking a quid pro quo from Tureaud and black leaders, Wright requested their support to counter those opposing his appointment. Tureaud promised to help and contacted Congressman William L. Dawson, from the First Congressional District of Illinois, who had the ear of the president. In 1949, President Harry Truman appointed Wright judge of the U.S. District Court for the Eastern District.

The junior Tureaud's case was discussed for more than two hours. LSU president Troy H. Middleton had been instructed by the board to report admission applications by Negroes to the board or to reject them unless otherwise instructed. A.P. Jr., a lean and well-dressed young man in a light blue wool suit, sat among the several spectators, white and Negro, in the courtroom during the lengthy court hearing. Emotions ran high for the student and his mother, who were appalled by the statements made by opposing counsel.

According to LSU attorney W. Scott Wilkinson Jr. of Shreveport, "Because of the history, tradition, customs, and the usages of the people of Louisiana, segregation of white and black is necessary in this state to preserve and to promote more friendly relations and mutual understanding between white and colored persons." The defense argued that "segregation has meant progress in the Negro race and the absence of race riots, which prove the wisdom of such practices." Perez continued in his accusations that young Tureaud was ungrateful for the expenditures that the state had spent to improve Negro education, as the some "3,000 happy students at Southern University" proved.[41] Perez was big, loud, and abusive in his defense. Taking a cue from his father, A.P. Jr. sat quietly, seeking to disguise how he really felt about the white attorneys' statements.

Perez, a wealthy land baron from Plaquemines Parish and a racist czar, was known throughout the state for his vigilant efforts to maintain the status quo. "Segregation forever" was the message communicated with regularity to his white constituents. His courtroom presentations included racial slurs and insults. Lucille was offended by Perez's language and demeanor and regretted attending the hearing with her son and husband. Tureaud told his son that these courtroom antics were designed to demean and anger the opposition, and he repeated a slogan often used by Thurgood Marshall when preparing NAACP lawyers for trial: "Lose your cool, lose your case."

The LSU attorneys attempted to show that SU had substantially the same courses as LSU. The group also predicted "dire consequences if Negroes were admitted to LSU."[42] A.P. Jr. was amazed by the malevolence directed at him by the opposition. Despite his father's advice, the young petitioner realized that this was the beginning of a difficult journey that would require personal fortitude and courage. He thought, "Can I do this?" The presence of his parents on either side of him was reassuring, and A.P. Jr. knew that when the going got tough, they would be there for him, as usual, unconditionally.

Judge Wright ruled in favor of the plaintiffs, and LSU's undergraduate school was to be desegregated. Happy with the success, Tureaud now experienced first-hand the anguish of having a child attend an all-white institution. He had counseled other Negro trailblazers who, as the result of his legal success against Jim Crow laws, had put them all in the forefront of making new laws. He had cared about these individuals, keeping in touch by letter, and, through his NAACP contacts, provided for them a network of support during their ordeal. For his son, he felt a heightened concern.

Going to college was an experience that young A.P. Jr. had dreamed about since he was in elementary school. "My parents talked a lot about their college days with me and my sisters and felt that it was one of the best times in their lives," A.P. Jr. recalled. "We enjoyed listening to my parents and their friends sharing stories about their years in college; their social life, fraternity and sorority activities, the challenges of rigorous courses, and the excitement of achievement. I wanted to have experiences like theirs and was excited about going to LSU."[43]

The exasperating events surrounding his son's enrollment as the first Negro undergraduate student at LSU were extremely trying for the senior Tureaud. A. P. Tureaud Jr. would be the only Negro student among thousands of white and international students. Anticipation made the first day very hard for members of the Tureaud household. After the legal challenges were squared away, young Tureaud was admitted as the result of a preliminary injunction. All of his friends in New Orleans had started school already, but A.P. Jr. had not been able to matriculate on time because of the legal problems.

After days of waiting, a date was set for him to enter LSU. "The car was packed with all of the usual items needed for dorm life and the trip to Baton Rouge seemed to take forever. My level of excitement and anxiety increased as we entered the campus," A.P. Jr. recalled.[44] Unfortunately the mood changed dramatically in the registrar's office when the Tureauds were informed by attorney Lawrence Brooks that LSU had applied for a new trial and A.P. Jr. would not be allowed to register.

"I was stunned and extremely disappointed," A.P. Jr. lamented. The drive back to New Orleans was gloomy even though his father was optimistic that this delay was a temporary setback and would be dealt with immediately. "As the car approached New Orleans I thought about my friends at Xavier, Dillard, and Southern and imagined that they were having a great time starting their college experience. At this moment I envied them and thought that perhaps I made a mistake," A.P. Jr. said of the emotionally charged events in the fall of 1953.[45]

At the new trial on September 16, Judge Wright set aside both motions entered by LSU and refused to rescind the injunction, which he had issued in A.P. Jr.'s favor. On September 18, A.P. Jr. registered at LSU as a freshman. Following registration and obtaining a class schedule, his parents accompanied him to his assigned dormitory, which was under the football stadium. Upon arrival, his dorm mates were eager to give A.P. Jr. the traditional freshman haircut. Trustingly, A.P. Jr. allowed the snipping off of his hair by the young white students. Before they left, his parents teased him about going bald like his father. The young student said a tender good-bye to his father and mother, assuring them that he felt fine and excited about beginning his college experience at LSU. Before returning to his room, he found a barber in the black neighborhood, several blocks from the north gates of LSU, to straighten out his haircut from the freshman ritual. The white-only barbershops that flanked the campus would not accommodate him.

The friendliness A.P. Jr. experienced during the peer rite promptly turned to taunting, ugly pranks, and cold isolation. He was assigned to a room for three students, yet he had no roommates. Loud music played by the white students blasted from stereo speakers they placed on the windowsill at night while he was trying to study or sleep. They also threw dead animals in front of his door. When he entered the showers, everyone left, whether they were finished showering or not. No one spoke to him.

A.P. Jr. was given the family car so that he could drive off campus to the safety of family friends in Baton Rouge or come home to New Orleans whenever he felt it necessary. Tureaud counseled his son during the harsh times on the LSU campus. He suggested that his son look for solace in the home of Howard alumnus Dr. Leo S. Butler, who lived in the south Baton Rouge neighborhood just beyond the LSU gates. According to A.P. Jr., "I was very unhappy and I depended a lot on my family to help me. It was the hardest thing that I had ever had to do."[46]

The media coverage was relentless. The first few days on campus were extremely trying for A.P. Jr. In recalling his initial exchanges with the press, he said, "From the date the suit was filed the press was active in reporting the progress of the case. Once I enrolled, settled in the dorm, and attended classes, the press was everywhere. Getting that much coverage made me very uncomfortable. I was trying to fit in as quickly as possible and I felt that continued media coverage would make it harder for me to make friends and become a part of the social activities on campus. I was also concerned that continued publicity might motivate crazy racists to do something stupid and violent."[47]

Several reporters called asking to take pictures of A.P. Jr. on campus. Others pumped him for information and quotes for their news stories. A magazine with national distribution wanted a story and pictures. The reporter also expressed an interest in posing A.P. Jr., the black LSU undergraduate, with a white female student. Offers of money and clothing were made to tempt A.P. to comply. His polite response to all the reporters was: "Sorry, but I really want to make this work and continued publicity makes it harder for me to do that. Please respect my privacy. Thank you."[48]

He had learned by watching his father deal with the press that it was important to be respectful and polite and not to compromise your values. He also heard his father warn young Negro lawyers against making "deals under the table, deals which he said would come back to haunt you." Tureaud advised them: "Be honest, be clean, or else you might be disbarred."[49]

Despite the young student's requests for a moratorium on publicity, the *Daily Reveille* kept the media beat alive. The black undergraduate's class schedule included English, math, Spanish, civilization, physical education, and Air Force ROTC. To fulfill a requirement on his first day of P.E. class, he was asked to swim the length of the swimming pool. The simple task became a full-scale media event. Almost every day there was an article about the first Negro undergraduate or about the university filing to revoke Tureaud's registration, as well as numerous letters to the editor.

A student letter to the editor suggested that in order to remove A.P. Jr. from the university, a Roman Colosseum party should be scheduled, with the Negro student and Mike, the LSU Bengal tiger mascot, battling it out in the football stadium. This letter also said that the audience of students and faculty would obviously cheer for Mike to be victorious.

White student Charlie Roberts, now head of the LSU Alumni Association, recalled that he attended ROTC class with A.P. Jr. and often wondered how the young black student tolerated the constant scrutiny by the press. "During his matriculation, he was constantly in the spotlight and treated like this spectacle." Roberts observed, "It had to be hard for him."[50]

Unlike the media, which hounded A.P. Jr. constantly, the students gave him the silent treatment. He remembered his father saying that there were always whites who aligned themselves with him in his efforts for equality but it often took longer for them to surface. A.P. Jr. kept hoping that such an alliance would materialize for him, but it never did. The closest he got to making a white friend on campus came in the form of a note. Found under the door of his dorm room, the note told him not to be discouraged and explained that, although its author wanted to be a friend, he could not because he would be blackballed from social activities and fraternities on campus. White students generally supported the silent treatment in the hope of isolating the lone black student so severely that he would leave LSU.

A.P. Jr. did make friends with a few of the black graduate students at LSU. One married couple lived in an apartment on campus and came to the dorm to meet him. They understood the difficulties he was going through, and a bond of friendship was forged almost immediately. Both were working on their master's degrees, and they too experienced racial indignities and isolation. The wife was visibly pregnant, expecting her baby during the first semester. As a young, attractive black woman, she felt vulnerable and shared stories about being called names by white males on campus. Crude comments were also made about her pregnancy. One white male student yelled at her as she walked to class in the busy quadrangle on campus that she would give birth to a monkey. A.P. Jr. was disappointed that many of the students at LSU were so mean-spirited and ignorant. He had hoped that the faculty would have set a better example of civility.

Instead, he found that many professors were distant, and a few were rude and racist. One of his teachers announced to the class the first day he met the group that "she had never taught a 'niggra' before and she didn't know how she was going to be able to manage the situation."[51] The teacher said she didn't even know whether she could touch his paper and made other crude comments to the class. A.P. Jr. was humiliated and insulted. Foreign students were enrolled in her class, and she taught them. She didn't think anything about correcting their papers. Needless to say, the young student had a terrible time in her class.

He was never called on or offered assistance by his teacher. He disliked her and did not seek out her help.

In the dining hall, students sat as far away from him as possible. "This was also true in my classes," A.P. Jr. told his father.[52] He expressed to attendees at a reunion for former LSU black students in 1989, "I was alone and became unhappy because this was not the college experience of my dreams. In fact it was more like a nightmare."

During his third week at LSU, A.P. Jr. realized that the pressure and stress he felt were taking their toll on his productivity. His studying was clouded by his feelings of sadness and isolation. One morning he arose early, unable to sleep once the banging on the walls had subsided. His dorm room was on the fifth floor under the football stadium, near the cage of Mike the Tiger. A.P. Jr. told his sisters on his first trip back to New Orleans that Mike was treated better than he was.

While sitting on a bench facing the street, he saw a pickup truck parked nearby. It was about 6 a.m. and foggy, so it was not clear who was in the truck. There were times when he thought about the possibility of being on the receiving end of a racially motivated act of violence, especially since the press kept the issue of his attendance alive. He stood up to leave when a black man, dressed in overalls, holding the hand of a boy about eight years of age, got out of the vehicle and walked toward him. He approached and asked A.P. Jr. if he was Tureaud, introduced his son, and stated that he had been on campus several times, hoping to find him. He was a farmer and a man of few words, but he wanted his son to see A. P. Tureaud and to know that LSU was now a possible college choice for him.

This experience had a tremendous effect on A.P. Jr. He realized, now more than ever, that his attendance at LSU could have a significant impact on desegregating all of the undergraduate programs in the state. He also realized that he was becoming a role model for college-bound Negro students in Louisiana.

After one month on campus, A.P. Jr. continued to be shunned by the students and barely tolerated by the faculty. He tried to place himself in environments and activities that encouraged social interaction, to no avail. As a Catholic, he attended Newman Club meetings at the Catholic center on campus. The students and priest were polite while he was there, but made no overtures to encourage future interaction.

As a member of the Air Force ROTC, he was approached by two upperclassmen who were his squad leaders and lived in a small room on his floor. They asked A.P. Jr. if he would consider changing rooms with them, since he had a larger room that was designed and equipped for three students. Realizing that these students never spoke to him before or acknowledged his existence, A.P. Jr. thought this gesture might be an opportunity to establish a positive relationship with them. Since the squad leaders' room did not have neighbors on either side of it, he would also eliminate the noise made by his neighbors. A.P. Jr. agreed to the switch, and the two guys helped him move into the smaller quarters. Once the change was made, the squad leaders never spoke to their black dorm mate again.

"Going home on weekends was the only happy times that I had while I was at LSU. To be a part of a large, gregarious, caring family was soothing beyond description; however, my weekend visits were very short because I had to leave New Orleans for Baton Rouge on Sunday afternoon. I had a Saturday morning physical education class, which I cut several times, in order to extend my weekends at home."[53] Tureaud felt that his concern for his son's safety, both physical and emotional, should be played down for the sake of A.P. Jr. When he spent weekends at home, A.P. Jr. could hear his father's attempts to console his mother, who feared for her son's safety while attending LSU. She was distressed that anyone, especially her son, had to endure such blatant mistreatment.

A.P. Jr. recalled, "Driving back to LSU was depressing, and the negative feelings increased as I got closer to the campus. I felt trapped in an untenable situation, one that I could not resolve. I thought about leaving but was not willing to admit defeat. I also believed that future cases to desegregate state schools would be hampered by my departure from LSU."[54]

After being at LSU a month, with no change in the silent treatment nightmare, A.P. Jr. began to think more about leaving the university and enrolling at Xavier University. These thoughts created new and intense conflicts for him. He later said of his dilemma: "The image of the farmer and his son put a face on desegregation for me, and I knew that I could not disappoint them, not to mention all of the other men and women of color who might want to attend LSU or one of the other state institutions supported by the taxpayers of Louisiana."[55]

One weekend in New Orleans, father and son had a long conversation at the office. In his usual soft-spoken and articulate manner, Tureaud told his son that he was not beholden to anyone but himself and that anytime he wanted to leave LSU he could. A.P. Jr. told his dad that he would stay the course and that he was failing math.

Norman Francis, a graduate of Xavier University with a degree in math, was one of the first black students to enroll at the Loyola University School of Law, becoming a law student there in 1953. Francis was a good friend of Dutch Morial, also a graduate of Xavier, and Robert Collins, who was Morial's roommate at LSU Law School. On weekends it was not unusual for the three law students to visit Tureaud's office.

Following graduation from LSU in 1954 and a stint in the military, Morial associated with Tureaud's law office. His legal career would include an appointment as Louisiana's first black assistant U.S. attorney (in 1965), first black juvenile court judge (in 1970), and first black judge of the Fourth Circuit Court of Appeals (in 1974). Morial's career took a turn to politics in 1967, when he was elected as the first black Louisiana legislator since Reconstruction. He later became the first black mayor of New Orleans, serving from 1978 to 1986.

Following law school graduation, military service, and the private practice of law, Collins went on to serve as a magistrate judge in New Orleans's Criminal District Court in 1972 and as an appointed federal judge in 1978.

Francis would graduate law school in 1955, serve in the military, and return to work at his alma mater, Xavier University. In 1968, he became president of Xavier and in 2009 enjoyed one of the longest tenures as president of one university in the history of the United States.

While studying in Tureaud's law office on weekends, Francis was informed of A.P. Jr.'s problem with math studies at LSU and agreed to tutor him. A few weekend sessions proved to be productive as A.P. Jr. set the curve on a subsequent math quiz. His LSU professor, the woman who told the class that she had never taught a "niggra," announced that the black student made the highest grade. In her demeaning, racist manner she told the class that she did not know how that could have happened. A.P. Jr., on the other hand, was delighted. He also noticed that in subsequent classes in that course students who used to sit as far away from him as possible now sat closer to him. He viewed this change as a positive sign, and his spirits were lifted.

LSU's first black undergraduate stayed at the university for only eight weeks because the judge's decision that permitted him to enroll was overruled. Tureaud joked with the LDF attorneys that eight weeks was about as long as his son could take it and as long as the LSU officials would let him stay there without the protection of a court order. On November 10, 1953, Tureaud called his son at LSU and informed him that he was coming to Baton Rouge that night. His son was unaware that the temporary injunction issued by the federal district court, under which he was admitted, was vacated and set aside by the court of appeals because of a technicality during the district court proceeding. When told of the mistrial, the undergraduate felt that a great burden had been lifted from his shoulders. Tureaud stayed with his son during his last night in the dorm, fearing repercussions after the court's decision was announced that he had to leave.

As the car headed south to New Orleans on Route 90, Tureaud informed his son that he had spoken with the registrar at Xavier University and that he could enroll immediately. A.P. Jr. was surprised but delighted with the news from his father. The mistrial for him was an honorable way to extricate himself from a counterproductive experience that could have created more emotional distress and failure.

Years later, Lucille Tureaud spoke with tears streaming from her eyes when discussing the mistreatment of her only son while attending LSU. The case proceeded through the court for two years. The U.S. Supreme Court finally settled the matter along with other appeals in southern desegregation cases. The undergraduate schools were legally open to Negro students. LSU's first black undergraduate student won on appeal; however, he refused to return to the campus. He attended and later graduated from Xavier University in New Orleans in 1957. Many years later, A.P. Jr. explained that he "never wanted to return to LSU."[56]

Much work had to be done to interest concerned citizens across the state in serving as plaintiffs for additional higher education and trade school cases. Support in generating this interest came from a variety of sources. Through his connections with other NAACP leaders, Tureaud cultivated an interested group of individuals with close ties to the organization. Doretha A. Combre of Lake Charles, who was elected the first female president of the state conference of NAACP branches, wanted to desegregate McNeese State College. She wrote to Tureaud on behalf of her own children and several others in Lake Charles who were interested in attending McNeese. From 1951 to 1954, Tureaud represented the plaintiffs in that lawsuit.

In 1954 Tureaud received the alumni award from Howard University for distinguished postgraduate achievement in law. Lucille, Tureaud, Sylvia, and A.P. Jr. traveled to Washington, D.C., for the black-tie event. Tureaud was among several alumni recognized at the award ceremony. Oveta Culp Hobby, U.S. secretary of health, education, and welfare, was the keynote speaker. Such events were heart-warming, and Tureaud greatly appreciated the acknowledgment of those who served to effect change.

In his acceptance speech, Tureaud stated:

> We in Louisiana are trying to keep pace with the other parts of the nation in its quest for the enjoyment of full civil rights. It was Louisiana which gave you *Plessy v. Ferguson*. We are not proud of the result of that case, but we at

least deserve credit for making an early attempt to strike down racial hatred and intolerance. It was an honest leadership, which found to its dismay that the "time was not ripe." . . .

At least one would think so but in the South precedents like the *Gaines, Sweatt, McLaurin, Sipuel,* and *Wilson* cases are not as readily accepted as they have accepted with binding force the doctrine of *Plessy v. Ferguson,* because:

> Vice is a monster of such hideous mien
> As to be hated needs but to be seen.
> Yet seen too oft, familiar with her face,
> We first endure, then pity, and then embrace.
> —Alexander Pope, "An Essay on Man"[57]

13

Desegregation of Primary and Secondary Schools

The LDF staff found that although it initially focused on universities and professional schools in its desegregation cases, the lawyers' interests in this area also included primary and secondary schools. As the lead local attorney for the NAACP, Tureaud filed primary and secondary school desegregation cases throughout Louisiana over a period of six to eight years. Tureaud knew the gravity of the situation. The parish school systems in Louisiana were unabashed in their support of segregated schools. School boards across the state were unwilling to admit to any wrongdoing and denied that children in Negro schools were receiving inferior educational opportunities.

As former chairman of the School and Playground Committee of the Federation of Civic Leagues, Tureaud developed a plan that outlined the need for public schools for Negro students citywide. According to the attorney, school board officials never seemed to include Negro schools in their annual projections: "They were just trying to make do with what they had."[1] In their book *Crescent City Schools: Public Education in New Orleans, 1841–1991*, historians Donald E. DeVore and Joseph Logsdon outline the interplay between Negro leaders interested in improving primary and secondary schools for all students and the all-white school board during the latter half of the 1940s. They confirm Tureaud's role in seeking better education for Negro students in Orleans Parish, which complemented his valiant pursuit for equal and desegregated school facilities throughout Louisiana. Tureaud and Daniel Byrd were among Negro leaders with whom New Orleans school superintendent Lionel J. Bourgeois, on taking office in 1946, established a dialogue in support of a consolidation and conversion program to address inadequacies of school facilities.[2] The consolidation and conversion program was to be accompanied by a massive building program financed through a millage increase, requiring legislative and voter approval. Both programs had opposition and spurned varying degrees of compromises and legal maneuvers.

The school consolidation and conversion program included plans to convert McDonogh No. 16 School and to reopen three public schools—Kruttschnitt; Zachary Taylor, located at Bellichade and Dryades streets; and Edward Douglass White (later renamed Langston Hughes), located near Esplanade Avenue, between Claiborne and Derbigny streets—that the school board had closed because white students no longer lived in the surrounding areas. Even though the three schools proposed to be reopened were dilapidated, Tureaud believed they were still in better condition than other buildings available in the Negro community. He also knew that there were fewer school buildings in neighborhoods occupied by Negro residents than in those occupied by whites.

There were white residents who were not pleased with any of the suggested conversions and consolidations. One after another they petitioned the school board against each of the conversions, even going so far as to file an injunction in civil district court to enjoin the school board from carrying out its intention to reopen the Zachary Taylor and Edward White schools.

As the result of this legal maneuver, state senator Arthur O'Keefe of New Orleans sponsored a bill requiring the school board to obtain permission from the people in the neighborhood whenever a school was to be converted from a white school to a Negro school or vice versa. The consent of at least two-thirds of the people living in the neighborhood would be needed, regardless of whether they were black or white. The bill, Act 463, was passed, and Governor Earl Long signed it into law in July 1948.[3]

Despite the law, the school board voted on November 30, 1948, to convert the Edward White School.[4] White residents reacted by again filing suit. Tureaud immediately proceeded to get Negro petitioners living within 300 feet of the school to intervene in the case on behalf of the school board. On an appeal to the Louisiana State Supreme Court, Act 463 was ruled unconstitutional in February 1949, and school officials proceeded with the conversion. Another suit filed by white patrons, this one pertaining to the Kruttschnitt School, suffered a similar fate, and that school was converted. These successful school conversions were the exception, however, not the rule.[5] Despite modest gains, "separate but equal" continued to be illusory.

Providing the momentum for the secondary school desegregation cases in Louisiana, Tureaud filed *Rosana Aubert v. Orleans Parish School Board* in 1948. At the time, the case in his home parish became one of the longest-running school desegregation cases, changing names twice, spanning a quarter of a century, and having more than thirty-five hearings. It became one of Tureaud's most publicized cases.

Wilfred S. Aubert Jr., a founder of the Ninth Ward Civic and Improvement League, was a dockworker and father of two. Aubert was growing increasingly angry with the apathy of the Orleans Parish School Board toward his children's schools.[6] He approached the NAACP duo Tureaud and Byrd, asking them to remedy the situation. The NAACP representatives were eager to accommodate Aubert with a lawsuit.

In a final attempt to allow the Orleans Parish School Board to provide fair treatment to Negro students, Tureaud delayed the filing of the school desegregation lawsuit until after an important vote on a bond issue in New Orleans to address the need for $40 million to build schools in the city. Projections were made concerning the need to spend a sizable portion of the money, as much as 63 percent, on Negro schools.[7] Encouraged that at least some of the board members seemed concerned about the lack of facilities for Negroes, Tureaud and others believed that filing the suit prior to the approval of the bond issue would create taxpayer resistance to it.

Bourgeois and the school board received the authorization for raising the needed funds when the millage hike was passed statewide; however, voters in New Orleans rejected it. A letter from an irate white parent accused Bourgeois of showing too much interest in Negroes. The superintendent was exasperated by such opposition. It would take another year's time and energy for him to persuade enough school board members, who did not want to alienate white voters, to authorize the millage increase.[8] In the meantime, Bourgeois was "thoroughly frustrated" because the community failed to adopt suitable measures to provide funds to allow him to build more schools for Negro students.[9]

The embattled superintendent called Tureaud to ask if he would do something to help the situation. In an ironic turn of events, the superintendent pleaded the case for the need for more schools for Negro students, explaining, "Vacant ones are not being used. We need the classrooms badly. We don't have any money to build any schools. It would take six or more years to complete, even if we went through the bond programs. I need the schools now." Bourgeois went so far as to ask Tureaud, "Why don't you go and file that suit that you have already written me about?" "It will be filed very shortly" was Tureaud's reply.[10] "It wasn't necessary for him to ask me to go ahead with the suit because I was going to file it eventually," Tureaud later recalled. The attorney knew that the Orleans Parish School Board and its superintendent were not so concerned about Negro education that they "merited that kind of criticism."[11] Incidents like this one were common, and for Tureaud, choosing when to file a case was a matter of political expediency.

Tureaud filed the *Aubert* case on May 30, 1948, with the U.S. District Court for the Eastern District of Louisiana. In the following six years, he also filed other public school cases that focused on school desegregation, such as *Clayton Guillory v. St. Landry Parish School Board* (1949), *Aaron Howard v. Lincoln Parish School Board* (1949), *Ardie Heard v. Ouachita Parish School Board* (1949), *Lawrence Hall v. St. Helena Parish* (1952), and *Clifford Eugene Davis v. East Baton Rouge Parish School Board* (1954).

Tureaud argued that under the equal protection clause of the Fourteenth Amendment to the U.S. Constitution, Negro students had the right to receive "instruction in courses of study including the use of modern and sanitary schools and school facilities, such as are provided by defendants for white children."[12] The attorneys for the Orleans Parish School Board waited more than a year before denying all of the allegations in Tureaud's complaint and demanding the case's dismissal.

On July 12, 1950, more than two years after the initial *Aubert* case was filed, Judge Herbert Christenberry denied the Orleans Parish School Board's request for dismissal and encouraged Tureaud to move forward with the case. During this time, Tureaud also represented a Negro group called the Citizens' Committee on Equal Education before the Orleans Parish School Board to complain about platooning, huge teacher loads, inferior facilities for Negro students, and other violations of the "separate but equal" principle in New Orleans schools. The "platoon" system of double shifts operated in several Negroe high schools in the city to ease heavy overcrowding. Some students attended school from 7 a.m. to noon, while others attended from 11 a.m. to 5 p.m. At the same time, some white schools had so few students that keeping them open made little economic sense. This waste infuriated Tureaud, especially since there was a great need for Negro schools. Reports published in the *Louisiana Weekly* estimated that a quarter of the city's Negro children were not in school.

Although they attended an all-black school, the Tureaud children received an enriched education at the Valena C. Jones School. By the time his children entered high school, it was obvious to Tureaud that all Negro public schools were not equal. Tureaud enrolled his daughters at the private Xavier Preparatory High School, located uptown near the Garden District. Xavier Prep was a coeducational Catholic high school, operated by the Sisters of the Blessed Sacrament. This order of nuns also operated Xavier University in New Orleans.

Katharine Drexel, a wealthy Philadelphia heiress, intent on improving educational opportunities for Native American and black children, became a Catholic nun and established the religious order. She used her inheritance to build and maintain forty elementary and secondary schools throughout the United States. Xavier University was established in 1915 because Mother Drexel realized that the graduates from her high schools needed a university that would readily accept them.

A.P. Jr. attended Joseph S. Clark High, a public school, which was named for the first president of Southern University in Baton Rouge. Because of extreme overcrowding in 1950, Clark was on the platoon system, consisting of two sessions, one in the morning and the other in the afternoon. Although the school had an outstanding faculty, it suffered inequities in funding and was supplied with cast-off furniture, books, and laboratory equipment from white public schools. Despite these conditions, Tureaud allowed his son to attend and graduate from Clark High, even though he could have enrolled him in Xavier Prep, which had a better academic reputation. Bayou Road School, which Tureaud had attended, was demolished in the 1930s, and a new school was erected that served white students. In the late 1940s, the building was converted to a high school for Negro students. Ironically, A.P. Jr. attended Clark High on Bayou Road, the site of his father's elementary school forty-two years earlier. Tureaud was confident that, despite the problems at Clark High, his son would receive an appropriate education. Perhaps he also realized that as the legal champion for public schools it would be prudent to have a child of his in one.

In addition, A.P. Jr. felt that his father realized the importance of having his son broaden his life experiences by attending school with classmates from a diverse range of socioeconomic levels, beyond the scope of the Creole community where he attended elementary school. At the time, only white students were bused to school. On the behalf of the New Orleans NAACP branch, Tureaud denounced these practices for making Negro residents second-class citizens.[13]

By the 1950s, Tureaud and other cooperating attorneys found less resistance to new schools for Negro residents. The school boards were offering schools, rather than risking legal action by the NAACP. "We were winning cases in different areas by making the school boards construct or put up facilities that were equal to the white schools," he said. "They were doing that without even reaching the question of whether separate but equal was unconstitutional. As fast as they could get the money, they would put the schools up," Tureaud said. "The school officials did not want to be sued because the lawsuits were becoming successful in knocking down segregation. School desegregation was one of the things that most white school officials did not want."[14]

The LDF's national office decided to change its focus in the school cases; discussing the idea with participants at an NAACP lawyers' conference in June 1950, it concluded that the time had come to test the constitutionality of segregation itself. At the 1950 conference, several southern lawyers, including Tureaud, expressed concern about being able to get suitable plaintiffs. He and the others realized that such action would force Negro students into white schools, instead of only achieving suitable school facilities for them. "Plaintiffs would be difficult to find," Tureaud wrote in a letter to E. A. Johnson, president of the Louisiana NAACP State Conference, "because parents would be putting their children at risk; they would be especially reluctant to offer their elementary-school aged children as guinea pigs."[15]

NAACP New Orleans field secretary Dan Byrd expressed the need to educate the branches about the shift in policy in 1951. "This is something entirely new and the branches are uninformed," he told those in the national office.[16]

Instead of starting from scratch, Tureaud approached Aubert and his fellow Ninth Ward Civic League activists about challenging Jim Crow outright. On November 6, 1951, league members met with Tureaud in the Ninth Ward's Macarty School, an aged and dilapidated facility that was the very example of educational inequality. A petition signed by more than ninety parents of high-school-age children in the ward declared that segregation is discrimination because Negroes always receive the "separate" but never the "equal." Six days later, busloads of Ninth Ward residents arrived at the school board's office to witness Tureaud presenting their petition to board members.

In the meantime, Tureaud met Oliver Bush, a local resident with children in public schools, through a neighborhood meeting sponsored by the local NAACP branch. The branch leaders were encouraging the parents of school children, like Bush, to give voice to their grievances against the Orleans Parish School Board for not giving them more suitable facilities. It was not uncommon for Tureaud to attend meetings to hear the complaints of the Negro residents in case he was able to assist by initiating legal action.

Bush was a successful insurance agent for the Louisiana Life Insurance Company. Active in the NAACP branch, Bush and his wife expressed their concern for all Negro children attending public schools. Their children attended McDonogh No. 19 in the Ninth Ward, just one of the city's overcrowded public high schools for Negro teachers and pupils. The board's solution to the severe overcrowding was to set up additional temporary buildings in the schoolyard.

Oliver Bush joined the *Aubert* case on behalf of his son, Earl Benjamin Bush. When Wilfred Aubert later dropped out of the case, the Bush family became the sole identifiable plaintiff. At least two of the Bush children graduated be-

fore Tureaud could get the school desegregation case on the docket. This situation caused the attorney to vary the ages and grade levels of plaintiffs in subsequent cases. Tureaud felt that an order that would desegregate not only the
high schools but also all of the schools in the public school system could be
achieved.

Reacting predictably in its denial of a petition by Tureaud demanding that
the board abolish its segregation policy, the Orleans Parish School Board on
November 28, 1951, announced "that such a radical change of policy could not,
at this time, serve the best interest of the system."[17]

Tureaud filed the *Bush* case on September 5, 1952. There were only two judges
in New Orleans at the time, and the Orleans Parish School Board requested a
three-judge court. Tureaud told the school board's legal counsel, "You will be
sorry, asking for a three-judge court in these cases," admitting years later that
he was just joking with them. "We couldn't wish for anything better," he said.[18]
Delighted, Tureaud knew that the three-judge court cases provided a direct appeal to the U.S. Supreme Court, and that was just what he and the other NAACP
lawyers wanted.

As the initial contact with the plaintiff in the *Bush* case, Tureaud was responsible for drawing up the petition, using the model approved by the LDF.
He had to ensure that the facts of the case were consistent with the Louisiana Constitution and relevant state laws. It was also his role to keep up with
case pleadings and hearings. The local attorney always worked coopera-
tively with Thurgood Marshall and the LDF staff, informing them when
he was ready to file suit and sending them pleadings for their modification.

Tureaud was confident that the *Bush* case would result in a favorable outcome. He felt that school superintendent Bourgeois had a slightly different approach to the problem of educational opportunities for Negroes than did the
other school superintendents he had encountered. He suspected that Bourgeois's training as a lawyer influenced his outlook. He had earned a law degree
from Tulane Law School.[19]

Sam Rosenberg, attorney for the Orleans Parish School Board, asked to be
excused from handling the desegregation case because of his regular duties for
the school board. Board member Emile Wagner convinced the state legislature
to appropriate $15,000 a year and the parish school board to appropriate $10,000
to retain a special counsel to handle the case. Tureaud suspected that the call
for special counsel might have been the result of school board skeptics who felt
Rosenberg, because of his Jewish background, would not have been aggressive
enough. With $25,000 a year for the school board to spend on a special counsel,

Tureaud knew that he and the other LDF attorneys could look forward to a long and drawn-out litigation.

In the original complaint filed in U.S. District Court for the Eastern District of Louisiana, on September 5, 1952, describing the inequities of the public schools operated in New Orleans, Tureaud wrote:

> 18. Defendants are maintaining and operating elementary and secondary public schools for approximately 34,950 white children, having a total plant evaluation in excess of $18,000,000; staffed with approximately 898 elementary teachers, averaging one teacher per 29 plus white elementary school pupils, and approximately 356 secondary school teachers averaging one teacher per 21 plus white secondary school pupils; having available 30,696 seats for 26,410 white elementary pupils and approximately 11,106 seats available for 8,180 white secondary pupils.
>
> 19. Defendants are also maintaining and operating elementary and secondary schools for approximately 30,740 Negro children having a total plant evaluation in excess of $5,000,000; staffed with approximately 584 elementary school teachers, averaging one teacher per 43 plus elementary school pupils, and approximately 188 secondary school teachers, averaging one teacher per 30 Negro secondary pupils: having available 19,172 seats for 25,141 Negro elementary pupils and approximately 4,933 seats available for 5,599 Negro secondary pupils.[20]

Tureaud believed that *Plessy v. Ferguson* could be overruled since the principles in *Plessy* had been eroded by other cases. He also felt that "separate but equal" would no longer stand because, even if facilities were equal, the fact that they were separate would be a denial of equal protection and due process of law. Tureaud wanted the *Bush* case, in his hometown of New Orleans, to be the Louisiana test case. Marshall determined that, nationally, the initial test case should be the South Carolina case, followed by cases filed in Topeka, Kansas, the District of Columbia and Virginia. These cases were part of the Legal Defense Fund's national strategy. The strategy paid off with the landmark U.S. Supreme Court decision in *Brown v. Board of Education of Topeka, Kansas.*

Tureaud carefully monitored the developments in the *Brown* case. He saw similarities between that case and the ones he filed for plaintiffs in Louisiana. The Topeka branch of the NAACP, headed by McKinley Burnett, was eager to assist in a case of a Negro third-grader named Linda Brown, who had to walk one mile through a railroad switchyard to get to her elementary school, even though an elementary school for white students was only seven blocks away.

Linda's father, Oliver Brown, tried to enroll her in the white elementary school, but the principal of the school refused. With Brown's complaint, Burnett felt the branch had "the right plaintiff at the right time."[21]

Other Negro parents joined *Brown,* and in 1951 the NAACP requested an injunction that would forbid the segregation of Topeka's public schools.[22] The U.S. District Court for the District of Kansas first heard the *Brown* case on June 25 and 26, 1951. The NAACP argued that segregated schools sent the message to Negro children that they were inferior to whites; therefore, the schools were inherently unequal. The board of education's defense was that, because segregation in Topeka and elsewhere pervaded many other aspects of life, segregated schools simply prepared black children for the segregation they would face during adulthood. The board also argued that segregated schools were not necessarily harmful to black children; great African Americans such as Frederick Douglass, Booker T. Washington, and George Washington Carver had achieved despite segregation schools. The lower court's decision stated that it felt "compelled" to rule in favor of the board of education because of the precedent set in *Plessy v. Ferguson.*

On appeal to the U.S. Supreme Court on October 1, 1951, *Brown* was combined with other cases that challenged school segregation in South Carolina, Virginia, and Delaware. The Supreme Court first heard the combined case on December 9, 1952, but failed to reach a decision. After a rehearing on December 7 and 8, 1953, the case was decided in the spring of the next year.[23]

On May 17, 1954, Chief Justice Earl Warren, speaking for the U.S. Supreme Court, unanimously declared that "in the field of public education the doctrine of 'separate but equal' has no place." In declaring that "separate educational facilities are inherently unequal," it explicitly overturned the reasoning of *Plessy v. Ferguson.*[24] The Supreme Court ruled in favor of the plaintiffs and required the desegregation of schools across America.

"We were first expecting really to use the *Brown* case as leverage in improving the schools for Negro children," Tureaud said.[25] In an NAACP lawyers' conference where they analyzed the backgrounds of each U.S. Supreme Court justice, the Negro attorneys determined that there would be a five-to-four decision.

Many others speculated on the outcome of the case. Marjorie Lawson, who was writing for the *Pittsburgh Courier,* expressed the fear that the NAACP lawyers were expecting too much from the Supreme Court. In response to Lawson's editorial, Tureaud wrote a telegram to the *Pittsburgh Courier* saying that the columnist could not speak for "those of us down south, because we looked forward to a declaration by the Supreme Court that would have invalidated deseg-regation." Surprised that the decision was unanimous, Tureaud admitted that the NAACP lawyers had their "fingers crossed" that the Court would decide in their favor.[26]

Sitting at the desk in his office, Tureaud tilted his swivel chair backward slightly as he read his incoming mail. Mostly routine, his new mail included a large white envelope containing an engraved invitation to the thirtieth reunion of the Howard University Law School Class of 1925. The event was scheduled for June 3, 1955, in the Faculty Dining Room of Baldwin Hall. Savoring the news, Tureaud reflected for a few moments on his experiences as a young man in D.C. He smiled as he remembered his first significant job at the Justice Department, graduating from high school, making lifelong friends, and his incredible experience studying the law. These were the years, he thought, that transformed him from an inquisitive, determined adolescent into a secure, goal-oriented professional. In an instant, he returned to his unread mail, but throughout the day images from his past life in Washington, D.C., came to mind. He would definitely attend the reunion.

At fifty-five years of age, Tureaud was at a good time and place in his life. He enjoyed being a father, husband, brother, uncle, and, at last, a full-time lawyer for the past twelve years. He was satisfied that his law practice allowed him to sufficiently support his family and that he was also able to use his legal skills to help his people seek freedom and justice. Tureaud anticipated the excitement of this reunion with old friends and professors.

This trip to the nation's capital for the Howard reunion would not be Tureaud's first since his earlier years as a student and young lawyer. Professionally and socially, he and Lucille visited Washington many times. But with the beginning of summer and the demands of a busy household, Lucille did not accompany her husband to Washington this time. Tureaud was delighted with the large turnout for the reunion. Almost all of the twenty-five members of his class attended, including one of two women, Isadora Letcher, who read the class prophecy. Letcher prophesized that when visiting the carnival city of New Orleans some decades after the 1925 Howard commencement, she would enter the office building of attorney Perry W. Howard and see Tureaud in his luxurious office surrounded by friends. "Suddenly there is great cheering, caused by the announcement of the complete election returns, electing Alexander P. Tureaud as Governor of Louisiana," she proclaimed.[27] Such a thought elicited hardy laughter from Tureaud. His former classmate's dream of the governor's race was perhaps a premonition of his impending race for the U.S. Congress in 1958.

Tureaud relished his time with his best friend and former roommate Eugene Davidson, who was toastmaster for the reunion. Davidson's father, Shelby, had died in 1931; the two reminisced about their time together and the influence the senior Davidson had on their involvement with the NAACP. Special moments were spent with his former professor, James Cobb, now a distinguished jurist. The reunion was all that Tureaud hoped it would be. After singing the alma mater, which ended the program, these legal pioneers, many actively involved in civil rights work in cities across the country, shared their successes and failures for hours, mixing pathos with humor. For some of them new networks were established, and for others old alliances were reinforced.

14
The Politician

National, state, and local politics affected the successes and failures of legal battles throughout the civil rights movement. Therefore, in his quest for equal rights, Tureaud found it prudent to focus not only on the courts but also on the political process. His involvement in the political arena dated from the years of the Long family dynasty in the 1920s.

Tureaud's role as a civil rights advocate extended beyond educating his colleagues about Louisiana lawyers and judges. He also sized up state and local politicians and their contributions to the cause, dismissed individuals with inflated egos, and admonished anyone who was self-serving. For example, Tureaud considered Huey Long, who had become governor of Louisiana in 1928, a year after he began to practice law in Louisiana, to be a brilliant lawyer and politician. Tureaud acknowledged with awe Long's ability to manipulate people. The attorney recalled, "He gave us the kind of leadership around here that had the poor people believing that everything he was doing was for the poor. A lot of it was for himself, but he didn't make a darn thing out of it because everything he got he either threw it away . . . or he spent it on politics trying to achieve . . . his political goals." Tureaud also discerned Long's vulnerability in spending his money on "too much alcohol and too many women."[1]

On September 8, 1935, at age forty-two, Huey Long was shot in the State Capitol building, allegedly by Baton Rouge physician Carl Weiss, and died two days later.

Both Long and Turreaud were lawyers, interested in history, owned newspapers and used the press to advance a cause, and both promoted alternatives to paternalistic leadership. The two willingly reproached institutions they felt impeded the rights of the underprivileged. Yet Long and Tureaud differed greatly in how they used their skills and attributes. History would show one as self-serving and the other as selfless.

Tureaud was interested in securing a notary commission from Governor Long. A political supporter of Long's who had recommended the young Negro attorney fell into disfavor with the governor the same day Tureaud visited Long's office to request the commission. Caught up in a web of political misfortune, his request was denied.

Long exploited the fears of white racists in order to obtain advantages for the Negro. For example, it was common knowledge that Negro nurses gained employment at Charity Hospital in New Orleans after the governor pointed out to legislators that white female nurses would have to treat Negro male patients. The race-baiting increased during the gubernatorial campaign of his brother Earl K. Long. Illustrating this fact is a stump speech Earl Long made during his run for reelection as governor in which he addressed the lack of voting rights for Negroes. "If they'd just leave us alone and quit brain-washing the colored people, we'd solve this [voting rights problem] ourselves. . . . I'm the best friend the colored man, the poor white man, and the millionaire, if he wants to do right, ever had in the state of Louisiana," Long proclaimed.[2]

Lieutenant Governor Earl Long succeeded Governor Richard W. Leche, who resigned his office in 1939. At the end of Earl Long's first term as governor, Tureaud received a notary commission. Sam Jones succeeded Long, and under his administration the commission was taken away from Tureaud. During Earl Long's second term as governor in 1948, Tureaud secured his notary commission permanently.[3]

Tureaud felt that race-baiting was not the only unscrupulous strategy used by the Longs. During Earl Long's administration, the Louisiana Legislature passed a bill banning mixed athletic contests, specifically targeting local baseball and boxing events. Governor Long was pressured by white owners of athletic teams and white investors in sporting events not to sign the bill. He gave the opposition an opportunity to defeat the bill by telling them that if they could get sufficient numbers of people to protest, he would refuse to sign it. They did not, so Long signed the bill.

As the bill was winding its way through the legislature, Tureaud received a call from one of the governor's business associates requesting that the two meet at his New Orleans apartment. "So, I went to see him and he said the governor would like for me to knock this bill out," Tureaud alleged.[4] The associate claimed that, for political reasons, the governor could not side with the white people who opposed the action. He proposed that Tureaud file a lawsuit and offered financial assistance to pay the legal fees. Having no interest in this scheme, Tureaud declined the offer. He knew without a doubt that if the Negro community voiced sufficient disagreement with this law he would file a suit and there would not be anyone in the white community offering to underwrite the litigation.

At that time, Tureaud openly admitted that in his mind this law was not hurting Negroes. "It was hurting the pocketbooks of the baseball teams and the operators of baseball clubs. They were the ones who were suffering from it. So in my opinion, just let them suffer because they didn't have enough guts to fight something like that [unjust law] in the legislature."[5]

As was his way, Tureaud refused to be involved in any of the initiatives of racist politicians and opponents of equal rights. He rationalized that Earl Long "had 'awakened [Negro residents] to the possibility of what an aggressive leader could do' and to what they themselves could do 'if only they could become a part of this aggressiveness and leadership.'"[6]

Tureaud began his political affiliation as a Republican and knew the history of Negro participation in the party of Abraham Lincoln. When Negroes gained the right to vote following the Civil War, they joined the Republican Party because of Lincoln's Emancipation Proclamation and legislation he helped to pass that sought to construct a new way of life without slavery in the South. "In those days, practically all Negroes were Republicans. Any Negro who was a Democrat was looked upon as someone who subscribed to the philosophy of racial discrimination," Tureaud recalled. "The Republican Party wasn't that good for Negroes either, but it had a sense of fairness and I would suppose that you would say a sense of justice," he conceded.[7]

Negro leaders in the South affiliated with the Republican Party from 1865 to the mid-1940s. Tureaud could name prominent Negro leaders who were active party members, men such as educator and college president Booker T. Washington of Alabama, K. W. Howard of Mississippi, Robert Church of Tennessee, and attorney Henry Lincoln Johnson of Georgia. His former law professor Judge Cobb was active in Republican politics in the District of Columbia. Cobb was frequently a member of the District of Columbia Negro delegation to Republican conventions.

Every four years there would be disagreements about the seating of the delegates from the South at the Republican National Convention. Negroes and white delegates would eventually form a coalition only because the national party would not permit the rejection of the Negro delegates. White candidates often sided with the Negroes in the hope of getting the nomination, especially those candidates who had not made any inroads with delegates prior to the convention. Tureaud believed white candidates typically favored these Negro delegates to ensure getting their vote.

In terms of actual participation in the election franchise, Tureaud knew that Negroes in the South had no real voting strength. Their numbers had been reduced from a majority following Reconstruction to practically a handful. According to Tureaud, "Those who escaped the calculated plan to disenfranchise numbered only about 400 or 500 in a large municipality like New Orleans. There were all kinds of devices used to disenfranchise the Negro."[8]

Walter Cohen, James Madison Vance, and Renee C. Metoyer, representatives of the Black and Tan faction,[9] struggled to keep the Republican Party in Louisiana alive during the earlier part of the twentieth century. They would distribute press releases to the local newspapers announcing official meetings of the party. Metoyer confessed to Tureaud that these meetings drew few members and may have consisted only of himself, Cohen, and Vance meeting on the bridge of the Old Basin Canal on their way home after work.

Tureaud believed Cohen, who served as secretary of the party under chairman Emile Kuntz, was by far the outstanding Republican in the state. Cohen had been recognized nationally at the convention for his party leadership. Tureaud admired his boss for his dedication to keeping the party alive and spending his money and time in the effort. Cohen's death in 1930 marked the end of Negro leadership in the Republican Party in Louisiana. The control of the party was stripped from Kuntz by John E. Jackson, a young white New Orleans attorney. Tureaud believed that Negroes were essential to Jackson's leadership in the Republican Party in Louisiana. The Democrats, and later the Dixiecrats, drew the majority of white members in states below the Mason-Dixon line because of their stand against equal rights for Negroes. "Except for Negroes in large numbers, there would not have been a Republican Party in the state," Tureaud insisted.[10] That fact was a constant source of annoyance for white Republicans.

Jackson was unappreciative of Negro patronage, a point he made clear at the first Republican State Convention under his leadership as the state's national committeeman. Although many Negroes, especially a large contingency from New Orleans, attended the 1934 convention, Jackson acquiesced to Louisiana's white Republicans who challenged the Negro delegates to the national convention. Tureaud felt that Jackson did nothing to help strengthen the Republican Party in Louisiana or in New Orleans. He could have attracted other followers who opposed the Cohen faction of the Republican Party, but he didn't. In 1936, the Louisiana attorney general issued an opinion recognizing Jackson's Lilywhite group as the official Louisiana Republican Party. Many of the remaining black Republicans, relics of the Black and Tan faction, defected to the Democratic Party.

Tureaud knew that involvement in political parties, whether Republican or Democrat, was successful, practically speaking, only if patronage led to jobs. Presidential appointments to key positions in Louisiana, such as that of postmaster, collector of internal revenue, the comptroller of customs, U.S. attorney, or occasionally judges, were given to those who the national body knew successfully managed to keep the party alive in Louisiana. Tureaud believed that Jackson sought no real following as long as he had control over the distribution of federal patronage positions. "There was just an army of a lot of generals and few soldiers," he said.[11]

During the early 1940s, Tureaud sought unsuccessfully to reactivate the Louisiana Republican Club, a corporation formed in 1930 by New Orleans Negro leaders to counter the white Republican leaders who sought to make the party a "Lilywhite organization." Tureaud wrote to Dr. Channing Tobias, a board member of the NAACP, "Among the many grievances is the failure of the Republican Party to break up the practice in the South of denying Negroes their registration certificates. As a result of this failure to act, more Negroes in Louisiana are registered as Democrats than are registered as Republicans. Negroes here seem to realize that their destiny is so tied up with the dominant party in the State that it is to their advantage to seek registration as a Democrat, and more especially because of the liberality of President Franklin Roosevelt and his wife, Eleanor."[12]

In April 1944, the Supreme Court declared the Texas white-only Democratic primary unconstitutional. Its opinion in *Smith v. Allwright* only increased the incentive of Negroes to register as Democrats. NAACP branches and Negro political organizations throughout Louisiana held successful voter registration drives.

Negroes in Louisiana had practically given up hope of achieving leadership in the Republican Party under John E. Jackson. Ferdinand Galleaud, who was listed as an at-large alternate in the Louisiana delegation to the 1948 Republican National Convention, and Ninth Ward resident Rev. Noah Copelin were two of a few remaining Negroes on the Republican Party Parish Committee. Tureaud noted that the Republican Party candidate Thomas E. Dewey lost to Franklin D. Roosevelt in 1944 and again to Harry S. Truman in 1948.

Jackson's leadership in the Louisiana Republican Party was successfully challenged by a young New Orleans lawyer, John Minor Wisdom, between 1948 and 1952, before the election of Dwight D. Eisenhower to the presidency. Tureaud considered Wisdom, a member of a prestigious law firm in the city, to be a leader in his profession and an individual of outstanding ability. Wisdom enlisted the assistance of Tureaud, though he had left the Republican Party, and insurance executive Alexander F. Laneuville, a black Republican who was an alternate delegate for the First District of Louisiana to the 1948 Republican National Convention. Laneuville had worked as an insurance agent for the Unity Life Insurance Company and later the Keystone Life Insurance Company. He was also one of the organizers of the Majestic Life Insurance Company. It was not the first time Tureaud was supportive of a Republican candidate, even though he was a registered Democrat. During the Louisiana gubernatorial election of 1948, Tureaud confided to a colleague, "I have . . . been approached on behalf of various candidates (Earl Long and Hale Boggs) who wanted my support." He confessed that he had "a foot in the camps of each faction."[13]

Over the objection of Jackson, Tureaud was assistant counsel on a suit filed in the district court challenging the legality of a party meeting. The suit spelled defeat for Jackson. Tureaud, who had attracted Wisdom's attention because of his civil rights legal work, was asked by Wisdom to convince Rev. Copelin and Galleaud to cast their parish committee votes in his favor. Tureaud approached them on a strictly personal level. He tried to convince them that the Republican Party of Louisiana could not succeed without aggressive new leadership. There was no monetary consideration, promise, or offer of anything in return for their support. Tureaud only sought to assure them that those who were supporting John Minor Wisdom felt that he could provide aggressive leadership. Tureaud did not convince Galleaud and Copelin to change sides. However, Wisdom's delegation was seated at the Republican Convention in Chicago in 1952, and Eisenhower was nominated as the Republican presidential candidate.

Alexander Laneuville was given a patronage job in 1954, described as an $8,200-a-year race relations adviser to the Veterans Administration.[14] Laneuville worked first in New Orleans and later went to Washington, D.C., where he resided until his death in 1970. Tureaud no longer sought to influence the Republican Party after his 1948 experience with Wisdom.

Following his success in getting Edward Hall and other black residents registered in St. John Parish, Tureaud decided that he wanted to be more active in Louisiana elections. He remarked, "I didn't want to just be among those counted. I wanted to be one who could be accounted for."[15] Drawing on his expertise in organizing civic leagues, Tureaud began to organize Democratic groups. One of the first groups was the Orleans Parish Progressive Voters League (OPPVL), founded in March 1949. Tureaud patterned the organization after a successful one in Texas under the leadership of Dr. Maynard Jackson, a Baptist preacher, who later moved to Atlanta. His son Maynard Jackson Jr. was elected the first black mayor of Atlanta in 1973. Tureaud had discussed this organization with Jackson while attending a Knights of Peter Claver convention in Houston.

As a Democrat, Tureaud took an active part in every election, whether it was for a local office or a national one. He supported candidates for governor, for mayor, for Congress, for the legislature, and even for the U.S. presidency. "We had participated in and conducted campaigns directly aimed at the Negro vote," he pronounced.[16] Campaigning for white politicians who were sympathetic to racial justice was part of the black leaders' strategy to further the goals of civil rights. It was part of the process to stimulate political participation by black voters. Constantly, Tureaud voiced his opinions about how to achieve political clout.

When De Lesseps "Chep" Morrison began campaigning for the office of New Orleans mayor in the 1940s, Tureaud and other supporters involved in the voter registration suits began working in the election campaign. An unknown at the time, Morrison did not readily attract all of the black political leadership. Tureaud felt that his opponent, Robert Maestri, did not court the Negro vote at all. Tureaud's support for Morrison included providing endorsements and securing substantial Negro votes. As a result, a majority of Negro voters registered in New Orleans voted for Morrison. Although these voters did not carry the election for Morrison, they did make quite an impression on him, and he sought out the Negro vote from that time on. Morrison ultimately became mayor of New Orleans in 1946.

Chep Morrison, a native of New Roads, Louisiana, was born on January 18, 1912. He was among many returning World War II veterans to gain political office after the war. The "reform" mayor of New Orleans between 1946 and 1961, Morrison dismantled the Robert Maestri "machine." As soon as his administration was sworn in, Morrison organized a biracial advisory committee. Tureaud was appointed to the committee but promptly recommended that it be abolished because it was an all-Negro committee. "It was basically Negroes sitting there talking to themselves," he told the mayor.[17] After the group recommended that all the city's public facilities be desegregated, there was nothing more for it to do.

All the same, throughout his political career, Morrison cultivated black support, becoming a catalyst for greater black participation in the political process. Tureaud admitted that Morrison "did not do a whole lot for Negroes."[18] He did stimulate their desire to participate in politics. Unlike many other white politicians, Morrison came to meetings with black groups and personally sought their endorsement.

Recognized as a Seventh Ward leader, Tureaud participated in OPPVL rallies held in every ward in New Orleans. While he was engaged in citywide campaigning, he was able to depend upon Seventh Ward workers to rally the support of candidates in his community. His citywide appearances were often held in churches, and he participated in a number of radio broadcasts. Sometimes, the rallies would include a cavalcade of automobiles and marchers in the streets. Citywide mass meetings would be attended by many of the candidates. Morrison was always there. Tureaud believed that Morrison's participation in Negro political events encouraged other white politicians to follow suit in order to get the Negro vote.

Other Negro political organizations were also established in New Orleans, including the Crescent City Independent Voters League (CCIVL), the New Orleans Voters League (NOVL), the Poor People's Defense League, the Louisiana Association for the Progress of Negro Citizens, the United Voters League, and the New Orleans Voters Association. Numerous splinter groups of these organizations made demands on white candidates running for office.

Difficulties with voter registration constantly stymied the efforts of Negro political groups. Dixiecrats, primarily white segregationists, were in power in Louisiana in 1948. The Democratic Central Committee in the state of Louisiana, which wanted to secure a win for the Democratic candidate in the national election, began taking a position on Negro voter registration. Republican presidential candidate Dwight Eisenhower was getting support from white Democrats. The state Democratic leadership saw an opportunity to get additional support by registering Negroes.

The Dixiecrats, including Louisiana state senator Willie Rainach, spearheaded statewide voter purging. In 1950 Rainach complained vehemently about the enfranchisement of Negro residents. He wanted all Negro voters off the rolls. He went into Washington Parish and purged the rolls of 1,300 black voters. A delegation of black residents from the city of Bogalusa met with Tureaud in his New Orleans office to see whether something could be done legally to regain their right to vote. Tureaud contacted the U.S. Department of Justice to register a complaint about the violation. He knew that complaints to the local registrar would provide limited relief at best. It was inconvenient for many black residents to travel the more than twenty miles from Bogalusa to Franklinton, which was the seat of government in Washington Parish, to register their complaints.

During several meetings held in Bogalusa, Tureaud discussed the efficacy of bringing a lawsuit on the registration issue. With the aid of friends in the city, Tureaud and NAACP field directors organized the voters who had been purged from the rolls, gathered their names, addresses, and qualifications, and were about to file the suit when Justice Department officials decided to take up the matter. Tureaud's efforts secured a Justice Department investigation that yielded findings favorable to the black cause. The investigation revealed that the white registrar himself was not a registered voter. Black voters were often purged from the rolls for such reasons as not properly crossing a "t" or dotting an "i." Federal district judge James Skelly Wright ordered that the voting rights for all black residents whose names were purged from the rolls be restored. Opponents appealed to the U.S. Supreme Court without success.

Mayor Morrison and Governor Earl Long became political enemies by the late 1940s and early 1950s. Long attempted to undercut Morrison's black support in southern Louisiana by forming an alliance with a New Orleans black attorney, Ernest Wright, and the People's Defense League (PDL). In 1949, Wright resigned his position with the Amalgamated Clothing Workers Union and became a full-time political organizer. Louis Berry, PDL's legal adviser, and Wright drummed up support for Long in and around New Orleans and tried to establish the PDL as a statewide organization. The PDL's loyalty to Long surpassed the OPPVL's support for Morrison.[19]

The Negro political organizations rapidly gained more sophistication and thus were able to better influence local, state, and national elections. They also began to demand monetary support from the candidates in exchange for their endorsements and vote-getting activities. Tureaud saw value in the Negro political organizations having to supplement their funds with money they received from the candidates they endorsed. As they became more experienced, black political groups targeted their activities and made more efficient and effective use of their resources.

Even candidates like Morrison could not supply finances for all the activities of the OPPVL. To carry on a sufficient campaign, OPPVL members volunteered their services and solicited funds in addition to those supplied by political candidates. Tureaud and OPPVL leaders, including Rev. A. L. Davis and Jackson V. Acox, used newspaper advertisements and recorded messages broadcast on radio to campaign for their candidates. The OPPVL's members would interview any candidates that sought black support in a campaign. This interview process was referred to as "schooling of the candidates."[20] Following these interviews, OPPVL members would caucus and then vote for or against endorsing the candidates. The membership did not always agree on one candidate.

No matter what office he ran for, Chep Morrison won OPPVL support each time. He became dependent upon Reverend Davis for his political support in the black community. Davis was a good stump speaker and made appeals for votes that energized people of color. With Davis, the OPPVL was able to command the attention of black voters.

The OPPVL had to compete with candidates who generated interest in their own campaigns by promising to improve opportunities for Negroes in the community. Some were successful in drawing away black voters who would have otherwise supported OPPVL candidates. The increase in politicians seeking endorsements made it more difficult for black political groups to decide on candidates to support, particularly when they were not part of the same ticket.

Sometimes three or four candidates would be running for the same office, each with a background of involvement with and concern for Negroes. On occasion, politicians like Morrison, who typically had the OPPVL support, would make up a slate of candidates and distribute a sample ballot, which excluded candidates favored by OPPVL. When that happened, the OPPVL would have to send out sample ballots of its own. A ballot with black letters on a gold background and other literature using the same colors became the symbol of OPPVL.

During Morrison's run for a second term in office he chose John J. Grosch for superintendent of police. Tureaud and the other OPPVL leaders could not accept Grosch because of his record of poor race relations as chief of detectives. Morrison's opponent in the mayor's race supported the candidate favored by the OPPVL.

OPPVL members also felt the need to support Negro candidates even when Morrison did not endorse them. The Negro political action group could not campaign for white candidates and deny Negro candidates a chance because that negated everything that was being done in the area of civil rights and community advancement.[21]

Following his 1958 reelection, Mayor Morrison dealt with members of the OPPVL and other Negro political action groups. Tureaud acknowledged that Morrison would readily accept an invitation and seemed to enjoy the opportunity to speak before Negro audiences. Tureaud and other Negro leaders found it easy to persuade the black voters to support Morrison because of his pleasing personality. Tureaud was a strong Morrison supporter and believed that the Democrat would give the state "a more progressive administration."[22] He also knew that Morrison was not hostile to Negroes participating in politics. Morrison was apologetic that he was unable to do more for his Negro constituents. He did not hesitate to point out that he and other white people wanted Negroes to gain the civil rights they sought. Morrison was keenly aware of the continuing threat of Leander Perez and his allies, who sought to elect staunch segregationists.

As mayor, Morrison responded to some of the demands made by his Negro constituents. Nonetheless, Tureaud sued the city during Morrison's administration in order to get a Negro on the New Orleans police force in 1950. Tureaud's lawsuit in the civil district court alleged racial discrimination after city officials refused to accept applications from Negroes. The lawsuit was dropped when Morrison agreed to work out a plan to allow for the first Negro policeman. The plan was finalized by Morrison's commissioner of public safety, Bernard J. Mc-Closkey, a lawyer whom Tureaud knew and had worked with before.

The administration of the New Orleans Civil Service Commission, responsible for hiring policemen and other city employees, would most likely deny Tureaud's version of how Morrison achieved the appointment of Negroes to the NOPD. A separate list of Negro applicants was established for use by the mayor's administration to guarantee appointment of a Negro policeman. Tureaud's announcement to the Negro press preempted Morrison's announcement, and the mayor publicly criticized the attorney for prematurely breaking the news. Carlton Pecot and John Raphael Sr. broke the racial barrier and became New Orleans policemen in 1950, the first Negroes hired since Reconstruction. Mayor Morrison assigned the new men to the juvenile bureau, dressed them in plain clothes, and tucked them away in a predominantly black district where very few white voters dared to venture. This cautious manipulation worked superbly for Morrison but not for Tureaud. The black policemen were hardly noticed.[23]

During Morrison's terms as New Orleans mayor, Negro taxicab bureau inspectors were hired, a park facility for Negro residents was developed, Negroes began to lease concessions at Pontchartrain Park, and city buses were desegregated. Tureaud admired Morrison's ability to publicize the assets of the city and referred to the mayor as an ambassador of goodwill. Mayor Morrison traveled throughout the country and overseas and invited individuals of power and influence to visit New Orleans. Tureaud was among the Negro leaders invited to dinners hosted by Morrison to meet some of the black dignitaries he brought to the city, including the secretary of state of Liberia and later the president of

Liberia William V. S. Tubman. On another occasion, Tureaud and others dined with President Haile Selassie of Ethiopia even though the dinner had to take place on a steamship on the Mississippi River because at the time Negroes were not allowed to eat in the restaurants of white hotels.

New Orleans businessman Clay Shaw represented the State Department when entertaining foreign visitors. Shaw also played an important role in the restoration of historic New Orleans sites and, in 1962, established the city's International Trade Mart. He was a member of the World Trade Development Committee and a member of the board of directors of Permindex, Permanent Industrial Exhibitions.[24] New Orleans district attorney Jim Garrison accused him of being involved in a conspiracy with the CIA to kill John F. Kennedy. In March 1967, Shaw was charged with conspiring to assassinate the president. A jury found Shaw not guilty of the charges in February 1969.

Shaw was responsible for protocol at events to which Morrison invited Tureaud and other black leaders. According to Tureaud, "Shaw was always very polite and respectful to the Negro guests in these situations."[25] He moved comfortably among all the invited guests, and that impressed Tureaud.

Mayor Morrison freely gave out the keys to the city to Negro visitors and issued many proclamations during events that black residents deemed significant. He could also be counted on to welcome Negro visitors to the city, such as Ralph Bunche, undersecretary for the United Nations. Bunche, a native of Detroit, was an educator and civil rights activist, famous for his service as adviser to the U.S. Department of State and to the United Nations, which began in 1946 as head of the Department of Trusteeship. He was awarded the Spingarn Medal by the NAACP in 1949 and was the recipient of the Nobel Peace Prize in 1950.

Bunche had participated in the Carnegie Corporation's well-known survey of the Negro in America, under the direction of the Swedish sociologist Gunnar Myrdal. Tureaud was familiar with this work as well and provided documents to Myrdal during his visit to New Orleans for that same research, which resulted in the publication of *An American Dilemma* in 1944.

As long as he did not have to compromise his morals, Tureaud provided valuable service to political organizations like the OPPVL. His support was not unconditional, however, and he reserved the right to dissent. In the 1950 U.S. Senate race, Morrison backed Malcolm Lafargue, the federal attorney who was the unsuccessful prosecuting attorney in the Minden, Louisiana, lynching case Tureaud investigated, instead of supporting incumbent Russell Long, the son of the late governor Huey Long. Tureaud and others resigned from the OPPVL because they supported Russell Long; Tureaud even appeared on a radio program with Ernest Wright. Long crushed Lafargue.[26] He later rejoined the OPPVL. Realist that he was, Tureaud still served as Morrison's Negro leader in the Seventh Ward.[27]

Congressman Hale Boggs's campaign for governor was the first statewide campaign in which Tureaud was involved. Tureaud's favorable assessment of Boggs was determined after many years of observing the political career of this New Orleans lawyer, who first entered politics as a Democratic leader in the anti–Huey Long movement. In 1941, four years after obtaining his law degree from Tulane University School of Law, Boggs was elected to the U.S. House of Representatives for the Second District of Louisiana. At age twenty-six, he was the youngest member of Congress. After an unsuccessful reelection bid in 1942, Boggs joined the U.S. Navy as an ensign and served in World War II. After the war, in 1946, he was elected to Congress and was reelected thirteen times.

After *Brown v. Board of Education,* Boggs signed the Southern Manifesto, which condemned desegregation. "I wish I could stand here as a man who loves his state, born and reared in the South, who has spent every year of his life in Louisiana since he was 5 years old, and say there has not been discrimination. But, unfortunately, it is not so."[28]

Tureaud observed Boggs's gradual transformation from one adamantly opposed to desegregation to a supporter of better race relations. Boggs's transformation was not unique in that several formerly staunch segregationist southern white Democratic politicians became more liberal and supportive of the civil rights movement.

The candidates in the 1952 Louisiana gubernatorial race were Congressman Boggs; Judge Robert Kennon of Minden; Lieutenant Governor William J. Dodd of Sabine Parish; former state registrar of lands Lucille May Grace of Plaquemine; New Orleans black pharmacist Kermit Parker; state senator Dudley J. LeBlanc of Vermilion Parish; archsegregationist businessman James McLemore of Alexandria; and the Long candidate, Judge Carlos Spaht of Baton Rouge. Governor Earl Long, who failed in his attempt to gain the right to run in this election, supported Spaht.

The statewide race proved to be a prototype of Louisiana's colorful political history, ripe with mudslinging and personal attacks. This campaign included the first woman to run for governor in Louisiana's history and the first Negro candidate to run for a statewide office in the twentieth century. Lucille May Grace was a longtime white politician who won election after election as registrar, along with the respect of the citizenry and the media for a successful career. As a Negro candidate, Parker would have been Tureaud's candidate of choice. However, Parker shunned the endorsement of the Negro political action committee in order to be considered as his own man. It was also rumored that Parker entered the race at the urging of Earl Long to draw Negro votes from Boggs.

Boggs was Morrison's choice. Tureaud and the OPPVL leadership were encouraged by Morrison to support Boggs, who was also supported by Congressman Russell Long. In an OPPVL radio broadcast endorsing gubernatorial candidate Hale Boggs, aired in January 1952, Tureaud, Jackson Acox, and Joseph O. Brien charged that Earl Long was responsible for a black voter registration "slowdown."[29]

Tureaud and Rev. A. L. Davis enjoyed political campaign activities and were popular on the campaign trail. Davis was a natural, drawing from his Baptist preaching style. Tureaud was noted for his earnest and compassionate appeals to the crowd for the advancement of human rights. By this time, Tureaud, Davis, and a committed cadre of Negro leaders throughout the state had established a reputation for organizing, executing, and delivering successful campaigns for local candidates. Together they established a viable network and developed campaign strategies that increased the awareness of the organization among Negro voters.

The OPPVL worked throughout the state for Boggs, spending money to get out the black vote. Tureaud and Boggs supporters traveled the political campaign trail to Shreveport, Monroe, New Iberia, Alexandria, Lafayette, and Baton Rouge. Tureaud knew that in places like Shreveport Negroes were not accustomed to seeing representatives of candidates at political rallies asking for their vote. On one occasion in Shreveport, Hale Boggs was speaking at a meeting in the public square, while Tureaud was speaking on his behalf at a black church. After the meetings, Tureaud and several Negro supporters went to a private home in Shreveport with Boggs to discuss the merits of his campaign. Present at the gathering was Ben C. Dawkins Jr., who was then president of the Caddo Parish School Board and a lawyer in Shreveport. Because of the prevailing social customs of the segregated South, Tureaud noted that all in attendance shared drinks, but not dinner, together.

Boggs lost in the first primary, capturing 19 percent of the vote. Most political insiders contributed the loss to a conspiracy between Earl Long and Lucille Grace, which prompted a Democratic State Central Committee hearing in 1951 to determine whether their charges were true that Boggs was a Communist. Though the charges were determined to be untrue, Boggs suffered from the negative publicity.

White politicians continued to seek the support of Tureaud and other black voters. When black political leaders campaigned in statewide elections, white candidates began to court competing black political organizations. With Morrison's encouragement, Tureaud and other OPPVL members held a meeting with Judge Kennon, who asked for their support. The usual promise was that he would try to improve opportunities for Negroes, in general, without political favors or special treatment for individual members of the group. Kennon, a former district attorney of Webster Parish, was a lawyer, a U.S. Army officer, a Presbyterian, and a Democrat. He previously held elective office as the mayor of Minden, Louisiana, and at the time was the youngest mayor in the United States. He was also a member of the state judiciary as a district judge and associate justice of the Louisiana Supreme Court.

Kennon made a wise decision by allowing Morrison to champion his campaign in New Orleans. He won the election, trouncing Republican Harrison Bagwell, on April 22, 1952. Governor Kennon would prove to be a great disappointment to Tureaud because he aided staunch segregationist Willie Rainach and Attorney General Fred LeBlanc in an assault on the NAACP in the mid-1950s. Kennon also supported the Louisiana State Legislature's effort to keep the public school system segregated and ordered the enforcement of laws supporting and strengthening segregation. He was unsuccessful in his second bid for governor in 1963.

The OPPVL was known for promoting the strengths of political candidates, instead of trying to discredit the opposition. Tureaud and others prided themselves in leaving the mudslinging to the opponent. They were quick to publicize the names of the candidates that segregationists like Perez were endorsing. No further publicity about the candidates or their credentials was needed. Any affiliation with Perez was sufficient for black voters to reject these candidates.

Candidates seeking OPPVL endorsement were required to go through a screening process. Appearing before the group, candidates would be asked if they were willing to bear a proportionate share of the cost for the OPPVL to support an endorsement. The answer was always yes; however, there were constraints based on the available funds of the candidates. Campaigns could be very expensive if they had to contribute to the coffers of every political organization that endorsed them.

OPPVL members developed a budget for each campaign, which clearly outlined the number of meetings, the approximate cost of each meeting, the number of mailings, and the postage costs. Also included in the budget were additional costs for transportation to and from places outside Orleans Parish and a reasonable allowance for the individuals involved.

The OPPVL never received the amount of money that political organizations were rumored to be getting. Its members sought to secure a $10,000 budget for statewide candidates, including those running for governor. They received no more than $10,000 for any state campaign and much less than that for a city campaign. It took just as much effort and time to organize and execute a campaign for a New Orleans mayor's race as it did for a statewide campaign for governor. Presidential elections required more money, and members would try to get it.

On the campaign trail throughout the state, the local Negro leaders introduced Tureaud and the OPPVL leaders to the crowds gathered at the various town meetings, the organizers highlighting their qualifications and their professional and political accomplishments in New Orleans. These introductions were sometimes inflated, Tureaud recognized, but it was done to stimulate voter interest.

Negro attorneys Edward Hines and Louis Berry were OPPVL allies and arranged meetings in Alexandria, Louisiana. Tureaud and Davis knew that their involvement meant a good meeting in terms of attendance, especially when both attorneys were working for the same candidate. In Shreveport, meetings drew church people who identified with Rev. A. L. Davis. In Lake Charles and Baton Rouge, black attorney Johnnie A. Jones and refinery worker Acie Belton were usually able to deliver an audience of respectable proportions.

Even when Tureaud was assured a good crowd, he had to depend on his own resources for transportation to the campaign rallies. In most cases, he and other organizers drove their own cars. If traveling by train or plane, they arranged to have ministers and other community leaders transport them locally because taxis were often not available to black patrons.

Despite the most careful travel planning, Tureaud and others would sometimes have to wait for hours before the meetings began. On one occasion, Tureaud slept in the train depot waiting for a train. Rallies for national candidates, such as those running for the U.S. Congress or for president, were sometimes included with candidates running for local office. In districtwide meetings, campaign workers in rural areas also came to speak. Tureaud knew that all the speakers had to be allowed to address the meeting: "If you didn't let them have their say, you wouldn't get the same results."[30]

Involvement in political campaigning could be dangerous. Tureaud almost always kept to himself the dangers in his travels around the state. In fact, he rarely told his wife, who was concerned for his safety, about times when he traveled alone. In 1952, Tureaud attended a rally for candidate D. J. Doucet, whom he supported for sheriff of Opelousas, Louisiana. While driving out of the town, located in the south-central part of the state, about fifty miles from Baton Rouge, Tureaud and his co-workers observed that they were being followed. They were told later that sheriff's deputies were escorting them out of the parish for their own protection. On another occasion, in Terrebonne Parish, Tureaud and others learned of the possibility of intimidation by their candidate's opponents. For their protection, they were again escorted by local law enforcement to the parish line.

Tureaud ran in the 1958 U.S. congressional election against the incumbent, F. Edward Hebert, a white supremacist, and two other candidates. The U.S. House election occurred in the middle of President Eisenhower's second term. The economy was suffering the Recession of 1958, which Democrats blamed on Eisenhower. The president's Republican Party lost forty-eight seats in this midterm election, increasing the Democratic Party's majority to a commanding level.

A New Orleans native, Hebert graduated from Tulane University in 1924. He pursued a career in public relations at Loyola University and in journalism for the *Times-Picayune* and the *New Orleans States*. As a front-page columnist and political editor, he covered the election of Huey Long to the U.S. Senate. His journalistic endeavors led to criminal convictions of Governor Richard W. Leche and LSU president James Monroe Smith. Hebert was thrust into the political limelight, which in 1940 led to his successful election as a Democrat to the Seventy-seventh U.S. Congress. Hebert was a protégé of Leander Perez and was a member of the House Un-American Activities Committee (HUAC) in 1943. He served in the House of Representatives until the end of the Ninety-fourth Congress, setting a record at the time as the longest period of service as a Louisiana representative. He chose not to run for reelection in 1976.

Congressman Hebert defeated Tureaud in 1958 by a handy majority. The 10,000 votes Tureaud received represented approximately 80 percent of the Negro vote in his congressional district. It was reported that Tureaud made one of the best showings in a race for Congress by a Negro since the turn of the century.[31]

Tureaud's campaign had major limitations, including lack of funds to put on a vigorous, widespread effort. O. C. W. Taylor, a local radio broadcaster and the first Negro public relations professional in New Orleans, served as Tureaud's campaign publicist. Junior law partner Dutch Morial, eager and enthusiastic but inexperienced, served as his campaign manager. Tureaud did most of the speaking on his own behalf at his rallies, which were limited to Orleans Parish. Because of the influence of Leander Perez, Tureaud knew that it would be counterproductive and dangerous to campaign in St. Bernard and Plaquemines parishes. He later heard from voters in those parishes that he received more votes than actually recorded for him in the returns.

Tureaud's opponents never failed to bring up the issue of race in their campaign speeches, and flyers circulated in the white communities. The headline of one flyer read: "It's as simple as black and white. Tureaud is the same black attorney who is associated with the NAACP."[32] The campaign flyer noted:

> Congressman Hebert is being opposed by the NAACP and its Negro candidate because during his tenure in congress, Hebert has fought against so-called civil rights legislation, against the usurpation of legislative powers by the United States Supreme Court, and he was one of the authors of the *Southern Manifesto* and among its first signers.
>
> During his years in Congress, he has advocated the economic and legal rights of all his constituents in the First Congressional District, but he has denounced the demagogic race hatred polices of the NAACP.
>
> The NAACP Negro candidate for Congress is a challenge to every white man and woman voter in our district.

Tureaud knew he had a slim chance of winning the congressional seat. The 17,000 Negroes registered to vote in his district could not overcome the 30,000 registered white voters. But Tureaud believed it was his responsibility to encourage others to follow his lead in public service. As he later explained, "There was no point in our urging Negroes to become registered voters simply for the purpose of voting and voting only for somebody that didn't concern themselves with their philosophy of government or the need for their representation in public office."[33]

In his run for U.S. Congress, Tureaud felt that he would at least have an opportunity to present to the Negro community the need for better representation. He wanted to raise the aspirations of Negroes to seek public office. A qualifying fee was the only requirement, besides age and citizenship, imposed by the U.S. Constitution for those who wanted to run for Congress. Tureaud reasoned, "If we never had a Negro candidate for Congress, they might well conclude that this was a position that many Negroes were not qualified to hold."[34]

Tureaud's campaign was a way to educate his community about the power and influence a member of Congress had over issues crucial to the community's welfare. Among other things, he informed his community of the congressional appointments made to the U.S. military academies in Maryland, New York, and Colorado, as well as other important federal posts. Congressman Hebert secured an appointment for his Negro chauffeur.

Although he conceded defeat early on election eve, Tureaud never passed up an opportunity to encourage Negroes to run for public office and to seek federal, state, and local government jobs. He and other black Democrats realized that, even as their ability expanded, their influence at the national level was, for the most part, limited to getting out the vote. The rewards for successful campaigns would go to Louisiana's white Democrats, many of whom were working directly against the interests of the national Democratic Party.

In the late 1920s, Tureaud's boss, Walter Cohen, dispensed patronage when the Republicans were in power on Capitol Hill. Democratic senators did not have the authority to approve Republican appointments, but many times these appointments were cleared through these senators from Louisiana, including the appointments made by Negro Republicans Cohen and Perry Howard of Jackson, Mississippi. Tureaud was in Howard's office in Washington more than once when he received calls from Democratic congressmen asking him to recommend candidates for positions that the Republican president would have to fill.

On trips to Washington, Tureaud always took time to go to the National Democratic Headquarters to express his concern about the appointment practices. In the 1960s, he joined a group of Negro leaders meeting in Atlanta to organize the Southern Democratic Association. The association hoped to reduce the power of white state senators who disapproved of the appointment of black men and women to federal posts.

In Tureaud's view, members of the U.S. Congress depended upon support from "their constituents to make them more responsive to the people." Senators Allen Ellender and Russell Long, who each served for more than thirty-five years, were "so tied up with the leaders of the Democratic Party in the state of Louisiana" that they would not recommend appointees without the state party's blessings.[35] The Louisiana Democratic Party wielded power through the U.S. senators who had the final veto power over a presidential appointment.

A black New Orleanian, Carl Walden, eventually received an appointment as an assistant U.S. attorney. This position did not require Senate confirmation. It is an appointment by the president, with the U.S. attorney making the initial nomination. Walden had the support of Louisiana congressman Hale Boggs, who was anxious to have a Negro as assistant U.S. attorney. Boggs was killed in a plane crash on October 16, 1972. Since that time Negroes have been appointed to the office of U.S. attorney in New Orleans.

Interaction in the courts between white and Negro lawyers forged relationships initially based on empathy; however, continued and frequent exposure to each other often led to relationships built on genuine respect. Tureaud delighted in federal appointments made to friends and colleagues, whether black or white. When Judge Frank Ellis was appointed to the U.S. District Court in 1961, Tureaud was pleased. Ellis made special arrangements for his friend Tureaud to have a seat in the courtroom during his swearing-in ceremony, even though seating was scarce and Tureaud was not a member of the judiciary or a significant political figure.

The collegial relationship between Judge Ellis and Tureaud was exemplary during a time when Jim Crow laws hindered the development of personal relationships between white and Negro residents. Tureaud appreciated Ellis's influence in delivering Louisiana in the successful presidential campaign of John Kennedy in 1960. The fondness between the two men existed even though Judge Ellis previously had been one of the Louisiana delegates to the Democratic Party's national convention who stood as the states' rights coalition or "Dixiecrats," opposing racial integration and fighting to preserve Jim Crow laws and racial segregation. Additionally, during his judicial tenure, Ellis approached civil rights litigation with a strong concern for the opinions of local white residents, even reversing and delaying desegregation efforts.

On election days, the Tureaud household resembled a local command center, busy from daybreak to midnight. The first to rise as the two morning newspapers hit the front porch, Tureaud began his day as usual by reading both dailies before preparing breakfast. Lucille prepared bag lunches for the older children who were "working the polls." Her large pots of red beans, rice, and meatballs, cooked the previous night, were ready as friends, colleagues, and relatives dropped by the house.

Lucille and the older girls distributed campaign literature and sample ballots. A.P. Jr., accompanied by his friend Castro Spears, operated a sound truck, which they drove in predominantly black neighborhoods, urging people to vote and to support particular candidates. Throughout the day and evening, Tureaud visited the polling places, where black volunteers assisted voters. These volunteers were also keen observers who reported voting irregularities or mistreatment of black voters trying to cast their ballots. Tureaud's office phones were always busy on election days, and his home phone was never unattended.

If only for a few minutes, Tureaud's presence as an unofficial poll watcher was reassuring to black voters. His relaxed manner and his ability to talk and sometimes joke with the white poll workers helped in reducing racial incidents in the key black polling stations in the city. When the polls closed, Tureaud drove home. Despite his inordinately long and exhausting day, he would attempt to stay up to listen to the results until all the winners were announced, though his family often caught him napping between election announcements.

15
Desegregation Battles after *Brown*

They want to throw white children and colored children into the melting
pot of integration out of which will come a conglomerated, mulatto
mongrel class of people! Both races will be destroyed in such a movement.
I for one, under God will die before I'll yield one inch to that kind of
movement.

—KKK leader, 1957

As the Legal Defense Fund lawyers cheered the tremendous victory in *Brown* and prepared for the enforcement of desegregation, the Louisiana Legislature immediately went to work in defiance of the *Brown* decision. The legislature proposed and the voters adopted an amendment to Art. XII, Sec. 1, of the state constitution, which provided that all public elementary and secondary schools should be operated separately for white and colored children under the exercise of the state police power to promote and protect public health, morals, better education, the peace, and good order. Legislative Acts 555 and 556 were then signed by Governor Robert Kennon in July 1954. The first act called for legally restricting state support to all but segregated public schools, and the latter authorized the local school board to assign pupils to schools on an individual basis. A provision in Act 555 also empowered the legislature to amend the Louisiana Constitution at any time, rather than every other year.

Initially, Tureaud's work on these school desegregation cases required going into court only two or three times a year. After *Brown,* in such cases, almost weekly court appearances were required of him. Considering that he was also working on other civil rights cases, one can only imagine the pressure Tureaud felt when giving time and effort to the specific details of each of the higher education and Louisiana trade school desegregation cases that he handled concurrently throughout the decades of the fifties and sixties. The Louisiana Education Association, headed by J. K. Haynes, who had been involved with the earlier teacher salary cases, joined with the NAACP to identify plaintiffs. Support also came from interested white persons, such as members of the faculty at Louisiana Tech who could see the value in offering Negroes a technological education. They raised their concerns with Tureaud and others about the need for black graduates with technical skills in their communities. The Southern University Law School faculty and administrators were also keeping abreast of these cases.

The lawsuit *Constantine v. Southwestern Louisiana Institute* (now the University of Louisiana at Lafayette) resulted in the first undergraduate desegregation of a previously all-white, state-supported college or university in the South.[1] Tureaud had filed suit against Northeast State College in Monroe, Louisiana (now the University of Louisiana at Monroe); McNeese State College (now a university) in Lake Charles, Louisiana; and the Southeast State College in Hammond (now Southeastern Louisiana University). All of these cases concluded after the *Brown* decision.

These colleges were among six state-supported institutions located across Louisiana in close proximity to areas with large populations of Negro high school graduates who could take advantage of them. Tureaud would later file suit to desegregate the other two regional state colleges, Northwestern State College in Natchitoches and Nicholls State College in Thibodaux (both now universities).

Prior to Tureaud's successful challenge to desegregate the state colleges, only Southern University in Baton Rouge and Grambling College (now Grambling State University) in Grambling were open to Negro students throughout Louisiana. Based on the principle laid down in *Gaines v. Canada,* the state had to provide educational opportunities to Negroes in the same manner in which it provided for whites. "We filed these suits as part of the policy of the NAACP because we could show without any difficulty that no provisions were made for Negro education above the high school level in any of the areas where these schools were located," Tureaud said. "There was no basis of equality. As a matter of fact, they had no schools, so there was no comparison."[2]

On January 4, 1954, Tureaud; Thurgood Marshall and Robert L. Carter of New York; and U. Simpson Tate of Dallas filed a class-action complaint against the Southwestern Louisiana Institute (SLI) governing board. Lafayette Parish residents Clara Dell Constantine, Martha Jane Conway, Charles Vincent Singleton, and Shirley Taylor sought admission to the school on September 15, 1953, and when they were denied, they appealed to the state board of education without results.[3]

In the complaint filed in the U.S. District Court for the Western District of Louisiana, the attorneys asserted that, by virtue of its whites-only admissions policy, SLI was in violation of the Fourteenth Amendment and of federal law, specifically the Ku Klux Klan Act of 1870 (Chap. 114, Sec. 16), which provided for the equal rights of all citizens. The three-judge panel for the case comprised Judge Wayne G. Borah of the Fifth Circuit Court of Appeals and newly appointed U.S. District Court judges Ben C. Dawkins Jr., of Shreveport, and Edwin F. Hunter, formerly of Alexandria but later residing in Lake Charles. The trial was scheduled for January 29, 1954, in New Orleans, despite a request by the state attorney general Jack Gremillion for a delay until after the U.S. Supreme Court ruled on the *Brown* case.[4]

On July 16, 1954, almost two months to the date after the *Brown* decision, the court issued a judgment permanently enjoining SLI from refusing to admit the plaintiffs. The judgment also covered "any other Negro citizen of the state, residing in Southwest Louisiana, and similarly qualified and situated."[5]

Judge Hunter wrote the court's opinion, which stated that six state colleges had been geographically located to attract greater enrollment because they allowed for a more affordable tuition and a reduced cost for those who could remain at home while going to school. Hunter said that Article 12, Section 1 of the Louisiana Constitution did indeed fail to address equality of treatment for black residents and the state had not provided equal accommodations in the vicinity of SLI.

An amicable settlement was worked out by consent decree for SLI and other regional institutions. Tureaud and his colleagues consented to a restriction that Negro residents could apply only to schools close to where they live, preventing the possibility of any one regional school getting an overabundance of Negro students coming from other sections of the state. Tureaud noted, however, that the schools in question and all other state colleges accepted white students from not only the local area but also from throughout the state, as well as other states and foreign countries. He agreed to the stipulation of this judgment because he felt bound by the argument of the plaintiffs' lawyers that the distance that Negro students traveled to Southern University was a violation of their rights under the *Gaines* decision to have the school within the immediate vicinity.

The attorney general's office identified for state superintendent of public instruction Shelby Jackson thirteen parishes considered to constitute southwestern Louisiana, and these were the parishes from which SLI president Joel L. Fletcher was advised to admit Negroes.[6] The first desegregated classes met on September 10, 1954, and the first Negro graduate, Christiana G. Smith, received her diploma during the 1956 spring commencement.[7]

In 1956, the Louisiana Legislature attempted to undermine progress in desegregating the state colleges and institutions when it passed Act 15. This act required all students applying for college to submit a certificate of good moral character signed by their high school principal and the local superintendent. A companion act made it a crime punishable by dismissal for any teacher or school official to favor integration. Signing a certificate of good moral character for a Negro student applying to a previously all-white college constituted favoring integration. Thus, the local principals and superintendents were prohibited from doing so.

In *Arnease Ludley v. Louisiana State University Board of Supervisors*, Tureaud successfully challenged these state laws. Judges Christenberry and Wright declared both acts to be unconstitutional in 1957, and the Fifth U.S. Circuit Court of Appeals upheld this decision the next year. It was a sweet victory for Tureaud, who remembered the sting of the first defeat when Wilson was dismissed from the LSU Law School. Often called "nigger lovers," Judges Wright, Christenberry, Borah, Dawkins, and Hunter took the brunt of criticism because of their support of civil rights. When newspaper accounts revealed that these judges had ordered the school boards to comply with their decisions to desegregate, they were subjected to threats and intimidations.

In fact, it was a civil court judge, Herman L. Midlo, who shared with Tureaud a simple way to get even with those who called all hours of the night with insults and threats. The judge kept a police whistle by his telephone, which he blew loudly into the receiver hoping to deter abusive callers. He encouraged Tureaud to do likewise. The Tureaud children got a kick out of blowing the whistle.

The case of Southeast State College in Hammond was assigned to Judge Christenberry. By 1955, the court of appeals held that these cases did not require a three-judge court. To convene a three-judge panel was a disadvantage to the court in handling its business. However, when only one judge was responsible, Tureaud found that cases lingered on the docket. When the case finally came up for settlement, attorney general Jack Gremillion, representing the state colleges in all of the desegregation cases, discussed the rules of residency with Tureaud. The attorney had prepared the decree in the same language that was used in the cases of SLI and McNeese, without the restriction that only students from the local residential area could be accepted. Tureaud knew that Judge Christenberry, who had supported civil rights in past cases, did not see a reason for the area restriction, and Tureaud was pleased that he had been assigned to this case.

On November 2, 1962, Pearl Jones Burton wrote to Tureaud describing her personal background and intentions to attend Northwestern State College in Natchitoches. Pearl Burton taught at St. Savior School of St. Savior Baptist Church and Gooch and Campti public schools. Currently a teacher at Central High School in Natchitoches, she wanted to earn a master's degree before she retired. This was not the first time Tureaud's services had been sought by the public school teacher. He recalled earlier correspondence when she requested legal help to use the mineral baths at Hot Wells, Louisiana. Her doctors had advised that the baths would be helpful to her arthritic hands. Burton wrote that she and her husband were denied use of the mineral baths, which were owned and operated by the state of Louisiana. On a trip to the spa, about fifty miles from her home, she was informed by spa attendants that if she brought her own jugs, they would fill them with the mineral water and she could carry them off the premises for use.

As a Louisiana taxpayer, she felt entitled to equal access to the baths and had requested assistance in this matter from her state legislator and other state officials, to no avail. Tureaud accepted the case with the understanding that Burton and other plaintiffs would settle for use of the baths only on a nonsegregated basis, as opposed to a possible agreement that the baths be opened to Negro patrons on a segregated basis. Tureaud wanted to further the goals of desegregation of public facilities, which was given new life with the U.S. Supreme Court's decision in *Brown*. In an effort to maintain segregation, Jim Crow arrangements were typical in the operation of public and some private facilities. Negro patrons were allowed use of facilities on specific days of the week, at separate hours, in certain areas of the building separate from white patrons. In the case of the spa at Hot Wells, Governor Jimmie Davis arranged for the baths to be operated by a private corporation, making the case in Tureaud's opinion null and void.

In her correspondence to Tureaud regarding her interest in attending Northwestern, Burton wrote, somewhat sarcastically: "Some might want to say that I am crazy, if I want to go to NSC." She assured Tureaud that she would seek and get a written review of her health status if he needed it. Tureaud found Burton to be a suitable plaintiff, confirmed by Dr. E. A. Johnson and Ben D. Johnson, both of the Natchitoches NAACP branch and Voters' League. She and her husband, Alton Burton, owned a local café, a gas station, and the Natchitoches Red Sox baseball team, which was organized with the intent to develop players who could potentially play in the Negro League. Burton was independent, spoke her mind, and was politically astute and active in the Democratic Party.[8]

The other plaintiffs in the Northwestern case were teachers Johnnye Brittain Page, Steve Jackson, Hyams J. Baptiste, James Johnson, Pearl Kirkland, and Mary Westminister and a nurse, Doris Rogue.

Tureaud received a phone call from New Orleans mayor Chep Morrison concerning the NSC desegregation suit. It was 1964, an election year. Natchitoches was similar to New Orleans and other southern Louisiana communities in that it had a substantial Catholic population, as well as a large and historically significant Creole community. Morrison was running for governor and asked the attorney if he would delay the case until after the election. The mayor felt he could get greater voter support without the publicity of a legal battle involving desegregation of a state college. Tureaud agreed to wait, but he also warned Morrison: "Make sure these delays that you are asking for will not be used to also further delay the case and to file these frivolous motions that usually followed."[9]

In return for his promise to delay the Northwestern case, Tureaud also requested that the defendants acknowledge that the college discriminated against Negro applicants so that it would be unnecessary for him to prove his case by testimony. The NAACP attorney knew that getting plaintiffs for desegregation cases was difficult enough because of the harassment and threats to their lives and livelihood. There was even greater apprehension for their safety when the plaintiffs were required to testify in open court. To his delight, Tureaud did receive assurances that there would be no dilatory tactics and that, when the time came, the attorney could get his judgment.

Morrison was defeated in the runoff with Public Service Commissioner John McKeithen of Columbia, Louisiana, in the governor's race. Just four months after his third attempt to win the Louisiana governorship, Mayor Morrison was killed, along with his son, John Randolph, in a plane crash in Mexico.

In 1965, Tureaud received a favorable decision from the courts in the Northwestern case. Despite the promises made by Morrison and his supporters, the plaintiffs' lawyers in the case experienced delay upon delay, even to the point that Tureaud filed a writ of mandamus to force Judge E. Gordon West to decide the case.[10] Tureaud was not surprised that Judge West seemed unwilling to act quickly on the case, as he did on many others. "He was adamant and outspoken about his disagreement with the U.S. Supreme Court decision on desegregation," Tureaud stated years later when reflecting on the conduct of judges that hampered his desegregation cases.[11]

Despite Judge West's stand on desegregation, Tureaud refused to let his frustration show and was careful to adhere to the rules of civility in his courtroom. Other attorneys were not so patient. In the St. Helena Parish school desegregation case, which by 1964 was already twelve years old, Judge West was offended by the conduct of Norman Amaker, a newly appointed Legal Defense Fund attorney who was working with Tureaud.

Tureaud knew Amaker to be a very capable young lawyer. He had attained notoriety as the lawyer on a successful appeal to the U.S. Supreme Court on behalf of a female witness in a case in Birmingham, Alabama. That appeal originated from a complaint in which the district attorney in the Alabama case was asked to stop referring to the NAACP witness by her first name. The witness had insisted that if the district attorney wanted a response from her, he would have to refer to her as "Miss." The judge did not agree that the district attorney would have to show her that courtesy. On the appeal to the U.S. Supreme Court, the Court ruled that the witness was entitled to be treated respectfully and that no witness should be abused in that manner.

Amaker had been the lawyer involved in several civil rights cases in Mississippi, and Tureaud found that he had an amicable rapport with Judge Harold Cox. Tureaud and other NAACP attorneys were known to hesitate going to the Mississippi judge fearing that Cox was not one to sign civil rights orders.

Amaker became annoyed with Judge West and let his frustration show when the judge repeatedly expressed his disagreement with the Court's decision in *Brown*. West later wrote to Tureaud asking him to remove himself and Amaker from the case unless they could conduct themselves more appropriately. In the nearly forty years that he had been practicing law, this was the first time that Tureaud had ever received a letter critical of his conduct in court. He wrote back to Judge West, stating that he did not think Amaker meant any offense to the court. Tureaud assured the court that at all times his actions would be consistent with that of a lawyer's ethical obligations, adding that he "would have to depend largely on the experiences which he had in the court at the time."[12] Without directly stating it, the New Orleans civil rights attorney was implying that, in the future, if the judge's behavior provoked flared tempers among the lawyers, he was not going to be apologetic about the lawyers' response. Clearly, the veteran attorney had witnessed that West had a way of offending members of the bar by rapping his gavel with annoying force and making what he felt were inappropriate and inflammatory comments.

Tureaud believed that delays should sometimes be granted for political reasons, a position he explained to the LDF staff. In a successful case on behalf of Edward Baker involving the desegregation of Nicholls State College in Thibodaux,[13] he felt a delay was warranted because the case was affecting the image of U.S. District Court judge Robert A. Ainsworth Jr. of the Eastern District of Louisiana, who was being considered for an appointment to the U.S. Court of Appeals by President Lyndon Johnson.

Judge Ainsworth was first appointed to the bench by President John F. Kennedy in 1961. A native of Gulfport, Mississippi, Ainsworth moved with his parents to New Orleans at an early age. He was a graduate of Jesuit High School and Loyola University Law School. Ainsworth joined the judiciary after serving eleven years as a Louisiana state senator, beginning in 1952. Tureaud observed: "Ainsworth was one legislator who tried to resist the blatant segregationist bills drafted by the majority of the Louisiana legislators during his tenure."[14]

Judge John Minor Wisdom of the Fifth Circuit held that, despite the Eleventh Amendment, federal courts had jurisdiction over state colleges and state boards of education. The Eleventh Amendment to the Constitution provides no haven for state agency when it violates federally protected constitutional rights.[15]

Tureaud's efforts eventually resulted in the desegregation of all the state colleges in Louisiana. Louisiana Tech was the only all-white state college that admitted black students without a lawsuit being filed against it, doing so in January 1966. Some cases took longer than others to settle. The case of Northwestern State College in Natchitoches dragged on for three years. The first suit filed against Northwestern in 1955 (*Hamp Williams et al. v. Northwestern State College et al.*) was dropped because of lack of interest on the part of the plaintiffs. These plaintiffs were schoolteachers who needed further studies to get or maintain their certification. Because of the time involved in litigation, many abandoned the idea of going to Northwestern in favor of accepting state grants to attend graduate school outside Louisiana.

Getting registration applications from college registrars was often difficult. Prospective students requested applications in writing instead of in person so that their race was not initially revealed. In some cases, white students applied for the forms for Tureaud and his colleagues.

It was important to obtain plaintiffs who would actually enroll in college after they were permitted to attend and be successful once admitted. Tutoring and other academic support services were provided to students who needed further assistance. One student interested in nursing did not have the necessary chemistry prerequisite. The NAACP branch made it possible for this plaintiff to attend a local high school class. Other students were provided with tutoring in mathematics and foreign languages. Teachers, priests, college seniors, and graduates were recruited to work with students who needed help. The extra tutoring and instruction were helpful, and each year a greater number of Negro students enrolled and progressed.

Grambling College president Dr. Ralph Waldo Emerson Jones called Tureaud to ask for his assistance in desegregating Grambling so that the school could qualify for federal money. Tureaud told Jones he would gladly help if white students applied to the school. A white student was identified and recruited through the network of NAACP branches.

Mary Jamison, who was teaching at a Catholic high school for Negroes in Lafayette, Louisiana, was interested in civil rights work. She applied to Grambling College, and in keeping with state board policy, her application was denied. Tureaud then filed a suit. The trial was heard in Baton Rouge before Judge West, who commented from the bench that the case could not be a genuine suit because "no white student who would really want to attend Grambling College." West then stated, "I don't believe that the plaintiff in this case is in court either," to which Tureaud immediately replied, "Yes, she is your honor, and she will testify," and he called Jamison to the stand.[16]

Judge West was not impressed with Jamison's testimony. He tried to find out whether she was sincere about going to Grambling College or whether she was part of an attempt to desegregate the institution. Jamison was a college graduate from a well-respected family in Long Island, New York. Her father was an engineer, and her mother was a schoolteacher. Jamison stated that she was accepting a job with Negro students and wanted to learn to relate and identify with some of their problems. "I could be a better teacher for them if I study at a Negro college and have selected Grambling College for that purpose," she stated.[17]

Jamison was admitted to summer school at Grambling, and Tureaud asked one of his twin daughters, Jane, to enroll and to be her roommate. Jane admitted that she was apprehensive about the situation, more so than Jamison. But their matriculation went off without any problems that summer, and they were great companions.[18]

The Louisiana Legislature announced that a branch of Southern University would be opened in New Orleans in 1958. Negroes complained that with this move the state board of education was trying to circumvent the admission of black students to the new LSU campus in New Orleans, with plans to open also in 1958. In 1956, Act 60 of the Louisiana Legislature established the LSU branch in New Orleans (currently named University of New Orleans, or UNO) in order to provide tax-supported higher education to the metropolitan area. One year later the U.S. Naval Air Station, on the shores of Lake Pontchartrain, was closed by the Department of Defense and was acquired by the Levee Board for the New Orleans campus of LSU.

In anticipation of the campuses' openings, Tureaud was asked by some of the news media whether the NAACP would accept a New Orleans branch of Southern University and whether the establishment of a New Orleans branch of LSU would have any bearing on what he was doing to advance the attendance of black students at LSU. Although some members of the NAACP petitioned the legislature not to open a branch of Southern in New Orleans, Tureaud did not oppose the opening of any school. In his view, there was an overwhelming need for educational facilities for Negroes, and the lack of facilities kept many Negro children out of school. Tureaud felt that in due course the problem of segregated schools would be resolved.

With his announcement to reporters that he was not opposed to the opening of Southern University in New Orleans (SUNO), Tureaud assured them that such a move would be answered by having Negro students enrolled at LSU in New Orleans (LSU-NO) on the day that it opened. That prediction came true as a result of his efforts. Anticipating the plan for admitting students to LSU-NO, the NAACP legal counsel asked interested Negro students to send in their applications and let him know if the university took any action to block their admission. If so, appropriate legal action would be taken.

An LSU attorney addressing the press outside the courtroom where the desegregation hearing was being held said, "The NAACP, which finances these suits, could very well spend some of that money sending these children to schools where they can get an education without harassing their white neighbors and without putting themselves up as an object of public ridicule and scorn."[19]

The court ordered LSU to accept applications from Negro students. Immediate registration was required, so a schedule was published in a black-owned weekly. On opening day, Tureaud found that the transcripts for many Negro students had not been sent to the university. In order to remedy this situation, NAACP volunteers were available to transport students to their high schools to get their transcripts so that they could be registered without difficulty or delay.

Classes at LSU-NO began in 1958. On the day the school opened, 1,460 freshmen registered; 40 were Negroes. It became the first public university in the South to open as a racially integrated institution. The registrar at the New Orleans campus told Tureaud that he was deputy registrar at LSU in Baton

Rouge at the time that Negroes were applying for admission. The registrar said he had helped prospective students secure the required certificates of eligibility and good moral character signed by the superintendent of their parish school boards. According to the registrar, some nuns from Italy who had applied to LSU in Baton Rouge faced being turned down for admission because they could not provide certificates of good moral character. Ironically, at the same time, individuals imprisoned at the Louisiana Penitentiary at Angola who applied to take courses at LSU were permitted to do so.

For the Negro students who initially desegregated the schools, threats and mistreatment were very real, and they were not given adequate security when confronted by angry white segregationists. Negro students were immediately suspended when provoked in altercations or perceived as a threat to safety. Tureaud felt it was important to maintain communication with students he had successfully represented in these cases. He wanted them to know that they were remembered and supported during these trying times. The chancellor of LSU-NO summarily suspended a Negro student who came to the campus with a knife in his pocket. The student's explanation, in Tureaud's appeal for his reinstatement, was that his brother had given him the knife to sharpen at a place located on his route to school. The attorney confirmed that it was not a pocket-knife; it was a kitchen knife.

Negro students attending the LSU-New Orleans campus had bottles thrown at them. White protesters set off fireworks in an attempt to intimidate them and chanted, "Niggers, go home." But Negro students stood their ground. They eventually took their grievance concerning segregation at an on-campus dining facility to Tureaud. Black student Raphael Cassimere, who later became a professor of history at his alma mater, described Tureaud as soft-spoken and a very good conciliator. Cassimere said Tureaud revealed his practical side during black students' attempt to desegregate the LSU-NO cafeteria by organizing a boycott and sit-in. Despite the prohibitions set forth in the *McLaurin* case of 1950, Tureaud told the students, "You are getting an education. And the cafeteria may not be desegregated the whole time you are there." However, as Cassimere explained, through the threat of a lawsuit handled by Tureaud, the university was challenged and opened the cafeteria on a nonsegregated basis. "The one thing he kept telling us is that we are winning," Cassimere said. Tureaud was "in it for the long haul."[20]

Realizing that many Negro students could not afford private universities in New Orleans, Tureaud was delighted that two public state schools were available in a city with a third of the state's population. Many Negro children would never have the opportunity to acquire an education unless tax-supported schools were open to them. He was fully aware that it had been necessary for him to leave the state in order to obtain higher education. Observing the success of urban tax-supported universities throughout the country, Tureaud understood that LSU-NO had the potential to become an outstanding school in a city that often ignored the education of minority students.

Ironically, the main campus of LSU in Baton Rouge, where Tureaud's son had enrolled, permanently admitted its first black undergraduates in 1964, six years after the desegregation of its new branch in New Orleans. To gain admission, a lawsuit was filed on behalf of six students: Louisiana residents Freya Anderson, Carlice Collins, Mason Ingram, Oliver F. Mack Jr., Clifford Ray Smith, and Adam Sterling III.

Some years later, A.P. Jr., a resident of New York, was in New Orleans visiting his parents. On a sunny spring afternoon Tureaud invited his son to drive with him to see the LSU-NO campus and how it had grown. As they approached the campus, A.P. Jr. recalled that Negroes were at one time allowed to swim and picnic only in a designated area along the shore of the lake. The site was off limits for Negroes then; however, it was a welcome experience for the first plaintiff in the LSU undergraduate-school desegregation case to see students of many colors and nationalities strolling the campus. With a modest sense of pride and accomplishment, Tureaud shared numerous facts and figures with his son about LSU-NO. In 1961 the school had become a full four-year institution. Within a few years new buildings were constructed, more land was acquired, the enrollment increased to 10,000, and the faculty became more integrated.

Before heading home from that trip to the LSU-NO campus, Tureaud, in an unusual display of parental affection, gave his son a verbal pat on the back by telling him that his contribution to LSU was a steppingstone to making an integrated LSU-NO a reality. In the next moment, A.P. Jr. noticed that a car behind him was close and moving closer, almost near his bumper, as he drove in the right lane on Elysian Fields Avenue. Through his rear-view mirror, A.P. Jr. saw several young white men in the car. Suddenly the car swerved into the left lane and began to move closer, forcing the car A.P. Jr. was driving to scrape the curb. Slowing down, A.P. heard the obscenities and racial slurs and the words "Nigger Tureaud" that were shouted as the car sped away.

Stunned, Tureaud and his son realized that the pleasurable mood of their campus visit was interrupted by the hash realities of racial intolerance. Not undone by the offensive behavior of the young men, who may have been students at LSU-NO, Tureaud told his son that he was more easily recognized by strangers now because of a significant increase in media coverage of his civil rights cases. Chuckling in his unique manner when confronted with racist behavior, Tureaud the lawyer eased himself into the role of father again, reminding his son that the challenge of change was constant and good men and women can and do make a difference. Always hopeful, Tureaud set a high standard for his son to follow.

They turned right off Elysian Fields Avenue and headed toward Pauger Street and home. Anticipating a dinner of Creole cuisine prepared by Lucille, the father and son were happy to be able to share a meal with relatives and a few friends.

16
Enforcing *Brown*'s Mandate in New Orleans Grade Schools

Success in the *Bush v. Orleans Parish School Board*, originally named *Rosana Aubert v. Orleans Parish School Board,* case would come only after numerous hearings and despite the state legislature's shenanigans. The NAACP lawyers were pleased to have Judge J. Skelly Wright as the judge in the case. LDF attorney Constance Baker Motley recalled that Judge Wright was one of the judges who supported the Supreme Court decision in *Brown.* He upheld the law, which was his duty as a federal judge. Motley noted, "The federal judge in some instances was the most hostile person in the community that we had to confront. However, that was not true in New Orleans and in that respect we were very fortunate."[1]

Tureaud received "a hell of a lot" of threatening letters during the litigation of the New Orleans school desegregation case. "It was almost a daily or nightly experience for me to get threats at home, my family, and everybody else," he said. "They'd call the neighbors, who would tell me not to sleep home at night because my house was going to get bombed. And they threw a lot of stuff on my damn doorstep, on the door of my home, . . . and on my office door. I would come here and find a lot of this damn voodooism stuff, grease, sand, all that kind of stuff. I don't know what the hell it was. . . . I would wipe it off and go on about my business," he fumed.[2]

The language of the abusive callers was so vulgar that many times Tureaud did not want his wife or children to answer the telephone. On one of many occasions when he was called derogatory names, a frustrated Tureaud responded to the caller invoking his usual dry wit, "Well I'm going to tell you something. I may be a son of a bitch, but I'm not a black son of a bitch."[3]

On February 15, 1956, Wright became the first district judge in the Fifth Circuit territory to enjoin a school board from continuing a policy of segregation in its public schools. Dismissing the 1954 Pupil Placement Act and the constitutional amendment mandating segregated public schools, he placed the Orleans Parish School Board under the specific requirement of the *Brown II* decision to admit children on a nondiscriminatory basis "with all deliberate speed." *Brown II,* handed down by the Supreme Court on May 31, 1955, created the methods by which school desegregation would be carried out, giving the discretion to federal district judges. History would reveal that the judges would take on the tasks with varying degrees of action. Many would delay the process. Legal historian Charles J. Ogletree Jr. of Harvard University School of Law would write years later: "The most recalcitrant judge and the most defiant school board were allowed to set the pace."[4]

Despite Judge Wright's ruling, the inactivity of the school board lingered for years. From 1956 through 1959, the Orleans Parish School Board made a great number of appeals. Many of these appeals, including an application for writs to the U.S. Supreme Court, which was subsequently denied, were made under the direction of school board special counsel Gerard Rault. Tureaud felt that his opponent was a decent attorney with a hard case to handle. All of the jurisprudence was against Rault, but Tureaud noted that the counselor did the best he could. Because of the numerous supplementary legal maneuvers, progress was extremely slow. The school board continued to delay in coming up with a plan. Tureaud surmised that Judge Wright felt that the process of litigation was necessary in and of itself. He felt that the time taken during the litigation process was necessary to allow New Orleans residents to prepare for desegregation.[5]

In addition to the delays caused by the Orleans Parish School Board or the state of Louisiana, the defense lawyers requested delays because they were busy in other courts. The Legal Defense Fund did not have a sufficient staff and relied on only a few lawyers, like Tureaud, who were running all its cases in states such as Arkansas, Tennessee, Alabama, Virginia, Oklahoma, Texas, and Louisiana.

Tureaud was distracted at the time by the outlawing of the NAACP in Louisiana, which resulted in a massive decline in the number of branches throughout the state. In March 1956, a temporary injunction was issued restraining Louisiana's NAACP on the grounds that the organization had failed to file a list of its members and contributors with the secretary of state in accordance with provisions of the Fuqua Law, a 1924 statute enacted to curb the Ku Klux Klan. Tureaud and others knew that the surrendering of its membership rolls would put those listed in grave danger. The risks were far too great.

Attacks on the Louisiana NAACP, other branches in other states, and the national office posed major problems. For NAACP counsel Robert Carter, handling the NAACP outlawing was one of his major responsibilities. In Louisiana, the case against the NAACP resulted in a hearing in state court before district judge Coleman Lindsey, ignoring a petition by Tureaud and Robert Carter requesting that the case be moved to federal court. Carter argued that the Fuqua Law was not only "vague and indefinite" but also an unconstitutional abridgment of free speech and association. He also charged that the state singled out the NAACP as part of "a major organized effort . . . to suppress all organized and individual opposition to racial segregation."[6]

Despite federal district judge J. Skelly Wright's assertion that the Louisiana court should not have issued the temporary injunction, he refused to vacate the order, saying that he could take no action until the case had been appealed to a higher court. The Louisiana State Supreme Court refused to review the case.

On April 24, Judge Lindsey made the injunction permanent. The court prohibited the states' NAACP branches from holding meetings or conducting regular meetings based on the Fuqua Law. NAACP leaders throughout the state feared violating the injunction. On November 26, 1956, the Louisiana Court of Appeal ruled that the lower court injunction was null and void and should never have been issued. The ruling was based on the technical point that since the NAACP had filed a motion in federal court prior to action by the state court, the latter bench had no right to hear the case or issue an injunction until the federal court acted.[7] Attorney general Jack P. Gremillion insisted that Lindsey's injunction still stood. He sent state troopers to Tureaud's office in the Peter Claver Building to prevent another meeting of the NAACP executive committee.[8] The raid on the NAACP offices heightened the tensions, the New Orleans branch was closed, Louisiana field secretary Clarence Laws was transferred out of state, and the NAACP national secretary, Roy Wilkins, suspended operations in Louisiana. As soon as the ban took effect, NAACP members from throughout the state sent their money to the national organization. As a result, the NAACP had few functioning branches in Louisiana between 1956 and 1962.

Tureaud had to be extremely careful as he remained under legislative and court scrutiny because his status as a lawyer was in serious jeopardy. However, a former Tureaud protégé, Revius Ortique of New Orleans, noted that other people—individuals the legislature could not retaliate against—assisted with obtaining plaintiffs and helped keep the struggle for desegregation going.[9]

On February 5, 1960, action by a three-judge panel comprising Judges Wisdom, Wright, and Christenberry permanently lifted the NAACP ban that had been based on the Fuqua Law.[10]

During the years of delay in the New Orleans school desegregation case, there was much tension in the Tureaud household because of the threat of violence to the family. Members of the family noticed men working on telephone and electrical poles around their home, particularly during Thurgood Marshall's frequent stays at the residence. A. P. Tureaud told his family that these men were actually FBI men watching the home for their protection. However, as threats to Tureaud and his family escalated, he and his wife made special provisions to have the twins, Jane and Janet, picked up from school. Both parents were anxious about their safety and required the Tureaud children to call home often to check in and assure their mother that they were safe.

The tension did not let up even when school was out for the summer. One afternoon a loud boom of something hitting the front of their home, scattering glass over the front porch, caused a tremendous scare at the Tureaud household. It was discovered that a baseball from neighborhood children playing in the street hit the window. An extremely relieved Carol Tureaud admitted that the incident was very upsetting at the time only because of the tension in the home caused by the recent round of threatening calls and rumors of their home becoming a target for a bomb, which was prompted by their father's pursuit of the *Bush* case.

The stress of his work seemed unrelenting, but giving in and doing nothing was unthinkable to Tureaud. On October 14, 1958, he learned the news of the death of his former law professor Judge James Cobb. The next day the U.S. District Court for the District of Columbia held a memorial service for Judge Cobb. Joel D. Blackwell, a member of the Howard class of 1938, officiating at the service, stated, "Judge Cobb on various occasions during his lifetime had taken great pleasure in assisting the newcomer to the Bar. He played a prominent role in judicial and legal circles, but he was quite active in civic activities in this city."[11]

Despite his grief over the loss of his former mentor, Tureaud found renewed spirit in those memorial statements. He would not let his mentor down and would continue the fight that Judge Cobb had instilled in him during his days in constitutional law class.

By 1960, the Orleans Parish School Board had done nothing toward desegregating the public schools. Tureaud wanted a desegregation plan and took on another round of court action seeking relief in the *Bush* case. Court decisions were favorable through the federal appeals process; however, there were numerous delays on school desegregation efforts. When the *Bush* case was reinitiated in the early 1960s, all three frontrunners in the Louisiana governor's race—

Earl K. Long, Willie Rainach, and Jimmie Davis—made the fight against desegregation a major issue. Tureaud was familiar with the race-baiting of Long
but considered the former governor's antics mild compared with those of Willie
Rainach, a state legislator from Claiborne Parish in northern Louisiana.

Many segregationists believed that Negroes were inferior to white people
and did not deserve treatment as equals; others did not want to give up or share
the privileges of the white majority to Negroes. Ultra-segregationists feared
amalgamation of the races if integration was allowed and declared that both
races would be destroyed with a resulting mongrel class of people. Such rhetoric was ridiculous to a person like Tureaud, who as a Creole embraced proudly
all parts of his race and ethnic background.

Like his associate Leander Perez, the ultrasegregationist attorney, Willie
Rainach, who would later commit suicide, equated integration with Communism. Rainach formed the first White Citizens' Council in Louisiana and was
the leader of the legislature's massive resistance to desegregation.

The gubernatorial candidate remarked in a speech at a campaign rally held
in the New Orleans Municipal Auditorium that "under the NAACP's timetable the integration showdown in New Orleans will come right here in New Orleans next fall." Amid the boos and hisses of the crowd, Rainach stated, "Federal Judge Wright has set next March the 15th as the deadline for your school
board to submit a plan to integrate your schools. According to the assistant attorney general of the state of Louisiana, NAACP attorney Tureaud, you know
who he is, told the assistant attorney general that the NAACP had deliberately
postponed this order until after the gubernatorial election. Tureaud said that
to bring the order up right now might elect Willie Rainach governor of Louisiana."[12]

Rainach was not elected governor; Jimmie Davis was. True to his campaign
pledge, Davis immediately took steps to ignore the law of the land and prevent
school desegregation in Louisiana. Louisiana Legislative Act 496 of 1960 authorized the governor to supersede any school board facing court-ordered integration and to run the schools under his own authority.

New Orleans school board's special counsel, Gerard Rault, in a press conference on June 20, 1960, stated, "We, therefore, without reservation endorse and
approve Governor Davis's assumption of control of the New Orleans schools.
Minority forces for integration, with the powerful help of the judicial pen, are
waging a strong attack on one of the state's most precious sovereign rights,
the right to establish, maintain, operate, and control its own public school
system."[13]

Since the legislative act had not yet been tested in the courts, Tureaud watched with dismay and amazement as the Louisiana Legislature authorized Governor Davis to abandon the entire public school system in New Orleans, closing schools in opposition to desegregation.

Save Our Schools (SOS) and the Committee for Public Education (COPE) were organized in New Orleans by white supporters seeking to keep the public schools open. SOS and COPE did not coordinate their efforts with those of Tureaud and other Negro civil rights leaders, although on rare occasions attorneys from the two sides discussed issues of mutual concern. Their members initially avoided the controversial issue of desegregation because anybody who sided with the integrationists could suffer social and political reprisals by the majority community leadership, which did not embrace race mixing.

The two groups received financial support from the Southern Regional Council (SRC), whose mission was to promote racial justice and the protection of democratic rights and expanded civic participation. Founded in 1919 as the Commission on Interracial Cooperation, the SRC engaged southern communities on issues of democracy and race. It promoted an end to the all-white primary in the 1940s, established state human relations councils to help desegregate southern schools in the 1950s, and founded the Voter Education Project to register African American voters in the 1960s. SOS also received funds raised in the black community by Dillard University president Albert Dent.[14]

Tureaud, through his relationship with Mary Sand, president of SOS, knew that her group did not have extensive support from the white business community, except for the Jewish business leaders represented by Betty Wisdom, niece of Judge John Minor Wisdom. The attorney also knew that Sand was one of the few white people who had an equitable working relationship with a Negro group.

Other SOS members well known among the black community as liberals were Urban League activists Rosa Keller, Helen Mervis, and Gladys Freeman Cahn, as well as Father Joseph Fischter of Loyola University and attorney John P. Nelson, both Catholics. Rosa Keller carried out an agenda of racial equity and civil rights while serving on the boards of the YWCA; Tulane and Dillard universities; Flint-Goodridge Hospital; and the Orleans Parish Library. Gladys Freeman Cahn was active in social welfare work in New Orleans, especially with the National Council for Jewish Women and the Urban League.

Nelson headed the public relations committee and even ran, though unsuccessfully, for a school board seat with SOS support. The extent of involvement of the SOS members was a surprise to Tureaud, but confirmed what he had told his son years earlier about support being forthcoming from white individuals who were willing to do the right thing in supporting equal rights. Despite being ostracized by neighbors and friends and receiving threatening phone calls, members of the SOS transported children to the public schools, braving the angry crowd of white people who demonstrated in the streets and on the sidewalks of the schools. They encouraged the parents to keep their children in the desegregated schools.

SOS hired a professional advertising agency to conduct a campaign to influence public opinion. The campaign, financed by the Stern Family Fund, focused on the potentially catastrophic damage that the shutdown of the public schools would have on the economy and social fabric of New Orleans. After its effort to keep the schools open experienced some success, the organization was disbanded.

COPE initiated the lawsuit *Williams v. Davis* against Governor Jimmie Davis in opposition to his takeover and closure of the New Orleans public schools. Admittedly, the LDF attorneys were hardly concerned about COPE members' lack of association with their efforts. LDF's position was that its own lawyers were best able to handle the school desegregation cases. They did not want anyone interfering in these cases. In fact, Tureaud knew that Thurgood Marshall was not always amenable to the U.S. Department of Justice entering desegregation cases because the department's participation might draw the court away from LDF's stance on these matters.

When the desegregation cases reached the U.S. Supreme Court and attracted national interest, the Department of Justice, through the Office of the Solicitor General, could intervene as a "friend of the court." At the time, Tureaud believed that when the Republicans were in office the Justice Department was reluctant to be involved in desegregation cases, fearing political reprisal. He felt that this resistance would change when the Democrats took over the Office of the President.

Despite ambivalence and lack of support from the white establishment, Tureaud's determination to fight was sustained by the support, though sometimes limited, he received from the Negro community. Disproportionately underprivileged, members of the black community had limited financial resources; however, many offered moral and emotional support, as well as hours of volunteering.

Frequently, opponents of integration maintained that the majority of Negroes did not want desegregation. Senator Russell Long was one white political figure to use the argument that there was Negro opposition to desegregation.

Long repeatedly stated that Negroes preferred their own schools. Such rhetoric required the NAACP to make sure that indifference and apathy did not influence the desired outcome of the New Orleans school desegregation case.

Civil rights advocates addressed PTA meetings and appealed directly to the Negro parents of public school students. Initially, the NAACP's appeal for action centered on parents and interested citizens who could stand up for desegregation. It used the personal testimonies of parents who supported school desegregation and followed through on its efforts believing that more and more Negroes would rise to the occasion as small but frequent victories were achieved.

Media coverage of the school desegregation issue was intense during the months and weeks leading up to the court decision in the *Bush* case, brought by the NAACP lawyers, and the *Williams* case, brought by COPE. Local and national radio, newspaper, and television reporters bombarded Tureaud's office with calls seeking statements and opinions on the *Bush* case. Tureaud repeatedly maintained that the legal action was an attempt on the part of the NAACP to make workable and enforce the Constitution of the United States, especially those laws pertaining to the desegregation of the public schools in Louisiana.

The Orleans Parish case was the priority case in Louisiana for the NAACP. Other states had been successful; now it was Louisiana's turn. The *Bush* case had many ramifications. It had taken on many collateral issues, and the Louisiana Legislature kept Tureaud and the LDF lawyers quite busy. Unlike Louisiana, other states did not have legislators seeking to circumvent court decisions every time such decisions were issued. Throughout the *Bush* litigation, Tureaud was in daily contact with the national office of the NAACP Legal Defense Fund.

The legislature was harassing the judge and the LDF lawyers. Whenever there was to be any change in an order, Judge Wright would call Tureaud and the opponents in for pre-trial conferences. Additionally, Tureaud would go to judge's chambers whenever orders needed to be signed. LDF attorney Jack Greenberg stated that "the defendants in the case really weren't litigating on the merits. They were using the courts as a way of stretching out forever the obligation to desegregate the schools."[15] The LDF lawyers' response to racists' clarion call "Segregation Forever" was "Litigation Forever."

Judge Herbert Christenberry heard part of the *Bush* case, along with other desegregation cases, such as the St. Helena Parish School case, which he presided over alternately with Judge Wright. But Wright presided almost entirely over the *Bush* case. Attorney General Gremillion was the adversary in the desegregation cases. Gremillion argued that the petitioners were asking for integration when they should have been satisfied with the earlier offer to open more schools and improve facilities for black students.

Tureaud was appalled at the way Gremillion dramatized these issues, acknowledging that the *Bush* and *St. Helena* cases involved state action of the egregious kind. Tureaud had little respect for Gremillion as a lawyer. As much as the Supreme Court had set out in clear and unmistakable language that the "separate but equal" doctrine had no place in law, Tureaud felt that the Louisiana attorney general should have acquiesced to the Court's ruling like the attorneys general of Virginia, Texas, and Arkansas did. As soon as the Court had spoken affirmatively on the rights, Arkansas invited and had Negroes graduating from not only the medical school but the law school as well. In fact, Tureaud's NAACP colleague Wiley Branton was a graduate of the law school at the University of Arkansas.

Tureaud felt that Gremillion should have displayed integrity and higher regard for his office than to lead a fight to appease the political leaders who were prolonging the resolution of *Bush* and other Louisiana school desegregation cases. Many issues were brought up that should have long been resolved because of the Supreme Court's decision in the *Brown* case.

"Here I was in the midst of a civil rights movement and nobody thought to ever ask me how I felt," Gremillion said years later in an interview about his role in the fight for desegregation. His assessment of his actions in desegregation cases and his relationship with Tureaud was quite different from the civil rights attorney's description. "I felt very conciliatory, but I had an official position to protect that always interfered with my conciliatory position," the attorney general said. According to Gremillion, if he had his way, he could have settled most of the lawsuits, "but that wasn't to be because the populace was much against it."[16]

He agreed with Tureaud that he sought any way possible to delay the action that the federal court seemed "dead set" on seeing done. However, not only did Gremillion express concern for the residents of Louisiana who did not want desegregation, but he also felt that the true victims in the middle of the issue were the Negro children.

Gremillion did not agree with the opposing side's assessment of Tureaud's role in the legal struggles, for he considered Tureaud to be a good friend. "I got along good with Tureaud. If they let Tureaud and I alone, we'd settle a lot of things. But Tureaud was a figurehead. He was doing what the lawyers for the NAACP . . . would tell him to do."[17]

Tureaud felt that Judge Wright hoped that a plan that had been successfully implemented in another state would be used in Louisiana. Some district judges called for state school plans starting at the first-grade level going up, some started at the first grade and the fourth grade, and some started at the twelfth grade going down. Judge Wright believed that children in the first grade would not be prejudiced and that younger children would more readily develop positive relationships when educated in an integrated environment. Thus, he proposed to integrate the schools one grade each year beginning with the first grade. Personally, Tureaud felt such a plan, desegregating one grade at a time, would be too slow.[18]

Despite Judge Wright's repeated meetings with the school board and establishing several deadlines by which the board had to submit its desegregation plan, little progress was made. On May 16, 1960, Judge Wright issued his own integration plan, decreeing that at the beginning of the next school year first-grade students would be permitted to enter either the nearest formerly all-white school or the nearest formerly all-Negro school, "at their option." The board realized that under such a plan almost two-thirds of the forty-eight white elementary schools might be desegregated.

On August 17, 1960, Governor Davis signed an executive order declaring that he had "superseded" the school board and taken over "control, management, and administration" of the New Orleans public schools. He appointed the Orleans Parish superintendent of schools James Redmond as his "agent" and ordered him to reopen the schools on September 8 on a segregated basis.

Davis's action directly challenged Wright's integration order, and the judge swiftly and decisively responded. On August 27, in a courtroom packed with black spectators, a three-judge panel comprising Wright, Herbert Christenberry, and Richard Rives heard arguments on *Williams v. Davis,* COPE's suit, now consolidated with the NAACP's *Bush* case. The nearly fifty black spectators in the federal courtroom and attorney Tureaud were very pleased. At last, Tureaud's many years of litigation were yielding positive results. Louisiana attorney general Gremillion was upset when the judges ruled against him, and he stormed out of the courtroom denouncing it as "a den of iniquity." Held in contempt, the attorney general later said he meant to say "den of inequity."[19]

NAACP attorney Jack Greenberg said Gremillion acted like "a lunatic in court." Greenberg said some lawyers like Gremillion thought "that by making a lot of noise and attracting a lot of attention, they would somehow be effective."[20] Both Tureaud and Greenberg agreed that the judges did not like such behavior and clients sitting in court saw that the attorney general was "making a fool of himself."[21]

During his hearing on the contempt charge, Gremillion confessed to telling the judges "they were nuts" on a point of law on which he was correct and was angry that "they didn't pay any attention to me." The attorney general was grateful to be represented by district attorneys, whom he called "fine lawyers," and to have his hearing before his former LSU schoolmate Judge Edwin F. Hunter. Gremillion stated that the situation "couldn't [have] be[en] played better in my backyard." "I had about $3,000 in my pocket that my friends had given me, anticipating a fine. And oh, I kept that money," he laughed.[22]

Judge Hunter found him guilty of contempt; however, he did not think a fine was necessary. He gave Gremillion a sixty-day suspended jail sentence and eighteen months' probation, provided that he obey the canon of ethics of the American Bar Association. The beleaguered attorney general boasted that he was a member of the ABA already and that was no sentence: "It furnished a big amount of news, but that was the end of it."[23]

In 1971, Gremillion was convicted on federal perjury charges in his dealings with the case of the bankrupt Louisiana Loan and Thrift Corp. He served fifteen months of a three-year prison sentence. Pardoned by Louisiana governor Edwin W. Edwards in 1976, Gremillion resumed his law practice. He died in 2001 in Baton Rouge after a long illness.

Wright's plan prompted the school board to propose its own plan based on the state's pupil placement law, initiated in Act 492 of the 1960 Louisiana Legislature. Judge Wright agreed and provided the board with a ten-week extension to put the plan in place. New Orleans public schools would open on September 8, 1960, but desegregation would be delayed until November 14, after the U.S. presidential elections. Years, later Wright explained his political consideration: "I had to work with Washington . . . because I knew that I was going to be alone, totally and absolutely alone."[24]

It was predicted that few black students would be admitted to white schools in Orleans Parish because of the school board's new plan, which required black students to apply for transfers to white schools and required approval of transfers based on seventeen criteria, including aptitude, intelligence, home environment, and other factors. The 137 applicants, including only one white student, had to submit to a battery of tests. A staff of school board employees, including teachers and psychologists, conducted the tests to determine the aptitude and the IQ of the students.

The plaintiffs were asked not to select any students for transfer who scored below 90. Only five girls had their requests for transfer approved. Judge Wright agreed to drop one student from this group when the school board discovered she was illegitimate. Many in the black community believed that only female students were chosen because they would not be as inclined to insight altercations.

Tureaud did not oppose testing Negro children to select students to desegregate the schools. He understood that Judge Wright was trying to have the school board select those who would be most likely to do well in class. However, the aptitude tests administered to the children measured skills such as matching boxes and colors and putting square pegs in square holes and round pegs in round ones—skills that Tureaud felt were not a true determination of a child's IQ and did not represent any of the criteria upon which admittance was supposed to be based.[25] Some of the Negro students attended public kindergarten. It so happened that the four who were selected attended preschool in one of the private schools.

On Monday, November 14, 1960, the first day of the opening of school under the desegregation order, Tureaud made a tour of the Seventh Ward. Police, some on horseback, were present where a demonstration was being held. A rumor spread that particular schools were going to be desegregated first. Named was McDonogh No. 16 at St. Claude and Pauger, in Tureaud's neighborhood. He went down to the demonstration, knowing that McDonogh wasn't going to be one of the schools.

He later drove to the Ninth Ward to the two schools that were going to be affected by the court-ordered desegregation. He reached the area just as federal marshals were escorting four black girls into McDonogh No. 19 and William J. Frantz schools. Six-year-olds Gail Etienne, Leona Tate, and Tessie Prevost enrolled in first grade at McDonogh No. 19. A few blocks away Ruby Bridges, with her signature hair ribbons, also six years old, entered grade one at the Frantz School. These young students became the national face of school desegregation. This particular Monday was referred to as "Black Monday" or "D-Day" (desegregation day). Only 2 of the 123 public schools in Orleans Parish, in which the city of New Orleans is the sole municipal entity, were desegregated. Both schools were located in working-class neighborhoods and until then were attended only by white students. The throngs of people gathered outside the schools were carrying on outrageously. White parents were storming the area to get their children out of the schools with black students.

Leander Perez went into McDonogh and Frantz schools on the first day to intimidate the schoolteachers. Perez told them that they should leave and not respond to the Orleans Parish School Board's order to be on the job that morning. State superintendent of education Shelby Jackson had declared the day a school holiday. What followed were weeks of protest by white segregationists who verbally and physically assaulted anyone, black or white, who did not respect the boycott of the schools. Angry mobs continued to gather outside the schools, shouting hateful things toward the black students. There were even louder shouts against white parents who had not removed their children from the schools.

Additional steps had to be taken to protect the first black children who integrated these schools. The father of one of the children was an attendant at a gasoline station on St. Roch Street. A crowd of white people raced there and began to vandalize the service station. Threatening the station operator, the protesters demanded that the Negro father be fired or they would continue to destroy the service station. The crowd didn't have to make good on its promise. The attendant was promptly fired.

Immediately the local NAACP leaders felt that they had to protect the students. Threats were made all over the city by roving bands of white students. One day it was widely reported that a mob was on its way from the school board office to protest in front of City Hall. Reports came in that the rabble consisted of residents of Jefferson, St. Bernard, and Plaquemines parishes, but there was no mention of anyone from Orleans Parish being in the crowd. It was also reported that the members of the vigilante crowd were rounding up Negroes and taking them to the police station under citizen's arrest.

Later that day, about noon, while sitting at his desk listening to the radio broadcast, Tureaud received a phone call from a group of Negroes whose determination was unquestioned. They asked him if he wanted them to go out on the street to retaliate against this mob. They wanted to offer protection to any Negro who might be arrested by the mob. Tureaud cautioned the caller not to take part in such action because the matter was in the hands of the police.

Police superintendent Joseph I. Giarrusso had been instructed by Mayor Morrison not to incarcerate the Negroes brought in by the mob. The mayor further directed the police to be on the alert for anything that might result in violence. He felt that tempers would soon be calmed with the passing of time.

Tureaud did not have much to say to Morrison during this time, feeling displeased that the mayor was always trying to appease the white populace. Such action diminished Morrison in the eyes of Tureaud. Louisiana legislators received erroneous reports that police riot squads on horseback were attacking white demonstrators with water hoses and police dogs, not unlike the tactics previously used to disperse Negro civil rights demonstrators. These reports incited the members of the all-white legislature to consider marching from Baton Rouge to New Orleans to intervene. However, television cameras revealed that policemen's hoses were actually turned up in the air and not aimed at any demonstrators. The cameras also captured the white mobs attacking Negroes in the street.

White students virtually abandoned McDonogh and Frantz schools and were being transported to schools in St. Bernard Parish or to private schools set up by Leander Perez and his supporters. As a result, there were three six-year-old Negro children left attending one of the schools, and the other, Ruby, was segregated from the few white children attending her school once she entered each day.

The NAACP became engrossed in all types of side issues, including the mob action, the threats and harassment of parents and friends of the Negro students who were integrating the schools, and the white children and their parents who were interested in staying in the public schools. One white family that lived in the neighborhood, Jimmy Gabrielle and his wife, Daisy, allowed their children to go to the local integrated school. Rev. Lloyd A. Foreman of the Methodist Community Center sought to have his son attend the school. They were so harassed that the Gabrielle family ultimately had to leave New Orleans. White residents attempting to provide transportation for white children who attended integrated schools were not only harassed but also beaten.

Tureaud had expected some resistance, but was surprised at the extent to which the segregationists opposed school desegregation. Leander Perez overtly challenged the authority of the U.S. government to enforce the court orders for desegregation. When President Eisenhower ordered the schools of the District of Columbia to comply fully with the Supreme Court decision, Perez went to the trouble and expense of distributing photographs of Negro and white students in fights around the D.C. public schools.

Black parents in New Orleans remained vigilant and presented a brave front publicly. One group appeared before television reporters who questioned them about how their children were doing and their intentions of leaving their children in the schools. One reporter asked a mother if she thought that her children understood the desegregation issue. The reply was, "I don't think she does. . . . She just thinks she's transferred from one school to another."[26]

The parents stated that their children were not frightened and were responding to the situation well. When asked if they were determined to have their children stay in school and to stick with it, they all said yes.

In reality, the parents of these four children faced tremendous harassment. They were frightened and sought assistance from Tureaud and the NAACP. One mother stated that a deputy sheriff from Plaquemines Parish had come to her home, threatening to fire her brother who worked in that parish if she did not withdraw from the case. Tureaud and the LDF lawyers persuaded her not to withdraw from the case and provided monetary support to the family.

The parents, the NAACP workers who helped them, and even family and friends were subject to threats of violence. Many changed their telephone numbers or had them unlisted to avoid the steady stream of abusive callers. The U.S. attorney also received abusive telephone calls, and because of the constant harassment, Judge Wright's residential telephone could no longer be listed in his name.

Posters hung in various locations around town implied that those who supported integration were Communists. The NAACP, Tureaud, and Judge Wright were listed as Communists on literature circulated in New Orleans's white neighborhoods. Newspapers published by hate groups from around the country were sent to Tureaud, as well as a postcard on which was printed, "Integrationists are communists."[27]

For more than five years, Judge Wright was reviled, cursed, and isolated because of his rulings on desegregation. He agonized over the ostracism meted out to his family, which weighed particularly heavily on his wife, Helen.

Gail Etienne and Leona Tate talked years later about the horror of their experience as the first black students at McDonogh No. 19.[28] The daily occurrences of angry white adults and children shouting obscenities, carrying signs with crude racist slogans on them, and making death threats, as well as incidents of physical abuse, frightened and confused them. Once the girls were inside the school, the faculty and staff did not provide a friendly and welcoming environment for them. Many of the teachers and administrators looked the other way as white children punched, kicked, and threw rocks at them on the playground and called them names. Unsupervised activities were moments of dread for all three girls, and after several incidents on the playground they hid in the trunk of an old tree to avoid being abused by their schoolmates. When they reported these incidents to their parents, they were told that if they retaliated they would probably be suspended or kicked out of school.

Their lives were dramatically changed at home as well. Because of the threats of violence, they were not allowed to play outdoors or to go shopping. Both girls stated that it took years for them to control their anxieties.

Many in the black community wondered why the first two schools to be integrated were both located in the Ninth Ward. The white children who attended the public schools in the Ninth Ward were formerly residents of rural St. Bernard and Plaquemines parishes. They migrated to New Orleans with their parents seeking better educational opportunities. However, now these families felt that because of their working-class status, they were chosen to bear the burden of forced integration with black people when the affluent uptown white residents did not. Tureaud and the other LDF lawyers were later told that the schools were chosen using the objective criteria that the test scores of the black applicants should equal or exceed the educational level of the white children who were attending the public schools in that district. Others, like historian and NAACP activist Raphael Cassimere, suspected that the school boards across Louisiana intentionally selected the schools whose integration would cause the greatest backlash. The proximity of the Ninth Ward to Perez and the White Citizens' Council members of St. Bernard Parish made their campaign of intimidation easier.

During the first year, hardly any white students attended the schools that were desegregated. The following year, Tureaud and other NAACP leaders were required to identify students who might want to attend integrated schools in different sections of the city. These children had to go through the same testing that had been used earlier. The second year, the number of Negro children submitted for testing to transfer to white schools dropped from 137 to 60.

Eight children were selected in the second year. Two of them entered a school in a mixed neighborhood near Carrollton Avenue. The PTA requested to have black students attend that school during the first year of desegregation, volunteering to escort the children to school if necessary and to create a rapport with their parents. The community support resulted in a smoother transition to desegregation.

The first four children to integrate New Orleans schools had to be accompanied by federal marshals. Tureaud believed that since John F. Kennedy was now president, more federal support would be forthcoming. Experience had taught Tureaud that the parents who were protesting desegregation knew which schools the Negro children would be attending because of the fanfare of police and U.S. marshals. In order to reduce the angry mob, Tureaud arranged for cab lines to transport these black pioneers to and from the schools so they could attend with less drama each day.

A cab company was selected whose drivers had a radio in their cabs and could broadcast immediately to a receiving station. Cab drivers would meet the children at the appointed hour, take them to the schools, and personally escort them to their classrooms. Once the children were safely inside, the driver would return to his cab, call into the cab's headquarters, and phone Tureaud to let him know that the children had been safely delivered. Tureaud would then inform Judge Wright. The specific times of the students' arrival and departure were not made public. The judge reluctantly agreed to this system, though he feared that the cab drivers would not be able to protect the children in the event of trouble.

The plan was so successful the first day that it immediately won Judge Wright's unconditional support. In one instance, a driver was five minutes late and Tureaud had not informed the judge that the children had been delivered. A worried Judge Wright phoned Tureaud and told him that the FBI agents stationed near the school noticed that one of the children had not arrived yet. It turned out that the child went in through the schoolyard rather than the usual entrance. Both Tureaud and the judge were greatly relieved.

Negro cab drivers transported these children for an entire term without accepting payment for their service. Tureaud was grateful because the success of his plan relieved the government of having to send so many U.S. marshals, which reduced hostility around the schools. "It was a whole lot less damaging for the children because all eyes were not on the them," Tureaud observed.[29] On one occasion, however, pranksters sent more than fifty taxicabs to the Tureaud home. "My parents called cab companies to tell them don't send any more cabs because they didn't ask for a cab," daughter Janet Tureaud recalled.[30]

Civil rights litigation did not bring Tureaud monetary wealth. It brought hate mail and harassing phone calls. The fight for civil rights did not bring Tureaud popularity; he had to search long and counsel hard to find and keep plaintiffs. It took sixteen years to desegregate the schools in Orleans Parish from the date the petition was filed to the date the final judgment was rendered. A. P. Tureaud worked on the case, along with many others, for the entire time.

Because of his involvement in the civic leagues and later in the NAACP, Tureaud would help initiate other changes in the public education system, including expanded curriculum offerings and the inclusion of Negro history in textbooks. The school board would increase its budget allocations in order to hire qualified Negro teachers and supervisors. These changes convinced Tureaud and his constituents that significant community improvement was possible when people worked together. His courage and determination in this effort would be tested many times. He viewed small victories as progress, and they inspired him to continue his fight for change and for a better life for his people.

17
Catholics and Desegregation

At the same time Tureaud worked through the courts to desegregate public schools, he worked to bring about racially integrated Catholic schools. The issue of separation of church and state required that his work in the church take on a different form than in the public arena. When Archbishop Joseph F. Rummel declared in a 1956 pastoral letter read at every mass in churches throughout the New Orleans Archdiocese that racial segregation was "sinful," Tureaud viewed the declaration as quite appropriate and received the news with great hope for change.

There had been several desegregation efforts by the church since 1953, when Rummel ordained Aubrey Osborne, the first black priest in the New Orleans Archdiocese. In 1948, Osborne had been one of two black students to enroll in the Notre Dame Seminary in New Orleans. A year later, Rummel ordered the removal of "White Only" and "Colored Only" signs from the churches in the archdiocese. He stated, "Let there be no further discrimination in the pews, at the Communion rail, at the confessional, and in parish meetings, just at there will be no segregation in the kingdom of heaven."[1]

Between 1956 and 1959 Tureaud acknowledged that Rummel backed off from his call for desegregation because of the outbreaks of violence throughout the Deep South. By the late 1950s the Catholic Church still had not desegregated its schools.

Tureaud supported efforts that paved the way for an easier transition toward desegregation. As a member of the Catholic Community of the South's (CCS) Commission on Human Rights, he took part in discussions that centered on problems associated with the desegregation of the parochial schools in Orleans

Parish. The CCS was the same group that warned black parishioners against the dangers of Communism after World War II. At that time, the association of liberals, civil rights activists, and union organizers was linked with Communist activities. Opponents of equal rights for Negroes and desegregation accused civil rights organizations of being Communist fronts in an attempt to weaken, discredit, and eliminate black leadership.

In the mid-1950s, the CCS's biracial commission met monthly to plan activities that would bring together black and white parishioners. The commission received mixed reactions. Its members visited churches in the archdiocese, celebrating mass and taking communion together. Initially, church leaders and parishioners were not notified in advance of such visits.

When the biracial group entered the white Catholic churches, ushers directed the black members of the group to the back pew of the church. The visitors objected, sometimes creating a disturbance with the ushers. White commission members later received complaints from their white friends at these churches. Tureaud opted for another approach, stating, "Needless to say, it was humiliating to the members and didn't help the cause for greater racial harmony."[2]

"We found that some of the churches felt that they should have been told that we were coming because it was upsetting the regular order of things," Tureaud stated. In addition to sitting together in the churches, commission members also had breakfast together. Acknowledging that the members' visits affected a church's usual routine, the commission began to advise each pastor in advance. After that, Tureaud recalled with satisfaction, "we got invitations to come, and there was an announcement at the mass and a welcome was extended."[3]

A biracial student group, the Southeastern Regional Interracial Commission, drew members from Sacred Heart College in Grand Coteau, Spring Hill College of Mobile, Alabama, and the colleges in New Orleans. Tureaud's son was involved in this group, which met to form social relationships and exchange ideas. A.P. Jr. was excited by the interest and positive interaction between black and white students. After attending one of the meetings, he returned home happy to tell his father that the group had planned social activities together. Tureaud asked his son, "Do you realize who the heroes here are?" Bewildered, A.P. Jr. asked his father what he meant by heroes. Tureaud explained by asking his son to think about what the young white students were willing to risk by being involved with black students. Voicing his opinion with conviction, he said, "They probably have been ostracized by their friends and maybe even by their families because they are doing something that is just and fair and involves being engaged with black students and trying to change the system."[4]

Tureaud told his son that the white students were the real heroes and he needed to understand and appreciate that. With great fervor, he advised, "You have to do it [be involved in civil rights activity], because you are caught in the struggle. They don't have to do it . . . but there always will be people who are willing to make that sacrifice."[5]

In discussing his civil rights work with his children, Tureaud revealed that he was motivated by the pursuit of justice and that a primary goal was to make things better. The Louisiana Creoles working in the construction trade faced roadblocks when they tried to secure major contracts. White construction workers continued to keep them out of the labor unions. Lack of employment opportunities prompted his father and brothers to eventually leave the South to secure jobs in their crafts as laborers, contractors, carpenters, and tradesmen. Tureaud was deeply disturbed when his sisters walked away from the family. He strongly desired that his whole family be able to live and thrive in New Orleans.

Archbishop Rummel announced in July 1956 that Catholic schools would be desegregated yearly, "grade by grade," beginning in 1957. Tureaud and other commission members, including attorney Dutch Morial, attorney Jack Nelson, and Dr. Leonard Burns, were working with the archdiocese to implement the desegregation plan. There was a large parochial school system in New Orleans, and Catholics, both black and white, attended in great numbers. Hoping to facilitate the effort on one particular occasion, Tureaud and white fellow member John McCain went to Holy Cross High School to speak with a group of students and their parents following the Supreme Court decision in *Brown*.

McCain, a lawyer, managed his family business on Baronne Street in the financial district of the city. He wanted to go further than some of the Negro commission members in accelerating desegregation, and his business suffered because of his outspoken support of the civil rights movement.

Holy Cross High School for boys was located in the city's Ninth Ward. McCain and Tureaud addressed a class and then opened up the meeting for discussion. The questions asked by some of the high school students indicated to Tureaud just how unprepared the white community was for the Supreme Court's decision on desegregation. "They did not understand it and couldn't sometimes make up their minds that they were going to get adjusted to desegregation," Tureaud remarked.[6]

The students asked questions and expressed their beliefs that Negroes were innately inferior and unable to achieve academic success. They honestly believed these were problems that they would have to resolve in order to have Negroes in class with them. Tureaud felt that blame for such stereotypes lay in the students' lack of exposure to Negroes, owing to the custom of separate education and religious worship. He confessed with hope, "By our going there, we sought to help change their prejudices about Negroes and helped to interpret the former segregation laws and the Court's new rulings."[7]

As the church became more insistent on desegregation, White Citizens' Council leaders Leander Perez and Jackson Ricau continually renounced it. Perez, a lawyer who had been a district judge, district attorney, and Democratic political boss of Plaquemines and St. Bernard parishes, gained attention as a nationally prominent opponent of desegregation. During the 1950s and 1960s, he wrote and researched much of the legislation sponsored by Louisiana's Joint Legislative Committee on Segregation.

In 1953 Archbishop Rummel rebuked Perez and other Catholic segregationists for keeping the archdiocese's schools all white. His pastoral letter of that year, "Blessed Are the Peacemakers," was read aloud in all of the diocesan churches. Perez and his allies didn't budge. When the archbishop threatened in 1956 to excommunicate them, they responded by withholding church contributions and staging protest rallies. At one point, a cross was burned on the archbishop's lawn. Again, staunch segregationists claimed Communist influence in order to discredit the archbishop. Men like Leander Perez were quick to call Archbishop Rummel a Communist. "He [Perez] called me a Communist. He called all of us [those proposing desegregation] Communists," Tureaud exclaimed.[8]

Citizens' Council leader Emile Wagner organized a countergroup to the Human Rights Commission composed of white Catholic laymen. The Association of Catholic Laymen viciously attacked Rummel and many activities of the HRC. Wagner challenged the archbishop to justify his call for school integration, while at the same time it was reported that the segregationist had a daughter attending school in the Northeast that enrolled Negro students.

When HRC members sponsored a lecture by New Yorker Hulan Jack, first borough president of Manhattan, on February 26, 1956, Wagner and his supporters picketed the event. It was Tureaud's fifty-seventh birthday, and Lucille had planned a typical birthday celebration at home for her husband with their children. She discovered that Tureaud had become so caught up in the activities surrounding the Jack lecture that he had not remembered it was his birthday.

Tureaud didn't want to miss the lecture, so Lucille, determined that the family would celebrate together, prepared herself and the children to accompany their father to the lecture hall. The picketers caused quite a disturbance that night. Tureaud flirted with danger many times when involved in activities and legal cases that provoked rabid racists. He confided to his family that racists' threats were the acts of cowards.

Keeping Archbishop Rummel informed of HRC activities, Tureaud felt that the archbishop had shown sufficient concern and interest in the issue of desegregation. He also believed that although Rummel gave the orders to desegregate the societies in the church, the archbishop would not defy the white majority. "I think he felt inclined to a more democratic way, but when he made this announcement, things didn't go too well," Tureaud concluded.[9]

Catholics had allowed Creoles their own schools and churches, which they established and continued to support. The archbishop's directives for desegregation were not always popular with the Creoles. Yet Tureaud knew they greatly appreciated the archbishop addressing the immorality of segregation.

On the other hand, Tureaud realized that many white Catholics believed that their overcrowded schools would not readily accept students other than those who belonged to their parish. "In that respect, we didn't have but a few who actually went to a desegregated school," he complained.[10] During this time, Rummel was becoming increasingly feeble, and Bishop John Cody was transferred from Kansas City to the New Orleans Archdiocese to help him with administrative duties. With Cody's assistance, the church began to act more decisively on the desegregation issue in 1962.

On March 23, 1962, Rummel announced that in the fall the city's Catholic schools would admit black students. When Perez and his allies persisted in their opposition, on April 16 the archbishop excommunicated Perez, state senator E.W. Gravolet, and activist B. J. Gaillot. By that fall, 104 black children were admitted to the city's previously all-white Catholic schools.

The area's Catholics and non-Catholics conceded to Rummel's delivery of the ultimate church penalty to Perez and the others. Some felt that the archbishop's courageous action was appropriate, sending a strong message to those who professed to be Catholics but refused to accept fundamental church teachings.[11]

The wives of Gravolet and Gaillot lamented that not only their husbands but also their immediate family members were made to feel the pain of the excommunication when their Catholic friends, and even some family members, shunned them. Unlike Gravolet and Gaillot, who never set foot in the church again, Perez reportedly continued taking communion and eventually repented.

Officials of the archdiocese began discreet inquiries after the death of Perez's wife, Agnes, in 1967 to determine whether he wished to return officially to the Catholic faith. Perez was informed that anything he might say in public that could be construed as "supporting the authority of the Church" would be sufficient to lift the censure.[12] One year before his death, Perez purportedly spoke to a small gathering, which included two priests, at the dedication of an incinerator plant in Plaquemines Parish. The priests apprised their superiors that he had ended his brief speech with a word of praise for the parochial school system and for Archbishop Philip Hannan. This statement was accepted as Perez's repentance. Soon after, the excommunicant was informed that he was absolved. Thus, when he died in 1969, Perez was given a Catholic burial.

Tureaud remembered visiting Washington, D.C., after the U.S. Supreme Court's decision on the school desegregation cases in *Brown v. Board of Education*. He and fellow members of Alpha Phi Alpha fraternity participated in a reception that night to celebrate the outstanding achievements of lawyers such as Thurgood Marshall, A. C. Hasting, Spotswood Robinson, Jack Greenberg, Robert Carter, George Hayes, and James Nabrit. Also in attendance was Mordecai Johnson, president of Howard University, who in commenting on one of the decisions took the position, "You know, you [Tureaud] didn't have as much trouble in Louisiana desegregating schools as we had in other states, because of the Catholic influence."[13] But the New Orleans attorney couldn't agree. Tureaud knew that parishioners were protesting every step of the way when the Catholic Church made plans under Archbishop Rummel to desegregate its schools. Catholic schools were desegregated after the public schools in New Orleans.

18
More to the Desegregation Mandate

There was more to the desegregation mandate than just the elimination of Jim Crow schools and public facilities and services. Tureaud's legal challenges ran the spectrum of individual and class action cases in criminal and civil matters. Addressing discrimination in numerous forms—among them, voting, employment, and public accommodations—required concurrent lawsuits that kept him in court for weeks, months, and years. Opponents vehemently railed against an attack on what they viewed as the sovereign rights of establishing and maintaining public schools, but often the ugliest battles were fought to break the chain of discrimination in housing.

Across the country, discrimination in housing was an issue of major concern for the NAACP. Tureaud witnessed a number of maneuvers by city officials, whether by restrictive covenants or in the name of improvement, that jeopardized quality housing for Negroes. State and federal government programs were also believed to be part of unscrupulous schemes that discriminated against Negro residents. Tureaud's involvement in these cases spanned the breadth of his legal career.

The Farm Security Administration (FSA), one of the agencies established by Democratic president Franklin D. Roosevelt to help rehabilitate the country after the Depression, took over more than 10,000 acres of land in Transylvania, Louisiana, from Negro residents in 1938, Tureaud recalled. Transylvania, owned by a Memphis company, was one of the richest farming areas in East Carroll Parish, as well as in the state of Louisiana. Before the end of slavery, the company left the farming to the Negro families who had lived in the area for nearly a hundred years, establishing a thriving all-Negro community with its own church, a Rosenwald school, and stores.[1] The FSA planned to move the approximately 250 black families out of Transylvania and resell the property to mostly poor whites from East Carroll and other northern Louisiana parishes.

The local FSA office had advised the regional office that no Negroes wanted to buy any of the land. Local FSA representatives had tricked black Transylvania residents into signing agreements to transfer to a resettlement project, Thomastown. Some twenty-five miles south of Transylvania in Madison Parish, Thomastown was a smaller tract of undesirable farmland. The unsuspecting signers were told that they were signing legal documents to continue living where they were.

According to former Transylvania native John H. Scott in his book *Witness to the Truth: My Struggle for Human Rights in Louisiana,* Tureaud helped to organize an NAACP branch in Transylvania to fight the FSA plans. The new branch members and the national NAACP office were able to express their true feelings about the project with the FSA national director and wrote to the U.S. president about their concerns. A compromise proposed by the FSA national office offered four other project sites to the Negroes who moved from Transylvania. These sites, unlike the Thomastown property, promised to have modern homes and churches, cotton gins and canning works, as well as new schools and a school bus. Tureaud turned down the compromise on behalf of the Transylvania residents, who sought the opportunity to purchase the land where they were currently living. By the end of the year, local officials begin issuing deadlines for the black families to leave their homes, and for many of them a chaotic move ensued. The NAACP protested the matter, with support from the National Baptist Convention, the Knights of Peter Claver, the Fraternal Council of Negro Churches, and the presidents of Southern University, Leland College, Dillard University, and the Louisiana Teachers Association.[2] The FSA eventually provided suitable resettlement projects for most Negro families, but not in Transylvania. Resilient and resourceful, the former black residents of Transylvania thrived over time in the resettlements that spread north of Lake Providence, near Tallulah, and in Thomastown in Madison Parish.

Constance Baker Motley of the Legal Defense Fund wrote to Shreveport attorney Jesse N. Stone instructing him on how to proceed with a notice of motion for preliminary injunctions and affidavits for a housing discrimination case, *Richard G. Stewart and John H. Wilson v. Clark Terrace Unit No. 1, Inc., et al.* The Shreveport housing discrimination case was a class action involving one hundred plaintiffs who had entered into an agreement on November 16 and 17, 1953, to purchase lots for new homes on the Clark Terrace Property, near the Libbey Glass Factory and Refinery. The new Clark Terrace subdivision, named for the late Southern University president Joseph S. Clark, was being developed as a cooperative housing development pursuant to Section 213 of the Fair Housing Act (FHA).

LDF attorney Motley was eager to work on the Shreveport housing discrimination case, knowing she had the enthusiastic cooperation of local Negro attorney Jesse Stone. Just four years out of Southern's law school, Stone was mentored by his former law professor Vanue Lacour and the more seasoned civil rights attorney A. P. Tureaud. Motley would also guide Stone's efforts on this civil rights case. Stone would later make a name for himself as a criminal defense lawyer, civil rights leader, law school dean, the first president of the historically black Southern University system, and judge pro temp of the Louisiana Supreme Court.

The Police Jury (the governing body) of Caddo Parish and white residents near the proposed site, particularly members of the Emmanuel Baptist Church and the Floral Heights Civic Association, opposed the site as a development of homes for middle-income Negroes because they felt it was too close to their neighborhood and businesses. The Police Jury adopted a resolution calling on the Shreveport city council to deny water and other facilities necessary for the development. Additionally, Sheriff J. Howell Flournoy wrote to Shreveport mayor Clyde Fant that there would be violence in the community if the site was developed for Negroes. With that warning, the sheriff allegedly threatened to refuse to perform his official duty to maintain order in the event of violence.

Depositions taken for the case brought on behalf of Stewart and Wilson outlined the course of events from March to October 1953 for the newly proposed housing development. FHA mortgage insurance and a Federal Housing Management Account (FHMA) agreement to purchase mortgages had been approved.[3] Land for the development was acquired, and the FHA inspected and approved the sale. Plans for construction, as well as the proposed charter and bylaws, were also in order.

In the spring of 1954, a meeting was called to discuss the concerns voiced by Emmanuel Baptist Church, Floral Heights Civic Association, and Police Jury of Caddo Parish against the proposed Clark Terrace project. In attendance were Sheriff Flournoy, Mayor Clyde Fant, Commissioner of Public Safety George D'Artoris, members of the City Council, and members of the Police Jury, as well as Shreveport black businessman and a representative for the purchasers Henry Allen and plaintiff John H. Wilson. As a result of this meeting, the proposed Clark Terrace site was moved to Line Avenue and Eighty-second Street, near the already established black neighborhood of Mooretown.

Following this meeting, the developers met with the Negro residents requesting that they sign new contracts transferring their deposits to sites in the new location. Wilson and Stewart refused the offer, wanting the original contracts to stand.

In addition to Tureaud, Motley, and Stone, other plaintiff attorneys on record were U. Simpson Tate of Dallas and Thurgood Marshall. The defense attorneys were Charles E. Tooke Jr.; the Booth, Lochard, Jack, and Pleasant Law Firm; U.S. Attorney T. Fitzhugh Wilson; and Charles M. Peters. Chief Judge Ben Dawkins Jr. was assigned to hear the case.

The major thrust of the housing case involved whether the defendants could lawfully deny the plaintiffs the right to purchase real property. Motley and Stone requested the court to prevent the defendants from denying the right and to decree that they honor the sales contract.[4] The plaintiffs' attorneys also requested a judgment of $6,000 for each of the parties in the suit. Their lawsuit ended in disappointment. Judge Dawkins declared no jurisdiction in the matter, and ultimately the suit was dropped.

Plaintiffs John H. Wilson and Richard G. Stewart were active participants in community affairs in Shreveport. Wilson was president of the Negro Chamber of Commerce and Stewart was a partner in a cleaning business, was also a salesman, and at the time of the suit was a letter carrier for the U.S. Postal Service.[5]

Motley was a guest in Wilson's home during her stay in Shreveport because there were no hotels that accommodated black people. Stewart volunteered to be Motley's driver. He drove her around town to talk with the community leaders about helping to finance the case. While riding with Stewart, Motley expressed her dismay regarding Negroes' refusal to talk with her about racial discrimination and mistreatment by local officials. She also stated that Negro lawyers did not cooperate with her and Stone as they developed the housing case. Tureaud knew well the peculiar nuances in race relations of specific locales throughout the state. This relationship dictated the degree of involvement and assistance he could expect from residents and members of the legal profession.

Motley surmised that fear of reprisal from white racists blocked cooperation and made it hard for Negroes to trust each other. Stewart traced the lack of trust in the Negro community to the antilynching campaigns and the violence that occurred during the struggle for voting rights for Negroes. "It was not always whites that blocked these efforts," he told Motley. "Negro women and men, prominent black people, such as school principals, were deputized by the local sheriff to work against our Negro civil rights leadership. The sheriff was one of the most powerful officials in the community, not the Mayor."[6]

Even if they were not undercover deputies, many Negro residents accepted the role of informants, or "snitches," Stewart acknowledged. Delivering mail to some 1,000 homes and more than 2,000 families, he noted residents on his route who received annual Christmas cards from "downtown," suggesting that he knew the sheriff's special relationship with these residents.[7]

In the late 1940s and 1950s, New Orleans mayor Chep Morrison pursued a program of slum clearance in the city to make way for housing developments and new construction in the Central Business District—including the areas now occupied by the Civic Center and the Union Passenger Terminal. The effort resulted in large numbers of Negro residents being displaced from their old neighborhoods. The racial policies of the time made it difficult for Negro residents to find new homes elsewhere. To help alleviate this problem, Jewish philanthropists Charles and Rosa Keller and Edith and Edgar Stern financed the construction of Pontchartrain Park, the city's first subdivision for middle-class African Americans. By 1955, nearly 250 homes occupied this once vacant land.

Tureaud opposed the Pontchartrain Park development because it continued the racial segregation that he abhorred. If the Kellers and Sterns had been willing to finance such housing on a non–racially segregated basis, perhaps within the various neighborhoods already established throughout the city, he would have had no objections. The establishment of segregated housing for middle-class black residents was just another opportunity for the white investors, developers, and construction companies to benefit. The housing construction industry's expansion into this once neglected market was occurring in a number of regions of the state.

Tureaud's actions reflected his belief in the evils of segregation, ineffectiveness of "separate but equal" policies and practices, and denial of black citizens' rights in a democracy. His motivation to eliminate legal barriers to opportunity and choice was based on asserting one's own competence and not acquiescing to superior or inferior distinctions in race and class. He believed strongly that white and black Americans would accept each other when the racial barriers were lifted. He was unprepared for a call for "voluntary separatism" by black Americans, reminiscent of the appeal of Marcus Garvey. Negroes were left frustrated when their communities, schools, and businesses were abandoned and felt even more powerless outside the confines of once black-only neighborhoods.

Tureaud and other civil rights advocates had been fighting for more than twenty-five years to remove the barriers to better jobs and to remove racial discrimination and racial distinction in employment of Negroes. "We have succeeded a great deal in that we've got Negroes in top-level positions in government and we've got them in industry that we have never had before," Tureaud said. He believed that amalgamation could reduce discomfort among groups growing up in the same government and that amalgamation would be more expedient than the separatist movement. "We can't have solid ethnic divisions of the people in America to succeed as a country. Everybody has to have his share of responsibility and enjoy the privileges and immunity that come with it," he stated. "We are going to have to develop and maintain an American culture."[8]

The only benefit of regrouping, Tureaud would advance, is to study the history of the Negro and his achievements and "to learn that he has done a great deal . . . of which we can be proud."[9] He was fiercely proud of his Creole heritage, and his insistence on retelling the stories of his mixed-race ancestry at times became problematic with those who felt that he was too proud of his white bloodline. Tureaud maintained a philosophy of group affiliation in the broadest terms throughout his religious, legal career, civic involvement, and social life. Those who got to know him appreciated his intentions and realized that his Creole pride motivated him in the longtime struggle for the rights of Negroes for which he dedicated his life.

In a number of news columns that he penned throughout his career, Tureaud challenged readers to be involved socially and politically and presented his perspectives on civil rights. In regular radio broadcasts, he provided legal tips to the community. These broadcasts provided a valuable community service, advanced public relations for the black lawyer, and fostered good relations between the public Tureaud and the community.

Tureaud felt that "there are those who evince a keener interest in public questions, and a stronger grasp of social forces." Speaking in poetic terms, he explained, "Their hearts are well kindled with social passion, with considerable definite scientific knowledge of the problems that now press for solution, and with an earnest purpose to have a hand in working them out." He believed that, "with their present attainment, they have splendid opportunity to make the world a better place in which to live."[10]

Tureaud's optimism stemmed from those in the Negro community who were not relating to the demand for black separatism. "They are actually integrating the social structure of America in intermarriage and interrelationships in all walks of life and are not following a set pattern of a black experience. They are identifying themselves with the establishment and are seeking their own goals in terms of the American dream. They are making their contributions to other nations of the world by lending their skills and expertise in the various ways that they have developed themselves," he professed.[11]

For him, whiteness was not a goal; he believed that many white Americans were not trying to be all white but were seeking identity with all ethnic groups. He maintained, "We have to mix. For those of us who want to observe these subcultures will only enhance the American culture by doing so."[12]

Tureaud believed that black individuals who were gaining advantages in an all-black experience would eventually have the authority to help themselves out of their inferior conditions: "They are developing a leadership group, but also as they develop, they would find it necessary to cross over into the majority American society. By wealth, by education, by contact, and experiences, they were bound to move out of black separatism into the larger class of Americans."[13]

Some of the same individuals who considered Tureaud to be wrong about the public protest movement, the value of the segregated housing for the Negro middle class, and assimilation also were convinced that Tureaud was misguided in his thinking involved free legal aid for the poor. Tureaud opposed the federal legal services for indigent residents, believing that they would take business from black lawyers, who relied on these clients for their livelihood. They also, in Tureaud's opinion, perpetuated a new kind of paternalistic control, this time from the federal government. Negro lawyers newly engaged in the practice of law could provide for this clientele, proving themselves in the profession and later engaging in the large firms and corporate practices developed on their own or in cooperation with white-owned firms as equals.

Justice Revius Ortique of the Louisiana Supreme Court gave this example: "We used to have sixteen black-owned and -operated insurance companies in this town. Today, I can think of only one locally owned and operated insurance company. A. P. Tureaud's position would have been, 'Let's look to the long-term; let's make sure we do these things methodically, making sure that we preserve what we've got and then make gains.'"[14]

Convinced that the Louisiana Bar routinely failed black entrants at least twice before allowing them to qualify, Tureaud acknowledged that even black-owned businesses, with a handful of exceptions, disdained black lawyers. Refusing to view himself as a victim, Tureaud did not dwell on setbacks, expecting those in the legal profession to rise to the occasion of justice and legal congeniality. He was a role model and set the standards for all attorneys because his ethics and integrity were above reproach. He stood out because many believed that he did not have a personal agenda. Tureaud did "what he did for the citizens of the city, state, and nation," white civil rights attorney Jack Nelson later said.[15]

In a research questionnaire seeking to disclose the treatment of black attorneys by the court system, Tureaud wrote that he didn't think he was treated any

differently than anyone else in court and that he was given the same consideration. Such a response was more pragmatic than truthful.

A paper titled "The Negro at the Louisiana Bar," presented by Tureaud to the
National Bar Association at its annual convention held in New Orleans in August 1953, noted that black residents began to practice law in Louisiana in 1865.
In the presentation, Tureaud provided information about educational opportunities for black law students at Straight Law School. He discussed the first law
graduates to gain distinction, the black lawyers' involvement in the *Plessy* case,
the first law school opened expressly for black students at Southern University
and its first graduates, and how black lawyers were treated by the Louisiana Bar.
According to Tureaud,

> Negro lawyers enjoy the respect of the members of the bar and the bench
> in all parts of this State. The judges and attaches of the Courts are courteous,
> kind, and considerate.
>
> I can truthfully say that I have never experienced any prejudice exhibited
> towards me or my clients in any case I have ever tried. The judges of all of
> the courts of Louisiana have been very helpful in those instances where the
> inexperienced lawyer required assistance.[16]

His pragmatism aside, Tureaud's assessment hardly matched up with the
complaints of Negro attorneys about having to endure considerable disadvan-
tages before the bench and bar, including requiring black attorneys to stand behind the rail when handling cases in the court and other humiliating and crude
discrimination. In the 1968 case brought by a white civil rights attorney Richard Sobol against the infamous segregationist Leander Perez,[17] one Negro attorney testified that a state judge told him when he appeared in court to try a case:
"I didn't know they let you coons practice law." The attorney also testified that
the judge dismissed Negro objections to being referred to as "nigger"" in court
because those using the term were only exercising their freedom of speech.[18]

Later in his career, Tureaud continued to compliment the Louisiana bench
and bar, stating that the state bar "never put any pressure on me because I conducted myself in an ethical manner, no matter what type case I was handling."
He stated, "One of the things that I can brag about, there is nothing you can
say to these judges around here unless I steal or rape or commit some offense.
. . . I made my place with those judges. I have won their respect and they know
they can call on me for professional opinions about certain phases of these [civil
rights] cases."[19]

Tureaud firmly believed that anybody who wanted to practice law had to ob-

serve the ethical standards required of lawyers. He rejected any activities or behavior that called into question the integrity and self-control of the individual.
He said,

> To hell with all that other damn stuff, because it didn't get you anywhere.
> This business of trying to brow beat somebody and carrying on . . . holler-
> ing and all this damn crap that I'm . . . being railroaded and all that don't get
> you anywhere . . . not as a lawyer.
>
> You may make those kinds of speeches to arouse the emotions of some of
> the people that you are talking to.
>
> I have the philosophy you can catch more flies with . . . honey or molas-
> ses, than you can with salt, or black pepper.[20]

Traveling due east from New Orleans on Highway 1, Lucille and her children
were en route to their vacation house in Pass Christian, Mississippi. As the black
four-door sedan cruised along the two-lane highway, Lucille checked with the
kids about the items they were responsible for putting in the car. Once she was
satisfied that her instructions had been followed, the conversation shifted to
plans for the weekend.

Upon arriving at the house near dusk, they unpacked the car, and everyone helped as Lucille prepared dinner. Serving pancakes had become the Fri-
day night ritual, which began when they purchased the house in Pass Christian.
Arriving at the vacation house for the first time, Lucille realized that all of the
provisions for dinner were frozen, so she made pancakes. Thus a tradition was
established.

Pass Christian, a small town sixty miles from New Orleans, was located in
Harrison County. In 2006, prior to Hurricane Katrina, Pass Christian claimed
a population of 8,000. In 1950 approximately 3,500 people lived there. The historic town is picturesque, with tall pines, azaleas, and stately mansions facing
the Gulf of Mexico. It has more than thirty miles of beaches with fine white
sand that parallel the highway from Bay St. Louis to Gulfport.

The tranquil shores of the Gulf of Mexico attracted city dwellers interested
in vacation homes and gracious living. Many wealthy white families developed
impressive estates, which were cared for by local black residents. Often black
families, including the fathers, mothers, and children, were employed as domestics, chauffeurs, handymen, and groundskeepers.

As in many cities and towns in the United States, people of color lived on the other side of the railroad tracks. Segregated Mississippi in the 1950s was proud of its tight and unrelenting grip of power that was perpetuated to maintain economic and social control over its nonwhite citizens.

One summer, Osceola and Daisy Blanchet made their vacation cottage in Pass Christian available to the Tureauds for two weeks. The Blanchets were renting an apartment on Riverside Drive in New York City on vacation that summer. The Tureauds enjoyed vacationing on the Gulf Coast and had rented houses in the nearby town of Bay St. Louis, where Lucille's mother and several family friends also owned vacation homes.

Next door to the Blanchets' cottage was a vacant house that was partially hidden by brush and trees. Clearing a narrow path at the rear of the house, the Tureaud children explored the uninhabited structure. Delighted, they reported to their mother that the house was in good condition. It had four large rooms, each with a fireplace; a bathroom; a large kitchen; and a screened porch on two sides of the structure. By the time Tureaud arrived by train to join his family, the empty house was a major subject of discussion. He listened as his family expressed intense interest in purchasing the house.

On their return to New Orleans, the discussions of the house waned; however, using his excellent research skills and his experience in the real estate business, Tureaud found the owner of the neglected house and purchased it. This arrangement was more to his family's liking than a previous home Tureaud had built in return for legal work. A.P. Jr. recalled many months of having to oversee the activities of a crew constructing a new home for the family not far from their existing home on Pauger Street in New Orleans. The new house was poorly designed and built. When Tureaud presented the idea to his wife of moving the family to the new home, Lucille refused to take up residency in the decidedly insufficient quarters.

Excited about the adventure of having a vacation house in "the Pass," Lucille, the children, family, and friends helped clear the brush; paint the house, inside and out; rescreen the porch; and update the bathroom and kitchen. Several friends donated furniture, and A.P. Jr. and his friends, with a borrowed pickup truck, took the furniture to the new vacation retreat. In short order the house was ready for a steady stream of fun-seeking visitors.

Beach parties, picnics, soft-shell crabbing at night, and days lounging on the screened porch were major activities enjoyed in Pass Christian. In addition to neighbors, the Tureauds entertained friends from New Orleans and other parts of the country. Occasionally the LDF lawyers working with Tureaud would spend the weekend at the Pass, enjoying Lucille's cooking in the relaxing and carefree environment of the Gulf Coast.

At this time, Pass Christian was a town of homes, a few stores, and churches. There were no movie theaters or malls. During the first summer, the children made many friends with locals and had lots of social activities centered on family and friends.

Frank Cook, a nearby neighbor, became friends with A.P. Jr. Frank's parents worked together at a large estate owned by a white family. Several times A.P. Jr. was at Frank's house when his parents came home from work. Frank's mother always sat in the back seat of the car, even though she was the only passenger. A.P. Jr. questioned his friend about this arrangement and was informed that because his mother looked like a white woman, it disturbed many in the town to see her sitting next to her dark-skinned husband. It was suggested by their employer that Mrs. Cook sit in the back seat of the car when riding alone with her husband.

Another family that the older Tureaud children socialized with had four daughters. The three oldest girls worked for a white family that owned an estate facing the Gulf. The house was designed for entertaining, with a long pier over the water and a swimming pool. The three sisters alternated between serving meals and cleaning the house. More than once when the owners were away, Sylvia and A.P. Jr. were invited to parties hosted by the sisters.

At Pass Christian, the children's first excursion to the beach, which was only a four-block walk from their house, was a unique experience. They swam and played on a section of the beach that was nearest to their home, only to be told by local policemen that colored people were not allowed on this section of the beach. The colored section of the beach was a narrow corridor, a short distance away, in a section called the rice fields.

Having a house in Mississippi at a time when the underpinnings of racial segregation were being dismantled by persistent legal action provided a unique opportunity for the Tureaud children. They understood that socially, racially, and economically, life here was lived differently than in a large city like New Orleans. Their interactions with locals, white and black, broadened their understanding of the good and bad codependence that existed between the races and helped them appreciate the hardships of their neighbors and friends. The getaway to their summer cottage in Pass Christian was a frequent respite for Tureaud and his family.

19
Reconstructing Public Education

Tureaud, like other desegregation proponents who celebrated finally achieving justice with the U.S. Supreme Court's decision in *Brown v. Board of Education,* experienced disappointment because of the slow pace of school desegregation. To them, "all deliberate speed,"[1] ordered in the second round of the *Brown* decision, appeared to mean no speed at all.

Even after Judge J. Skelly Wright mandated the integration of grades one through six, public schools in New Orleans were not being desegregated. The school board was busing white children out of their assigned school districts as a means to circumvent desegregation. "No white child, I might say, had been to any Negro school until a long time after the implementation of desegregation," Tureaud noted several years later.[2]

White children had outnumbered Negroes in the New Orleans public schools when the desegregation process began in 1960, but shortly thereafter just the opposite was true. The parochial schools in Orleans Parish were not able to absorb the large number of white children who fled the public schools. White parents were moving to Jefferson, St. Bernard, and Plaquemines parishes, where public schools were desegregated but the majority of students were white.

Previous attempts to get state aid for parochial and private schools to accommodate this increase in students had been unsuccessful. Several plans had been aggressively presented in the Louisiana House and Senate at the behest of the archbishop of New Orleans. After three attempts, a limited funding plan was finally approved for parochial schools. Tureaud was disappointed by this turn of events.

Private schools in New Orleans, established to accommodate the white students whose parents did not want them to go to desegregated schools, immediately took measures to get similar state support. Legislators created a "grant-in-aid" program that provided financial support to the parents who wanted to move their children from the desegregated public schools to segregated private schools. There seemed to be no lengths to which white legislators were not willing to go to stop desegregation.

Initially, Tureaud thought that insufficient funds would render Louisiana's grant-in-aid movement impotent. Despite his efforts to prevent them, private schools sprang up like mushrooms as a result of financial support from the grant-in-aid program of the 1960s. The Legal Defense Fund had attacked similar laws in other states. Nonetheless, Tureaud feared that the U.S. Supreme Court might uphold grant-in-aid programs in Louisiana. He monitored the development and enrollment of the parochial schools across the nation. Some were Catholic, but others were Baptist, Episcopalian, and Methodist, and they enrolled a large number of students. Tureaud knew that if all the parochial schools operated by the Catholic Church were to close in Orleans Parish, the public schools would be unable to accommodate these children. The state subsidy paid to parochial schools was much less than the costs to accommodate these children in public schools.

Tureaud believed that the grant-in-aid program could be viewed as a public subsidy and would be a unique test case not only for parochial schools but also for nonreligious private schools. Louisiana's subsidies included a school lunch program, free textbooks, and transportation to Catholic schools. The federal government subsidized educational programs, such as Head Start and Operation Upgrade. He surmised that the courts might determine that the grant-in-aid program in Louisiana would not be a violation of the First Amendment, which prohibits the establishment of religion with public funds.

Again short on resources, but with unrelenting determination, an undaunted Tureaud challenged the actions of the Louisiana Legislature. The litigation in the grant-in-aid program would last almost ten years in the courts.

The first grant-in-aid law passed in 1958 under Act 258, he fumed, was "patently unconstitutional on its face."[3] On the first occasion a court reviewed this legislation, it observed, "This is not the moment in history for a state to experiment with ignorance," and it held that the grant-in-aid program, administered jointly by the Louisiana State Board of Education and the parish or city school boards, ran afoul of the equal protection clause.[4]

Members of the legislature amended their first law, but Tureaud and the other plaintiffs' attorneys saw clear reasons to attack the second law, Act 3 of the Second Extraordinary Session of 1960. If the 1958 scheme was a blatantly discriminatory state action, Tureaud knew that the second tuition grant program did not solve the constitutional inadequacies of the earlier one. He argued that the law was designed for the express purpose of making school desegregation ineffective.

In the 1960 act, the Louisiana Legislature eliminated the provision that availability of tuition grants was dependent on the integration of the public schools in the parish and restricted grants to nonprofit schools. The legislature preserved the substance of the program, including provisions for closing the public schools. Proponents stated that the grants were earmarked for salaries of educators who were teaching nonreligious subjects in the parochial schools. They argued that these were the same courses taught in the public schools. The teachers' association and the state superintendent of education opposed benefits offered to teachers who left the public schools in Orleans Parish to teach in the private schools in Plaquemines Parish. The Louisiana Legislature, however, stated that the program would not be implemented by any appropriations other than those which had been set aside for the private schools.

Tureaud realized another disheartening situation that developed as a result of public subsidies used to create private schools. Funds were also earmarked to teach students with special needs. Both Negro and white owners established schools for this purpose. Many of these schools were started in private homes, garages, and other inadequate facilities. Some had only one toilet, or two at the most, to serve as many as fifty to one hundred students. Staff-to-student ratios were minimal, and many staff members were not trained in special education. Overcrowded classrooms made instruction impossible.

The law firm of Breazeale, Sachse, and Wilson of Baton Rouge represented the Louisiana Legislature. In court, the defendants maintained that they were not getting grant-in-aid money to operate a segregated school or to facilitate racial discrimination, noting that Negroes were also receiving funds from the state for their private schools. Tureaud felt that Negro children benefited because there were no facilities available to provide educational and support services to them.

School desegregation orders affirmed by the Fifth Circuit Court of Appeals in 1961 were met with Act 2 of the Second Extraordinary Session of the Legislature on the same day. Act 2 allowed parish school boards to close a parish's schools if a majority of voters were in favor of doing so and to dispose of the school's property as the board deemed appropriate. A 1958 act that created educational cooperatives could acquire this property and operate schools with the money the state furnished under the grant-in-aid program allowed in Act 3 of

1960. Two additional acts of that year (Acts 9 and 10) helped shore up funds for the grant-in-aid program, with a one-time $2,500,000 transfer from the Public Welfare Fund and $200,000 monthly from the sales tax collections to the Education Expense Grant Fund.

Act 147 of 1962 eliminated provisions for closing public schools, transferred administration of the grant-in-aid program from the state board of education to the Louisiana Financial Assistance Commission, and provided for grants to be made to the students and parents rather than directly to the private schools. Accordingly, the defendants contended that the statute was essentially different from the earlier statutes considered by the court and that it represented legislative acceptance of the decisions of this court and of the U.S. Supreme Court. The legislative theory of the law is that state aid to the student is not aid to the school.[5]

On January 30, 1964, Tureaud filed *Bryan Poindexter et al. v. Louisiana Financial Assistance Commission* (LFAC) in federal court in New Orleans. The LFAC filed for dismissal, stating that the plaintiffs lacked standing to sue and that the three-judge court lacked jurisdiction. The dismissal was denied.[6] Between 1966 and 1968, the three-judge federal panels, comprising Judges John Minor Wisdom, Herbert W. Christenberry, and Robert A. Ainsworth, struck down Louisiana's attempts to undermine desegregation with the grant-in-aid program.

Tureaud applauded the U.S. Department of Justice for doing a tremendous job of taking statements and testimony in the 1967 grant-in-aid trial.[7] The class action case was initiated under the Civil Rights Act of 1871, one of the most important federal statutes for civil rights litigation. The act allowed individuals to sue other individuals for violation of civil rights set forth in the U.S. Constitution and federal statutes.[8] Civil rights lawyers increasingly used this statute after 1961 when the Supreme Court of the United States in *Monroe v. Pape,* 365 U.S. 167, articulated that the statute could be used to "override certain kinds of state laws."[9] It allowed the civil rights lawyers to avoid the state courts and try their cases in federal court, where they felt justice would be more readily provided. The defendants in the case moved for dismissal using tactics prevalent during civil rights challenges that would require trial in the state courts.

The Louisiana Financial Assistance Commission and its members, the Louisiana State Board of Education and its members, the state superintendent of public education, the Orleans Parish School Board and its members, and the superintendent of the Orleans Parish School Board were all named as defendants in the case. The complaint also named as defendants the Ninth Ward Elementary School, the Carrollton Elementary School, and the Garden District Academy, which were the three private schools chartered by the commission. The court later dismissed these defendants from the suit on a motion by the plaintiffs.

Tureaud notified plaintiff Lorraine Ambeau of New Orleans about the trial, which was scheduled to begin in the U.S. District Court, 400 Royal Street, at 10 a.m. on Monday, March 20, 1967. He requested that she arrange her schedule so that she would be ready to testify when called upon.

Representatives from more than fifty private schools testified before the three-judge federal panel that they had no Negro children in their schools because none had applied. Some 7,000 white children received state "grants-in-aid," including the 1,171 pupils of the Ninth Ward Cooperative School. Tureaud revealed that there were no Negro children who had been approved to receive grants. According to the plaintiffs, the state paid $360 to each student attending a private school—but allocated $257 a year for each student attending a public school in Orleans Parish.

Fortunately for Tureaud and the other lawyers for the plaintiffs, the court ruled that the defendants' argument rested on a misunderstanding of the nature of the plaintiffs' rights. The ruling stated that the plaintiffs were not suing as taxpayers objecting to the legislature's violation of the state constitution; it asserted that their federal rights protected by the U.S. Constitution were being violated. The court further stated that the plaintiffs were concerned that the state had established with the grant-in-aid program a second school system, one that was segregated.

Finally, the court took judicial note of the Civil Rights Act of 1964, 78 Stat. 241, 42 U.S.C., 1971. This act directs the attorney general, on the complaint that children have been denied admission to a public school by reasons of race or color, "to initiate and maintain appropriate legal proceedings to achieve desegregation of the school."

Judge Wisdom stated in the court's opinion that there is a due process argument that public funds derived, at least in some part, from taxes paid by the plaintiffs should not be appropriated to nonpublic purposes in deprivation of the plaintiffs' right to a desegregated state school system. The plaintiffs emphasized the equal protection clause as justification for their suit. The state-supported "white" private schools denied them admission on the ground of race, and the very existence of a second and quasi-public school system endangered bona fide public schools and damaged Negro pupils. It damaged public schools by diverting teachers, students, and funds into a competitive system.

It tended to dilute the right of Negro children to attend integrated schools. It placed the stamp of state approval on the stigma of Negro inferiority, perpetuating the humiliation of Negroes implicit in segregated education. That, in substance, was the basis for the plaintiffs' suit. The court found that the grant-in-aid law, Act 147 of 1962, was invalid because it was designed to negatively affect desegregation of the public schools.[10]

At least one resident, a New Orleans attorney, appreciated the decision of the three judges on the panel. In a letter of gratitude, C. Ellis Henican, of Henican James & Cleveland Attorneys at Law in New Orleans, commended the judges for "this tremendous public service." He complimented Tureaud on his success and wrote, "I wish to pay due response to all of you for a courageous, very intelligent, and highly desirable decision."[11]

The three-judge panel's decision was affirmed by the U.S. Supreme Court on appeal from the U.S. District Court for the Eastern District of Louisiana, January 15, 1968.[12] The Louisiana Legislature responded by passing Act 99, which created an Education Commission for Needy Children to aid parents not wishing to enroll their children in public schools where there was "an increase in juvenile delinquency, juvenile crime rates, and schools dropouts." Citing that "Act 99 must go the way of its predecessors [Acts 147, 3, and 258]," Judge Wisdom and the other judges on the panel declared the legislation in violation of the equal protection clause.[13] The judgment was affirmed by the U.S. Supreme Court on October 14, 1968.[14]

To improve school desegregation, Tureaud and his LDF colleagues wanted not only students but also teachers and administrators to be a part of the process. Their next legal demand sought to require the transfer of white teachers to Negro schools and vice versa. White teachers were transferred first, and eventually, a limited number of Negro teachers were assigned to white schools. Soon administrators and teachers of both races were working side by side in the public school system; however, the process was not without significant drawbacks—for example, many Negro teachers and administrators were demoted in the transfer or lost their jobs.

Tureaud contested a number of firings of Negro teachers and the replacement of them with white teachers. One of the cases he handled was against the Madison Parish School Board, *Linda Williams v. George Kimbrough*,[15] in which four former elementary school teachers, Linda Williams, Doris Cockerham, Hosea Atkins, and Flora Martin, alleged that they were unfairly dismissed by the school board. Tureaud argued that their dismissals were in violation of the equal protection and due process clauses of the Fourteenth Amendment.

The four teachers were dismissed from their jobs in the spring of 1968, as the Madison Parish School Board was preparing for court-ordered faculty integration for the following school year. In the 1968–69 school year, all but two schools in Madison Parish either integrated their faculties for the first time or increased their number of teachers of the opposite race. It is particularly noteworthy that Wright Elementary School had no white teachers in the 1967–68 school year but employed four for the 1968–69 school year, the same number of Negro teachers dismissed.

The principal at Wright met separately with Linda Williams and Doris Cockerham, telling them both that because of integration they would be replaced at the school by white teachers. Superintendent M. A. Phillips followed up with a letter to Williams and Cockerham stating that because the board was required to place several white teachers in the formerly all-Negro school, their employment was terminated. The two Negro teachers made a personal call to Phillips's office seeking a transfer rather than dismissal. The superintendent told them that it was against the school board's policy to transfer replaced teachers.

One of Phillips's aides overheard the discussion. Shortly after the teachers left Phillips's office, the aide advised the superintendent that his action with reference to the replaced teachers was in violation of a decree of the U.S. District Court of the Western District of Louisiana issued on April 7, 1967, outlining faculty employment and past assignments in elementary and secondary public schools.[16] To correct this mistake, Phillips sent letters to Cockerham and Williams, notifying them that they had been assigned to Anderson Island School, a one-room school located on a plantation approximately sixty miles from Tallulah, Louisiana. Twenty-three Negro students in grades one through eight attended the school and were taught by one teacher. The school was built and paid for by the plantation owner, who maintained the building and surrounding grounds. A room attached to the school provided basic housing for one person but was inadequate for a teacher with a family.

After visiting the school and the attached room, Williams, when given the choice of taking the Anderson Island position and being dismissed from the Madison Parish School System, chose the latter, as did Cockerham.

Also in April, Hosea Atkins and Flora Martin, both teachers at Wright, received word of their dismissal in individual letters from Phillips. Included with the dismissal letter to both teachers was a copy of correspondence from the superintendent to the school board recommending that Atkins and Martin not be reemployed as teachers in the Madison Parish schools for 1968–69 because their work was not satisfactory. Tureaud believed that their dismissals were based on weak, if not questionable, offenses. Atkins was cited for unprofessional conduct on a school field trip to a state park. When several students were unruly and destroyed park property, Atkins was alleged to have informed the park's management that he was not responsible for the pupils' actions. Martin's dismissal stemmed from an unsatisfactory evaluation during observation by another teacher.

The lawsuit filed on behalf of the four teachers was amended in 1968–69 from an earlier class action on behalf of Negro students in Madison Parish initiated by Tureaud in 1965, seeking injunction relief against the operation and administration of its public schools on a racially discriminatory basis. Tureaud amended the suit taking into account a portion of the court's April 7, 1967, decree, conforming exactly to the model decree set forth in the *Lee* case in Jefferson Parish, in which the plaintiff was offered her job back and was awarded back pay.

He asked that the plaintiffs be immediately reinstated to their teaching positions and be awarded back pay, together with compensation for any loss suffered by them as a result of their allegedly unlawful discharge. The suit also requested the awarding of reasonable attorneys' fees.

Sensitive to the problems and issues inherent in school desegregation, the court ruled that a disproportionate number of Negro teachers were dismissed. The court also indicated that the burden of proof to rehire these teachers was to be borne by the school district and that the proof must be clear, nondiscriminating, and convincing. Refusing to uphold the school district, the court declared that the board of education failed to meet its burden with respect to all of the dismissals.

The court decreed that at the beginning of the next school year the four teachers were to be given an opportunity to be considered for teaching positions for which they qualified and they were not to be considered merely as prospective new applicants. If there were no openings, they were to be objectively compared with all other teachers currently in the system. If they were found to be superior to any, they were to be given a position and the least qualified dismissed. The court declared that the wrongful dismissals of teachers also entitled them to recover provable damages, including salary differences in intervening employment and moving expenses to new jobs.

It was a victory for desegregation and civil rights, but a bittersweet one for the civil rights legal practitioners. The court rejected the plaintiffs' claims for attorneys' fees, stating that such fees are rarely granted where neither statute nor contract calls for them. It would be years later that Tureaud's work would help Negro lawyers become civil rights lawyers and earn a living.

Throughout the 1960s white residents continued to flee the public schools in New Orleans. Negro students enrolled in schools that were formerly all white; gained better facilities, classroom space, and proximity to the schools; but did not attain a racially mixed school environment. Although the public schools in Orleans Parish were not closed down like schools in other states in the South, legislation to combat desegregation began gradual reconstructing of public education. Years later the New Orleans public schools were populated by a predominance of black students, with diminished support, resources, and leadership.

20
More Direct Action

Now, it's true; New Orleans didn't burn down. But it didn't burn down because people like A. P. Tureaud were here saying to the white community,
"Look, you've got to give. You can't stand still, you've got to give."
   And he was saying to the black community, "That is not the way to accomplish it. The courts are the means by which we can accomplish it."

   —Justice Revius Ortique, in *Journey for Justice: The A. P. Tureaud Story*

The NAACP became the symbol of progressive action for
Negroes throughout Louisiana in the 1940s and 1950s. Although Tureaud was
involved in political activity and diplomatic biracial appeals during this time, it
was the legal battles in which he and other NAACP attorneys across the country
were engaged that resulted in reforms and expanded civil rights. The demands
of the 1960s called for new strategies and approaches to eliminating racial bias.
Many of the organizations that appealed to the younger black activists emerging on college campuses called for nonviolent direct action. This new approach
was a strategic problem for A. P. Tureaud. Direct-action tactics for continued
civil rights gains included street demonstrations, picketing, sit-ins, and other
displays of public protest. Tureaud persevered with his usual zeal in the courts
while young college students carried the fight to the streets. Thus the streets became another civil rights battleground during the 1960s.

   The new generation of activists felt that the legal system was too slow. These
activists also rejected the local and state governments that resisted implementation of court-ordered mandates. Tureaud held to the philosophy of the NAACP
Legal Defense Fund to use the law for social change. He and the NAACP lawyers
saw the U.S. Supreme Court's decision in *Brown* as not only defeat for school
desegregation but as a means to chip away at racial discrimination in all areas
of society.

   The advocates of public protest increased the burden of civil rights lawyers
already overwhelmed and overworked. Defending the students involved in the
sit-ins of March 1960 in Baton Rouge was an example of the added responsibility civil rights lawyers like Tureaud were required to take on.

Major Johns, a twenty-year-old student at the Baton Rouge campus of the historically black Southern University, convinced fellow students to join others from across the nation who had participated in sit-ins. In his speeches to students, Johns exclaimed that they should protest local laws that required them to enter the back door of public places and that denied them equal job opportunities, the right to vote, or any privilege granted to a full citizen.

On the afternoon of March 28, 1960, seven Southern University students— Janette Hoston of Monroe, Louisiana; John W. Johnson of Cullen, Louisiana; Kenneth L. Johnson of Mississippi; Jo Ann Morris of Shreveport, Louisiana; Donald T. Moss of Winnfield, Louisiana; Marvin Robinson of Chicago; and Felton Valdry of Port Allen, Louisiana, sat at the lunch counter of the Kress department store in downtown Baton Rouge and were arrested for disturbing the peace.

The next day, nine more students staged sit-ins, also downtown. Mary Enola Briscoe, Eddie Charles Brown Jr., Lawrence Hurst, and Sandra Ann Jones of Baton Rouge; Larry L. Nichols of Shreveport; Charles L. Peabody of Atlanta; and Mack Jones of Alexandria, Louisiana, sat at Sitman's Drugstore on Main Street. John B. Garner and Vernon J. Jordan of Baton Rouge sat at the Greyhound bus terminal. Both groups were arrested and also charged with disturbing the peace.

At the university, there were mixed reactions regarding these demonstrations and what position the administration would take in response to the students' acts of civil disobedience. Rev. T. J. Jemison, a leader of the 1953 Baton Rouge bus boycott, raised bail money for the students from contributions by the black community. Then, on March 29, 1960, Pastor Jemison introduced four of the sit-in participants to a standing-room-only meeting at the Mount Zion First Baptist Church. Their speeches served to rally support for their actions and highlighted the recognition of their courageous and worthwhile commitment to seeking access to public accommodations.

The arrested students were leaders on the campus, and many were honor students. Their popularity increased on the campus and in the community as a result of their heroic action. On March 30, hundreds of Southern University students staged an hour-long prayer meeting at the state capitol on their behalf.

Positive reactions were short lived. In addition to their arrests, time spent in jail, and pending criminal charges, the student demonstrators were suspended from Southern. SU president Felton G. Clark announced the suspension of the arrested students, along with Major Johns, who was the primary strategist for the sit-ins. The students needed legal representation, and Southern University Law School graduate Johnnie Jones, the attorney who handled the 1953 Baton Rouge bus boycott, was their initial legal counsel.

Jones called on Tureaud for assistance. Initially, exasperated by the turn of events with public protest strategies sweeping the nation in the fight for civil rights, Tureaud said he had more important things to do than represent students involved in acts of civil disobedience. Indeed, he was very busy and immersed in a number of civil rights cases, including the New Orleans public school desegregation case. In these cases, he was confronting Louisiana state superintendent of education Shelby Jackson, the state district judges, and Louisiana Supreme Court justices. Tureaud felt that representing student demonstrators could harden the decisions and actions of these same authorities when he went before them to address school desegregation. Despite his reservations, Tureaud, with the support of the Legal Defense Fund, joined Johnnie Jones in representing the students. Conversely, the increasing civil disobedience would become the impetus for speeding up civil rights progress in the courts.

The first trial was in the Nineteenth Judicial District Court located in Baton Rouge. The court found the students guilty as charged, and on appeal the Louisiana Supreme Court upheld the lower court's ruling. Such action was no surprise to Tureaud and Jones. They were eagerly prepared to take the case to the U.S. Supreme Court.

LDF attorneys had initial concerns about the number of issues raised in the brief. In a July 13, 1960, letter, LDF lawyer James M. Nabrit III suggested that Tureaud and Jones seek to raise only three lines of defense before the court. Nabrit's first line of defense was the Motor Carriers Act, prohibiting passenger discrimination in facilities "operated or controlled by" the carriers. Secondly, he proposed the Commence Clause of the Constitution, which prohibits discrimination during interstate travel. The third line of defense was the Fourteenth Amendment argument for violation of due process that Tureaud and Jones had used before the state court.[1]

Garner v. Louisiana was the U.S. Supreme Court's first decision concerning lunch counter sit-ins. Chief Justice Earl Warren delivered the opinion for the Court. Issues brought up in the separate concurring opinions written by three associate justices, Felix Frankfurter, William O. Douglas, and John Marshall Harlan II, disclosed the significance attached to this case in the dismantling of Jim Crow laws. Tureaud thought that the manner in which Justice Warren set out the issues of due process in the following exchange with state's attorney John F. Ward was brilliant:

Justice Warren: Mr. Ward, suppose a man running this store does have a custom of segregation, but he doesn't want to offend the Negroes to the point that they won't come into his store and buy his other articles. And, when a thing of this kind [sit-in] happens, he says, "Well it's not my practice or my custom to do this but I don't want to offend these people and I am not going to order them out of my place. I will just tell them it is not my custom to serve them." And he takes that attitude and objects no further to their being there and then the police comes in to see no disturbance of any kind and put the people in jail for disturbing the peace. Is that the violation of the law?

Ward: You would have that situation only in the *Garner* case.

Justice Warren: In the *Garner* case, yes; but you defend the *Garner* case very strongly and I want to know how you do it and that is the reason I am asking these questions. Isn't that the *Garner* case?

Ward: I don't know that in reading of the testimony of Mr. Wilkes the owner of Sitman's Drug store, where the *Garner* case took place, you can draw the conclusion necessarily from the testimony he was not asking the person to leave. We contend that he was, even though he did not say those specific words "Please get up and leave." We contend that the inference, the only inference, that you can draw from that testimony . . . is that he was in fact asking the person to leave because he had no place to serve him and he was taking up space which his other customers might have been using under those circumstances.

Justice Warren: He did not say that!

Ward: No, that is correct. In so many words specifically, no sir, he did not.

Justice Warren: Well if you have two inferences that can equally be drawn, one of them guilt and one of innocence, what one do you choose in your state?

Ward: Normally, in criminal cases you choose the presumption of innocence.

Justice Warren: Innocence, that is what we have here.[2]

The justices found no evidence that the defendants' quiet, peaceable behavior of sitting at the counters would have supported a finding that their conduct would have disturbed the public. The Court held that the convictions were in violation of the defendants' due process of law guaranteed them by the Fourteenth Amendment to the U.S. Constitution. Chief Justice Warren pointed out that shortly after the arrest of the sixteen students who sat in at the lunch counters, the Louisiana Legislature amended its "disturbance of the peace" statute in an obvious attempt to encompass the type of activity involved in these cases.

The Court acknowledged that there was a deep-seated pattern of segregation of the races in Louisiana, going back at least to *Plessy v. Ferguson* in 1896, when the Supreme Court sanctioned the "separate but equal" doctrine. The Louisiana Legislature in Act No. 630 restated it in 1960.

Tureaud was well aware of the history of southern politicians who enacted laws that sought to restrict equal rights for Negroes. Litigating a case similar to *Garner*, Thomas Morris Chester, who in 1873 became one of the first black lawyers to be admitted to the Louisiana Bar, represented a black man who was refused service at a soda fountain in New Orleans. Chester won the suit, nearly a century before the 1960s sit-ins. "It is fatal to liberty," Chester said, "when the color of a man's skin, deepened by the sun of heaven . . . ostracizes him . . . from the public places and outlaws him in public estimation."[3]

Justice Felix Frankfurter, a native of Vienna, Austria, agreed with the general approach of Chief Justice Warren regarding the lack of evidence in the law of disturbing the peace but thought the Louisiana statute had to be construed to cover peaceful activity that might lead to violence.

Justice William O. Douglas, who was considered a member of the court's "liberal wing," disagreed on the question of possible violence arising from the sit-ins because these demonstrations had raised racial tensions considerably in Louisiana and other states. Justice Douglas responded that restaurants, whether in drugstores, department stores, or bus terminals, are a part of the public life of most communities. Although they are private enterprises, they are public facilities in which the state may not enforce a policy of racial segregation. The justice also indicated that "the authority to license a business for public use is derived from the public. Negroes are as much a part of that public as are whites."[4]

Justice John Marshall Harlan II, whose grandfather had previously served on the Court and dissented in *Plessy v. Ferguson,* said he believed that Louisiana had invaded the realm of free expression of opinion by imposing criminal sanctions on persons participating in sit-in demonstrations. Harlan declared the statute under which the demonstrators were arrested unconstitutionally vague. In his opinion, it was obvious that a state had an interest in preserving peace and harmony within its borders, but Justice Harlan declared: "When a state seeks to subject to criminal sanctions conduct which, except for demonstrated paramount state interest, would be a range of freedom of expression assured by the 14th Amendment, it cannot do so by means of a general and all-inclusive 'breach of the peace prohibition.'"[5]

Attorney Ward's closing remarks in the *Garner* case were more revealing of the thoughts of the contemporary leadership in Baton Rouge:

> These are times that require understanding, good will, and patience, regardless of how hard sometimes these things may come to some among us.
>
> The recognition and acceptance that really count cannot be hastened or ever won by any action that creates alarm, destroys goodwill, or alienates the different groups in the community. Our society may have its imperfections, as do all things of human design. But this is not the way improvements will be brought about.
>
> Time and orderly evolution can bring progress. Force can bring none.[6]

On December 11, 1961, the U.S. Supreme Court overturned the convictions of the sixteen former Southern University students. The civil rights community hailed the Court's decision in favor of the "Southern sixteen" as an overwhelming victory. "I thought we didn't have a ghost of a chance in that *Garner* case, but, we won it," Tureaud said.[7] In a congratulatory phone call to Jones in Baton Rouge, a jubilant Tureaud stated, "The stone that was rejected became the cornerstone."[8] A.P. Jr. believes that although his father did not approve initially of the public protest movement and its subsequent demonstrations, "he later on saw the value . . . that it did push the legal avenues too, into a more consolidated effort. So, he did some growing too."[9]

In the late 1950s Tureaud had begun to cultivate relationships with younger black activists, recognizing that they were the future leaders in their community. He gave them the benefit of his wisdom and experience but yielded to some of their demands. To this end, he started with the NAACP Youth Council, organized in his office during the summer of 1960. Raphael Cassimere, one of the Youth Council's presidents, described Tureaud as soft spoken, a good conciliator, very determined, modest, good humored, and practical. Tureaud's qualities impressed Cassimere. His relationship with Tureaud motivated him to be more focused, less hot tempered, and more willing to direct his frustrations into positive actions.

As Tureaud remarked years later, he never relinquished his belief that a legal strategy was best in the overall fight for civil rights. "I didn't put on one demonstration and I got all these things. Demonstrations did not desegregate anything but lunch counters, and we had to make it possible for them to carry those out by litigation."[10] Such a victory made Tureaud more committed to using traditional legal methods for redress. However, winning in court made younger activists initiate more demonstrations and feel that they were an integral and vital part in the civil rights movement, despite their continued arrests. In time, the NAACP leadership began to acquiesce to the younger crowd, fearing the loss of more branch membership and support for the organization as a whole.

Tureaud had been asked by a subcommittee of the New Orleans NAACP to file suit against Acts 70 and 80 of 1960, the Louisiana Legislature's laws prohibiting sit-ins. He declined, stating that such action was "not practical," perhaps because it would interfere with the negotiations the NAACP was pursuing with members of City Hall. He also was awaiting the decision in *Garner*. Tureaud, a Young Turk in the 1920s, was by the 1960s viewed as the Old Guard of the New Orleans branch. A new generation of Young Turks wanted to do things its own way.

In a second wave of Louisiana demonstrations, orchestrated in 1961 by the newly founded Congress on Racial Equality (CORE), Southern University students and other individuals were arrested and jailed in Baton Rouge. Unlike in the *Garner* case, which argued the due process clause of the Fourteenth Amendment, in *Cox v. Louisiana* Johnnie Jones and the CORE attorneys put forth an argument before the U.S. Supreme Court that overturned the convictions using the First Amendment's freedom of speech.

Tureaud continued in his belief that law was an effective tool for social change, stating, "I am more in favor of that than all this damn stuff they are carrying on in the street."[11] There were those who applauded Tureaud's leadership style. He was "understated" and "low-keyed" but very resolute, recalled Sybil Morial, wife of his protégé Ernest "Dutch" Morial. "I don't know that being flamboyant and offensive would've worked in the forties and fifties," she said. "I don't think that he compromised himself when he went in the court and said 'sir' and it wasn't in a way that . . . demeaned him. And I think it worked and, little by little, gains were made in the courts. The judges respected him. Who knows . . . what would have happened if you had someone . . . who was . . . a little more fiery."[12]

Tureaud identified his own personal struggle to establish himself as a lawyer with the advancement of the black legal profession as a whole, and this was not a self-serving belief. Knowing the power of group action, he began the Louis A. Martinet Society, a statewide organization of black lawyers, in 1957. According to Tureaud, "Negroes had nothing to fight with. They didn't have any of the materials of war. They only had their physical being and whatever persuasion they could bring to bear by group activity or something like that. We in Louisiana had to depend upon our own resources for whatever we could achieve or whatever gains we could make."[13] Tureaud's interest in organizing this group could be regarded as inconsistent with his call for desegregation, but in reality he was organizing his colleagues so that they could learn to be effective advocates in the years ahead. As civil rights gains were made, Tureaud was even more committed to desegregation.

When he finally established himself in full-time practice, he nurtured the careers of many young attorneys. Tureaud took Morial, one of his favorites, into his law practice. They worked many nights from dawn to dusk on civil rights cases with many of the leading civil right lawyers from across the country. Morial sharpened his political skills during his involvement with the NAACP, Alpha Phi Alpha fraternity, and the Knights of Peter Claver. He shared membership in these and other organizations with his mentor, Tureaud.

Morial embraced the strategies of his generation more readily than Tureaud. He was one of the leaders in the New Orleans's Freedom March on September 30, 1963, the largest protest demonstration in the city's history. In an interracial effort, 10,000 black people and 300 whites marched from Shakespeare Park to the New Orleans City Hall. The white business elite cooperated with the Freedom March, securing a parade permit for it and also warning the White Citizens' Council not to provoke the marchers. With Morial were A. L. Davis, Milton Upton, Avery Alexander, and A. J. Chapital, along with Oretha Castle, who addressed the crowd. Not one city official greeted the marchers at City Hall.

Picketing and demonstrations continued through 1965. CORE activists picketed segregated theaters and other facilities, and the NAACP Youth Council picketed the downtown stores in defiance of the older black leaders of the Citizens' Committee who had reached an agreement with the white storeowners. Raphael Cassimere said the merchants on Canal Street had not delivered as many jobs as they had promised.

Tureaud readily acknowledged that civil rights gains would be made with not only the efforts of Negro activists but also the leadership of white Americans, who were often willing to accept abuse and ridicule for their attempts to help Negroes achieve equal rights.

By the late 1960s biracial political and civic groups were making overtures to black leaders, who remained diplomatic in their dealings with the majority while fighting for equal rights. Tureaud was part of these groups, and many of the black attorneys he mentored gained leadership in these biracial efforts. When Governor John McKeithen formed the first state biracial commission, he tapped the black Shreveport attorney Jesse N. Stone to be co-director with white attorney Jack Martzell, who was one of Judge Wright's former law clerks. When white attorney Bascom Talley, with whom Tureaud had been acquainted during his work on cases in Bogalusa, Louisiana, became president of the Louisiana State Bar Association and wanted black attorneys to participate in the annual conventions of the state bar, he encouraged Tureaud's involvement. All practicing lawyers in the state were required to join the Louisiana State Bar and pay an annual membership fee. However, Jim Crow laws made it legal for black attorneys to be prohibited from attending association meetings and annual conventions.

When the Louisiana Bar Association allowed black lawyers to attend its meetings for the first time in the mid-1960s, association leaders changed the location of the meetings to Mississippi, a state known for its extreme racism and severe segregation and hostility toward black people. Tureaud and several younger lawyers went to a conference held in Biloxi, Mississippi. At the conference dinner, the black lawyers were directed to a separate dining room. The younger attorneys stormed out, requesting that their banquet fee be refunded.

Tureaud stayed, despite the criticism of his younger colleagues who did not understand his willingness to remain. Later he chastised them, stating that their behavior was "impolite" and "ill-mannered" because they had voluntarily paid to attend the meeting. He told them, "They didn't send for you, you came. You paid your money and now you are going to make this scene, and everybody is going to know about it."[14]

Many years later in New Orleans, Tureaud's son A.P. Jr. met Lawrence Lehmann, the grandson of Judge Herman L. Midlo. Lehmann told A.P. Jr. that his grandfather and Tureaud shared a mutual respect for each other as lawyers, activists, and residents of New Orleans. Lehmann stated that his grandfather was at the Louisiana State Bar Association meeting in Biloxi. Upon seeing Tureaud eating in the designated room alone, he decided to join him. Before the evening was over, several white lawyers joined them for dinner.

Because there was money to be made, white southern lawyers were eager to represent black clients in civil and criminal cases. However, they refused to be involved in civil rights cases, fearing censure and possible loss of white clients.

Also, there was little or no money for civil rights challenges. The white members of the bar in Louisiana had literally abdicated their responsibility regarding civil rights, except very few, such as New Orleans attorneys John P. Nelson, Benjamin E. Smith, and Herman Midlo. Judge Midlo was known for his involvement in black voter registration in the 1940s.[15]

In fact, the Louisiana State Bar was involved in the censure of white civil rights attorney Richard B. Sobol as late as 1968. Sobol, while on leave of absence from his Washington, D.C., law firm, Arnold and Porter, and temporarily residing in New Orleans, was working voluntarily with the Lawyers Constitutional Defense Committee (LCDC). The LCDC was a New York charitable corporation formed by CORE, the American Civil Liberties Union, American Jewish Congress, and other organizations to provide much-needed additional lawyers, particularly in Louisiana, Alabama, and Mississippi, to handle civil rights litigation in the South emerging from the Civil Rights Act of 1964. LCDC associated with a local law firm, where it offered legal representation in civil rights matters. Sobol was and had been associated with the New Orleans black law firm of (Robert) Collins, (Nils) Douglas, and (Lolis) Elie since 1964.

While representing a civil rights plaintiff in Plaquemines Parish, Sobol was arrested and charged with practicing law without a license. A three-judge court held that state court prosecution of Sobol was unlawful and undertaken for the purpose of harassment. The United States intervened on his behalf because it considered Sobol's relief vital to the national interest. The United States took the position that the arrest and prosecution of Sobol constituted a form of harassment, undertaken without basis in law or fact, for the purpose of deterring him and other lawyers from helping to provide legal representation in civil right cases.[16]

Political, social, personal, and economic reasons kept white lawyers from accepting civil rights and social welfare cases. The core of Sobol's suit was that there were not enough Louisiana lawyers willing to assist and defend the state's Negro population.[17]

In 1963, Tureaud's protégé Ernest Morial was one of five lawyers representing Louisiana in a White House meeting on the subject of civil rights. At the invitation of President John F. Kennedy, Morial accompanied state bar leaders Bascom Talley, immediate past president Oliver Stockwell, Harry Kelleher, and John G. Weinmann to the meeting of more than 240 lawyers from across the country. Talley later wrote in his president's message published in the *Louisiana Bar Journal* that the president and vice president made one point that in his estimation was thematic to the whole conference:

They emphasized the basic fact that we, as lawyers, have our obligation, too, and that obligation is to uphold final judgments of our Courts, whether we like or dislike them.... I don't know a single lawyer who hasn't at some time or another had to give bad news to a client that his case had been lost. There is no legal or moral reason that I know of to make a distinction between ordinary judgments and judgments involving civil rights.

I feel deeply that, no matter how much we may dislike a final judgment, we, as lawyers, are obligated to uphold it publicly and privately, if our system is to endure.[18]

By June 11, 1963, President Kennedy decided that the time had come to take stronger action to help the civil rights struggle. He proposed the new Civil Rights Bill to Congress and appeared on national television to ask Americans to end segregation. "One hundred years . . . have passed since President Lincoln freed the slaves, yet their heirs, their grandsons, are not fully free," he stated.

On August 27, 1963, Tureaud heard the news of the death of ninety-five-year-old W. E. B. Du Bois, then a naturalized citizen of Ghana, Africa. In November of that year, President Kennedy was assassinated in Dallas. Tureaud was deeply disturbed that many prominent civil rights leaders were assassinated during the 1960s, including Malcolm X, Martin Luther King Jr., and President Kennedy's brother Robert F. Kennedy. These political leaders were the victims of extremists who resorted to violence to retain the status quo of white supremacy. Despite these tragic events, Tureaud continued his frontal assault on injustice, even though members of his family were concerned for his safety.

The 1960s proved to be a turbulent time for race relations, with intermittent bouts of, on the one hand, discrimination and massive resistance to civil rights and, on the other, legal victories and high marks of achievements in biracial efforts and social and political inclusion.

21

Courts Are the Way

During his career of more than forty-five years, Tureaud
gained the respect of federal judges Herbert W. Christenberry, J. Skelly Wright,
and John Minor Wisdom. At the time of his first judicial appointment, Wright,
thirty-eight, had the distinction of being the youngest judge on the federal bench.
Christenberry, Tureaud, and Wisdom, at least a decade older than Wright, were
about the same age and in the 1960s felt that retirement was in the distant future. The three men shared many experiences in the civil rights arena, which
were resolved in and out of court. When anyone challenged Tureaud's knowledge of civil rights matters, he was proud to inform them that these judges supported the work he had done with many cases for some time and that they recognized him as someone who was well informed in these matters.

Tureaud respected Christenberry, Wright, and Wisdom, along with Judge
Richard T. Rives, who were responsive to the demands of the times and supported the U.S. Supreme Court decisions. Many of the cases that they decided
set legal precedents, particularly in civil rights, which the U.S. Supreme Court
upheld. Tureaud believed that these judges were forthright in their decisions. "I
never had to appeal any of their decisions except when in certain cases we felt
that they were a little too conservative on the issue of desegregation," the attorney said in an interview in 1969. "That was never very often," he recalled. "The
few appeals were made because the Legal Defense Fund had a deadline to reach
and didn't want these judges to stymie these efforts."[1]

Judge Wright observed after serving on the court and supporting desegregation: "I never have been a gregarious type, and I've become much less so in
the past few years. You never know whether people really want to talk with you
and I don't see a lot of people any more."[2] The Irishman, who was a Catholic,

was proud of his heritage and shared a special relationship with his mother. She was a forthright person and commanded respect. Several of his relatives were city politicians. His middle name came from that of a commissioner in city government, Joe Skelly. Tureaud noted that Wright was an efficient, able judge who acted very responsibly when problems were brought to his attention.

Tureaud felt that Christenberry was quick to decide that constitutional rights were clear. In 1957, President Dwight D. Eisenhower had considered Christenberry for appointment to the U.S. Court of Appeals for the Fifth Circuit, but Christenberry's rulings in civil rights cases ruined his chances, and the seat went to John Minor Wisdom, who had not previously served as a judge. In 1965, Christenberry received national attention for citing police in Bogalusa, Louisiana, for contempt of court because they persistently refused to obey his prior order directing them to protect civil rights marchers from assaults by local whites. That same year, it was Judge Christenberry who swore in the first Negro assistant U.S. attorney, Ernest Morial, and Tureaud was present to witness this occasion and have his picture taken with the judge and his protégé. Because of Christenberry, Tureaud also attended several receptions of the Federal Bar Association, even though he was not a member. Christenberry served as a federal district court judge until his death in 1975.

The U.S. Supreme Court refused to review most school desegregation suits; therefore the circuit court, with three judges from the Fourth Circuit and seven from the Fifth, was the last resort for most of these cases.[3] The Fifth Circuit Court of Appeals had its headquarters in the Central Business District of New Orleans. The court heard appeals from sixteen district courts in Georgia, Florida, Alabama, Mississippi, Louisiana, and Texas and handled a large number of civil rights cases.[4] Because a number of vacancies occurred and were filled on the court in the 1950s, by 1961 only two of its seven judges, both Democrats, were appointed by a president other than Eisenhower.

Christenberry and Wright did not make it to the Fifth Circuit bench. When Judge Wright was appointed in 1962 to the U.S. Court of Appeals for the D.C. Circuit, Tureaud believed that Wright would have preferred to remain in New Orleans if political circumstances had permitted. Louisiana's senators Allen Ellender and Russell Long had blocked Wright's appointment to the Fifth Circuit by President John F. Kennedy. Tureaud hoped President Kennedy would consider Judge Wright for any vacancy that came up on the U.S. Supreme Court. Judge Wright was considered to be very aggressive, and U.S. Supreme Court justice Hugo Black, who was also from the South and a former member of the KKK, concurred with many of his opinions.

Judge Wright and attorney Tureaud developed a collegial relationship over the years and felt comfortable with each other as they engaged in conversations about political and personal issues. In their discussions, Tureaud shared his belief with Wright that perhaps Justice Black was staying on with the Court despite his eligibility for retirement in the hope that someone with similar opinions would get the nod as his replacement. Wright maintained that the president of the United States selected Supreme Court justices based on his personal preferences and not on those of the retiring justice.

Tureaud had other reasons for supporting Judge Wright for a possible position on the Supreme Court. He saw it as an opportunity to put a justice on the Court who was familiar with and trained in the Louisiana Civil Code. Tureaud felt that the Supreme Court had not been well equipped to analyze the civil code since the time a New Orleanian, Edward Douglass White, served as chief justice, from December 19, 1910, to May 19, 1921. Tureaud also believed that President Kennedy, a liberal, would want to place a qualified candidate on the Court who shared his views on civil rights. Certainly, Judge Wright merited serious consideration on this account. Others shared Tureaud's view, although Judge Wright was doubtful.

President Kennedy did not have the opportunity to make many judicial appointments. When a D.C. Court of Appeals position opened up, Tureaud conceded that Judge Wright got it with the blessing of both state senators, who wanted Wright out of Louisiana. Out of respect for Judge Wright, Tureaud maintained that the judge was elevated to the position solely because he deserved the promotion.

When Tureaud congratulated Judge Wright on his appointment, the judge told him that he was glad to receive the promotion, although he felt he could have better served in a specialty area. Tureaud knew that in addition to his very fine record in civil rights, Judge Wright had "a certain pride in his ability in admiralty law and that was the field that he liked a great deal." Going to Washington, where he would largely deal with administrative law, with many government cases, would be an adjustment for Wright.[5]

In 1957, John Minor Wisdom, who had not previously served as a judge, was appointed to the Fifth Circuit by President Eisenhower. The then junior member of the Fifth Circuit was the most atypical member of the court.[6] It was Wisdom, the Republican national committeeman from Louisiana, who first worked with Tureaud in his attempt to take over the Republican Party in Louisiana. Wisdom became a strong supporter of school desegregation and civil rights in general and later was known as one of the "Fifth Circuit Four." He and his colleagues,

Chief Judge Elbert Tuttle, Richard Taylor Rives, and John Robert Brown, were viewed as the four judges of the Fifth Circuit in the 1950s and 1960s who issued the series of decisions crucial to civil rights.

Judge Rives, a former president of the Montgomery and the Alabama State Bar associations, was appointed by President Harry Truman and served as chief judge from 1959 to 1960. The Alabama native was the sole Democrat among the "Fifth Circuit Four." Impatient with delaying maneuvers, Chief Judge Rives frequently reminded his fellow southerners that they had to obey the law whether they liked it or not.

Judges Rives, Christenberry, and Wright in a strongly worded opinion in the *Bush* case stated: "Interposition is not a constitutional doctrine. If taken seriously, it is illegal defiance of constitutional authority." Quoting from Chief Justice John Marshall, the federal jurists said: "If the legislature of the several states may, at will, annul the judgments of the courts of the United States, and destroy the right acquired under these judgments, the Constitution itself becomes a solemn mockery and the Nation is deprived of its own tribunals."[7]

Tureaud and other civil rights attorneys who sought relief through the courts were fortunate to have federal judges Wright, Wisdom, Rives, and Christenberry review and rule on their cases. Unfortunately, they also had to contend with Judge E. Gordon West and judges of the Western District, under whose jurisdiction most of Louisiana's sixty-seven school districts fell. President Kennedy appointed Judge West, and no other federal judge in Louisiana was as flagrantly contemptuous of the *Brown* decision as West. The other judges of the Western District—Richard Putnam, Edwin Hunter, and Ben Dawkins—were likewise unenthusiastic about integration.

Judge West was a native of Massachusetts, where he attended primary and secondary schools, and followed in the footsteps of his grandfather, eventually becoming a lawyer. After a work transfer from Gulf States Utilities in Beaumont, Texas, in the mid-1930s to the Baton Rouge Electric Company, he enrolled at LSU, earning an accounting degree in 1941 and a law degree in 1942, a year after successfully passing the bar. On June 10, 1942, he received orders to active duty in the U.S. Navy, serving until late 1945. On his return to Baton Rouge, he practiced law first as an attorney with the Louisiana Revenue Department and then in private partnership with his former law school classmate Russell Long. From 1952 to 1961 he was in partnership with Byron Kantrow, in the firm that became Kantrow, Spaht, West, and Kleinpeter. His appointment to the federal bench in September 1961 received the approval of both Louisiana senators, including his former law partner Long, which assured his confirmation.

West strongly believed that many problems were created by the federal courts' involvement in matters that were for state courts and issues never intended to be federal matters. His biggest complaint was the injection of the federal courts into moral and social matters that were outside their purview. He believed that "if they have to be involved because of a Supreme Court ruling, the federal courts should carefully limit their involvement to what is absolutely required by the statutes of the rulings of the Supreme Court."[8]

In open court, Tureaud endured Judge West's comments against the Supreme Court's ruling in *Brown*. West maintained that the Supreme Court was wrong in its decision and that there was no legal justification for some of the decisions of the Supreme Court. West said that the Court's decision was not "the law of the land" but the "law of the case."[9] He believed that significant harm had resulted from these Court decisions, but he also recognized the authority of the high court and reluctantly complied with its mandates.

Although Tureaud agreed that Judge West was one of the most conservative federal judges he had to face in the Louisiana desegregation cases, he also stated that West was a capable judge. However, Tureaud objected to the manner in which the judge conducted his court. West wrote not only the opinions but also his own decrees, outlining the method of desegregation instead of following the usual pattern in these cases, where the attorneys were requested to hammer out the decrees. Keeping his criticism of the judiciary to himself as was his usual custum, Tureaud did not make public comments about West, as did some civil rights attorneys. According to Tureaud, in less formal settings with Judge West, the judge stated that as an easterner he had no prejudice against the Negro but he felt that he had to defer to the southerners' prevailing attitudes regarding race. Tempering plans for desegregation, Judge West felt he was protecting the Negroes. Tureaud chuckled at such thoughts and hoped that one day he could tell West what he really thought of his spineless decisions regarding civil rights matters. He also believed that Judge West may have lost his chance to be seriously considered for an appointment to the U.S. Court of Appeals because of his actions in desegregation cases.

Tureaud was particularly sensitive to activities that might alienate members of the legal community. He always reacted decisively when the strategies of the LDF lawyers and local civil rights attorneys were under attack by black or white militants. The attorney felt strongly that legal leadership was critical to the continued success of the movement and that it would fail miserably without the efforts of the cadre of lawyers responsible for achieving desegregation. Although Tureaud was easygoing and positive in his outlook, those who knew him personally realized that his lifelong interest in seeking justice was a significant part of his emotional, social, and spiritual life. He was more animated and verbal when his caseload was heavy and demanding.

As he did with Communist sympathizers, Tureaud distanced himself from those who publicly criticized members of the judiciary. Part of Tureaud's success was his diplomatic approach and his ability to negotiate. "And it doesn't mean that he was an Uncle Tom or that he went with hat in hand," according to political scientist Frank Ransburg of Southern University in Baton Rouge. "There were probably some businessmen who supported him politically, but could not let it be known, because many of their white patrons would not give them business anymore."[10]

In fact, Tureaud and others met with white business and political leaders to carry out as peacefully as possible, even if secretly, the initial desegregation of libraries, buses, parks, and schools. Announcements of plans to desegregate were often suppressed in the local newspapers until after black patrons had entered the public facilities. The objective was to avoid having angry segregationists gather in protest at such sites. Reports after the fact emphasized nonconfrontational and peaceful resolution.

Tureaud sought to temper the professional behavior of several younger black lawyers. He warned them against actions that could result in being disbarred. One such lawyer was Revius Ortique, a graduate of the Southern University Law Center, who would become the first black justice elected to the Louisiana State Supreme Court. Ortique did not want to obey the segregation laws governing public accommodations. Once, he and another black lawyer were criticized by some of the judges for going into the courthouse restroom designated for whites only. Tureaud called Ortique into his office and warned him that breaking the law in using the white water fountain and restroom could result in his license being revoked and he would then not be able to help others as a lawyer.[11]

Realizing that by the 1960s he was now one of the premier civil rights advocates in Louisiana and a member of the Old Guard, Tureaud reluctantly accepted the criticism and disdain of the young black activists. He had been a Young Turk in the 1920s and as a result of his youthful experiences ignored the current criticism and name-calling. New Orleans attorney Lolis Elie, involved in civil rights work for more than forty years, believed Tureaud's work paved the way for succeeding generations of lawyers to be paid for practicing civil rights law. Elie cited New Orleans's long tradition of rebellion and its historic position as one of the most literate African American communities as contributing to its success in the struggle for equality.[12]

About his constituency and his role as a black leader, Elie said that Tureaud drew strength and support from the Creole community, in terms of its leadership and legacy in the civil rights arena, as early as the antebellum period. He also was able to establish supportive relationships in the uptown African American community by aligning himself with men like Rev. A. L. Davis, president of an important black Baptist association. His personal and professional relationship with Davis forged new ground for political coalitions, helping to allay the prejudices, often based on color and religion, that often existed between African Americans and Creoles.

Typically, Creoles used their political capital with members of their own culture; however, in order to consolidate the entire community of color, Tureaud knew that it was necessary to expand the boundaries. Even though he looked white, members of the African American community knew that he was committed to securing justice for all. In addition to consolidating the black community in New Orleans, he was able to garner the resources and abilities of middle- and upper-middle-class Negroes throughout the state. As a law school graduate, he had the ability to connect with well-educated men and women, both black and white, to advance equality. His nonconfrontational style of leadership deflected criticism or rejection of him even by those in the white community who were hostile toward desegregation. A singular quality that carried him through his many years of service was the development of collegial relationships with members of the judiciary, who respected his knowledge of constitutional law and conferred with him on legal strategies.

Also in the 1960s, many black civil rights lawyers accomplished broader roles in local, state, and federal positions in the judiciary and legislative offices. Constance Baker Motley left the LDF office in 1964 to pursue a political career in New York, serving in the state senate and as the first female president of the borough of Manhattan. Tureaud was thrilled to hear the news in 1966 that Motley had been appointed the first African American woman to a federal judgeship. He applauded President Lyndon Johnson's choice of his former NAACP colleague. He was sure that she would bring her sensitivity to civil rights issues to the bench as she did in the courtroom as a lawyer and in City Hall and the statehouse as a lawmaker. Judge Motley would serve in the U.S. District Court for the Southern District of New York, obtaining senior status in 1986.

After unsuccessful electoral races in 1959 and 1963, Ernest Morial became the first black member of the Louisiana State Legislature since Reconstruction after being elected in 1967 to represent an uptown district in New Orleans. Morial became the first black juvenile court judge in Louisiana in 1970. When he was elected to the Louisiana Fourth Circuit Court of Appeals in 1974, he was the first black American to have attained this position, and in 1978 he was sworn in as the first black elected mayor of New Orleans.

On June 13, 1967, President Johnson appointed Thurgood Marshall to the U.S. Supreme Court upon the retirement of Justice Tom C. Clark. Johnson stated that this was "the right thing to do, the right time to do it, the right man and the right place."[13] Marshall was confirmed as an associate justice by a Senate vote of 69–11 on August 31, 1967. Tureaud was extremely proud to see his good friend sworn in as the ninety-sixth person to hold the position and the first African American.

If white judges lauded Tureaud for his expertise and stellar practice in civil rights law, one could only imagine the accolades Tureaud received from the black judiciary, whose members he toiled with as a colleague and mentor. Out of respect for his long and successful legal career, friends and colleagues affectionately called him "Judge." In 1969, at the age of seventy, Tureaud was appointed an ad hoc traffic court judge in New Orleans by Mayor Moon Landrieu. The affectionate title was no longer honorary.

In 1970, another Tureaud protégé, Israel M. Augustine Jr., became the first African American elected as judge in Orleans Criminal District Court. In 1971, Augustine presided over the Black Panther trial, a case that brought him national attention.

Fellow LDF attorney Robert Carter, a 1940 graduate of Howard, was appointed to the bench by President Richard Nixon as a judge of the U.S. District Court for the Southern District of New York in 1972.

22
Race against Time

During the year that the 1964 Civil Rights Act became law, Tureaud, his wife, Lucille, and three of their children, Carole, Jane, and Janet, embarked on their first trip to Europe, which began in London and ended in Paris. While traveling from England to Holland, Tureaud became ill and was advised by the physician who examined him to return home immediately. Having anticipated traveling to Europe for many years, Tureaud decided against cutting his summer trip short and endured the intermittent pain he was experiencing. In addition to touring the capital cities of western Europe, Lucille and Tureaud did not want to miss their once-in-a-lifetime audience with Pope Paul VI, arranged by Archbishop Philip Hannan of New Orleans.

In Rome, the Tureauds were briefed regarding the protocol for the audience and were transported to Castel Gandolfo, the summer residence of the pope. Once the guests were inside the imposing structure and settled in the reception room in their assigned seats, Pope Paul VI appeared and greeted them. An interpreter introduced Tureaud and his wife to His Holiness, highlighting Tureaud's civil rights career, including his service as a Catholic layman. The official Vatican photographer captured the memorable moment when Tureaud and his wife greeted the pope. Lucille noted that "Pope Paul VI was a thin man, with an expressive face and the most compassionate eyes I've ever gazed into; they were large, crystal clear and reassuring. It was a moment that I will never forget."[1]

Meeting the pope and experiencing the pomp, splendor, and power of the church up close in the magnificent setting of the Italian countryside was a singular experience for the Tureauds. Upon returning from Europe, the Tureauds briefly visited their son and daughter-in-law at their home in White Plains, New York. Fay and A.P. Jr. were expecting their first child in January. The New York layover was enjoyable. However, Lucille and the children were concerned about Tureaud's medical problem and were anxious to return home so that he could undergo a comprehensive medical exam.

New Orleans doctors informed the sixty-five-year-old Tureaud that he had prostate cancer. He accepted the news stoically and immediately began treatment. His loved ones rallied around him, and family gatherings became a priority. Visits became more frequent with his children, grandchildren, and close friends.

The Grands, as their grandchildren called Lucille and Tureaud, developed meaningful relationships with each one of them, even though several lived in other states. Tureaud was a conscientious letter writer. Receiving a letter and a $1 bill from Grand became a weekly treat for the members of the "Grandfather's Club." These weekly *billets-doux* were enhanced for birthdays and special holidays, as Grand fattened up the usual weekly allowance. Needless to say, the "Club" accomplished its goal as Tureaud maintained regular contact with his grandchildren.

On Sunday, August 17, 1969, Camille, the strongest hurricane to directly strike the U.S. mainland in the twentieth century, severely damaged the Tureauds' house in Pass Christian, Mississippi. More than two hundred people died as a result of this intense storm, which devastated the Gulf Coast. As Tureaud's health deteriorated, going to the Pass was not high on the list of priorities for Lucille. Sylvia and Elise lived in Maryland, A.P. Jr. was in New York, and Carole was in Nebraska. Jane and Janet remained in New Orleans.

The Tureauds' Thanksgiving of 1969 was celebrated at Split Rock Lodge in the Pocono Mountains of Pennsylvania. This festive gathering included all of the children, their spouses, and seven grandchildren. Louie and Doward Patterson, of Dundalk, Maryland, the in-laws of Tureaud's oldest daughter, Sylvia, also joined the group. Sitting at the long, festively decorated table, laden with small pumpkins, gourds, brightly colored fall foliage, and candles that cast a warm glow on the faces of the members of the Tureaud clan, A.P. Sr. smiled and joked as each course of the oversized meal on Thanksgiving Day was served by the two waiters assigned to their table.

Lucille and Tureaud were delighted to see all of their progeny and their grandchildren together, which was not a common occurrence. Lucille was also pleased that everyone had made a special effort to participate in the holiday weekend. Although his medical intervention was helping to decrease the progression of the deadly disease, a cure was not forthcoming for her husband. As a result of his strong constitution, Tureaud was only beginning to show the outward manifestations of his illness.

Sylvia, the oldest, was there with her husband, Theodore Patterson, an accomplished physician in Maryland, and her three children, Gina, Chavis, and Tina. A graduate of Xavier University of Louisiana, Sylvia had taught elementary school in New Orleans, married, and moved to Dundalk with her husband, Ted, who was one of the first black graduates of the University of Maryland Medical School. Together they confronted the racial biases during the modern civil rights era and evolved as role models for many in their community.

A.P. Jr. and his wife, Fay Darensbourg, a native of Baton Rouge, traveled from White Plains, New York, with their son Alexander Pierre III, named in honor of his grandfather. A.P. Jr., after graduating from Xavier and Columbia universities, married and moved to New York, where he worked as a special education teacher at White Plains High School. Fay, a graduate of Xavier University in New Orleans and Drexel University in Philadelphia, worked as a librarian. A second son, Andrew, would join the family a few years later, and A.P. Jr. became director of special education for the White Plains schools, working in this capacity for twenty-eight years, retiring in 1996.

Carole, a medical technology graduate of Xavier University, received her master's degree in the same field from St. Louis University. After graduation, she traveled to the Philippines to visit a classmate from graduate school. Returning to New Orleans on a freighter that accommodated passengers, she enjoyed many interesting ports of call. Living at home, Carole invited the captain and crew to dinner with her family, and they came. Lucille and Tureaud became friends with the captain and enjoyed his company on several return visits to New Orleans. Eventually they went to visit the captain in the Philippines.

As a young woman, Carole entered a religious order in the Midwest; however, she did not remain in the religious community and subsequently entered the field of medical technology. She would later settle in Omaha, Nebraska, where she worked for the major portion of her career. In her retirement, she would return to her native New Orleans.

Elise, a dietician and the fourth Tureaud to graduate from Xavier University, received a graduate degree from Howard University in Washington, D.C., the beloved alma mater of her parents. Always interested in human rights and politics, she participated in a Crossroads to Africa experience while in undergraduate school. She married Kenwin Nicholls, a Howard University Medical School graduate and a native of Trinidad.

At the time of the celebration at the lodge, Elise and Kenwin had two daughters, Vanessa and Lisa. A third daughter, Kimberly, would be born a few years later. The family lived in New York City and eventually moved to Silver Springs, Maryland. After a divorce, Elise worked as a dietician in programs for senior citizens and eventually became the director of a center in D.C. that provided comprehensive services to seniors. She retired from that position in 2009.

Jane and Janet, the beloved twins, were the youngest members of the family. Despite their identical appearances Jane and Janet were always distinct individuals, each with their own interests and personas.

Janet, a single parent, attended the event at the lodge with her daughter, Ronda. Several years later as the wife of Edward Davis, Janet would give birth to her second daughter, Monique. After being a stay-at-home mom until her children were older, she would work for the City of New Orleans in several capacities before retiring.

As a teenager Jane developed an interest in tennis and received notice in the region as an excellent player. One of Lucille's younger brothers, Burel Dejoie, was an outstanding tennis player. Jane sharpened her tennis techniques by playing with and being coached by Uncle Bo. For a brief time she left New Orleans and moved to Detroit. At the time of the Thanksgiving weekend she was living at home in New Orleans, working and studying. Her most recent employment is at Dillard University in New Orleans.

Skeet shooting, swimming, and walks in the scenic countryside kept everyone entertained that Thanksgiving holiday. Mealtime in the baronial dining room, which was warmed by a roaring fire, was the best part of each day. There were serious conversations, humorous jokes, and silly banter as the Tureaud clan drew closer and realized that in the near future family gatherings would be different.

Family members who had not seen Tureaud for some time were disturbed to see his once full face now gaunt. Substantial weight loss was a telltale sign that his illness was progressing. Yet he complained infrequently. As the holiday visit came to an end, sadness permeated the group, and saying good-bye was hard. Tureaud's positive attitude helped his family members keep their emotions in check. Elise recalled, "As we left, I looked at him longingly, thinking about what lay ahead for him and for us. Leaving Daddy was a very sad time for me, but I was very happy about the family gathering and the good memories we were creating."[2]

Tureaud accepted his illness with the dignity that characterized his entire life. He was his mother's son and reflected her calm demeanor and her devout religious beliefs. As he began to feel the debilitating impact of his illness, Tureaud organized his personal papers and finalized his will.

The ailing attorney realized that his days of having a front-row seat in the civil rights arena were behind him. He told his son that his age and physical condition prohibited his being considered for a significant judgeship, although he enjoyed his brief tenure as ad hoc judge for traffic court. "That's life. If I were younger and in good health, a judgeship would be a welcome transition at this time in my life. I've been lucky and have done most of the things I wanted to do," Tureaud said.[3]

In the fall of 1971, Tureaud's gait was deliberate and slow as the intensity of his pain escalated. "He carried a raw potato in his pocket or under his arm, saying he didn't know if the old wives' tale was true, but it couldn't hurt," said Raphael Cassimere. Tureaud believed that a sliced raw potato placed on the body might alleviate pain. The prevailing belief was that eating potatoes leaches nutrients from one's body and so placing potatoes on boils and other skin conditions would pull toxins from the body. Under his arm, where many of the body's glands are located, would have been the most appropriate place to apply the potato to counteract disease.[4]

Each day, getting to his office was a struggle. Although he had limited energy, Tureaud completed paperwork and returned phone calls. When stronger dosages of medication were prescribed, he reduced his office hours and refused to accept new clients. As his condition continued to deteriorate, he reluctantly announced his retirement.

A.P. Jr., during a visit to New Orleans, accompanied his father to City Hall to secure legal documents. While there, they made an unscheduled visit to the courtroom of his protégé and former law partner Ernest "Dutch" Morial, then the first black juvenile court judge in New Orleans. Despite the differences in their ages, Morial and Tureaud were devoted to each other as colleagues and friends. According to Sybil Morial, Tureaud and her husband enjoyed a close relationship, "like father and son."[5]

Dutch was delighted to see his mentor and A.P. Jr., but saddened by Tureaud's deteriorated physical appearance. As the father and son exited the building, a young white lawyer rushing by called out, "Hey, Tureaud, haven't seen you in some time. Where the hell have you been?" Tureaud said hello, introduced his son, and inquired about a legal matter. Other comments were exchanged, and upon parting the lawyer said, "Man, you shouldn't work so hard. You look like you need to take a break." After walking a short distance in the opposite direction, Tureaud turned to his son and said, "Damn fool, doesn't he know I have cancer?"[6] A.P. Jr. was surprised by his father's reaction to the innocent inquiry. The lawyer was obviously unaware that Tureaud was gravely ill. It had been a long time since A.P. Jr. heard his father react emotionally. It was also the first and only time that he witnessed a negative response from his father regarding his illness.

Although Tureaud was officially retired, his office remained open for clients requesting personal documents and legal papers. Antoine Marcell "Mutt" Trudeau, a partner and colleague, was available to help. Tureaud's devoted sister Victoria, a secretary in his office for many years, opened and closed the office daily, answered the phone, and attended to necessary clerical work.

During 1971, Dr. Joseph Logsdon, professor of history at LSU in New Orleans, began a series of tape-recorded interviews with Tureaud from his sickbed. As the interviews progressed, so did the cancer, and frequently the pain was unbearable. Yet with a clear mind and a determined will, the ailing attorney looked forward to his sessions with Logsdon. Tureaud knew that this would be his final opportunity to record the events of his life and to reflect on his family, his work, and his unique point of view regarding the history of the civil rights struggle in Louisiana.

To ease his extreme discomfort, stronger dosages of medication were administered. At the same time, Logsdon escalated the interview process. Tureaud was always proud of his uncanny ability to remember detailed information, and fortunately during these taped sessions his memory did not fail him.

As the days passed, Tureaud summoned incredible will to complete the interviews. It seemed to members of his family that he was determined to live until he had completed telling the story of his life, in his way and in his words. With Logsdon's insightful questions and Tureaud's detailed responses, the trials and tribulations, as well as the joys and sorrows, of this exceptional human being were recorded for posterity. In addition to his own life story, he and Logsdon chronicled the history of the civil rights movement in Louisiana, from the time of his birth in 1899 to his death in 1972.

Although conserving his energy for the sessions with Joseph Logsdon, Tureaud maintained his passion for collecting and preserving historical documents related to Creole culture and the contributions of black citizens in Louisiana. He cofounded with Charles Rousseve, and was president of, the local Archives of Black History in 1971.[7]

Also in the same year he retired, Tureaud was inducted into the Tulane Law School Order of Coif, a national law school honor society. The Tulane law faculty bestowed this honor in recognition of Tureaud's professional accomplishments. Tulane Law School, the twelfth oldest law school in the country, was founded as a private institution in 1847. It joined the Order of Coif in 1931. The school was desegregated in 1963.

On January 22, 1972, at the age of seventy-two, Tureaud died at his home on Pauger Street. His prolonged illness had been a painful journey. Several months before dying, he told his son that he hoped he would die soon because he had nothing to look forward to but intense pain. He summed up his life by saying that it was a good one and insisted that he always tried to do his best.

Lucille, his primary caretaker, was emotionally and physically drained from the months of constant home care that preceded her husband's death. Several weeks before Tureaud passed away, she informed the doctor that one persistent bedsore, near the base of his spine, was not responding to various interventions. After his death, Lucille was informed that the area in question was not a bedsore. The cancer had penetrated the sacral area, destroying bone and tissue, leaving an opening in that part of his diminished body.

His children, reflective and sorrowful upon hearing of their father's death, were also relieved that his suffering was over. Within twenty-four hours of his passing, all of his children and grandchildren were reunited in New Orleans.

The pastor of Corpus Christi Church, along with Archbishop Hannan and the leaders of the Interdenominational Ministerial Alliance, conferred with Lucille regarding plans for a morning funeral mass. Dan Byrd informed the family that Tureaud's longtime friend and ally Justice Thurgood Marshall of the U.S. Supreme Court would give the closing eulogy. Following the funeral mass on January 29, 1972, Tureaud was buried at St. Louis Cemetery No. 3, on Esplanade Avenue.

At a concelebrated high mass in Corpus Christi Church, Archbishop Hannan, accompanied on the altar by eighteen Catholic priests and Protestant ministers, offered the last rites of the church to A. P. Tureaud. In addition to family and friends, the church was overflowing with black and white citizens, from high-ranking officials to day laborers. Lucille noted that Corrine, one of Tureaud's sisters who had left the family to live as white, was sitting in the rear of the church.

The celebrants reflected on the philosophy of the pioneering civil rights attorney, whose life was devoted to racial and religious equality. Many of these priests and ministers were colleagues of Tureaud, who had worked for many years to develop religious coalitions to combat racial injustice. Thurgood Marshall ended the service with the following words: "He was a great man. In this age of civil rights, we got where we are today by the efforts and dedication of men like A.P. Tureaud, who made himself a leader."[8]

The funeral procession to the graveyard was extensive. Marshall rode in the limousine with Lucille, A.P. Jr., and several other family members, under the watchful eye of the Secret Service. The solemn ride was briefly interrupted by the banter that had become customary between Marshall, the prankster, and businesslike Lucille. Marshall's tongue-in-cheek request for a short detour to a local pharmacy to get a medication for his glaucoma was tersely rejected by Lucille, who said, "First we must take care of burying Tureaud, then we will take care of your eyes."

Once inside St. Louis Cemetery, the mourners, lead by a priest, recited brief prayers. The casket was placed inside the marble and stone crypt that Tureaud had purchased several years earlier. After the interment, the family members gathered at home to comfort each other and to enjoy the support of friends and relatives. Leah Chase, owner of Dooky Chase's Restaurant, prepared food for the gathering.

Notes

1. Underestimated and Misperceived

1. The term "colored" has been used to describe Americans of black or African ancestry. Throughout American history, the acceptable racial terms for persons of black or African ancestry have been "Negro," "colored," "black," "Afro-American," and "African American." In this book, these terms will be used interchangeably and with regard to the appropriateness of the time period in which the term was used. Tureaud was also a Creole, referencing a particular group of Americans of mixed heritage that will be discussed extensively in chapter 2. It is important to note that Tureaud lived through periods of time when "Negro," "colored," and "black" were acceptable terms. He preferred the use of "Negro" and "colored," not "black."

2. Of Creole Heritage

1. The term "Creole" has been defined in many ways and may be interpreted differently; however, several scholars agree that the word is derived from the Portuguese word *crioulo*, which means a slave of African ancestry born in the Americas, or the New World. See Arnold R. Hirsch and Joseph Logsdon, eds., *Creole New Orleans: Race and Americanization* (Baton Rouge: Louisiana State University Press, 1990), 60. *Webster's New World Dictionary of American English* (Hoboken, NJ: John Wiley and Sons, 1998), 347, defines a Creole as a person of French, Spanish, or Negro descent born in the Americas. In *The Free People of Color of New Orleans: An Introduction* (New Orleans: Margaret Media, 1994), 60, Mary Gehman notes: "The term Creole is a linguistic anomaly whose true meaning continues to be debated today. Most scholars agree that it comes from the Spanish or Portuguese criollo or crioulo meaning created in America, in the New World, as opposed to being created or born in Europe." In Adam Fairclough, *Race and Democracy: The Civil Rights Struggle in Louisiana, 1915–1972* (Athens: University of Georgia Press, 1995), 2, "Afro-Creole," "Creole of color," and "Black Creole" are synonymous terms that identify a multiracial person of color born in the New World. "White Creole" refers to a child of European parents born in the New World. After the Civil War, whites of French and Spanish ancestry attempted to claim exclusive use of the term "Creole"; however, people of color identified themselves as Creoles and used the designation to set themselves apart from the other cultures in the region. The Afro-Creole cul-

266 Notes to Pages 4–13

ture evolved in Louisiana as the French and Spanish settlers mated with African slave women, producing mulatto children. Native Americans, indigenous to the region, also contributed to this process of multiracial blending, as runaway slaves frequently found refuge among local tribes.

2. The term "mulatto" is used for a person with Caucasian and African ancestries.

3. The Black Code in Louisiana was modeled after the original code of King Louis XIV, which was enacted for slaves in the French islands.

4. Charles E. O'Neill, foreword to *Our People and Our History: Fifty Creole Portraits,* by Rodolphe Lucien Desdunes, trans. and ed. Sister Dorothea Olga McCants (1973; Baton Rouge: Louisiana State University Press, 2001), x.

5. Money from the John McDonogh estate significantly aided the New Orleans public school system. McDonogh, a wealthy white merchant, planter, and real estate speculator, died in 1850 and left most of his estate to the cities of New Orleans and Baltimore for education purposes. New Orleans school administrators established the first McDonogh School for white children during the antebellum period. McDonogh Schools, grades two through six, were opened during Reconstruction, and both Negro and white students attended these schools.

6. Harnett T. Kane, *Plantation Parade: The Grand Manner in Louisiana* (New York: Bonanza Books, 1945), 67–71.

7. Emilie Ganet-Leumas, researcher, St. James Clerk of Courts, Conveyance Book 20, 295–96. "Aurora Trudeau, widow of George Mather of the parish of St. James, La., for and in consideration of the sum of Twelve Hundred Dollars, to be paid in the lawful money of the United States, does by this instrument transfer and alienate all her rights, title, and interests in the said slave Josephine, a colored girl eighteen years and her child Adolphe, being her separate property; to Augustin Tureaud."

8. In Louisiana, the Act of Manumission, with its prescribed procedures, was recorded and filed in the appropriate parish office, usually the courthouse or city hall. A register of free colored persons entitled to remain in the state was kept in the New Orleans mayor's office.

9. Gehman, *Free People of Color,* 87.

10. St. James Parish Clerk of Courts, Conveyance Record Book 63, 487–88, folio 4745. In 1925, many years after his death, Adolphe's heirs sold his share of the land. Louis Tureaud, Alex's father, was not a legitimate heir and therefore was not a beneficiary of Adolphe's property.

11. A $1 rental receipt for a "wall box, good for one year," issued in 1899 from the St. Vincent De Paul Cemetery, later found among family papers, is believed to be for the crypt of this child, whose name is not recorded on census documents or in family papers.

12. Alex was named for his paternal uncle James Alexander Slater and his paternal grandmother, Caroline Pierre. Alex was baptized on April 2, 1899, in St. Augustine Church by the assistant pastor, Father L. Henrionnet. He was sponsored by his maternal aunt Marie Helena Dejan and his paternal uncle James Alexander Slater, who became his *marraine* and *parraine,* or godmother and godfather. Godparents are important religious mentors in the lives of Creoles, often providing emotional and financial support to their godchildren.

13. Tureaud Tape A. Joseph Logsdon, a former University of New Orleans history professor, taped interviews with A. P. Tureaud between 1968 and 1971. After Logsdon's death, the audiotapes were donated by the Logsdon family to Rachel L. Emanuel and A. P. Tureaud Jr. for use in writing this biography. Privately held by the authors, they are cited here in the notes as labeled on the cassette tapes: Tureaud Tape A, Tureaud Tape B, and so on. A transcription is available at Earl K. Long Library, University of New Orleans. (See n. 5 of chap. 3 notes.)

3. Educating Alex

1. Gehman, *Free People of Color*, 25.

2. René J. Le Gardeur, *The First New Orleans Theatre, 1792–1803* (New Orleans: Leeward Books, 1963), 10–14.

3. Desdunes, *Our People and Our History*, 92.

4. A. E. Perkins, ed., *Who's Who in Colored Louisiana* (Baton Rouge: Douglas Loan Co., 1930), 66. See also *Dictionary of American Biography*, s.v. Lafon, Thomy.

5. A. P. Tureaud Interview, Earl K. Long Library, University of New Orleans, container list 164-1, photocopy of typescript of interview of A. P. Tureaud by Dr. Joseph Logsdon (hereafter cited as Logsdon, "Tureaud"), 63.

4. Southern Exodus

1. Editorial, *Chicago Defender*, July 22, 1916.

2. Edgar A. Toppin, *The Black American in United States History* (Boston: Allyn and Bacon, 1973), 198–99.

3. Barbara A. Worthy, "The Travail and Triumph of a Southern Black Civil Rights Lawyer: The Legal Career of Alexander Pierre Tureaud, 1899–1972" (Ph.D. diss., Tulane University, 1984), 27.

5. Preparing for a Legal Career

1. Tureaud Tape B.

2. Ibid.

3. Ibid.

4. Clifford Muse (archivist, Moorland Spingarn Research Center, Howard University), telephone conversation with A. P. Tureaud Jr., April 1, 2005.

5. Rayvon Fouché, *Black Inventors in the Age of Segregation: Granville T. Woods, Lewis H. Latimer, and Shelby J. Davidson* (Baltimore: Johns Hopkins University Press, 2003), 138.

6. Ibid., 140.

7. Ibid., 142.

8. In a written complaint to William H. Lewis, Davidson wrote: "If you will be able to do some good in this matter, your help will not be confined alone to me and mine, but there are others who will feel the benefits arising from this effort. I wish it understood that I do not contend that any place in government gives one a title thereto, but it has and is the practice where one has labored and wrought to let them have the fruit of their labors and not by displacement . . . to one who had done nothing to deserve it." Shelby J. Davidson, personal communication to Honorable William H. Lewis, U.S. assistant attorney general, 6, Shelby J. Davidson Collection, Moorland-Spingarn Manuscript Collection, Howard University.

9. Fouché, *Black Inventors*, 212.

10. Ibid., 145.

11. Ibid., 146.

12. Jack Greenberg, *Crusaders in the Courts: How a Dedicated Band of Lawyers Fought for the Civil Rights Revolution* (New York: Basic Books, 1994), 14.

13. "The Rise and Fall of Jim Crow," Educational Broadcasting Corp., www.pbs.org/wnet /jimcrow stories_events_niagara.html (accessed April 27, 2010).

14. Tureaud Tape B.

15. "The Black Renaissance in Washington, D.C., 1920–1930s," www.dclibrary.org/blkren/ (last updated June 20, 2003).

16. Tureaud Tape E.

17. Ibid.

18. The Howard Theatre opened its doors on August 22, 1910, with a seating capacity of 1,200 and displaying an Italian Renaissance façade and Spanish baroque architecture. W. H. Smith was the first manager of the Howard Theatre. The Howard closed its doors in 1929, at the onset of the Great Depression. Dunbar Theatre opened in 1920 and closed in 1960.

19. Tureaud Tape D.

20. Ibid.

21. Dennis S. Nordin, *The New Deal's Black Congressman: A Life of Arthur Wergs Mitchell* (Columbia: University of Missouri Press, 1997), ix.

22. Tureaud Tape B.

23. Ibid.

24. Nordin, *New Deal's Black Congressman*, x.

25. Tureaud Tape B.

26. Liva Baker, *The Second Battle of New Orleans: The Hundred-Year Struggle to Integrate the Schools* (New York: HarperCollins, 1996), 50.

27. Tureaud Tape B.

28. Ibid.

29. Ibid.

30. J. Clay Smith, *Emancipation: The Making of the Black Lawyer, 1844–1944* (Philadelphia: University of Pennsylvania Press, 1993), 47.

31. Tureaud Tape B.

32. Ibid.

33. Hart v. State (Md. 1905), 60 A. 457, 463 (1905).

34. Tureaud Tape B.

35. Ibid.

36. Ibid.

37. Ibid.

38. Ibid.

39. Ibid.

40. Ibid.

41. www.medicolegal.tripod.com/blackstone.htm (accessed May 27, 2010).

42. Tureaud Tape B.

43. The statue was intended to be a gift from the American Bar Association to the English Bar Association, but after it was cast, it was found to be too big to fit in the Hall of Courts in London. This casting was donated to the U.S. government, and a smaller copy was made for the English.

44. Tureaud Tape B.

45. Genna Rae McNeil, *Groundwork: Charles Hamilton Houston and the Struggle for Civil Rights* (Philadelphia: University of Pennsylvania Press, 1983), 22.

46. "Negro Gets $5,000 Office: President Appoints Walter L. Cohen Customs Controller [sic] at New Orleans," *New York Times*, November 5, 1922.

47. Stafford Tureaud (nephew of A. P. Tureaud Sr.), interview by Rachel L. Emanuel, May 1993.

6. Return to New Orleans

1. Quotation from Louisiana Legislature, Act 81, Sec. 1 (1870).

2. Smith, *Emancipation*, 282.

3. Tureaud Tape B.

4. "Negro Gets $5,000 Office" (see n. 41 of chap. 5 notes).

5. John M. Barry, *Rising Tide: The Great Mississippi Flood of 1927* (New York: Simon and Schuster, 1997), 234, 244, 345, 385.

6. Stafford Tureaud interview.

7. Donald E. DeVore and Joseph Logsdon, *Crescent City Schools: Public Education in New Orleans, 1841–1991* (Lafayette: University of Louisiana at Lafayette, 1991), 192.

8. Ibid., 184.

9. Lee Sartain, "We Are but Americans: Miss Georgia M. Johnson and the National Association for the Advancement of Colored People in Alexandria, Louisiana, 1941–1946" (paper presented at the annual conference of the British Association for American Studies (BAAS), Manchester, England, April 2004), 32. This paper is now a journal article: "We Are but Americans: Miss Georgia M. Johnson and the National Association for the Advancement of Colored People in Alexandria, Louisiana, 1941–1946," *North Louisiana History* 25 (Spring–Summer 2004): 108–34.

10. A. P. Tureaud Sr., interview by Robert Wright, "Howard University Civil Rights Documentation Project," 1969, Moorland-Spingarn Research Center, Howard University, Washington, D.C. (hereafter cited as Wright, 1969).

11. Rachel L. Emanuel and Denise Barkis-Richter, *Journey for Justice: The A. P. Tureaud Story*, DVD, directed by Rachel L. Emanuel, Baton Rouge: A. P. Tureaud Chapter of the LSU Alumni Association/Louisiana Endowment for the Humanities (LEH), 1996; Lolis Elie (New Orleans attorney), interview by Rachel L. Emanuel, March 1993.

12. Judge Constance Baker Motley (U.S. District Court for the Southern District of New York), interview by Rachel L. Emanuel, April 1993; Emanuel and Barkis-Richter, *Journey for Justice*.

13. A. P. Tureaud Sr., correspondence with New Orleans Branch NAACP, March 26, 1929, box 8, folder 1, Tureaud Papers, Amistad Research Center, Tulane University, New Orleans (hereafter cited as Tureaud Papers, ARC).

14. A. P. Tureaud, personal correspondence with Walter W. White, October 2, 1931, box 3, folder 27, Tureaud Papers, ARC.

15. Tureaud Tape A.

16. A. P. Tureaud, personal correspondence with Robert Bagnell, October 24, 1931, box 8, folder 2, Tureaud Papers, ARC.

17. Hirsch and Logsdon, *Creole New Orleans*, 270.

7. Meeting Lucille

1. Historically, black and white residents living in uptown New Orleans were influenced by the English who developed that part of the city after the United States purchased Louisiana in 1803.

Downtown residents, including those living in the Vieux Carré, Faubourg Tremé, Faubourg Marigny, and the Seventh Ward, retained the French and Spanish cultures and mores predominant in
Louisiana prior to the United States' annexation of the territory.

2. Fairclough, *Race and Democracy,* 14.

3. Emanuel and Barkis-Richter, *Journey for Justice.*

4. Frank Dow, correspondence with John J. Kennedy, November 9, 1936, box 20, folder 18, Tureaud Papers, ARC.

5. A. P. Tureaud Sr., correspondence with John J. Kennedy, November 17, 1936, box 20, folder
18, Tureaud Papers, ARC.

6. Cyprian Davis, *The History of Black Catholics in the United States* (New York: Crossroad,
1990), 236–37; Fairclough, *Race and Democracy,* 14.

7. W. Charles Keyes Jr., executive director, Knights of Peter Claver, personal communication to
Rachel L. Emanuel, February 13, 2003, in possession of the author.

8. Knights of Peter Claver Web site, www.kofpc.org (last viewed May 24, 2010).

9. Thurgood Marshall, correspondence with Thomas R. Lee Jr., national secretary, National
Council Knights of Peter Claver, October 1957. "Thank you for $300 contribution from National
Council Knights of Peter Claver and continued support." Box 4, folder 38, Tureaud Papers, ARC.

10. A. P. Tureaud Jr., interview with Rachel L. Emanuel, April 1993.

11. A. P. Tureaud Sr., commencement address to graduates of Xavier Preparatory School, New
Orleans, 1956 (on file with the authors).

8. Growing Community Involvement

1. DeVore and Logsdon, *Crescent City Schools,* 207, 209.

2. Ibid., 212–15 n. 56; Alonzo G. Grace, "Tomorrow's Citizens: A Study and Program for the
Improvement of the New Orleans Public Schools," New Orleans, 1939, 28, 32. Amistad Research
Center at Tulane University holds Monograph 4, pt. 3, General Program for Colored Children.

3. The national PTA organization was founded in 1897 in Washington, D.C., as the National
Congress of Mothers by Alice McLellan Birney and Phoebe Apperson Hearst. The national PTA
movement was created to better the lives of children.

4. Tureaud Tape A.

5. Ibid.

6. Ibid.

7. Ibid.

8. Hirsch and Logsdon, *Creole New Orleans,* 265.

9. Tureaud Tape H.

10. Ibid.

11. Wright, 1969.

12. Fairclough, *Race and Democracy,* 64.

13. Ibid., 56.

14. John Rousseau (former New Orleans newspaper reporter), interview by Rachel L. Emanuel,
May 1993.

15. Hirsch and Logsdon, *Creole New Orleans,* 272.

16. Tureaud Tape E.

17. Fairclough, *Race and Democracy*, 37; Tureaud Tape E.

18. A. P. Tureaud, correspondence with George W. Johnson, March 14, 1941, box 8, folder 10, Tureaud Papers, ARC.

19. Fairclough, *Race and Democracy*, 59; *Louisiana Weekly*, April 20, 27, and May 11, 1940.

20. Rousseau interview.

21. Tureaud Tape 1/BB.

22. Wright, 1969.

23. Ibid.

24. Sybil Morial, interview by Rachel L. Emanuel, May 1993.

25. Raphael Cassimere (charter member of NAACP Youth Council, New Orleans), interview by Sheila Cooper, February 1993.

9. The War Years

1. A. P. Tureaud Sr., "Our Freedom," undated speech (on file with the authors).

2. *New Orleans Sepia Socialite*, November 7, 1942, 6.

3. Ibid., 8.

4. Tureaud Tape A.

5. Ibid.

6. *New Orleans Sepia Socialite*, November 7, 1942, 6.

7. *U.S. Supreme Court Adams v. U.S.*, 319 U.S. 312 (1943); *Adams et al. v. United States et al.*, No. 889.

8. Sartain, "We Are but Americans"; Georgia Johnson, correspondence with Ella Baker, director of NAACP branches, April 30, 1945, group 1, box B-60, 2:0001, Papers of the NAACP, Manuscript Division, Library of Congress, Washington, D.C. (hereafter cited as Papers of the NAACP).

9. Georgia Johnson, correspondence with Ella Baker, director of NAACP branches, March 25, 1946, group 1, box B-60, 2:0001, Papers of the NAACP. The Japanese attack on Pearl Harbor had taken place a month previously, and in the spirit of wartime unity and patriotism, the federal government suppressed and censored the full story of the Alexandria riot. So successfully was it censored that in most historical works that mention the event, only a line or paragraph of detail was devoted to it. See Fairclough, *Race and Democracy*, 78, and Harvard Sitkoff, "Racial Militancy and Interracial Violence in the Second World War," *Journal of American History* 58 (1971): 667–69.

10. Fairclough, *Race and Democracy*, 77.

11. A. P. Tureaud Sr., FBI Report, file no. 100-428855 (hereafter cited as Tureaud FBI Report); files were obtained in 1995 by Rachel L. Emanuel through the Freedom of Information Act. Most of the information in the forty-page document was blacked out.

12. Lee Finkle, "The Conservative Aims of Militant Rhetoric: Black Protest during World War II," *Journal of American History* 60 (1974): 694, 699, 705; Jerry Purvis Sanson, *Louisiana during World War II: Politics and Society, 1939–1945* (Baton Rouge: Louisiana State University Press, 1999), 246, 265.

13. Tureaud FBI Report, entry June 4, 1958.

14. Julia Dejoie (former secretary of A. P. Tureaud Sr.), interview with Rachel L. Emanuel, April 2001.

15. Formed in 1919 in the United States, the Progressive Educational Association evolved from

a broad progressive concept advocated by Columbia University philosopher John Dewey. The group promoted ideas of child-centered learning, racial understanding, democracy, citizenship, and social justice. This approach was conceived in response to the contemporary school curriculum, which was seen to be run on the basis of efficiency management and rote memorization of information. It was believed that a progressive education would instill in children human values and good moral habits that would equip them for a rapidly changing industrial society. However, so radical did these views seem to the establishment, especially the avocation of national economic planning, that they were attacked for being wholly collectivist and undermining beliefs in private enterprise.

16. A. P. Tureaud FBI Report, Memorandum File No. NY 100-7629 SUB C, p. 2.

17. Ibid.

10. NAACP Lawyer

1. Fairclough, *Race and Democracy*, 61–62; Adam Fairclough, "'Being in the Field of Education and Also a Negro . . . Seems . . . Tragic': Black Teachers in the Jim Crow South," *Journal of American History* 87 (2000): 13; Merline Pitre, *In Struggle against Jim Crow: Lula B. White and the NAACP, 1900–1957* (College Station: Texas A&M University Press, 1999), 57; Darlene Clark Hine, "Black Professionals and Race Consciousness: Origins of the Civil Rights Movement, 1890–1950," *Journal of American History* 89 (2003): 1279–80; Monica A. White, "Paradise Lost? Teachers' Perspectives on the Use of Cultural Capital in the Segregated Schools of New Orleans, Louisiana," *Journal of African American History* 87 (Spring 2002): 270, 279–80.

2. Worthy, "Travail and Triumph of a Southern Black Civil Rights Lawyer," 42.

3. Thurgood Marshall, correspondence with A. P. Tureaud, December 15, 1941, box 49, folder 22, Tureaud Papers, ARC.

4. *Louisiana Weekly,* February 4, 1942.

5. A. P. Tureaud, correspondence with Thurgood Marshall, February 25, 1942, box 49, folder 23, Tureaud Papers, ARC; A. P. Tureaud to Thurgood Marshall, April 10, 1942, box 49, folder 23, Tureaud Papers, ARC.

6. A. P. Tureaud, personal communication, July 29, 1942, Papers of the NAACP.

7. J. Clay Smith, interview by Rachel L. Emanuel, April 1993; Emanuel and Barkis-Richter, *Journey for Justice.*

8. Thurgood Marshall, personal communication, July 30, 1942, Papers of the NAACP.

9. Raphael Cassimere Jr., "Equalizing Teachers' Pay in Louisiana," *Integrated Education* 15 (July/August 1977): 3–8.

10. A. P. Tureaud, correspondence with Thurgood Marshall, October 2, 1942, box 49, folder 23, Tureaud Papers, ARC.

11. Thurgood Marshall, correspondence with Donald Jones, September 19, 1942, box 49, folder 23, Tureaud Papers, ARC.

12. Juan Williams, *Thurgood Marshall: American Revolutionary* (New York: Three Rivers Press, 1998), 99.

13. A. P. Tureaud, correspondence with Donald Jones, September 19, 1942, box 49, folder 23 Tureaud Papers, ARC.

14. Editorials, *New Orleans Sepia Socialite,* August 29 and September 5, 1942.

15. Worthy, "Travail and Triumph of a Southern Black Civil Rights Lawyer," 48.

16. Ibid.; A. P. Tureaud, correspondence with J. Bernard Cookes, October 27, 1942, box 49, folder 23, Tureaud Papers, ARC.

17. Tureaud's commencement address, Xavier Preparatory School, 1956, on file with the authors.

18. Emanuel and Barkis-Richter, *Journey for Justice.*

19. Louis Berry, correspondence with A. P. Tureaud, November 14, 1946, box 19, folder 15, Tureaud Papers, ARC; Minutes of NAACP Branch Activities, Alexandria, April 28, 1941, box 12, folder 9, Tureaud Papers, ARC; Thurgood Marshall, memorandum to New York office, September 11, 1945, box 23, folder 27, Tureaud Papers, ARC

20. Fairclough, *Race and Democracy,* 106.

21. A. P. Tureaud, correspondence with Thurgood Marshall, September 29, 1944, box 56, folder 7, Tureaud Papers, ARC; A. P. Tureaud, correspondence with Eula Mae Lee, August 24, 1945; Eula Mae Lee, correspondence with A. P. Tureaud, October 10, 1946; A. P. Tureaud, correspondence with Thurgood Marshall, July 30, 1948; A. P. Tureaud, correspondence with Eula Mae Lee Brown, July 30, 1948, box 37, folder 22, Tureaud Papers, ARC.

22. Motley interview.

23. Jack Greenberg, interview by Rachel L. Emanuel, April 1993.

24. Wright, 1969.

25. Tureaud Tape E.

26. *Louisiana Weekly,* April 13, 1946.

27. Wright, 1969.

28. A copy of the telegram is on file with the authors.

29. Rousseau interview.

30. Ibid.; Emanuel and Barkis-Richter, *Journey for Justice.*

31. Fairclough, *Race and Democracy,* 116.

32. Ibid., 113–18. Fairclough provides the account of the trial based on *Louisiana Weekly,* March 1, 1946; *PM,* February 25, 1946; *Shreveport Times,* February 26, 27, 28, March 1, 2, 1946; *Shreveport Journal,* February 24, March 1, 1946; and Martha Wilson, correspondence with Roy Wilkins, February 25, 1946, in Daniel E. Byrd, "Report of Investigation of Lynching of John C. Jones," pt. 7, series A, folder 2-A-398, Papers of the NAACP.

33. Gilbert King, *The Execution of Willie Francis: Race, Murder, and the Search for Justice in the American South* (New York: Basic Books, 2008), 118.

34. Rousseau interview.

35. John P. Nelson, interview by Rachel L. Emanuel, May 1993. A decorated war veteran and a devout Catholic, Jack Nelson was the rare white lawyer who embraced civil rights at the time. He was influenced by Father Louis J. Twomey, a Jesuit priest and president of Loyola University.

36. A. P. Tureaud Jr. interview, April 1993.

37. Rousseau interview.

11. Law and Fatherhood

1. Jane Tureaud (daughter of A. P. Tureaud Sr.), interview by Rachel L. Emanuel, November 1993.

2. Ibid.

3. Carole Tureaud (daughter of A. P. Tureaud Sr.), interview by Rachel L. Emanuel, November 1993.

4. A. P. Tureaud Jr., interview by Rachel L. Emanuel, June 2005.

5. Sylvia Tureaud Patterson (daughter of A. P. Tureaud Sr.), interview by Rachel L. Emanuel, November 1993.

6. A. P. Tureaud Jr. interview, June 2005.

7. Jane Tureaud interview.

8. Ibid.

9. A. P. Tureaud Jr. interview, April 1993.

10. Fairclough, *Race and Democracy,* 49.

11. Ibid.

12. Tureaud Tape E.

12. "Separate but Equal" Strengthened in the Face of Desegregation

1. Williams, *Thurgood Marshall,* 174–75.

2. Mark V. Tushnet, *Making Civil Rights Law: Thurgood Marshall and the Supreme Court, 1936–1961* (Oxford: Oxford University Press, 1994), 123–25.

3. Louis Berry, interview by Rachel L. Emanuel, March 1993.

4. *Louisiana ex rel. Viola M. Johnson v. Board of Supervisors, Louisiana State University,* No. 25414, 19th JDC, Parish of East Baton Rouge (1946).

5. Evelyn Wilson, *Laws, Customs and Rights: Charles Hatfield and His Family—A Louisiana History* (Westminster, MD: Willow Bend Books, 2004), 129.

6. Judge Robert Carter (U.S. District Court for the Southern District of New York), interview by Rachel L. Emanuel, April 1993.

7. Walter Lynwood Fleming, *Louisiana State University, 1860–1896* (Baton Rouge: Louisiana State University Press, 1936), 153.

8. Wilson, *Laws, Customs and Rights,* 131.

9. Ibid.

10. Editorial, *The Reveille,* December 17, 1946.

11. *State of Louisiana, ex rel. Charles J. Hatfield, Relator v. Board of Supervisors of Louisiana State University and Agricultural and Mechanical College, et al.,* 19th JDC, East Baton Rouge Parish (1946).

12. Louisiana Legislature (1880), Act 87, amended by Louisiana Legislature (1888), Act 90, 2459.

13. Wright, 1969.

14. "New NAACP Prexy Tureaud Installed," *Louisiana Weekly,* January 14, 1950, 1.

15. Ibid.

16. Editorial, "We Salute Honored Citizens," *Louisiana Weekly,* January 21, 1950, 14.

17. "Nine Apply for Admission to LSU—Board to Act on Negro Admission at August Meeting," *Louisiana Weekly,* July 15, 1950, 1.

18. Clarence A. Laws, "Citizens Comment on Supreme Court Ruling," *Louisiana Weekly,* June 17, 1950.

19. *Henderson v. United States Interstate Commerce Commission and Southern Railway Co.,* 339 U.S. 816 (1950). Elmer W. Henderson, a black man, filed a complaint against the Interstate Commerce Commission (ICC). The Court held that the plaintiff had been denied equal access in violation of the Interstate Commerce Act. After finding that the plaintiff had been discriminated against by the railway's failure to furnish him with service equal to that provided to white passengers, the Court dismissed the complaint on the finding that the situation had been corrected by the amendment of an ICC regulation.

20. Laws, "Citizens Comment on Supreme Court Ruling."

21. Ibid.

22. Nine applied for admission to LSU on July 12, 1950, and subsequently three more students applied. The applicants were Nephus Jefferson, Dan Columbus Simon, Willie Cleveland Patterson, Charles Edward Coney, Joseph H. Miller Jr., Roy Samuel Wilson, Lloyd E. Milburn, Lawrence Alvin Smith Jr., James Leo Perkins, and also Edison George Hogan, Harry A. Wilson, and Anderson Williams.

23. "LSU Board Says 'No' to Negro Applicants; Vote to Deny Admission to 12," *Louisiana Weekly,* August 5, 1950, 1; editorial, "LSU Board Rejects Responsibility," *Louisiana Weekly,* August 5, 1950, 10.

24. Trial details from "LSU Suit Taken under Advisement," October 7, 1950 (quotation); "Court Orders LSU to Admit Negro School Plans Appeal to U.S. Supreme Court," October 14, 1950, all in *Louisiana Weekly.*

25. Fairclough, *Race and Democracy,* 218.

26. Raymond Floyd (retired Southern University professor), interview by Rachel L. Emanuel, March 1998.

27. Greenberg interview.

28. Motley interview.

29. "Court Orders LSU to Admit Negro—School Plans Appeal to U.S. Supreme Court," *Louisiana Weekly,* October 14, 1950.

30. "Wilson Meets the Press at LSU," *Louisiana Weekly,* November 11, 1950, 1.

31. "Tureaud Levels Blasts at Roy Wilson 'Critics,'" *Louisiana Weekly,* January 27, 1951, 1.

32. Thurgood Marshall, correspondence with A. P. Tureaud, January 12, 1951, box 10, Tureaud Papers, ARC.

33. Editorial, "Fumbling Around in the Dark," *Louisiana Weekly,* October 20, 1951, 10.

34. "Collins, Morial Win Moot Court Trials at LSU," *Louisiana Weekly,* May 3, 1952.

35. Motley interview.

36. A. P. Tureaud Jr. interview, April 1993.

37. Ibid.

38. Ibid.

39. Worthy, "Travail and Triumph of a Southern Black Civil Rights Lawyer," 85.

40. Greenberg interview.

41. "Leander H. Perez, LSU Counsel Causes Tirade," *Louisiana Weekly,* September 19, 1953, 1.

42. Ibid.

43. A. P. Tureaud Jr. interview, April 1993.

44. Ibid.

45. Ibid.

46. Ibid.

47. Ibid.

48. Ibid.

49. Ibid.

50. Charlie Roberts, interview by Rachel L. Emanuel, November 1989.

51. A. P. Tureaud Jr. interview, April 1993.

52. Ibid.

53. Ibid.

54. Ibid.

55. Ibid.

56. Ibid.

57. A. P. Tureaud speech, Charter Day, Howard University, March 2, 1954, in possession of Emanuel and the Tureaud family; Alexander Pope, *An Essay on Man,* 4 vols. (London, 1733–34), E-10 1503 Fisher Rare Book Library, Toronto. Tureaud's reference no doubt was taken from the judge's opinion in *Besig v. United States,* 208F.2d142 (9th Cir. 1953): "Appellant thinks our opinion is 'unclear as to whether the test of obscenity is that it *repels* or that it *seduces.*' We observe no contradiction in any of these expressions. They aptly describe the quality of language, which the word 'obscene' is meant to suggest. Of course, language can be so nasty as to repel and of course to seduce as well. Appellant's argument tempts us to quote Pope's 5 quatrain about the Monster Vice which, when too prevalent, is embraced."

13. Desegregation of Primary and Secondary Schools

1. Tureaud Tape 2/AA.

2. DeVore and Logsdon, *Crescent City Schools,* 221.

3. Ibid., 224.

4. Ibid.

5. Ibid., 225.

6. Baker, *Second Battle of New Orleans,* 152.

7. Fairclough, *Race and Democracy,* 108.

8. DeVore and Logsdon, *Crescent City Schools,* 221.

9. Tureaud Tape C.

10. Ibid.

11. Ibid.

12. *Bush v. Orleans Parish School Board,* 188 F.Supp. 916 (E.D. La., 1960). A. P. Tureaud first filed *Rosana Aubert v. Orleans Parish School Board,* on May 30, 1948. It was later combined with the *Bush* case, until Aubert dropped out of the case.

13. "NAACP Raps School Board for Clark Platoon System Plan," *Louisiana Weekly,* August 26, 1950, 1.

14. Tureaud Tape F.

15. Fairclough, *Race and Democracy,* 156; A. P. Tureaud, correspondence with E. A. Johnson, July 15, 1950, box 10, folder 8,Tureaud Papers, ARC.

16. Fairclough, *Race and Democracy,* 156; Dan Byrd, correspondence with Thurgood Marshall, September 12, 1951, box 1, folder 2, Dan Byrd Papers, Amistad Research Center, Tulane University, Baton Rouge.

17. O. Perry Walker to A. P. Tureaud, November 28, 1951, box 43, folder 21, Tureaud Papers, ARC.

18. Tureaud Tape F.

19. Ibid.

20. *Bush v. Orleans Parish School Board,* 188 F.Supp. 916 (E.D. La., 1960).

21. Edward W. Knappman, ed., *Great American Trials* (Detroit: Visible Ink, 1994), 467.

22. Ibid.

23. Benjamin Munn Ziegler, ed., *Desegregation and the Supreme Court* (Boston: Heath and Co., 1958), 78.

24. *Brown v. Board of Education,* 347 U.S. 483 (1954). This case was argued on December 9, 1952, reargued on December 8, 1953, and decided on May 17, 1954.

25. Tureaud Tape F.

26. Ibid.

27. *The Bison* (Howard University yearbook), 1922, 104.

14. The Politician

1. Wright, 1969.

2. Earl Long Campaign for Governor stump speech, WDSU-TV, 1960, Louisiana State Archives, Baton Rouge.

3. The Louisiana Notary Commission lists Tureaud as being licensed from January 1, 1939, to December 31, 1944, and again from October 1, 1948, to December 31, 1970.

4. Tureaud Tape H.

5. Ibid.

6. Fairclough, *Race and Democracy,* 44-45.

7. Tureaud Tape E.

8. Ibid.

9. Frederick J. Dumas, "The Black and Tan Faction of the Republican Party in Louisiana, 1908 to 1936" (MA thesis, Xavier University, 1945), 14.

10. Tureaud Tape E.

11. Ibid.

12. A. P. Tureaud, correspondence with Dr. Channing Tobias, October 4, 1944, box 1, folder 12, Tureaud Papers, ARC.

13. Fairclough, *Race and Democracy,* 135.

14. "GOP Considers 2 Negroes for Top Dixie Posts," *Jet,* September 16, 1954, 8.

15. Tureaud Tape H.

16. Ibid.

17. Ibid.

18. Ibid.

19. Fairclough, *Race and Democracy,* 181.

20. Tureaud Tape H.

21. Ibid.

22. Tureaud Tape BB.

23. Edward F. Haas, *DeLesseps S. Morrison and the Image of Reform: New Orleans Politics, 1946–1961* (Baton Rouge: Louisiana State University Press, 1974), 77-78.

24. Permindex was a corporate front, headed by Major Louis M. Bloomfield of Canada. Clay Shaw operated a division of Permindex in New Orleans at the International Trade Mart.

25. Tureaud Tape H.

26. Fairclough, *Race and Democracy,* 182.

27. Hirsch and Logsdon, *Creole New Orleans,* 279.

28. Transcript, Hale Boggs Oral History Interview, March 13, 1969, by T. H. Baker, Lyndon Baines Johnson Library, Austin, Texas; online: www.lbjlib.utexas.edu/johnson/archives . . ./oral-history . . ./BoggsH/boggs-h1. pdf (accessed April 3, 2005). Transcript, Bess Abell Oral History Interview I, May 28, 1969, by T. H. Baker, 27, Lyndon Baines Johnson Library, Austin, Texas; online: www.lbjlib.utexas.edu/johnson/archives.hom/oralhistory.hom/AbellB/Abell01.pdf (accessed January 14, 2002).

29. OPPVL radio broadcast script, box 19, folder 8, Tureaud Papers, ARC.

30. Tureaud Tape BB.

31. A. P. Tureaud Jr. interview, April 1993.

32. Campaign flyer, box 19, folder 9, Tureaud Papers, ARC.

33. Tureaud Tape H.

34. Ibid.

35. Tureaud Tape C.

15. Desegregation Battles after *Brown*

1. After the 1953 LSU case, black undergraduates did not enroll at LSU until a suit was filed in 1964.

2. Tureaud Tape C.

3. *Constantine v. Southwestern Louisiana Institute* (hereafter cited as *Constantine v. SLI*), Complaint, 8.

4. A. P. Tureaud, correspondence with Robert L. Carter, January 19, 1954, box 65, folder 21, Tureaud Papers, ARC.

5. *Constantine v. SLI,* Judgment, July 16, 1954.

6. Michael G. Wade, "Four Who Would: *Constantine v. Southwestern Louisiana Institute* (1954) and the Desegregation of Louisiana's State Colleges," in *Higher Education and the Civil Rights Movement: White Supremacy, Black Southerners, and College Campuses,* ed. Peter Wallenstein (Gainesville: University Press of Florida, 2008), 66.

7. "Old Times There Are Not Forgotten: USL's First Black Recalls Commencement 1956 with Mixed Emotions," *USL Alumni News,* Fall 1966, 12.

8. Johnette Williams (niece of Pearl Burton), e-mail message to Rachel L. Emanuel, October 1, 2004.

9. Tureaud Tape BB.

10. Ibid.

11. Ibid.

12. Tureaud Tape C.

13. *Louisiana State Board of Education et al., Appellants, v. Edward Baker et al., Appellees,* No. 21138, Fifth Circuit Court of Appeal, decided December 11, 1964.

14. Tureaud Tape C.

15. U.S. Constitution, Amendment XI.

16. Tureaud Tape C.

17. Ibid.

18. Jane Tureaud interview.

19. Emanuel and Barkis-Richter, *Journey for Justice;* WDSU news clip (New Orleans), 1958.

20. Cassimere interview.

16. Enforcing *Brown*'s Mandate in New Orleans Grade Schools

1. Motley interview.

2. Wright, 1969.

3. Fairclough, *Race and Democracy,* 246.

4. Charles J. Ogletree Jr., *All Deliberate Speed: Reflections on the First Half Century of Brown v. Board of Education* (New York: W. W. Norton and Co., 2005), 127.

5. Tureaud Tape C.

6. Fairclough, *Race and Democracy,* 197.

7. Ibid., 208.

8. Ibid., 209.

9. Emanuel and Barkis-Richter, *Journey for Justice.*

10. Fairclough, *Race and Democracy,* 225.

11. Memorial Exercises in Memory of Judge James Cobb, U.S. District Court, Washington, D.C., October 15, 1958.

12. Emanuel and Barkis-Richter, *Journey for Justice.*

13. News clip, WDSU, June 20, 1960.

14. Fairclough, *Race and Democracy,* 236.

15. Emanuel and Barkis-Richter, *Journey for Justice.*

16. Jack Gremillion, interview by Mary Hebert, Oral History Project, Louisiana State University Special Collections, 4700.0532, tape 959, side A, LSU, Baton Rouge.

17. Ibid.

18. Tureaud Tape F.

19. Gremillion interview.

20. Greenberg interview.

21. Tureaud Tape F.

22. Gremillion interview.

23. Ibid.

24. Fairclough, *Race and Democracy,* 238; Jack Bass, *Unlikely Heroes* (Tuscaloosa: University of Alabama Press, 1995), 132–34.

25. Tureaud Tape F.

26. News clip, WDSU, June 20, 1960; Emanuel and Barkis-Richter, *Journey for Justice.*

27. Tureaud Papers, ARC.

28. "From *Plessy* to *Brown,*" a symposium sponsored by the Amistad Research Center, Tulane Law School, and the Black Law Students Association of Tulane University, New Orleans, September 25, 2004, celebrating the fiftieth anniversary of *Brown v. Board of Education.*

29. Tureaud Tape F.

30. Janet Tureaud interview.

17. Catholics and Desegregation

1. Fairclough, *Race and Democracy,* 171; Joseph Francis Rummel, "Blessed Are the Peace Makers," March 15, 1953, box 19, folder 15, Louis Twomey Papers, Loyola University of the South, New Orleans.

2. Tureaud Tape 3/CC.

3. Ibid.

4. Emanuel and Barkis-Richter, *Journey for Justice.*

5. Ibid.

6. Tureaud Tape 3/CC.

7. Ibid.

8. Ibid.

9. Ibid.

10. Ibid.

11. James Conaway, *Judge: The Life and Times of Leander Perez* (New York: Knopf/Random House, 1973), 189.

12. Ibid.

13. Tureaud Tape 3/CC.

18. More to the Desegregation Mandate

1. John H. Scott with Cleo Scott Brown, *Witness to the Truth: My Struggle for Human Rights in Louisiana* (Columbia: University of South Carolina Press, 2003), 82. Rosenwald schools were funded under a rural school building program established by Illinois philanthropist Julius Rosenwald, who was a partner and board chairman of Sears Roebuck and Co., to improve the quality of public education for African Americans in the early twentieth-century South.

2. Ibid., 91.

3. J. S. Baughman, communication to J. H. Wilson, president of FHMA, October 7, 1953, Papers of the NAACP.

4. Pursuant to Title 28, U.S. Code, Sec. 2201.

5. Richard G. Stewart is the father of Louisiana judges Carl E. Stewart, Fifth Circuit Court of Appeals, and James E. Stewart, Louisiana Court of Appeals.

6. Richard G. Stewart, interview by Rachel L. Emanuel, October 3, 2004.

7. Ibid.

8. Tureaud Tape A.

9. Ibid.

10. Ibid.

11. Ibid.

12. Ibid.

13. Ibid.

14. Justice Revius O. Ortique Jr., interview by Rachel L. Emanuel, September 1993.

15. Nelson interview.

16. A. P. Tureaud, "The Negro at the Louisiana Bar" (paper presented to the National Bar Association at its annual convention held in New Orleans, August 1953), box 77, folder 49, Tureaud Papers, ARC.

17. *Sobol v. Perez,* Civil No. 67–243, 19 (E.D. La., filed July 12, 1968).

18. Ernest Gellhorn, "The Law Schools and the Negro," *Duke Law Journal* (1968): 1069, 1075–76. Other Negro attorneys, detailing harassment and threats of physical harm, testified to their "unwillingness or reluctance to go to Plaquemines Parish, especially in civil rights cases." *Sobol v. Perez,* Civil No. 67-243, 19 (E.D. La., filed July 12, 1968).

19. Wright, 1969.

20. Ibid.

19. Reconstructing Public Education

1. "All deliberate speed" is a phrase referenced in *Brown v. Board of Education of Topeka, Kansas.* While the NAACP lawyers had proposed to use the word "forthwith" to achieve an accelerated desegregation timetable, Chief Justice Earl Warren adopted Justice Felix Frankfurter's suggestion to use a phrase associated with the revered Oliver Wendell Holmes, "with all deliberate speed." Ogletree, *All Deliberate Speed,* 3. Shortly after Warren retired from the Court, he acknowledged that "all deliberate speed" was chosen as a benchmark because "there were so many blocks preventing an immediate solution of the thing in reality that the best we could look for would be a progression of action." It became clear over time that critics of desegregation were using the doctrine to delay compliance with *Brown,* and in 1964 Justice Hugo Black declared in a desegregation opinion that "the time for mere 'deliberate speed' has run out"; www.loc.gov/exhibits/treasures/trr007.html (accessed May 27, 2010).

2. Tureaud Tape F.

3. Tureaud Tape C.

4. *Bryan Poindexter et al. v. Louisiana Financial Assistance Commission,* 258 F.Supp. 158 (E.D. La., 1966), 160.

5. *Borden v. Louisiana State Board of Education,* 168 LA 1005, 123 So. 655 (1929).

6. *Poindexter v. Louisiana,* 1966.

7. Henry Aronson, correspondence with Hugh Fleisher, Department of Justice in New Orleans, April 19, 1967, box 69, folder 18, Tureaud Papers, ARC.

8. The Civil Rights Act of 1871 reads: "Every person who under color of any statute, ordinance, regulation, custom, or usage, or any State or Territory or the District of Columbia, subjects, or causes to be subjected, any citizen of the United States or other person within the jurisdiction thereof to the deprivation of any rights, privileges, or immunities secured by the Constitution and laws, shall be liable to the party injured in an action at law, suit in equity, or other proper proceeding for redress, except that in any action brought against a judicial officer for an act or omission taken in such officer's judicial capacity, injunctive relief shall not be granted unless a declaratory decree was violated or declaratory relief was unavailable" (42 U.S.C. § 1983).

9. Karen M. Blum and Kathryn R. Urbonya, *Section 1983 Litigation* (Washington, D.C.: Federal Judicial Center, 1998), 2 (quoting *Monroe v. Pape*).

10. *Poindexter v. Louisiana,* 1966, 275 F.Supp. 833 (1967).

11. C. Ellis Henican (Henican James & Cleveland, Attorneys at Law), correspondence with Wisdom, Ainesworth, Christenberry, August 30, 1967, box 69, folder 18, Tureaud Papers, ARC.

12. *Louisiana Financial Assistance Commission v. Bryan Poindexter et al.,* 389 U.S. 571 (1968).

13. *Bryan Poindexter et al. v. Louisiana Financial Assistance Commission,* 296 F.Supp. 686 (1968).

14. *Louisiana Education Commission for Needy Children et al. v. Bryan Poindexter et al.,* 89 S.Ct. 48 (1968).

15. *Linda Williams v. George Kimbrough,* 415 F.2d 874–Court of Appeals, Fifth Circuit (1969).

16. On April 7, 1967, the district court entered a decree patterned after the Fifth Circuit Court's mandate in *United States v. Jefferson County Board of Education,* 5 Cir., 372 F.2d 836, aff'd with modifications on rehearing en banc, 380 F.2d 385, cert. denied sub nom. *Caddo Parish School Board v. United States,* 389 U.S. 840, 88 S.Ct. 67, 19 L.Ed.2d 103 (1967): "(a) Faculty Employment. Race or color shall not be a factor in the hiring, assignment, reassignment, promotion, demotion, or dismissal of teachers and other professional staff members, including student teachers, except that race may be taken into account for the purpose of counteracting or correcting the effect of the segregated assignment of faculty and staff in the dual system. Teachers, principals, and staff members shall be assigned to schools so that the faculty and staff is not composed exclusively of members of one race. Whenever possible, teachers shall be assigned so that more than one teacher of the minority race (white or Negro) shall be on a desegregated faculty. Defendants shall take positive and affirmative steps to accomplish the desegregation of their school faculties to achieve substantial desegregation of the faculties in as many of the schools as possible for the 1967–68 school year notwithstanding that teacher contracts for the 1967–68 or 1968–69 school years may have already been signed and approved. The tenure of teachers in the system shall not be used as an excuse for failure to comply with this provision. The defendants shall establish as an objective that the pattern of teacher assignment to any particular school not be identifiable as tailored for a heavy concentration of either Negro or white pupils in the school. . . . (c) Past Assignments. The defendants shall take steps to assign and reassign teachers and other professional staff members to eliminate the effects of the dual school system."

20. More Direct Action

1. James A. Nabrit, correspondence with A. P. Tureaud, July 13, 1960, box 9, Tureaud Papers, ARC.

2. *Garner v. State of Louisiana,* 368 U.S. 157 (1961). Audiotaped recording of hearing, U.S. Supreme Court Archives, Washington, D.C.

3. David Lander, "The Civil War Correspondent, Thomas Morris Chester, Reporter, Lawyer, and Lecturer, Battled Bigotry with an Arsenal of Eloquence," *American Legacy* 12 (2006): 14.

4. *Garner v. State of Louisiana,* 368 U.S. 157 (1961).

5. Ibid.

6. Editorial, "Pressure Tactics Don't Help," *Baton Rouge State-Times and Morning Advocate,* March 31, 1960, 8A; Rachel L. Emanuel and Denise Barkis-Richter, *Taking a Seat for Justice: The 1960 Baton Rouge Sit-Ins,* DVD, directed by Rachel L. Emanuel, Baton Rouge: Southern University Law Center (SULC)/Louisiana Endowment for the Humanities (LEH), 2006; *Garner v. State of Louisiana,* 368 U.S. 157 (1961), audiotaped recording of hearing.

7. Tureaud Tape F.

8. Johnnie A. Jones Sr., interview by Rachel L. Emanuel, March 30, 2005; Emanuel and Barkis-Richter, *Taking a Seat for Justice.*

9. A. P. Tureaud Jr. interview, April 1993.

10. Wright, 1969.

11. Ibid.

12. Sybil Morial interview.

13. Wright, 1969

14. Ortique interview.

15. Fairclough, *Race and Democracy*, 420.

16. *Sobol v. Perez*, 289 F.Supp. 392 (E.D. La. 1968).

17. Gellhorn, "Law Schools and the Negro," 1075–76.

18. *Louisiana Bar Journal* 11 (August 1963): 116–17.

21. Courts Are the Way

1. Wright, 1969.

2. William E. Giles, "Judge Wright: In the Center of the New Orleans Controversy," *Wall Street Journal*, November 10, 1960.

3. J. W. Peltason, *58 Lonely Men: Southern Federal Judges and School Desegregation* (New York: Harcourt Brace, 1961), 28.

4. Effective October 1, 1981, Alabama, Georgia, and Florida were split off into the U.S. Court of Appeals for the Eleventh Circuit.

5. Tureaud Tape F.

6. Peltason, *58 Lonely Men*, 27.

7. *Bush v. Orleans Parish School Board* (*United States v. State of Louisiana*), D.C., 188 F.Supp. 916, 926.

8. Janice Hornot, "A Candid Conversation with Judge E. Gordon West," *Around the Bar*, Baton Rouge Bar Association, January 1986.

9. Discussion of Judge West in this and the following paragraphs is from Tureaud Tape C.

10. Tureaud Documentary Scholars' Panel, Xavier University, New Orleans, February 26, 1993.

11. Ortique interview.

12. Elie interview.

13. www.millercenter.org/academic/americanpresident/events/06_13.

22. Race against Time

1. A. P. Tureaud Jr. interview, April 1993.

2. Elise Tureaud interview, by Rachel L. Emanuel, November 1993.

3. Ibid.

4. Cassimere interview; Phoenix Salvage, interview by Rachel L. Emanuel, September 7, 2005.

5. Sybil Morial interview.

6. A. P. Tureaud Jr. interview, April 1993.

7. Worthy, "Travail and Triumph of a Southern Black Civil Rights Lawyer," 190.

8. Thurgood Marshall, "Eulogy, for A. P. Tureaud, Sr.," *The Claverite*, January–February 1972, 28–29. (A copy is on file at the Amistad, Tureaud Papers, box 6, folder 39.)

Index

Acox, Jackson V., 169
Adams, Frank W., 39, 48
Aeolian Hall, Old, 31
Ainsworth, Robert A., Jr., 189, 232
Alexander, Avery, 245
Alpha Kappa Alpha sorority, 68–70, 82
Alpha Phi Alpha fraternity, 39, 69, 75, *photo following 116*, 217, 245
Amaker, Norman, 188
Ambeau, Lorraine, 233
Anderson, Marian, 38, 88, 89
Archives of Black History (New Orleans), 262
Armstrong, Louis "Satchmo," 22
Association for the Study of Negro Life and History, 81
Association of Catholic Laymen, 215
Atkins, Hosea, 234
Atlanta University, 37, 130
Aubert, Wilfred S., Jr., 152, 155
Aubert v. Orleans Parish School Board, 151, 153, 155, 195
Augustine, I. B., 78
Augustine, Israel, 101, 256

Bagatelle Plantation, 6, 8, *photo following 116*
Bagnell, Robert, 37
Baranco, Dr. Beverly V., 77, 79
Baton Rouge, La., 146, 147, 154, 176, 239; sit-ins, 239
Bauduit, Agnes Leonie, 17, 34
Bauduit, William, 34
Bell, Louis A. 55

Bennett, Kirt, *photo following 116*
Berry, Louis, 112, 127, 169, 176
Bigard, Barney, 22
Bigard, Eric, 22, 23
Birney, Charles, 47
Birth of a Nation, The (Griffith), 39
Black, Hugo, 51, 85, 95
Black Code. *See* Code Noir
"Black Monday" (or "D-Day," desegregation day), 206
Blackstone, William, 48–49
Blackstone Hall, 49
Blackstone Society, 48
Boggs, Hale, 166, 173, 174, 179–80
Booth, Felton Whitlock, 47
Borah, Wayne G., 102–103, 104–105, 107, 134, 184, 185
Bourgeois, Lionel J., 150, 152, 156
Bourgeois, Nanine (aka Ann Slater), 7–9, 75, *photo following 116*
Brandeis, Justice Louis, 32
Brazier, Dr. Aaron, 86
Bridges, Ruby, 206
Bringier, Aglae, 6
Bringier, Elizabeth "Betsy," 6
Bringier, Emanuel Marius Pons, 6
Brisco, Mary Enola, 239
Brown, Eddie Charles J., 239
Brown, Linda, 157
Brown, Oliver, 158
Brown, Suzie, 70
Brown v. Board of Education, 157, 158, 173,

Brown v. Board of Education, continued
    182–84, 186, 188, 195, 203, 217, 229, 238,
    252
Brown II, 196
Bunche, Ralph, 172
Burns, Dr. Leonard, *photo following 116,* 214
Bush, Oliver, 155
Bush v. Orleans Parish School Board, 155–57,
    195, 198, 202–204, 252
Byrd, Daniel "Dan," 78, 88, 101, 106, 110, 113,
    114, 150, 152, 155, 263
Byrd, Mildred, 110

Carey, Archibald, 78
Carter, Robert, 124, 183, 256
Carver, George Washington, 38
Cassimere, Raphael, 91, 192, 210, 243, 245, 261
Castle, Oretha, 245
Catholics, and segregation: cross burned on
    archbishop's lawn, 215; desegregation of
    schools, 214, 216; dissatisfaction with con-
    tinued segregation in schools and churches,
    79; policy of racial segregation, 13; racial
    segregation declared "sinful," 212; removal
    of "Whites Only" and "Colored Only" signs
    from churches, 212; "War of the Pews," 12
Chapital, Arthur, 59, 78, 88, 245
Chase, Leah, 264
Chester, Thomas Morris, 242
Chicago, Ill., 22–29, 32
Chicago Defender, 26, 28, 32, 42
Christenberry, Herbert W., 107, 134, 137, 153,
    185, 197, 202, 204, 232, 249, 250, 252
Civil rights acts: of 1866, 5; of 1871, 232; of
    1964, 233, 247
Clark, Felton G., 239
Clark, Joseph S., 220
Claverite, The, 77, 78
Cobb, James A., 34, 44, 45, 51, 160, 163, 198
Cockerham, Doris, 234–35
Code Noir, 4, 266n3
Cody, Bishop John, 216
Coghill, Dora, 17
Cohen, Walter, 51, 55–56, 63, 64, 111, 164, 179
Coleman, Edward Maceo "Red," 30
Collins, Douglas, 247
Collins, Robert, 137, 147, 247
Combre, Doretha A., 148

Commentaries (Blackstone), 48–49
Committee for Public Education (COPE),
    200–202, 204
Congo Square, 18
Congress of Racial Equality (CORE), 244,
    245, 247
Congressional election of 1958, 177–78
*Constantine v. Southwestern Louisiana Insti-
    tute,* 183
Cook, Frank, 228
Cooper, Ollie Mae, 43
Cornell University, 39
Corps d'Afrique, 8
Corpus Christi Church (New Orleans), 71, 72,
    75, 263
Couvent, Marie, 19
Cox v. Louisiana, 244
Crawford, George W., 39
Creole(s): Afro-Creole culture, 4; antebellum
    renaissance, 30; brown paper bag test, 13–
    14; community, 4, 8, 13–14, 154, 187, 225;
    cottage, 11; in Crescent City, 18, 22, 67, 109,
    168; cuisine, 1, 14, 19, 194; culture, 3, 20,
    88, 87, 99, 223, 262; definition of, 265n1;
    downtown Creole community, 21, 71, 80,
    123; jazz band, 31; and Jeunes Amis Hall,
    14; and Joe "King" Oliver, 14; lawyers, 53.
    See also New Orleans
Creole Voices, 30
Crescent City Independent Voters League
    (CCIVL), 168
Crisis, The, 38, 40, 65

Daily Reveille (LSU), 136, 143
Darensbourg, Fay. *See* Tureaud, Fay (daugh-
    ter-in-law)
Daughters of the American Revolution (DAR),
    88
Davidson, Eugene "Gene," 35, 39–40, 160
Davidson, Leonora Coates, 36
Davidson, Shelby, 35–36
Davis, Edward, 260
Davis, Jimmie, 186, 199–201, 204
Davis, Monique, *photo following 116,* 260
Davis, Rev. A. L., 89, 169, 170, 174, 176, 245,
    255
*Davis v. East Baton Rouge Parish School
    Board,* 153

Dawkins, Ben C., Jr., 184
Dejan, Marie Eugenie. *See* Tureaud, Marie
  Eugenie Dejan (mother)
Dejan, Louisa (Mamere), 12, 19
Dejan, Marie Helena, 266
Dejoie, Burel, 260
Dejoie, C. C., 67, 82
Dejoie, Julia, 82, 97, 98
Dejoie, Lucille Albertine. *See* Tureaud, Lucille
  Albertine Dejoie (wife)
Delarosa, Augie, 28
Delarosa, Oscar, 25–26, 33
DePriest, Oscar, 28, 43
Desdunes, Rodolphe L., 19, 30, 53–55
Desegregation, 90, 110, 115, 116, 127, 128, 138–
  40, 147, 148, 154, 187. *See also* Segregation
Dillard University, 200, 219, 260
Direct-action tactics, 238
Dixiecrats, 164, 168, 180
Dooky Chase's Restaurant, 124, 264
Douglas, Nils, 247
Drew, Dr. Charles, 38
Drexel, Katharine, 153–54
Du Bois, W. E. B., 37, 38, 40, 62, 65, 99, 248
Dunbar Theatre, 40

Education Commission for Needy Children,
  234
Eisenhower, Dwight D., 166, 168, 177, 208,
  250, 251
Elie, Lolis, 62, 247, 254, 255
Ellington, Edward "Duke," 38
Emancipation Proclamation, 5
Etienne, Gail, 206, 209

Farm Security Administration (FSA), 218–19
Fat Tuesday. *See* Mardi Gras Day
Faubourg Marigny, 1, 10, 11, 15, 269–70n1
Faubourg Tremé, 9–13, 269–70n1
Fifteenth Amendment, 44, 113
Fletcher, William, 34
Flint-Goodridge Hospital (New Orleans), 74,
  87, 117, 137, 200
Foister, Daryle, 132, 137
Fourteenth Amendment, 44, 153, 183, 234,
  240, 242, 244
Francis, Norman, 146
Frankfurter, Felix, 240, 242, 281n1

French Hospital (New Orleans), 121–22
French Quarter, 9, 14, 18, 57, 109
Fuqua Law, 196–97

Gaillot, B. J., 216
Gaines v. Canada, 128, 132, 149, 183, 184, 241
Gallagher, Buell G., 93
Garner, John B., 239
Garner v. Louisiana, 240–44, 255
Garvey, Marcus, 31, 222
Gayle, James, 86
Gens de couleur libres (free people of color),
  4, 66
Grace, Alonzo G., 81
Grambling College. *See* Grambling State University
Grambling State University, 183, 190
Grant-in-aid program, 230–33
Gravolet, E. W., 216
Great Migration, 23, 24, 30
Green, S.W., 58
Greenberg, Jack, 108, 124, 135, 139, 202, 204,
  217
Gregory, Thomas Ralph, 32
Gremillion, Jack P., 184, 185, 197, 202–205
Grimké, Angelina Weld, 38–39
Grimké, Archibald, 38
Grimké, Francis, 38
Grimké, Sarah Stanley, 38
Group, The, 86, 87–89
Guerand, Charles, 63
Guillory v. St. Landry Parish School Board, 153

Hall v. Nagel, 111
Hall v. St. Helena Parish School Board, 153
*Hamp Williams et al. v. Northwestern State
  College et al.,* 189
Hannan, Archbishop Philip, 217, 257, 263
Hardin, Dr. Joseph, 59
Harding, Warren G., 55
Harlan, John Marshall, II, 240, 242
Harlem (N.Y.), 19, 29, 30, 51, 31
Harlem Renaissance, 30
Harris, Albert "Sonny Man" Jr., 113–14
Hart, William Henry Harrison, 33, 46–47
Harvard University School of Law, 196
Hasting, A. C., 217
Hatfield, Charles, 127, 130, 131

Haydel, Dr. C. C., 77, 81, 119
Hayes, George, 217
Haynes, J. K., 78, 108, 182
Haywood, Jules, 20
Heard v. Ouachita Parish School Board, 153
Hebert, F. Edward, 177–79
Henderson, Edwin B., *photo following 116*
Herget, G. Caldwell, 130
Hill, Veronica Brown "Connie," 101
Hines, Bridgette, 17
Hirsch, Arnold, 64
History of Negro Physicians in New Orleans,
    The (Tureaud and Haydel), 81
Hobby, Oveta Culp, 148
Holmes, Oliver Wendell, 32
Hoover, J. Edgar, 96–97
Hoston, Janette, 239
Houdini, Harry, 20
Houston, Charles Hamilton, 49, 62, 63, 101,
    105, 127, 131
Howard Theatre, 40, 268
Howard University, 34–36, 39, 47, 66, 68, 69,
    139, 148, 259; School of Law, 34, 45, 57, 148,
    217
Howard v. Lincoln Parish School Board, 153
Human Rights Commission, 215
Hunter, Edwin F., 184, 185, 205, 252
Hurst, Lawrence, 239

Illinois Central Railroad, 23, 25, 43
Interdenominational Ministerial Alliance, 263

Jack, Hulan, 215
Jackson, John E., 164–66
Jackson, Maynard, 167
Jackson, Maynard, Jr., 167
Jackson, Shelby, 184, 206, 240
Jamison, Mary, 190
Jemison, Rev. T. J., 239
Jim Crow laws, 15, 19, 47, 54, 116, 128, 135, 141,
    180, 240, 246
Johnson, Ben, 186
Johnson, Dr. E. A., 155, 186
Johnson, Georgia, 96
Johnson, James Weldon, 38, 40, 62, 63
Johnson, John W., 239
Johnson, Kenneth L., 239
Johnson, Lyndon B., 189, 255, 256
Johnson, Mordecai, 217

Johnson, Robert, 38
Johnson, Viola M., 127; *Johnson* case, 130–31
Jones, Carrie Lee, 115
Jones, Donald, 87
Jones, John, 113–15
Jones, Johnnie, 176, 240, 244
Jones, Mack, 239
Jones, Ralph Waldo Emerson, 190
Jones, Sandra Ann, 239
Jones, Ralph Waldo Emerson, 190
Jordan, Vernon J., 239

Keller, Charles, 222
Keller, Rosa, 200, 222
Kennedy, John F., 189, 247, 248, 250
Kennedy, Robert F., 248
Kennon, Robert, 173, 175, 182
King, Dr. Martin Luther, Jr., 40, 81, 248
Knights of Columbus, 33
Knights of Peter Claver, 76–78, 121, 125, 219,
    245
Knights of Pythias, 57, 58–59, 66
Knights of the White Camellia, 51
Ku Klux Klan, 31, 51, 183–84, 196
Kuntz, Emile, 164

Labat, George, 56, 64
Lacour, Vanue, 220
Lafon, Thomy, 20
LaGarde v. East Baton Rouge Parish School
    Board, 107
Lake Pontchartrain, 14, 191
Landrieu, Moon, 256
Lawyers Constitutional Defense Committee
    (LCDC), 247
LeCesne, Archibald T., 77
Lee, Eula Mae, and teacher salary equalization
    case, 107, 236
Lee Street riots, 95–96
Legal Defense Fund (NAACP), 6, 105, 112,
    124, 128, 131, 182, 188, 196, 202, 219, 230,
    238, 240, 249
Les Cenelles, 30
Lewis, John G., 78
Lincoln University School of Law, 128
Locke, Alain, 38
Lockett, Johnson, 59
Logsdon, Joseph, 64, 150, 262
Long, Earl K., 162, 169, 173

Long, Huey P., 134, 161–62, 172, 177
Long, Russell, 173, 179, 201, 250
Longe, George, 97, 101
Louis Armstrong Park, 19, 37
Louisiana Association for the Progress of
    Negro Citizens, 168
Louisiana Bar Journal, 247
Louisiana Financial Assistance Commis-
    sion, 232
Louisiana Progressive Educational Associa-
    tion (LPEA), 98
Louisiana's Joint Legislative Committee on
    Segregation, 215
Louisiana State Constitution of 1898, 129
Louisiana State University (LSU), 36–47, 128,
    129, 132, 133, 192, 193; law school, 127, 134–
    37, 147, 185; medical school, 128, 137
Louisiana State University–New Orleans
    (LSU-NO), 190–93
Louisiana Tech University, 182, 189
Louisiana Weekly, 89, 131, 93, 133
L'Ouverture, Toussaint, 6
Loyola University Law School, 116, 146, 189
Lucas, Dr. George W., 56, 63–64
*Ludley v. Louisiana State University Board of
    Supervisors,* 185
Lynching. *See* Minden lynching

Magnolia Housing Project, 89
Malite (Tureaud's great-great-grandmother), 7
Malveaux, Vincent, 77
Mardi Gras Day, 13, *photo following* 116, 123,
    124
Marshall, Thurgood, 38, 40, 50, 56, 63, 78, 87,
    94, 100, 101, 109, 111, 114, *photo following*
    116, 124, 127, 131, 141, 156, 183, 201, 221,
    256, 263
Martin, Flora, 235
Martinet, Louis A., 19, 53, 55, 245
Mason, Anna Mae, 94–95
Mather, Aurora, 6
Mather, Celestine, 8
Mather, Josephine, 6, 7
Mather, Noel, 8
Mather Plantation (Belle Alliance), 8
McCleave, Madame Florence C., 31
McCray, Hattie, 63
*McLaurin v. Oklahoma State Regents for
    Higher Education,* 131, 192

McMillan v. Iberville Parish School Board, 107
McNeese State College/University (Lake
    Charles, La.), 148, 183, 185
Meritt, Watson, 86
Metoyer, Rene, 57–58, 164
Midlo, Herman, 185, 246, 247
Miles, Lizzie, 72
Minden lynching, 113–15, 171
Mitchell, Arthur W., 41–43
Mitchell v. Wright, 112
Moliere, Nicole, *photo following* 116
Mollay, Alexander, 59
Monroe v. Pape, 232
Morgan State University, 30
Morial, Ernest "Dutch," *photo following* 116,
    124, 126, 137, 147, 177, 214, 244, 245, 247,
    250, 255, 261
Morial, Sybil, 126, 244, 261
Morial, Walter, *photo following* 116
Morris, Jo Ann, 239
Morton, Jelly Roll, 72
Moss, Donald T., 239
Motley, Constance Baker, 62, 72, 108, 124, 135,
    138, 195, 219–21, 255
Mulatto(es), 4, 6, 9, 20, 266n2
Mutual Housing Association, 41, 42

Nabrit, James M., Jr., 78, 217
Nabrit, James M., III, 240
National Association for the Advancement of
    Colored People (NAACP), 31, 36–40, 43, 50,
    58, 59, 61–65, 70, 72, 75–78, 80, 83, 85–107,
    110, 111, 133, 136–38, 141, 148, 150, 152,
    154–60, 165, 169, 172, 175, 178, 182, 183,
    186–91, 195–97, 199, 202–204, 207–11, 218,
    219, 238, 243–45, 255; New Orleans branch,
    56, 61, 63, 64, 86, 96, 97, 99, 131 132, 154,
    244. *See also* Legal Defense Fund (NAACP)
Nelson, John P. "Jack," 115, 200, 214, 224, 247
Nelson, Medard, 21
New Orleans, 54–58, 60. *See also* French Quar-
    ter; Vieux Carré
New Orleans Crusader, 55
New Orleans Municipal Auditorium, 86, 88,
    93, 199
New Orleans Sentinel, 89
New Orleans Times Picayune, 32, 83, 136, 177
New Orleans University, 74
New Orleans Voters Association, 168

New Orleans Voters League (NOVL), 168
Newstadter, Marcus, *photo following 116*
New York City, 25, 29–31, 33, 50, 227
Niagara Movement, 37
Nicholls, Elise. *See* Tureaud, Elise Eugenie
    (daughter)
Nicholls, Kenwin, 259, 260
Nicholls, Kimberly, 260
Nichols, Larry L., 239
Nicholls State College/University (Thibodaux,
    La.), 183, 188
Nicholls, Lisa, *photo following 116,* 260
Nicholls, Vanessa, *photo following 116,* 260
Ninth Ward Civic and Improvement League,
    152
Nixon, Richard, 256
North Carolina Central School of Law, 128
Northeast State College (Monroe, La.), 183,
    215
Northwestern State College/University
    (Natchitoches, La.), 110, 183, 185–87, 189

Ogletree, Charles, 196
Oliver, Joe "King," 14, 31
Orleans Parish Progressive Voters League
    (OPPVL), 166, 168–70, 174–76
Orleans Parish School Board, 102, 152, 153,
    155, 156, 196, 198, 232
Ortique, Revius, 197, 224, 238
Osborne, Aubrey, 212

Pass Christian, Miss., 226–28, 258
Patterson, Chavis, *photo following 116,* 259
Patterson, Doward, *photo following 116,* 258
Patterson, Gina, *photo following 116,* 126, 259
Patterson, Louie, *photo following 116,* 258
Patterson, Sylvia. *See* Tureaud, Sylvia Louise
    (daughter)
Patterson, Theodore (Ted), *photo following
    116,* 125, 259
Patterson, Tina, *photo following 116,* 259
Paul VI, *photo following 116,* 257
Payne, Lutrill, 132, 137
Peabody, Charles L., 239
Pearson v. Murray, 128
Pecot, Carlton, 171
Perez, Agnes, 217
Perez, Leander, 139, 171, 178, 199, 206, 208,
    215, 225

Perez, Manuel, 72
Perry, Dr. E. B., 79
Petit, Buddy, 72
Petite, Eric, 14
Pierre, Caroline, 266
Pierre, Hugh, 85
Pierre v. Louisiana, 85
Pittsburgh Courier, 158
Place Du Cirque, 18
Place Des Negres, 18
Plessy, Homer, 19
Plessy v. Ferguson, 3, 5, 19, 54, 60, 133, 149, 157,
    158, 242
*Poindexter et al. v. Louisiana Financial Assis-
    tance Commission,* 232
Poor People's Defense League, 168
Pontchartrain Park, 171; housing develop-
    ment, 222
Powell, Adam Clayton, Jr., 40
Prevost, Tessie, 206
Pythian Temple, 58, 66, 130

Rachel (stage play), 39
Rainach, Willie, 168, 175, 199
Raphael, John, Sr., 171
Rault, Gerard, 196, 199
Reconstruction, 45, 67, 82, 111, 129, 164; Loui-
    siana legislature during, 5, 8
Richards, William Henry, 45
Richardson, Mason N., 47
Robinson, Henry Warmouth, 64
Robinson, Marvin, 239
Robinson, Spotswood, 217
Roosevelt, Eleanor, 88, 165
Roosevelt, Franklin D., 43, 95, 165, 218
Rousell, Ignace, 85
Rousseau, John E., 88, 89, 90, 113
Rousseve, Charles, 262
Rummel, Archbishop Joseph Francis, 78, 212,
    215, 216, 215, 217

St. Augustine Catholic Church, 9, 12, 13, 19
St. James Parish, 5–6, 8–9, 94
St. John's College, 33
St. Louis Cemetery, 263, 264
St. Roch Cemetery, 75
Save Our Schools (SOS), 200–201
Schools: Bayou Road School, 17, 18, 20, 60, 62,
    54; Bucket of Blood School, 18; Carroll-

ton Elementary School, 233; Clark High School, 154; Dunbar High School (Washington, D.C.), 38; Edward White School, 151; Garden District Academy, 233; Holy Cross High School, 214; Kruttschnitt School, 151; Joseph Craig School, 60; Marigny School, 17; McDonogh School No. 16, 34, 151; McDonogh School No. 19, 206, 208, 209; Medard Nelson School, 21; Myrtilla Miner Normal School (Washington, D.C.), 39; Ninth Ward Cooperative School, 234; Ninth Ward Elementary School, 232–33; Thomy Lafon School, 20–21, 68; Valena C. Jones School, 60, 71, 153; William J. Frantz School, 206, 208; Wright Elementary School, 235; Xavier Preparatory High School, 68, 153; Zachary Taylor School, 151

Segregation, 1, 3, 5, 12, 13, 15, 25, 27, 29, 36, 40, 54, 63, 78, 82–83, 92–93, 110, 115, 129, 133, 140, 154, 156, 158, 175, 192, 197, 212, 242, 254. *See also* Desegregation

"Separate but equal" doctrine, 5, 19, 82, 108, 127, 139, 151, 153, 157, 203, 222, 242

Sepia Socialite, 89, 105

Seventh Ward Civic League, 59, 60, 72

Sipuel, Lois Ada, 128

Sipuel v. Board of Regents of Oklahoma, 128, 149

Sit-ins, 238; Baton Rouge, 239–43, 244

Slater, Alexander, 8

Slater, Ann. *See* Bourgeois, Nanine

Slater, James Alexander, 8, 25, 75, *photo following 116,* 266

Slater, Robert Manuel, 31, 75

Smith, Christiana G., 186

Smith, Frank B., 57

Smith v. Allright, 165

Sobol, Richard, 225, 247

Social clubs: Autocrat Social and Pleasure Club, 58–59, 87; Bulls Aid and Social Club, 21; Eatmores, 119, 120, 121; Informal Club, 40; Junior Eatmores, 121; Knights of Pythias, 57–59; Mu-So-Lit Club, 36; Pen and Pencil Club of Washington, 36; San Jacinto Club, 56; Zulu Social and Pleasure Club, 123

Sorrell, E. W., 101

Southeastern Regional Interracial Commission, 213

Southeastern Louisiana University (Hammond, La.), 183, 185

Southeast State College. *See* Southeastern Louisiana University (Hammond, La.)

Southern University (Baton Rouge), 102, 129, 130–31, 135, 139, 140, 154, 183, 186, 219, 220, 225, 239, 243, 254; law school, 183, 240, 254

Southern University–New Orleans (SUNO), 190, 191

Southwestern Louisiana Institute (SLI), 183

Spears, Castro, 180

Spears, Mack, 81

Spingard Medal, 38, 171

State of Louisiana, ex. rel. Charles T. Hatfield, Realtor v. Board of Supervisors Louisiana State University and Agricultural and Mechanical College, 130, 131

Stern, Edgar, 222

Stern, Edith, 222

Stewart, Richard G., 221–22

Stewart v. Clark Terrace Unit No. 1, Inc., 219

Stone, Jesse N., 218, 220, 246

Straight College, 17, 54, 74, 130; law school, 55, 57, 225

Sweatt, Heman Marion, 132

Sweatt v. Painter, 131, 132, 149

Talley, Bascom, 246, 247

Tate, Leona, 206, 208

Taylor, O. C. W., 177

Teacher salary equalization cases, 101, 104, 107–108, 110, 134

Terrell, Judge Robert Heberton, 45–46

Terrell, Mary Church, 46

Thirteenth Amendment, 44

Thirteenth Street Boundary Association, 41

Thomas, Joseph, Dr., 125–26

Thomas, Julius A., Jr., *photo following 116*

Thomastown, 219

Thompson, Frederick, 126

Thornton, Joseph A., 51, 57, 58, 111–12

Times Picayune. See New Orleans Times Picayune

Transylvania (East Carroll Parish, La.), 218–19

Trudeau, A. M. "Mutt," 56, 58

Trudeau, Antoine M., 55

Trudeau v. Barnes, 63–64

Tulane Law School, 139, 173

Tureaud, Adolph (brother), 9, 15, 19–20, 25, 29–31, 51, 74, 75

Tureaud, Adolphe (grandfather), 6, 7, 8, 266

Tureaud, Alexander Pierre, Sr.: family legacy, 5–9; family life, 10–13, 21–22; life in Seventh Ward, 10–13, 13–14; and Catholic Church, 11, 13, 70, 257; Creole culture, 13–14, 94, 255, 262; early education, 15, 17–18, 20–22; work in Chicago, 24–27, 99; dry wit, 28, 90, 109–10, 112, 195; in New York, 30–31; on black separatism, 31, 223–24; work in Washington, D.C., 32, 40–41; legal education, 34, 39, 43–50; Alpha Phi Alpha fraternity, 39, 69, 75, photo following 116, 217, 245; and NAACP, 40, 61, 63, 64, 85–87, 101, 131–32, 208–209; and newspapers, 40–41, 89–90, 105–106; with Arthur W. Mitchell, 41–43, 83–84; Customs House job, 51, 55–56, 65, 70, 73; sisters who crossed the color line, 52; Creole leadership, 54, 56, 80; practicing law in New Orleans, 57–58, 59, 70, 73, 101, 124; and Autocrat Club, 58–59; and civic leagues, 59–61, 150, 211; with Lucille, 71, 74–76, 81, 117–19, 123, 124–26; Knights of Peter Claver, 76–79, 212–16; views on paternalism, 82, 225; professionalism and ethics in legal profession, 91, 162–63, 187–88, 225–26, 243, 246, 254; courtroom style, 91, 108, 135; FBI files, 96, 98–99; and war loans and bond drives, 97–98; Communism and Communist Party, 99, 209; and teacher salary equalization, 101–104, 107–108; and Thurgood Marshall, 101, 108–10; and voting, 110, 164; voting rights cases, 111, 112, 169; Minden lynching, 113–15; and desegregation of LSU, 117, 130–31, 132, 133–35, 137, 138–42; with Eatmores, 119–21, 226–28, 258; and desegregation of other state colleges and universities, 148, 182–87, 188–89, 191–93; and Orleans Parish public school desegregation, 151, 153, 155, 195, 198, 202–205; and politics, 161, 180–81; on Huey Long, 162; with Republican Party, 163–66, 179; political organizations, 166–68, 169–70, 175–77; with Democratic Party, 167, 179; on Chep Morrison, 170, 171–72, 174, 207; campaign for Congress, 177–79; on attack on NAACP, 196–97; and desegregation of housing, 218–21, 222; on grants-in-aid, 230–34; legal strategies for civil rights, 238, 243–44, 245, 249, 253; and sit-ins, 239; children, 259–60; death of, 263–64

Tureaud, Alexander Pierre, Jr. (son), 75, 76, 108, 113, photos following 116, 116–19, 122, 125; and desegregation of LSU, 138–48; and family, 257–59, 261–62, 264; high school education, 154, 180, 193, 213, 227–28, 243, 246

Tureaud, Alexander Pierre, III (grandson), photo following 116, 259

Tureaud, Andrew (grandson), 259

Tureaud, Augustin Dominique (A.D.; great-great-grandfather), 5–6, 7

Tureaud, Augustin Marius (A.M.; great-grandfather), 6, 7

Tureaud, Benjamin, 6

Tureaud, Blanche (sister), 9

Tureaud, Carmen Louise (sister), 9, 52, 74

Tureaud, Carole Lucille (daughter), photo following 116, 117, 118, 125, 257, 258, 259

Tureaud, Corinne (sister), 9, 52, 74

Tureaud, Edward ("Eddie"; brother), 9, 15, 22, 52, 74

Tureaud, Edward (great-uncle), 6, 9

Tureaud, Elise Eugenie (daughter), 75, 76, 123, 125, 258, 259, 260

Tureaud, Emile (brother), 9, 52, 53, 74, photo following 116

Tureaud, Fay (daughter-in-law), photo following 116, 257, 259

Tureaud, Henry, 6

Tureaud, Jane Victoria (daughter), photo following 116, 117, 121–23, 125, 190, 198, 257, 260

Tureaud, Janet Katherine (daughter), photo following 116, 117, 125, 198, 257, 260

Tureaud, Louis (father), 7, 8, 9–12, 14, 15, 16, 19, 21, 22, 50, 75, 76, photo following 116, 118, 266

Tureaud, Louis "Willie" (brother), 9, 10, 15, 22, 51, 52–53, 72, 74, 75, photo following 116

Tureaud, Lucille Albertine Dejoie (wife), 66–71, 76, 81–82, 92, 100, 108, photos following 116, 117–20, 122–24, 138, 140, 148, 158–59, 173–74, 180, 194, 216, 226–27, 257–59, 263–64

Tureaud, Marie (great-aunt), 6
Tureaud, Marie Eugenie Dejan (mother), 7, 9, 10–13, 15–16, 19, 22–23, 50–53, 72, 74–75, 76
Tureaud, Marie Louise (sister), 9, 52, 74
Tureaud, Ronda (granddaughter), *photo following 116*, 260
Tureaud, Stafford (nephew), 52, 57, 72
Tureaud, Sylvia Louise (daughter), 74, 75, 117, 123, 125, 126, 148, 228, 258, 259
Tureaud, Victoria (sister), 9, 31, 52–53, 70, 74, 75, *photos following 116*, 262
Tureaud, Virginia (sister), 9, 52, 74
Tuskegee Normal and Industrial Institute, 37

U.S. Customs House, 51, 55, 57, 59, 65, 70, 73, 101
U.S. Department of Justice, 32
U.S. Department of the Treasury, 36
U.S. Supreme Court, 5, 32, 43, 63, 85, 95, 128, 131–32, 134, 148, 156, 158, 169, 184, 186, 188, 196, 201, 230, 232, 234, 240, 243, 244, 249, 250, 256, 263, 271
United Voters League, 168
University of Arkansas, 203
University of Louisiana at Lafayette, 183
University of Louisiana at Monroe, 183
University of Maryland, 128
University of Missouri School of Law, 128
University of New Orleans, 190
University of Oklahoma School of Law, 128
University of Texas School of Law, 131–32
Upton, Milton, 245

Valdry, Felton, 239
Vance, James Madison, 164

Vieux Carré, 9–11, 15, 57, 109, 123. *See also* New Orleans

Wagner, Emile, 215
Walling, William English, 37
Ward, John F., 241
"War of the Pews," 12
Warren, Earl, 158, 240–42
Washington, Booker T., 37, 92, 158, 163
Washington, D.C., 22, 32, 34, 36, 39, 51
Washington Daily American, 35, 40
Waterhouse, Priscilla, 17–18
West, E. Gordon, 187, 188, 190, 252–53
White, Edward Douglass, 32, 151, 158, 251
White, Walter W., 63, 87
Williams, Fannie C., 17–18, 60, 80
White Citizens' Council, 215
White Hall Plantation, 6
Williams, Linda, 234
Williams v. Davis, 201
Wilson, John H., 220–21
Wilson, Roy, 132, 135–36, 137
Wisdom, John Minor, 165–66, 189, 197, 200, 232–34, 249–52
Woodson, Carter G., 38
Wright, J. Skelly, 89, 139, 140–42, 173, 185, 195–97, 199, 202–206, 209, 211, 229, 249–52

Xavier University, 68, 77, 98, 127, 139, 146, 148, 154, 259

Young, Andrew, 38, 81, 120
Young Men's Christian Association (YMCA), 28
Young Women's Christian Association (YWCA), 82